Understanding
the New European
Data Protection Rules

T0384079

Understanding the New European Data Protection Rules

Paul B. Lambert

CRC Press
Taylor & Francis Group
Boca Raton London New York

CRC Press is an imprint of the
Taylor & Francis Group, an **informa** business

AN AUERBACH BOOK

CRC Press
Taylor & Francis Group
6000 Broken Sound Parkway NW, Suite 300
Boca Raton, FL 33487-2742

First issued in paperback 2020

© 2018 by Taylor & Francis Group, LLC
CRC Press is an imprint of Taylor & Francis Group, an Informa business

No claim to original U.S. Government works

ISBN 13: 978-0-367-65768-0 (pbk)
ISBN 13: 978-1-138-06983-1 (hbk)

This book contains information obtained from authentic and highly regarded sources. Reasonable efforts have been made to publish reliable data and information, but the author and publisher cannot assume responsibility for the validity of all materials or the consequences of their use. The authors and publishers have attempted to trace the copyright holders of all material reproduced in this publication and apologize to copyright holders if permission to publish in this form has not been obtained. If any copyright material has not been acknowledged please write and let us know so we may rectify in any future reprint.

Except as permitted under U.S. Copyright Law, no part of this book may be reprinted, reproduced, transmitted, or utilized in any form by any electronic, mechanical, or other means, now known or hereafter invented, including photocopying, microfilming, and recording, or in any information storage or retrieval system, without written permission from the publishers.

For permission to photocopy or use material electronically from this work, please access www.copyright.com (http://www.copyright.com/) or contact the Copyright Clearance Center, Inc. (CCC), 222 Rosewood Drive, Danvers, MA 01923, 978-750-8400. CCC is a not-for-profit organization that provides licenses and registration for a variety of users. For organizations that have been granted a photocopy license by the CCC, a separate system of payment has been arranged.

Trademark Notice: Product or corporate names may be trademarks or registered trademarks, and are used only for identification and explanation without intent to infringe.

Library of Congress Cataloging-in-Publication Data

Names: Lambert, Paul, 1971-, author.
Title: Understanding the new European data protection rules / Paul Lambert.
Description: Boca Raton : CRC Press, 2017. | Includes bibliographical references.
Identifiers: LCCN 2017013868 | ISBN 9781138069831 (978-1-138-06983-1)
Subjects: LCSH: Data protection--Law and legislation--European Union countries. | Privacy, Right of--European Union countries.
Classification: LCC KJE6070 .L36 2017 | DDC 346.24/0664--dc23
LC record available at https://lccn.loc.gov/2017013868

**Visit the Taylor & Francis Web site at
http://www.taylorandfrancis.com**

**and the CRC Press Web site at
http://www.crcpress.com**

"The nature of the internet means data protection is clearly a global matter."*

"European data protection laws have some of the highest standards in the world."†

"Under the new agreement, the EU–US Privacy Shield, the Federal Trade Commission will continue to prioritize enforcement of the framework as part of our broader commitment to protect consumers' personal information and privacy. We will continue to work closely with our European partners to ensure consumer privacy is protected on both sides of the Atlantic."‡

---

* Irish data protection supervisory authority (DPC), Annual Report 2014, 23 June 2015.
† Peter Heim, "The Quest for Clarity on Data Protection and Security," *Network Security* (2014:2) 8.
‡ Federal Trade Commission Chairwoman Edith Ramirez, statement on EU-US Privacy Shield, February 2, 2016, at https://www.ftc.gov/news-events/press-releases/2016/02/statement-ftc-chairwoman-edith-ramirez-eu-us-privacy-shield.

Contents

NOTES		xix
ABBREVIATIONS		xxi
CHAPTER 1	NECESSARY TO CONSIDER EU RULES	1
	Introduction	1
	EU Data Protection Rules Are Important for US Businesses	2
	Comparable Analysis Beneficial	4
	Pre-Problem-Solving Works in EU and US	5
CHAPTER 2	US–EU SIMILARITIES, DIFFERENCES, AND BRIDGES	9
	Introduction	9
	History	9
	Similarities and Differences	12
	Similarity Bridges	15
CHAPTER 3	THE NEED FOR DATA PROTECTION	23
	Introduction	23
	Growing Importance of Data Protection	24
	Fundamental Right	24
	Digitization	25
	Online Abuse	25
	Benefits	26
	Applies to All Organizations	27
	Fines	28
	Data Breach and Data Loss	28
	Requirements to Report Data Breaches	29
	Prosecutions	31
	Proactive Official Audits	31

CHAPTER 4   NEED FOR UPDATING DATA PROTECTION   35
               Introduction   35
               EU Commission   37
               Update and New and Enhanced Provisions   42
               DPD95 Repealed   57
               Conclusion   57

CHAPTER 5   EU DATA PROTECTION CONCEPTS   61
               Introduction   61
               Personal Data   61
               The Parties   62
               Personal Data Use and Compliance   63
               Describing Data Protection   64
               The Data Protection Regime   66
               Outward-Facing Data Protection Compliance   67
               Inward-Facing Data Protection Compliance   69
               A Rights-Based Regime   73
               National Data Protection Supervisory Authorities   74
               Data Protection Rules Introduced   74
               Data Protection Concepts   76
               General Criteria for Data Processing   78
               Legitimate Processing   79
               Definitions   79

CHAPTER 6   THE INSTRUMENTS   83
               Introduction   83
               Data Protection Laws   83
               Legal Instruments   83
               General Provisions in the DPD95   84
               General Provisions in the GDPR   85
               Data Protection Principles   86
               Legitimate Data Processing Conditions for Lawfulness of
               Processing   88
               GDPR Background Recitals   89
               Consent Conditions   94
               Freely Given Consent   94
               Consent for Processing: Conditions for Consent   95
               Withdrawing Consent   96
               Conclusion   96

CHAPTER 7   THE NEW RULES   99
               Introduction   99
               Repeal of DPD95   100
               Context of GDPR   100
               Fundamental Right   101
               Formal Nature of Regulations and Directives   101
               Introducing the New GDPR Changes   102
               Processing of Criminal Convictions and Offenses Data   104

Processing Not Requiring Identification   104
Controllers and Processors   104
Responsibility of the Controller   105
Joint Controllers   105
Processor   106
Processing under Authority of Controller and Processor   106
Processing Not Allowing Identification   106
Exemptions   106
Conclusion   108

CHAPTER 8   DEFINITIONS   111
Introduction   111
Categories of Personal Data   111
General Personal Data   112
Sensitive Personal Data   112
Data Protection Definitions   115
New Definitions in GDPR   115
    Restriction of Processing   115
    Profiling   116
    Pseudonymization   116
    Personal Data Breach   116
    Genetic Data   116
    Biometric Data   116
    Data Concerning Health   117
    Main Establishment   117
    Enterprise   117
    Group of Undertakings   117
    Binding Corporate Rules   118
    Data Protection Supervisory Authority   118
    Supervisory Authority Concerned   118
    Data Protection Supervisory Authority   118
    Cross-Border Processing of Personal Data   119
    Relevant and Reasoned Objection   119
    Information Society Service   119
    International Organization   119
    Child   120
Updated Definitions in the GDPR   120
    Personal Data   120
    Sensitive Personal Data   120
    Background Guidance   121
    Legal Rule   122
    Data Subject   124
    Processing   125
    Filing System   125
    Controller   125
    Processor   126
    Recipient   126
    Third Party   126

	Data Subject's Consent	126
	Representative	127
	Relevant Filing System	127
	Conclusion	127
CHAPTER 9	PRINCIPLES	131
	Introduction	131
	Background Guidance on Lawful, Fair, Transparent	132
	Data Protection Principles	136
	Processor	140
	How to Collect and Process Personal Data	140
	Conclusion	140
CHAPTER 10	PRIOR INFORMATION CONDITIONS	143
	Introduction	143
	The General Data Protection Regulation (GDPR) Changes	143
	Prior Information Requirements: Directly Obtained Data	145
	Prior Information Requirements: Indirectly Obtained Data	146
	Timing of Information	148
	Conclusion	149
CHAPTER 11	LEGITIMATE PROCESSING CONDITIONS	151
	Introduction	151
	Lawfulness of Processing: General Legitimate Processing Conditions	152
	Lawfulness of Processing: Sensitive Personal Data Legitimate Processing Conditions	154
	Conclusion	156
CHAPTER 12	KEEPING RECORDS	159
	Introduction	159
	Liability and Measures to Demonstrate Compliance	159
	Maintaining Records	159
	Records Requirement	161
	The Principles' Record Requirements	162
	Cooperation with the Data Protection Supervisory Authority	163
	Conclusion	163
CHAPTER 13	REPRESENTATIVES OF CONTROLLERS NOT ESTABLISHED IN EU	165
	Introduction	165
	Representatives/Non-EU Controllers	165
	Background Guidance	165
	Article Requirement	166
	Conclusion	167
CHAPTER 14	RIGHTS OF INDIVIDUAL DATA SUBJECTS	169
	Introduction	169
	Recipients of Rights	170

Issues   170
Background Guidance   172
Legal Rules and Rights   173
Conclusion   177

CHAPTER 15 RIGHTS OF CONFIRMATION AND RIGHT OF ACCESS   179
Introduction   179
Right of Confirmation   179
   Background Guidance   180
   Legal Rule   181
Right of Access   182
   Background Guidance   183
   Legal Rule   184
   Access: What Must Be Supplied   185
   Time Limits for Access   185
   Making Request for Access   185
   Dealing with Access Requests   186
   Response to Access Requests   187
   Possible Access Exceptions and Issues   188
Conclusion   189

CHAPTER 16 RIGHT TO RECTIFICATION   191
Introduction   191
Background Guidance   191
Legal Rule   193
Conclusion   194

CHAPTER 17 RIGHT TO ERASURE AND RIGHT TO BE
            FORGOTTEN   197
Introduction   197
Background Guidance   197
Legal Rule   200
Conclusion   205

CHAPTER 18 RIGHT TO RESTRICTION OF PROCESSING   209
Introduction   209
Background Guidance   209
Background Guidance on Methods to Restrict Processing   210
Legal Rule   211
Conclusion   211

CHAPTER 19 RIGHT TO OBJECT TO PROCESSING   213
Introduction   213
Background Guidance   213
Legal Rule   215
Conclusion   217

CHAPTER 20 NOTIFICATION OBLIGATION REGARDING
RECTIFICATION, ERASURE, OR RESTRICTION ... 219
Introduction ... 219
Legal Rule ... 219
Conclusion ... 219

CHAPTER 21 RIGHT AGAINST AUTOMATED INDIVIDUAL
DECISIONS AND PROFILING ... 221
Introduction ... 221
Background Guidance on Profiling ... 222
Legal Rule ... 222
Conclusion ... 223

CHAPTER 22 RIGHT TO PREVENT DIRECT MARKETING
PROCESSING ... 225
Introduction ... 225
Background Guidance ... 225
Legal Rule ... 226
Conclusion ... 226

CHAPTER 23 PORTABILITY ... 229
Introduction ... 229
Background Guidance on Automated Processing and
Portability ... 229
Legal Rule ... 230
Conclusion ... 231

CHAPTER 24 OUTSOURCING TO THIRD-PARTY DATA PROCESSORS ... 233
Introduction ... 233
Background Guidance ... 234
Legal Rule ... 236
Processing under Authority ... 237
Processors and Security ... 238
New Processor Requirements ... 238
Controller Records ... 239
Processor Records ... 240
Conclusion ... 241

CHAPTER 25 CHILDREN ... 243
Introduction ... 243
Background Guidance ... 244
Children Merit Specific Protection ... 244
Transparency and Children ... 245
Legal Rules ... 245
Age ... 245
No Legitimate Interest Processing of Personal Data of
Child ... 247

Child's Consent and Conditions for Information Society
Services   247
Transparency and Children   248
Codes of Conduct and Certification   248
Data Protection Supervisory Authority   249
Conclusion   249

CHAPTER 26 INCREASED PENALTIES AND FINES   251
Introduction   251
Background Guidance   251
Fines of Ten Million   253
Fines of Twenty Million   254
Fines for Non-Compliance with Data Protection
Supervisory Authority Order   254
Impact   256
General Conditions for Imposing Administrative Fines   257
Penalties   259
Enforcement   260
Conclusion   260

CHAPTER 27 CODES OF CONDUCT AND CERTIFICATION   263
Introduction   263
Background Guidance: Codes of Conduct   263
Codes of Conduct   263
Monitoring Approved Codes of Conduct   265
Details of Codes of Conduct   266
Certification Seals and Marks   268
Background Guidance   268
Legal Rule   268
Conclusion   270

CHAPTER 28 SECURITY OF PERSONAL DATA   271
Introduction   271
Background Guidance   272
Risk and Damage   272
Breaches   274
Risk Evaluation   275
High Risks   275
Risk and Damage   276
Legal Rule: Appropriate Security Measures   277
Notification of Data Breach to Data Protection Supervisory
Authority   282
Communication of Personal Data Breach to Data Subject   283
Data Protection Impact Assessment   284
Prior Consultation   286
Ensuring Appropriate Security Measures   287
Employees and Security   288

Engaging Processors and Security Issues   289
Legislative Data Protection Reviews   291
Specific Public Interest Prior Consultations   291
Security Directive   291
Security Awareness   292
Data Protection Supervisory Authorities Guides   292
Security and Article 29 Data Protection Working Party
(WP29)/EDPB   294
Organizational Security Awareness   295
   Identifying and Controlling Organizational IT
   Security   295
   Appraising Employees   296
   General Policy   297
   Email   297
   Internet Access   297
   Mobile Telephones and Devices   297
   Vehicles   297
   Internet Social Media   298
   Software Installation and Management   298
   Password Security   298
   Connecting Hardware   298
   Remote Access   298
   Bring Your Own Device (BYOD)   299
Organizational Security Measures   299
Breach Laws to Consider   300
Third-Party Security Providers   301
Disposal of Computer Hardware   302
Conclusion   303

CHAPTER 29 DATA BREACHES   305
Introduction   305
Data Breach Incidents in Context   305
Background Guidance   306
   Data Breach   306
   Notifying Data Breach to Individual Data Subjects   306
   Notifications and Measures re Data Breaches   307
Legal Rule   307
   Notification of a Data Breach to Data Protection
   Supervisory Authority   307
   Communication of a Data Breach to the Data Subject   309
Employee Data Breaches   310
Notification Timelines   310
Notification Processes   310
Security Standards   310
Incident Response   312
Conclusion   312

CHAPTER 30 DATA PROTECTION IMPACT ASSESSMENT AND
           PRIOR CONSULTATION   315
           Introduction   315
           Background Guidance   315
              High Risks   315
              Data Protection Impact Assessment   316
           Legal Rule   318
           Reasons for Assessments   321
           Assessment Reports   323
           Assessment Characteristics   323
           Steps and Methodologies   325
           Prior Consultation and Risk   326
           Conclusion   327

CHAPTER 31 DATA PROTECTION BY DESIGN   329
           Introduction   329
           Background   329
           Principles of Data Protection by Design   330
           Legal Rule: Data Protection by Design   331
           Conclusion   333

CHAPTER 32 DATA PROTECTION AS DEFAULT   337
           Introduction   337
           Legal Rule   337
           Assessments   337
           Certification   339
           Conclusion   339

CHAPTER 33 CROSS-BORDER TRANSFERS OF DATA   341
           Introduction   341
           Background Guidance   342
              Cross-Border Flows   342
              Transfer Agreements and Mechanisms   343
           Legal Rule   349
           Permitting Transfers via Adequacy Decision   350
           Adequate Protection Exception   352
           Transfers via Appropriate Safeguards   353
           Creating Adequacy through Consent, Contract   354
           Transfers via Binding Corporate Rules (BCRs)   355
           Transfers or Disclosures Not Authorized by EU Law   359
           Transfers via Derogations for Specific Situations   359
           Exceptions   361
           Issues   362
           Establishing Whether the Ban Applies   363
           Schrems, EU–US Safe Harbor, and EU–US Privacy
           Shield   365
           Conclusion   368

CHAPTER 34 RIGHT TO BE INFORMED OF THIRD-COUNTRY
SAFEGUARDS 371
Introduction 371
Background Guidance 371
Legal Rule 373
Conclusion 374

CHAPTER 35 TRANSPARENCY 375
Introduction 375
Background Guidance 375
Legal Rule 380
Conclusion 383

CHAPTER 36 HEALTH DATA 385
Introduction 385
Health-Related Definitions 385
Data Concerning Health 385
Genetic Data 386
Biometric Data 386
Pseudonymization 386
Profiling 387
Legal Rule: Special Data 387
Health Research 388
Right to Be Forgotten Exception 389
Conclusion 390

CHAPTER 37 ePRIVACY 393
Introduction 393
Background 394
DPD95 and ePD 396
Scope of ePD 396
Security 397
Confidentiality 398
Traffic Data 399
Non-Itemized Billing 399
Call Line Identification 399
Location Data 400
Directories 400
Unsolicited Communications, Direct Marketing, and Spam 400
The Spam Problem 402
Spam Internationally 402
Unsolicited Communications 402
Marketing Default Position 403
Limited Direct Marketing Permitted 404
Direct Marketing to Existing Customers' Email 404
National Marketing Opt-Out Registers 405
Deceptive Emails: Marketing Emails Must Not Conceal
Identity 405

Marketing Emails Must Provide Opt-Out   405
Marketing Protection for Organizations   406
ePrivacy Regulation Proposal   406
Conclusion   407

CHAPTER 38 COURTS   413
Introduction   413
Civil Sanctions   414
Background Guidance   416
New GDPR Remedies, Legal Rules, Damage, and
Compensation   419
Right to Effective Judicial Remedy against Controller or
Processor   420
Right to Compensation and Liability   420
Right to Lodge Complaint with Data Protection
Supervisory Authority   422
Right to an Effective Judicial Remedy against a Data
Protection Supervisory Authority   422
Representation of Data Subjects   423
Organizational Privacy Groups   424
    Background Guidance on Representative Data Subject
    Organizations   424
Jurisdiction Issues   425
    Controller or Processor in EU   425
    Controller or Processor Not in EU   425
    Monitoring   426
    Jurisdiction, Main Establishment, Groups   426
    Investigation and Evidence   428
Conclusion   428

CHAPTER 39 SOME SPECIFIC ISSUES IN GDPR   429
Introduction   429
Specific Data Processing Situations   429
Employment Data   430
Processing National Identification Numbers   431
Public Authorities   431
Processing and Freedom of Expression and Information 431
Safeguards and Derogations: Public Interest Archiving/
Scientific or Historical Research/Statistical Processing 432
    Background Guidance   432
    Legal Rule   435
Obligations of Secrecy   436
Churches and Religious Associations   437
eCommerce Directive   437
General Registration/Notification Requirement Removed 437
Conclusion   438

CHAPTER 40 DATA PROTECTION SUPERVISORY AUTHORITIES   441
Introduction   441
Data Protection Supervisory Authorities   441
Tasks   442
Investigative Powers   444
Corrective Powers   445
Authorization and Advisory Powers   446
Independence   447
Cooperation with National Data Protection Supervisory
Authorities   449
Enforcement Powers of Data Protection Supervisory Authority   449
Investigations by National Data Protection Supervisory
Authorities   449
Power to Obtain Information   450
Power to Enforce Compliance with the Data Protection Laws   450
Power to Prohibit Overseas Transfer of Personal Data   450
Powers of Authorized Officers to Enter and Examine   451
Prosecution of Offenses   451
Notifying Data Breach to Data Protection Supervisory
Authority   452
European Data Protection Board   452
Background Guidance   452
Legal Rule   453
Conclusion   453

CHAPTER 41 THE DATA PROTECTION OFFICER   457
Introduction   457
New Data Protection Officers   457
Position   459
Article 39 Tasks   459
Group Data Protection Officer   461
Qualifications and Expertise   461
Contact Details   461
Duty of Confidentiality   462
Reporting   462
Independent in Role and Tasks   462
Resources   462
Data Protection by Design and Data Protection by Default   463
Conclusion   464

APPENDIX I: THE SOURCES OF DATA PROTECTION LAW   467

APPENDIX II: HOW TO COMPLY WITH THE DATA PROTECTION
REGIME   487

APPENDIX III: GENERAL DATA PROTECTION REGULATION
SECTIONS   491

INDEX   499

Notes

EU Directive: This is a legal instrument that applies generally in the European Union (EU) nut requires individual implementing laws in each individual member state. The main EU data protection law was and EU Directive from 1995, the DPD95.

EU Regulation: This is a legal instrument that applies generally and directly in all EU member states without the need for any individual implementing measures in the EU member states.

Recitals: The Recitals to the GDPR are interpretative aids to a regulation but do not form part of the formal legal rules. They are, however, instructive and help describe the background and context to the introduction of the GDPR, in particular the need or an updating of the data protection regime on foot of new issues, concerns, and challenges. Some of these themes are referred to below.

Articles: The Articles to the GDPR are the legal rules or legally binding parts of the regulation.

Personal data: Any data or information identifying or relating to the individual data subject. (In the United States, personal data is often referred to as personally identifiable information [PII]).

Data subject: The individual who the personal data relates to.

Controller: The organization collecting, processing, and holding the personal data.

Processor: An outsourced third-party organization or related entity carrying out certain defined outsourced activities for and on behalf of the main data controller with the personal data for example outsourced payroll, outsourced direct marketing, and so on.

Supervisory authority: An official data protection supervisory authority of one of the respective EU member states, such as the Data Protection Commissioner (DPC) in Ireland or the Information Commissioner's Office (ICO) in the United Kingdom.

Data retention: Note that the data protection regime is separate to the issue of mandated retention of certain telecommunications data for access in relation to terror law investigations—which is known as data retention law. This book refers to data protection only and not data retention issues. See further details in Appendices.

PII: Personal data is often referred to as personally identifiable information or PII in the United States.

TFEU: Treaty on the Functioning of the European Union.

Abbreviations

These abbreviations shall be used throughout:

GDPR: Regulation (EU) 2016/679 of the European Parliament and of the Council of 27 April 2016 on the protection of natural persons with regard to the processing of personal data and on the free movement of such data, and repealing Directive 95/46/EC (General Data Protection Regulation) Official Journal of the European Union, 4.5.2016, L 119/1.

  (The GDPR replaces the DPD95 and is directly effective throughout the European Union without the need for separate sets of national implementing legislation.*)

DPD95: EU Data Protection Directive 1995 (Directive 95/46/EC of the European Parliament and of the Council of 24 October

---

* The original draft for the GDPR was proposed by the EU Commission and is officially entitled: Proposal for a Regulation of the European Parliament and of the Council on the protection of individuals with regard to the processing of personal data and on the free movement of such data (General Data Protection Regulation) COM(2012) 11 final. Note also the various amendments in the versions as they advances, such as EU Data Protection Regulation (Regulation (EU) No xxx/2016 of the European Parliament and of the Council on the protection of individuals with regard to the processing of personal data and on the free movement of such data (General Data Protection Regulation) (the text of the tripartite agreed version of December 2015).

1995 on the protection of individuals with regard to the processing of personal data and on the free movement of such data).

DPO: Data protection officer.

WP29: EU Article 29 Working Party (replaced by GDPR with the EDPB).

FTC: US Federal Trade Commission.

EDPB: European Data Protection Board.

ePD: ePrivacy Directive*; dealing with, for example, data protection for phone, email, SMS text, and Internet. (Note: There is a new proposal to replace the ePD with a new ePrivacy regulation [ePR]). The draft proposal is entitled *Proposal for a Regulation on Privacy and Electronic Communications* [2017]).

Member state: A member state of the European Union.

EU Commission: The European Commission.

EEA: European Economic Area, comprising the EU member states plus Iceland, Liechtenstein, and Norway. The EEA applies similar data protection rules to the EU. (Note: Switzerland also has a similar type arrangement with the EU.)

Charter: Charter of Fundamental Rights of the EU.

TFEU: Treaty on the Functioning of the European Union.

Human Rights Convention: European Convention for the Protection of Human Rights and Fundamental Freedoms.

Data Protection Convention: Convention for the Protection of individuals with regard to automatic processing of personal data at Strasbourg on 28 January 1981 (Council of Europe Convention).

---

* As amended by Directives 2006/24/EC and 2009/136/EC.

1

NECESSARY TO CONSIDER EU RULES

Introduction

Commercial imperatives and what is expected by employees, customers, and users mean that data protection is a fast-growing global compliance issue. Organizations and businesses must respect personal data and data protection issues as regards their employees', customers', and users' data. As part of this, organizations also need to be aware of new European rules in relation to personal data and data protection. EU rules that were already in existence dating from 1995 have been replaced and enhanced. The 1995 data protection directive (DPD95) was replaced in 2016 with a new wider data protection regulation. The new regulation is formally referred to as the EU General Data Protection Regulation (GDPR). The GDPR is the single most important personal data and data protection set of rules to arrive in over 20 years. It strengthens the applicable rules as well as introducing many new ones. The GDPR is one of the most important developments for EU, US, and other organizations to be aware of. This is also important for those who professionally advise organizations. Understanding what is required in the new EU data protection rules is essential.

Under the EU data protection rules, an organization is referred to as a "controller" (i.e., the data controller). (An outsourced organization carrying out certain defined activities for and directed by the main data controller organization is referred to as a "processor" [i.e., data processor for the controller organization]).

EU Data Protection Rules Are Important for US Businesses

Why are EU data protection rules important for US businesses? Some of the reasons include

- The EU accounts for approximately 20% of worldwide exports and imports.
- The EU is the largest (or second largest, depending on figures) worldwide importer.
- The EU is made up of 28 states (with standardized rules making it streamlined and easier for business).
- Even after Brexit, EU or EU equivalent data protection legal standards will apply in the UK—including the new GDPR.
- The EU market is approximately 510 m people (third largest world population after China/India).
- EU data protection rules apply across all relevant organizations (regardless of size).
- EU data protection rules apply to controller organizations.
- EU data protection rules apply to processor organizations.
- EU data protection rules apply to and protect all relevant individuals.
- EU data protection rules require compliance from all US organizations based in the EU.
- EU data protection rules apply to US organizations exporting to EU consumers.
- EU data protection rules apply to proposed transfers or exports of personal data from the EU to the US.
- The EU data protection rules have been modernized and enhanced significantly in the new GDPR.
- There are new requirements in relation to the growing problem of data breach issues.
- There are new and enhanced compliance rules.
- There are mandated Data Protection Officers in organizations.
- There are new rights for individuals against businesses.
- Most striking perhaps is the new penalties and fines regime.
- Non-compliance or inadequate compliance can result in penalties of up to €20 m or 4% of *global annual turnover*.
- This is a lightning bolt for US, EU, and other organizations assessing and understanding the new EU data protection rules.

So, EU data protection rules can apply from the smallest to the largest US businesses when they seek to exploit the EU consumer marketplace.

Transatlantic business is significant, including Internet, eCommerce, aeronautics, technology, computing, finance, services, and so on. The Internet means that data protection is "clearly a global matter."*

Even where a US company is not dealing directly with EU consumers, such as processors, outsource companies, and cloud storage entities such as third-party data processors that hold or deal with the EU consumer or employee data for the organization, it must note that EU data protection rules can also apply.

As indicated in the preceding list, the new fines rules are very significant and present a risk for organizations in the EU, dealing with the EU, and/or receiving data from the EU.

Therefore, EU data protection rules can be directly relevant for many US businesses, and compliance is required. The new EU rules are also important for other reasons. The previous EU rules (in the DPD95) were viewed around the world as the best standard for data protection and for other countries modeling their own data protection rules. European data protection laws are frequently recognized as being "of the highest standards in the world."† There have also been calls for the US to adopt similar rules. Indeed, certain US state rules have been described as similar to some of the EU rules.

Any processing of personal data in the context of the activities of an establishment of a controller or a processor organization in the EU should be carried out in accordance with the GDPR, regardless of whether the processing itself takes place within the EU.‡

To ensure that persons are not deprived of protection, the processing of personal data of individual data subjects who are in the EU by a controller or a processor not established in the EU is subject to the GDPR where the processing is related to offering goods or services to such individual data subjects (irrespective of a payment).§

---

* Irish data protection supervisory authority (DPC), Annual Report 2014, June 23, 2015.
† Peter Heim, "The Quest for Charity on Data Protection and Security," *Network Security* (2014) (2014:2) 8–10.
‡ GDPR Recital 22.
§ GDPR Recital 23.

Processing of personal data of individual data subjects who are in the EU by a controller or processor not established in the EU should also be subject to the GDPR when it is related to the monitoring of the behavior of such individual data subjects (including tracking and profiling) insofar as their behavior takes place within the EU.*

The new GDPR also provides for a one-stop-shop mechanism to facilitate organizations in an efficient non-duplicatory manner. "Businesses will only have to deal with one single [data protection] supervisory authority. This is estimated to save €2.3 billion per year."† This will facilitate US–EU business and organizations doing business with the EU.

Comparable Analysis Beneficial

All US organizations operating in or targeting the EU or receiving EU data need to be aware of and compliant with EU data protection rules. Even if not directly applicable to certain US organizations (e.g., not operating in or targeting the EU or receiving EU data), it is still beneficial to consider the EU data protection regime. The nature of these rules means that they apply generally and across the board to *all* EU personal data. In the US, comparable rules do not apply wholesale, but rather are limited to specific sectors or specific sectoral types of personal data, for example health data, genomic data, financial data, data involved in certain types of data breaches, and so on. The EU rules are general, wide, and all-encompassing. The US rules are limited and case specific—thus naturally leaving many gaps. How the EU regime deals with data in areas not yet expressly covered in the US can be insightful, instructive, or of assistance to organizations, officers within organizations responsible for dealing with personal data, and external advisors. It is also useful to review and compare how the EU deals with issues that also arise and are of concern in the US.

---

* GDPR Recital 24.
† European Commission—Press release, "Agreement on Commission's EU Data Protection Reform Will Boost Digital Single Market," Brussels (December 15, 2015), at http://europa.eu/rapid/press-release_IP-15-6321_en.htm.

Pre-Problem-Solving Works in EU and US

While there is a long history and evolution of data protection concerns, the current increase in security, hacking, data breach, and data loss brings data protection issues to the fore. When issues go wrong, there can be litigation, lost sales, customer drop-off, diminished goodwill and brand reputation, and so on. There can be direct tangible financial effects. Corporate officers and even managing directors are in the spotlight in ways that have not occurred before. Sometimes they can be sued. There are increasing examples of corporate officers and managing directors losing their positions as a result of not adequately dealing with or preventing data breach issues.

The EU data protection regime now expressly mandates compliance with the concept of data protection by design.* This is the concept of formally considering data protection issues and implications at all stages of development and roll out of new products and services—versus an add-on consideration at the very end of development. In the latter instance, if problems arise, it may mean costly amendments, delaying go-live, cancelling a launch, major revisions, or worse, cancelling the product entirely. It can be worse if the product has actually launched, with withdrawal, lost sales, and so on arising. Incorporating data protection by design is a form of pre-problem solving, ensuring that speed bump or road block problems do not arise at a critical stage later on. US companies who transact with the EU can benefit by pre-problem solving US and EU issues all at once, avoiding potential problems in advance as well as gaining associated efficiencies, customer goodwill, and commercial advantage over competitors. In any event, data protection by design (and privacy by design) is increasingly recognized and popular in technology organizations in Canada, the US, and Europe. Microsoft has adopted and promoted this concept for many years. Other multinational organizations such as Intel and McAfee also favor the concept. Dr. Anne Cavoukian, Ontario data protection commissioner, is credited with developing and promoting the concept as well as tools for applying the concept to

---

* Data protection by design (DPbD) is also sometimes referred to as privacy by design (PbD).

real life situations. The book *The Privacy Engineer's Manifesto, Getting from Policy to Code to QA to Value** also promotes this concept.

As indicated on Page 1, where US organizations and businesses collecting or receiving EU personal data fail to comply with the EU data protection regime, the bottom line can suffer directly from very significant official fines and penalties—quite apart from the potential for users, customers, or representative bodies to pursue litigation in addition.

This guide is essential for all US businesses and organizations that directly or indirectly deal with EU personal data, as well as those who aim to expand their markets. It is also essential to seek to reduce or avoid data incidents arising regardless of where the organization is located.

REGULATIONS AND DIRECTIVES

On a technical note, the import of an EU "regulation" is that it is applies across all EU member state countries once initiated, as opposed to an EU "directive," which must wait until each member state enacts its own national laws to bring in or effect the directive. The previous rules from 1995 applied via a data protection directive (DPD95) which was required to be implemented on a case-by-case basis in each EU member state. The new rules in the GDPR apply directly without the need for country-by-country legislation to implement them.

RECITALS AND ARTICLES IN REGULATIONS AND DIRECTIVES

The new GDPR, like all formal EU regulations, is divided into "recitals" and "articles." The recitals provide background interpretative context but are not legally binding. The articles are the legally binding rules of the regulation. It is recommended to

---

* Finneran Dennedy, Fox, and Finneran, *The Privacy Engineer's Manifesto, Getting from Policy to Code to QA* (Aspen Open, 2014).

consider both so as to better understand the rational and legal import of the new EU data protection rules.

FURTHER READING

- Ciriani, "The Economic Impact of the European Reform of Data Protection," *Communications & Strategies* (2015) (97) 41.
- Fuster, *The Emergence of Personal Data Protection as a Fundamental Right of the EU* (Springer, 2014).
- Gilbert, "EU General Data Protection Regulation: What Impact for Businesses Established Outside the European Union," *Journal of Internet Law* (2016) (19:11) 3.
- Gilbert, "European Data Protection 2.0: New Compliance Requirements in Sight—What the Proposed EU Data Protection Regulation Means for US Companies," *Santa Clara Computer and High Technology Law Journal* (2012) (28:4) 815.
- Lambert, *The Data Protection Officer: Profession, Rules and Role* (Routledge, Taylor & Francis, 2017).
- Lynskey, *The Foundations of EU Data Protection Law* (OUP, 2015).
- Victor, "The EU General Data Protection Regulation: Toward a Property Regime for Protecting Data Privacy," *Yale Law Journal* (2013) (123:2) 513.
- Voss, "Looking at European Union Data Protection Law Reform through a Different Prism: The Proposed EU General Data Protection Regulation," *Journal of Internet Law* (2014) (17:9) 12.

2

US–EU Similarities, Differences, and Bridges

Introduction

There is a long history of concern over and protection for privacy. More recently, there is concern over and particular protections for informational protection or data protection. These concerns are not unique to the EU or, indeed, to the United States. Most countries share these concerns.

However, there are some differences in how protection is achieved and how wide specific protections are. One avenue is to establish protection for personal data generally across all sectors of the economy, while another approach may be to provide for individualized data protections, sector by sector. The EU favors the former approach, while the United States in general favors data protection sector by sector or issue by issue.

History

The legal discussion in relation to privacy is frequently linked to Warren and Brandeis's legal article in 1890 entitled "The Right to Privacy," published in the *Harvard Law Review*.* Warren and Brandeis were notable jurists and academics in the United States.

Arguably, data protection is (part of) the modern coalface of the discussion in relation to privacy and privacy protection.† Data protection, in many respects, can be wider than privacy rights and is an express stand-alone fundamental right. The EU data protection

---

* Warren and Brandeis, "The Right to Privacy," *Harvard Law Review* (1890) (IV) 193.
† See Rule and Greenleaf, eds, *Global Privacy Protection: The First Generation* (Elgar, 2008).

regime can be seen as setting standards in certain areas of informational privacy protection, which have come to be followed in other jurisdictions internationally, beyond the EU,* and even followed by or influencing US states.

The growth of the processing of information relating to individuals in electronic computer data format from the 1970s onwards led to ever-increasing concerns regarding such processing. Existing laws were "insufficient to deal with concerns about the amount of information relating to individuals that was held by organizations in electronic form."[†]

The impetus for formal national data protection laws began in Germany, and has since spread. Originally, the main EU data protection instrument was the DPD95.[‡] The purpose is largely to promote openness and transparency to individuals of information held about them in filing systems, whether manual or computerized, and

---

* See Birnhack, The EU data protection directive: An engine of a global regime, *Computer Law & Security Report* (2008) (2) at 512. However, the data protection regime is separate and distinct from privacy. Data protection and data protection rights exist as stand-alone enumerated fundamental rights in the EU, separate from privacy. Data protection is, in many respects, more explicit and enumerated than privacy rights. There have also been calls for international-level data protection rules. Certainly, if this were to come to pass, it could bring greater certainty for both organizations, industry, and individual data subjects. There are frequent comments in relation to disparities between US and EU protection for personal data. While this is frequently correct, there are also frequent similarities as well as, it has to be said, certain instances where US laws may be more explicit than EU data protection laws. More recently, there is also an endeavor called "privacy bridges," whereby academics are trying to link up the similarities and common interest of protection between the US and EU in relation to personal data concerns. Spiekermann and Novotny, "A Vision for Global Privacy Bridges: Technical and Legal Measures for International Data Markets," *Computer Law and Security Report* (2015) (31:2) 181. Peter Heim states that "European data protection laws have some of the highest standards in the world," Heim, "The Quest for Clarity on Data Protection and Security," *Network Security* (2014) (2014:2) 8.

† Carey, *Data Protection, A Practical Guide to UK and EU Law* (OUP, 2009) 1. Also, Bainbridge, *Data Protection* (CLT, 2000) 2.

‡ The EU General Data Protection Regulation (GDPR) and previously the 1995 data protection directive (DPD95) are the main EU measures. However, there was previously the Council of Europe Data Protection Convention in relation to personal data (1981). Various EU states also enacted personal data legislation nationally. For example, the German state of Hessen enacted a data protection law in 1970, and a federal German data protection law was proposed in 1971.

to protect their data protection interests and rights in relation to such information.*

Even prior to the DPD95, concern for informational privacy in the computer environment was recognized in an early data protection regime. The Council of Europe proposed and enacted the Data Protection Convention in 1981.† National data protection laws were enacted following on from the Data Protection Convention. Subsequently, these were updated and amended to also implement the DPD95.

The Data Protection Convention sets out the following principles and requirements: personal data must be

- Obtained and processed fairly and lawfully.
- Stored for specified and legitimate purposes and not used in a way incompatible with those purposes.
- Adequate, relevant, and not excessive in relation to the purposes for which the personal data are stored.
- Accurate and, where necessary, kept up to date.
- Preserved in a form that permits identification of the individual data subject for no longer than is required for the purpose for which those data are collected and stored.‡

In addition, the Data Protection Convention provides that

- Personal data that reveal racial origin, political opinions, or religious or other beliefs, as well as personal data relating to health or sexual life, or criminal convictions, may not be processed automatically unless member state law provides appropriate safeguards.
- Appropriate security measures must be taken to protect personal data stored in automated data files against accidental or unauthorized destruction, accidental loss, and unauthorized access, alteration, or dissemination.

---

* MacDonald, *Data Protection: Legal Compliance and Good Practice for Employers* (Tottel, 2008) 33.
† Data Protection Convention, at http://conventions.coe.int/Treaty/en/Treaties/Html/108.htm. Also, "Convention for the Protection of Individuals with Regard to Automatic Processing of Personal Data," *International Legal Materials* (1990) (20) 317.
‡ Convention Articles 5–8.

- Any data subject is entitled to establish the existence of an automated personal data file, its main purposes, as well as the identity, habitual residence, or principal place of business of the controller.
- Any data subject is entitled to obtain at reasonable intervals and without excessive delay or expense confirmation of whether personal data are stored in the automated data file as well as communication to the individual data subject of such data in an intelligible form.
- Any data subject is entitled to obtain rectification or erasure of such data if these have been processed contrary to the provisions of domestic law giving effect to the basic principles set out in the Data Protection Convention.*
- Any data subject is entitled to have a remedy if a request for confirmation, communication, rectification, or erasure is not complied with.†

Similarities and Differences

The United States and the EU both have data protection rules. Importantly, in the United States, these are generally only on an issue-by-issue basis. The US issue-by-issue approach therefore leaves many gaps and areas not covered by data protection in the United States.

The EU data protection regime and the laws referred to in the previous section generally operate at a wide general level to cover all types of personal data. They govern all personal data collection and processing use by an organization.

This differing approach to types of personal data, and what is and is not covered by the data protection regimes, is a significant difference between the EU and the United States.

One of the most notable examples of a specific data protection type law in the United States is the Video Privacy Protection Act of 1988. This specific act was introduced after Judge Robert Bork was asked embarrassing questions relating to his alleged video rentals during his Supreme Court nomination hearing. The Act was introduced as a

---

* Articles 5 and 6 of the Data Protection Convention.
† ibid.

reaction to ensure that in future, personal data relating to an individual's personal video rental history would remain protected, personal, and confidential.

As yet, the US approach to data protection for an individual's personal information and data is on a case-by-case basis. There is no wide, general, uniform law in the United States across all types of personal data.

While there is no general overall federal law governing the collection and use of all personal data or personally identifiable information (PII), there are a growing number of individual state laws. These state laws are also frequently issue specific.

Certain federal data protection–focused laws relate to the collection, use, and processing of certain types of personal data. These include financial or health information and electronic (marketing) communications. The following federal legislation relates, whether directly *or* indirectly, to personal data issues

- Federal Trade Commission Act (FTCA).*
- Title V of Gramm–Leach–Bliley Act (GLBA).†
- Children's Online Privacy Protection Act (COPPA).‡
- Fair Credit Reporting Act (FCRA).§
- Controlling the Assault of Non-Solicited Pornography and Marketing Act (CANSPAM Act).¶

---

* Federal Trade Commission Act (FTC Act) 15 USC §§41–58. The FTC may agree mutual agreements of understanding with data protection supervisory authorities or regulators in other countries. One such example is the bilateral agreement between the FTC and the national official data protection supervisory authority in Ireland, entitled the Data Protection Commissioner. The official agreement is the Memorandum of Understanding with US Federal Trade Commission (FTC–Irish Data Protection Commissioner).

† Financial Services Modernization Act (Gramm–Leach–Bliley) (GLB) Act 15 USC §§6801–6827.

‡ Children's Online Privacy Protection Act (COPPA) 15 USC §§6501–6506.

§ As amended by the Fair and Accurate Credit Transactions Act.

¶ The Controlling the Assault of Non-Solicited Pornography and Marketing Act (CANSPAM Act) 15 USC §§7701–7713 and 18 USC §1037. See Reid, "Recent Developments in Private Enforcement of the Can-Spam Act," *Akron Intellectual Property Journal* (2010) (4) 281.

- Health personal data such as Health Insurance Portability and Accountability Act (HIPAA).*

Organizations also need to note, for example, the

- Electronic Code of Federal Regulations.
- FTC Self-Regulatory Principles for Online Behavioral Advertising.

While various states have some form of data protection–related legislation, California law and policy frequently lead the way in relation to personal data and data protection. Other states sometimes follow the lead of the California initiatives in this area: for example, the California Security Breach Notification Law and the California Online Privacy Protection Act. California was the first state to enact a security breach notification law.† This requires that organizations disclose breaches of security to individuals whose personal information was acquired by an unauthorized third party. The California Shine the Light law‡ requires organizations to disclose details of the third parties with whom they have shared their personal data. The California data security law§ requires organizations to implement security procedures to protect personal data against unauthorized access, destruction, use, modification, or disclosure. On occasion, the approach of Californian data protection laws is compared to the EU data protection model. Presidents Obama and Trump favor initiatives (including an Executive Order) in relation to federal agency data security.

Some of the contrasts and similarities between US and EU data protection law include

- Under EU data protection law, a legal basis and a legitimate purpose are needed before personal data may be processed.
- In the United States, commercial data may be processed unless there is some legal rule preventing it.
- The EU recognizes data protection as a fundamental right.

---

* Health Insurance Portability and Accountability Act (HIPAA) 42 USC §1301.
† California Civil Code §1798.82.
‡ Shine the Light law, Cal. Civil Code. §§1798.83-1798.84.
§ Data security law, Cal. Civil Code §1798.81.5.

- Lawful conditions on collecting and processing personal data apply as well as consent for the use of personal data.
- The EU also places emphasis on the principle of proportionality and expectations of data protection.
- While the issues and concerns for individuals may be the same in the United States, the EU, and elsewhere, the form of regulating is somewhat different: that is, general versus specific.
- The EU applies a high level of data protection.
- Enforcement, however, is often left to individuals and to data protection supervisory authorities. This is not at all dissimilar to the United States, where individuals, class actions, and Federal Trade Commission (FTC) actions can apply.
- The United States has a large number of privacy laws, both federal and state, as well as the federal prosecutors and even state prosecutors/attorneys general.
- The FTC has emerged as the leading data protection regulator in the United States.
- It engages in investigations, consent orders, and prosecutions.
- Enforcement actions also arise under HIPAA legislation.*

Similarity Bridges

A recent project seeks to identify, elucidate, and promote areas of common interest between the United States and the EU in relation to data protection concerns.† The project was sponsored and facilitated by Massachusetts Institute of Technology (MIT) and the Institute for Information Law of the University of Amsterdam. The project issued a report, which listed 10 areas for commonality and bridges between

---

* See *Privacy Bridges, EU and US Privacy Experts in Search of Transatlantic Privacy Solutions* (Massachusetts Institute for Technology Computer Science and Artificial Intelligence Laboratory, Cambridge, MA, United States) and the Institute for Information Law of the University of Amsterdam (Amsterdam, the Netherlands) (September 2015) 19.

† *Privacy Bridges, EU and US Privacy Experts in Search of Transatlantic Privacy Solutions* (Massachusetts Institute for Technology Computer Science and Artificial Intelligence Laboratory, Cambridge, MA, United States and the Institute for Information Law of the University of Amsterdam, Amsterdam, the Netherlands) (September 2015).

US and EU data protection. Referring to the need for bridges, the data protection bridges report states that there are indeed areas of commonality, but also differences, thus demonstrating a need for bridges and related research.

These data protection bridges are

- BRIDGE 1: DEEPEN THE ARTICLE 29 DATA PROTECTION WORKING PARTY (WP29)/FEDERAL TRADE COMMISSION RELATIONSHIP—The EU WP29 and the US FTC should commit to regular, public dialogue and policy coordination on leading data protection challenges faced in the transatlantic region. This bridge would institutionalize the working relationship between the WP29 and the FTC via a memorandum of understanding (MOU). This MOU will foster better cooperation and more efficient policy development and enforcement by these regulators, thereby delivering enhanced data protection to individuals on both sides of the Atlantic.

- BRIDGE 2: USER CONTROLS—Users around the world struggle for control over their personal information. This bridge calls on technology companies, data protection regulators, industry organizations, data protection scholars, civil society groups, and technical standards bodies to come together to develop easy-to-use mechanisms for expressing individual decisions regarding user choice and consent. The outcome should be usable technology, developed in an open standards-setting process, combined with clear regulatory guidance from both EU and US regulators, resulting in enhanced control by users over how data about them are collected and used.

- BRIDGE 3: NEW APPROACHES TO TRANSPARENCY—This bridge recommends that the WP29 and the FTC rely on the MOU described in Bridge 1 to coordinate their recommendations on data protection notices and then jointly encourage an international standardization process. By pooling the insights that they gained from earlier and ongoing standardization efforts, and drawing on lessons learned by other industries on required notifications (e.g., nutrition labeling), they can develop more definitive guidance on transparency and thereby achieve a necessary condition for the user controls described in Bridge 2.

- BRIDGE 4: USER-COMPLAINT MECHANISMS: REDRESS OF VIOLATIONS OUTSIDE A USER'S REGION—Users interact with web-based services from all around the world. When they have complaints, they should have an easy path to resolution. This bridge encourages all online services to provide contact information and calls on the appropriate EU and US public agencies to cooperate on the creation of a directory of basic information about relevant jurisdictions and how and to whom complaints concerning data protection may be brought.

- BRIDGE 5: GOVERNMENT ACCESS TO PRIVATE SECTOR PERSONAL DATA—This bridge offers guidance to, in particular, telecommunication and Internet services faced with surveillance from their own and foreign governments. Specifically, it recommends that all such companies establish uniform internal practices for handling such requests regardless of jurisdiction, citizenship, and data location; report on practices relating to government access requests on a regular basis; and adopt best practices based on international standards (such as those of the Global Network Initiative), with the goal of developing a framework for assessing and responding to requests for data originating outside national territory.

- BRIDGE 6: BEST PRACTICES FOR DE-IDENTIFICATION OF PERSONAL DATA— De-identification of personal data is a critical tool for protecting personal information from abuse. This bridge calls on EU and US regulators, who already share common views about de-identification, to identify concrete, shared standards on de-identification practices. Common standards will improve data protections on both sides of the Atlantic while enhancing legal certainty for both EU and US organizations that follow these recommendations.

- BRIDGE 7: BEST PRACTICES FOR SECURITY BREACH NOTIFICATION—Although information security breaches have a global impact on users, given that many of them reside in different jurisdictions than those of service providers, there is a lack of uniformity in security breach notification laws, both domestically (across distinct sectors) and even more so internationally. This bridge recommends that the relevant authorities cooperate when dealing with multi-nation breaches, both in terms of enforcement and in establishing a more harmonized breach-reporting regime. It also recommends that firms complement their reporting obligations by adopting robust information governance systems, which should result in an increase in the level of data protection of end users.
- BRIDGE 8: ACCOUNTABILITY—Both EU and US regulators have accepted the idea of organizational responsibility (or "accountability") as a means to assure data protection and for firms to satisfy domestic legal obligations. This bridge identifies the common elements of enforceable corporate accountability programs. It recommends that the WP29 and FTC harmonize their approaches while emphasizing the need for the private sector to develop more effective means for external verification and scaling of accountability programs for use by small and medium enterprises. The hoped-for outcome is an improvement in actual data processing practices that not only benefits individuals but also offers companies more effective compliance guidelines for international operations.
- BRIDGE 9: GREATER GOVERNMENT-TO-GOVERNMENT ENGAGEMENT—This bridge proposes that in parallel with the MOU suggested in Bridge 1, EU and US executive agencies and decision-making bodies engage in active dialogue and, where appropriate, effective coordination of their regulatory activity. Such government-to-government engagement seems especially valuable in a number of new sectors in the transatlantic economy (an interesting example is the development and use of drones) that pose acute data protection challenges. The exchange of information on a regular basis and development of transparent platforms for

active discussion and practical policy development will yield a variety of benefits to governments, individuals, and commercial actors alike.

• BRIDGE 10: COLLABORATING ON PRIVACY RESEARCH PROGRAMS—Finally, this bridge encourages the growth of common perspectives on data protection in the EU and the United States by fostering collaborative, multidisciplinary engagement of data protection researchers on both sides of the Atlantic. It identifies barriers to bringing together academics to work on joint data protection research projects in a variety of fields and suggests ways to overcome them.

The WP29 is made up of representatives of each of the respective national data protection supervisory authorities in the EU. The reference to the WP29 changes under the new GDPR, where the WP29 is replaced by a new European Data Protection Board (EDPB).

The data protection bridges report states that

> These ten data protection bridges are all practical steps that require no change to the law yet will result in better-informed, and more consistent, regulatory cooperation, policy guidance, and enforcement activity. Our mandate as a group is to produce recommendations that can be acted upon without changes in the legislative environment of either the EU or the United States.*

The data protection bridges report adds that

> While many members of the expert group that produced these recommendations have strong views about the future direction of US and EU rules, here we seek to surmount challenges facing the information society, without entering into divisive debates on changes to underlying constitutional or statutory frameworks. Changing the law is an arduous

---

* *Privacy Bridges, EU and US Privacy Experts in Search of Transatlantic Privacy Solutions* (Massachusetts Institute for Technology Computer Science and Artificial Intelligence Laboratory, Cambridge, MA, United States) and the Institute for Information Law of the University of Amsterdam (Amsterdam, the Netherlands) (September 2015).

and lengthy endeavour, and waiting for it to happen can become simply an excuse for inaction. Ideally, this report will bring about improvements in protection due to positive actions not only by governments and regulatory authorities, but also by the private sector, civil society, and others, all of whom may implement its recommendations.*

Organizations and individuals must assess their expanded rights and obligations under the new GDPR, as well as initiatives referring to the commonality between the US and the EU, such as the data protection bridges initiative.

KEY CONCEPTS

There are differences between the US and the EU on data protection; however, there are also many similarities. The issues of concern facing organizations, individuals, and regulators are similar across an increasingly connected globe. Pre-problem-solving is a shared interest regardless of borders.

KEY WORDS

- Similarities and differences.
- Data bridges.
- WP29, EDPB, and FTC.
- User self controls.
- Increased transparency.
- Complaint and redress mechanisms.
- De-identification.
- Breach notifications.
- Accountability.
- Germany.
- Council of Europe.
- Warren and Brandeis.

---

* ibid.

FURTHER READING

- "Convention for the Protection of Individuals with Regard to Automatic Processing of Personal Data," *International Legal Materials* (1990) (20) 317.
- Data Protection Convention.
- de Hert and Papakonstantinou, "The Council of Europe Data Protection Convention Reform: Analysis of the New Text and Critical Comment on its Global Ambition," *Computer Law & Security Review* (2014) (30:6) 633.
- de Terwangne, "The Work of Revision of the Council of Europe Convention 108 for the Protection of Individuals as Regards the Automatic Processing of Personal Data," *International Review of Law, Computers & Technology* (2014) (28:2) 118.
- "Draft Convention for the Protection of Individuals with Regards to Automatic Processing of Personal Data," *International Legal Materials* (1980) (19) 284.
- Electronic Communications Privacy Act and the Computer Fraud and Abuse Act.
- Fairclough, "Privacy Piracy: The Shortcomings of the United States' Data Privacy Regime and How to Fix It," *Journal of Corporation Law* (2016) (42:2) 461.
- Gilbert, "European Data Protection 2.0: New Compliance Requirements in Sight—What the Proposed EU Data Protection Regulation Means for US Companies," *Santa Clara Computer and High Technology Law Journal* (2012) (28:4) 815.
- Glosson, "Data Privacy in Our Federalist System: Toward an Evaluative Framework for State Privacy Laws," *Computer and Internet Lawyer* (2016) (33:8) 1.
- Greenleaf, "Modernizing Data Protection Convention 108: A Safe Basis for a Global Privacy Treaty," *Computer Law & Security Review* (2013) (29) 430.

- Harrell and Rothstein, "Biobanking Research and Privacy Laws in the United States," *Journal of Law, Medicine & Ethics* (2016) (44:1) 106.
- Health Insurance Portability and Accountability Act (HIPAA) 42 USC §1301.
- Heim, "The Quest for Clarity on Data Protection and Security," *Network Security* (2014) (2014:2) 8.
- Hess, *Protecting Privacy in Private International and Procedural Law and by Data Protection: European and American Developments* (Ashgate, 2015).
- Hurwitz, "Data Security and the FTC's Uncommon Law," *Iowa Law Review* (2016) (101:3) 955.
- Kierkegaard, Waters, Greenleaf, Bygrave, Lloyd, and Saxby, "30 Years On: The Review of the Council of Europe Data Protection Convention 108," *Computer Law & Security Review* (2011) (27) 223.
- MacDonald, *Data Protection: Legal Compliance and Good Practice for Employers* (Tottel, 2008).
- Mantelero, "Competitive Value of Data Protection: The Impact of Data Protection Regulation on Online Behaviour," *International Data Privacy Law* (2013) (3:4) 229.
- Phan, Flo, and Patel, "Recent Trends in the FTC's Data Security and Privacy Enforcement Actions," *Journal of Internet Law* (2016) (19:9) 18.
- *Privacy Bridges, EU and US Privacy Experts in Search of Transatlantic Privacy Solutions* (Massachusetts Institute for Technology Computer Science and Artificial Intelligence Laboratory, Cambridge, MA, United States and the Institute for Information Law of the University of Amsterdam (Amsterdam, the Netherlands) (September 2015).
- Purtova, *Property Rights in Personal Data, a European Perspective* (Kluwer, 2012).
- Reid, "Recent Developments in Private Enforcement of the Can-Spam Act," *Akron Intellectual Property Journal* (2010) (4) 281.
- Warren and Brandeis, "The Right to Privacy," *Harvard Law Review* (1890) (IV) 193.

3
THE NEED FOR DATA PROTECTION

Introduction

Why do we have a data protection regime? There is a data protection regime because of the legal and political recognition that society respects the personal data protection and informational data protection of individuals. In the context of data protection, that means respect for, control of, and security in relation to informational personal data. Data protection protects personal data relating to individuals, which includes employees, contractors, customers, and users. Personal data issues apply to every individual and every organization.

Data protection rules exist to ensure

- Protection in relation to personal information.
- Obtaining consent from individuals to collect and process personal data.
- Security in respect to personal information.
- Protection against personal informational abuse.
- Protection against personal information theft and identity theft.
- Protection against unsolicited direct marketing.
- Protection for the data protection rights of individuals.
- Increased protection in recognition of new technological and Big Data issues.
- Transparency in collection.
- Transparency in use and processing.
- Pre-problem-solving.
- No waiting for a problem issue to arise and reacting to it, whether breaches, incidents, or access requests.

Growing Importance of Data Protection

Data protection compliance is important for all organizations, large and small. One example of this importance is data protection supervisory authority investigation of various organizations in relation to specific data protection issues. The commercial reality of cross-border transfers of personal data is also recognized in transfer mechanisms created for the default transfer ban on transferring personal data outside of the EU (as many countries have lower standards of personal data protection). The Intel group, for example, has been approved under the EU binding corporate rules (BCR) transfer procedure to exempt it from the EU transfer ban in relation to transferring personal data.*

Fundamental Right

The protection of natural persons' personal data is a fundamental right. Article 8(1) of the EU Charter and Article 16(1) of the EU Treaty provide that everyone has the right to the protection of their personal data.† The principles and rules on the protection of individuals' personal data must, whatever the nationality or residence of natural persons, respect their fundamental rights, notably their right to personal data protection.‡ The right to personal data protection may

---

* This examination and approval process occurred under the auspices of the Irish data protection supervisory authority (DPC). The BCR procedure is one of the mechanisms by which an organization can export or transfer personal data outside of the European Economic Area (EEA). Without the BCR (or a similar exemption mechanism), the organization would not be permitted to make such a transfer. These transfers are sometimes referred to as trans-border data flows or cross-border data flows. The default position is that trans-border data flows may not occur from the EEA to non-EEA countries unless exempted. See "Commissioner Approves Intel Corporation Binding Corporate Rules," DPC.

† EU General Data Protection Regulation (GDPR) Recital 1. Charter of Fundamental Rights of the European Union; Treaty of the European Union.

‡ GDPR Recital 2. It should contribute to the accomplishment of an area of freedom, security and justice and of an economic union, to economic and social progress, the strengthening and the convergence of the economies within the internal market, and the well-being of individuals; ibid.

sometimes be balanced with other fundamental rights in accordance with the principle of proportionality.*

Digitization

The increasing "centralisation of information through the computerisation of various records has made the right of [data protection] a fundamental concern."† Data protection is important, increasingly topical and an issue of legally required compliance for all organizations. More importantly, it is part of management and organizational best practice. Individuals, employees, and customers expect that their personal data will be respected. They are increasingly aware of their rights, and increasingly enforce their rights. "[D]ata protection issues are never far from the horizon at the moment. There are waves of discussion in this area ... and ... that wave is riding high."‡ The significant attention focused recently on the fallout of the EU–US Safe Harbor transfer regime being declared void,§ its impact on transatlantic business, and the complex political negotiations required for the new EU–US transfer regime entitled EU–US Privacy Shield highlight the mainstream commercial and political significance of data protection law and the importance of US–EU trade.

Online Abuse

The issue of online abuse, which involves, among other things, harassment, threats, revenge porn, and data protection, has also been hitting the headlines.¶ Data protection issues are also in the headlines

---

* GDPR Recital 3.

† Personal data protection and privacy, *Council of Europe*, at www.coe.int/t/dghl/standardsetting/dataprotection/Default_en.asp.

‡ Editorial, Saxby, *Computer Law & Security Review* (2012) (28) 251.

§ Ni Loidean, "The End of Safe Harbor: Implications for EU Digital Privacy and Data Protection Law," *Journal of Internet Law* (2016) (19:8) 1.

¶ Tragically, such online abuse can, and does, result in and contribute to actual suicide. This is a particular concern in relation to children and teenagers. See, generally, Lambert, *Social Networking, Law, Rights and Policy* (Clarus, 2014); Lambert, *International Handbook of Social Media Laws* (Bloomsbury, 2015); Philips, *This Is Why We Can't Have Nice Things: Mapping the Relationship Between Online Trolling and Mainstream Culture* (MIT Press, 2015).

because of public and official data protection supervisory authority concerns with the problem of the damage of certain permanent data online. The EU Court of Justice, on the foot of such concerns, issued an important decision in a "right to be forgotten" case directing that certain personal data online had to be deleted from search engine listings.* This case received major media attention both inside and outside of the EU. Issues of takedown, deletion, and forgetting have been increasing in importance, and sometimes also urgency, for many years. The award-winning book *Delete: The Virtue of Forgetting in the Digital Age* highlights some of these issues.[†]

Benefits

A further reason why data protection is important, and increasingly the focus of press attention, is that organizations are increasingly using security and respect for data protection as an advantage and commercial differentiator in the marketplace. Apple has repeatedly announced that it does not operate on a *data-intrusive model* collecting user data. In fact, it has even criticized some of its technology competitors. Most recently, Apple has had a skirmish with the FBI in relation to mandated new software to access iPhone data. Microsoft has for many years promoted the data protection–friendly policy of data protection by design. Separately, Microsoft has also had an official skirmish in relation to protecting and preventing access to personal data held on its servers outside of the US.

Post Snowden, many US technology companies have been heavily lobbying the US administration for a roll back of certain data collection and data retention activities and practices, particularly those argued to be extra-judicial, extra-legal, and/or hidden-legal, on the basis that they will disadvantage the US-based data-, cloud-, and cloud storage–driven industries.

---

* See *Google Spain SL, Google Inc v Agencia Española de Protección de Datos (AEPD), Mario Costeja González*, Court of Justice (Grand Chamber), Case C131/12, May 13, 2014.
[†] Mayer-Schönberger, *Delete: The Virtue of Forgetting in the Digital Age* (Princeton, 2009). Also see Lambert, *International Handbook of Social Media Laws* (Bloomsbury, 2015) and the international comparisons and issues highlighted therein.

Many companies have been highlighting the fact that they are non-US based. Companies are now promoting the fact that they have or are building EU-based cloud storage facilities, and in some instances, that EU data will remain located in the EU.

Applies to All Organizations

All organizations collect and process personal data. Whether they are big organizations or new start-ups, they need to comply with the data protection regime. Bear in mind also that even a new technology start-up can scale relatively quickly to millions of users. Many issues enhance the importance of getting the organizational data protection understanding and compliance model right from day one. These include legal obligations; director, board, and officer obligations; investigations, fines, penalties, prosecutions, being ordered to delete databases, and adverse publicity on the front pages of the press media; commercial imperatives, and even positive commercial advantages. If one also considers some of the recent large-scale data breach incidents, there are examples of chief technology officers as well as managing directors/CEOs losing their employment positions as a result of the incident. On a separate issue, Apple, for example, sees the commercial (and ethical) values in protecting personal data.

In addition, organizations often fail to realize that data protection compliance is frequently an issue of dual compliance. They need to be looking at both *inward* and *outward* data processing issues.

Internally, organizations have to be data protection compliant in relation to all of their employees' (and contractors') personal data. Traditionally, this may have related to personnel files and employee contracts, but it now includes issues of electronic communications, social media, Internet usage, filtering, monitoring, on-site activity, off-site activity, company devices, employee devices, vehicles, location services, and so on. The consequences of getting it wrong are now more significant.

Separately, organizations have to be concerned about personal data relating to persons outside of the organization, for example customers, prospects, and so on. Comprehensive data protection compliance is also required for those outward-facing issues. The consequences of non-compliance are significant.

Fines

Substantial fines have been imposed in a number of recent cases. Fines, and frequency of fines, are increasing. In some instances, organizations have been ordered to delete their databases. In a new technology start-up situation, this can be the company's most valuable asset. The consequences, therefore, cannot be overstated. Data protection is also one of the most important due diligence issues to consider when businesses are being bought and sold.

A data protection supervisory authority can also impose significant fines for a non–data loss incident. A financial organization was fined for mixing up details of financial data relating to two separate individuals. This would have caused financial loss and damage for one of the individuals, as they were not credited with all of their payments and contributions.[*] The account details were not kept accurate and up to date. This was despite complaint correspondence to the financial organization from one of the individuals over a period of time. The data protection supervisory authority comments:

> We hope this penalty sends a message to all organizations, but particularly those in the financial sector, that adequate checks must be in place to ensure people's records are accurate. Staff should also receive adequate training on how to manage and maintain them, with any concerns fully investigated in order to ensure problems are addressed at an early stage.[†]

Data Breach and Data Loss

Data protection is also increasing in coverage in mainstream media. This is due in part to the large number of recent data loss and data breach incidents. These have involved the personal data of millions of individuals being lost by commercial organizations and, perhaps more worryingly, by trusted government entities.

---

[*] See the UK data protection supervisory authority Information Commissioner's Office (ICO), "Prudential Fined £50,000 for Customer Account Confusion," November 6, 2012.

[†] ibid.

Up until recently, the issue of data loss was a proverbial small back page story. More recently, however, the loss of personal data files of tens of millions of individuals in a single instance—including from official governmental sources—make data loss a front page issue. There is increased scrutiny from the data protection supervisory authorities and others, and new regulation of data security issues, preparedness, and reactivity. Organizations must look at security issues with increasing rigor. Organizations can face liability issues in breach incidents but also in the aggravating situation where a vulnerability may have been already known and highlighted internally but was not acted on, thus contributing to the breach incident. As well as official investigations, fines, penalties, and sanctions, organizations also face liability issues to users and in some instances, potential liability to banks and financial intermediaries also. Target, for example, was sued not just by individual data subjects but also by financial intermediaries. Examples such as this are likely to increase.

Class actions, in relation to both data protection and other issues, have been a common theme in the US landscape for many years. While these are less common in the EU, they will likely increase in future as the new GDPR expressly recognizes the possibility of individual data subject representative organizations.

Requirements to Report Data Breaches

There are enhanced obligations to report all data breaches and data losses.* There are also enhanced financial penalties. In some instances, personal director responsibility for data loss can arise. The need for compliance is now a boardroom issue and an issue of senior corporate compliance. Proactive and complete data protection compliance is also a matter of good corporate governance, brand loyalty, and a means to ensuring user and customer goodwill.

The frequency and scale of breaches of security are increasing. There are many examples, such as breaches at

- Yahoo (two breaches affecting 500 million and one billion users, respectively).

---

* Unless exempted.

- Adobe.
- TalkTalk.
- Target.
- Home Depot.
- Sony PlayStation (70 million individuals' personal data affected in one instance and 25 million affected in another*).
- Sony *Interview* breach.
- Office of Personnel Management (OPM) (official, 22 million affected).
- Insurer Anthem (80 million affected).
- Affair dating website Ashley Madison (37 million affected).
- Hotels.
- Even security firms; for example, hacking firm Hacking Team.
- Children's' toymaker VTech.
- and others.

These examples emphasize the increasing importance of data security compliance for personal data. The UK Revenue and Customs loss of discs with the names, dates of birth, and bank and address details for 25 million individuals[†] and the hack of federal employee databases in the US highlight that official breaches also occur. There are already many examples of substantial fines for data protection breaches,[‡] including commercial and official organizations.

---

[*] See, for example, "Martin, Sony Data Loss Biggest Ever," *Boston Herald*, 27 April 2011; Arthur, "Sony Suffers Second Data Breach with Theft of 25 m more User Details," *Guardian*, 3 May 2011.

[†] See, for example, "Brown Apologises for Record Loss"; "Prime Minister Gordon Brown Has Said He 'Profoundly Regrets' the Loss of 25 Million Child Benefit Records," *BBC*, November 21, 2007.

[‡] The Brighton and Sussex University Hospitals NHS Trust had a fine of £325,000 imposed by the ICO in relation to a data loss incident. See, for example, "Largest Ever Fine for Data Loss Highlights Need for Audited Data Wiping," *ReturnOnIt*. Zurich Insurance was fined £2.3 million for losing data in relation to 46,000 individual customers. See, for example, Oates, "UK Insurer Hit with Biggest Ever Data Loss Fine," *The Register*, August 24, 2010. This was imposed by the Financial Services Authority (FSA). Text spammers are often investigated; for example, see Arthur, "Spam Text Senders Face Fines of up to £500,000," *Guardian*, October 1, 2012. A police authority has been fined £120,000 in relation to a data breach involving unencrypted personal data; see "Police Force Fines £120,000 after Theft of Unencrypted Data," *Guardian*, October 16, 2012.

Prosecutions

The data protection supervisory authorities in the US, EU, and elsewhere prosecute breaches. This ability to prosecute includes directors as well as companies. Errant outsource private investigators have also been prosecuted. Many large organizations have been prosecuted and fined in relation to data breach incidents.

Proactive Official Audits

Data protection supervisory authorities are increasingly proactive and undertake audits of data protection compliance as well as incidents of breaches.* They can also be critical of organizations and the data protection policies and practices of organizations.† The phone hacking scandal in the United Kingdom also highlights the importance of personal data.‡ A major news organization had to close down. There has been previous criticism from data protection supervisory authorities of the abuse of official databases by unauthorized access by police and civil servants, sometimes for personal reasons and on other occasions being paid for data by external third parties. A previous Minister for Justice also criticized unauthorized police access of an official police database for personal or non-official use.

---

* Facebook international has been audited by the Irish data protection supervisory authority (DPC). The audit relates to Facebook internationally, outside of the United States and Canada. See first stage of the audit report, of December 21, 2011, *Facebook Ireland Limited, Report of Audit*.

† See, for example, letter from WP29 and the EU data protection supervisory authorities to Google at https://dataprotection.ie. The UK data protection supervisory authority (ICO) is also involved in dealing with personal data issues relating to the recent press phone hacking scandal, which is also the separate subject of the Leveson Inquiry, at www.levesoninquiry.org.uk/. The ICO investigation is called Operation Motorman. For more details see Operation Motorman: Steve Whittamore Notebooks, ICO, at https://ico.org.uk.

‡ This resulted in the Leveson Inquiry and a large number of data subject litigation cases against newspapers, as well as a separate ICO investigation.

KEY CONCEPTS

The need for data protection was identified in numerous different locations over a long period of time. The advent of computer data has enhanced the need and concern for such protections. More recently, Web 2.0 and now Big Data issues enhance this need even further.

KEY WORDS

- Need for data protection.
- Increasing computerization.
- Increasing amalgamation of data.
- Online abuse issues.
- Deletion, takedown, and forgetting.
- Data breach-reporting need.

FURTHER READING

- "Brown Apologises for Record Loss, Prime Minister Gordon Brown Has Said He 'Profoundly Regrets' the Loss of 25 Million Child Benefit Records," *BBC*, November 21, 2007.
- Cohen, "The Regulatory State in the Information Age," *Theoretical Inquiries in Law* (2016) (17:2) 369.
- *Encyclopaedia of Data Protection* (Sweet and Maxwell).
- "Largest Ever Fine for Data Loss Highlights Need for Audited Data Wiping," *ReturnOnIt*.
- Rodata, "Data Protection as a Fundamental Right," in Gutwirth, Poullet, de Hert, de Terwangne, and Nouwt, *Reinventing Data Protection?* (Springer, 2009) 77.
- "Personal Data Protection and Privacy," *Council of Europe*, at http://www.coe.int/t/dghl/standardsetting/dataprotection/Default_en.asp.
- "Police Force Fined £120,000 after Theft of Unencrypted Data," *Guardian*, October 16, 2012.

- Schachter, *Information and Decisional Privacy* (Carolina Academic Press, 2003).
- Spanish EU Court of Justice "right to be forgotten" case.*

---

* *Google Spain SL, Google Inc v Agencia Española de Protección de Datos* (AEPD), Mario Costeja González, Court of Justice (Grand Chamber), Case C131/12, 13 May 2014.

4

NEED FOR UPDATING
DATA PROTECTION

Introduction

The EU General Data Protection Regulation (GDPR) is overhauling and modernizing the data protection regime. Organizations throughout the EU and elsewhere will be affected and will have to prepare for the new rules.

The 1995 data protection directive (DPD95) in the EU dates from 1995. Obviously, therefore, there have been many changes since. For example, it pre-dates online social networking. Cloud computing, Big Data and wider Web 2.0 services, online abuse such as revenge porn, and so on did not exist in 1995. Modern activities such as drones, vehicle data, and self-driving vehicles were not envisaged at the time of the 1995 rules.

Threats to personal data and informational data protection have increased in line with the increased ease with which personal data can be collected and transferred electronically. This has increased further with digital technology, computer processing power, Web 2.0,[*] aggregation, Big Data, Internet of things (IoT), localization data, and social media.[†] The Internet continues to develop and also brings up new challenges.[‡]

---

[*] That is, the second generation of Internet websites and Internet services.

[†] Note, generally, comments of the UK data protection supervisory authority the Information Commissioner's Office (ICO) in relation to privacy by design (PbD) and the report *Privacy by Design* at https://ico.org.uk. The GDPR refers to data protection by design, art. 23. Also note Information and Privacy Commissioner, Ontario.

[‡] Blume, "It Is Time for Tomorrow: EU Data Protection Reform and the Internet," *Journal of Internet Law* (2015) (18:8) 3. On the general developments and threats, note, for example, Fishleigh, "Is Someone Watching You? Data Privacy and Protection: Current Issues," *Legal Information Management* (2015) (15:1) 61.

The whole area of transfers of personal data outside of the EU (known as cross-border transfers)* is regularly changing; for example, new countries are added to a white list of permitted data export countries in relation to the default transfer ban after having been examined by the EU Commission. This is one of the cross-border data transfer mechanisms. There are also other changes, such as contractual clauses and binding corporate rules. If an organization needs to consider the possibility of data transfer exports to non-European Economic Area (EEA) countries, the most up-to-date transfer rules should be assessed, and appropriate professional advice should be sought. It may be necessary to have specific legal contracts in place. These rules may also be sector specific for certain industries; for example, airlines flying to the United States from Europe.

Further topical issues are regularly being analyzed by the Article 29 Data Protection Working Party (WP29) and now the European Data Protection Board (EDPB). The WP29 has also recently referred to

- The implementation issues for the new GDPR.[†]
- The consequences of the *Schrems* EU Court of Justice case.[‡]

Some of the areas of concern that the GDPR seeks to address[§] include

- The data protection regime in the online age.
- Social media.
- Cloud computing.
- Minimum/maximum standards.
- The data protection principles.[¶]

---

[*] Previously known as trans-border data flows.

[†] WP29, February 2, 2016, at http://ec.europa.eu/justice/data-protection/article-29/documentation/opinion-recommendation/files/2016/wp236_en.pdf.

[‡] WP29, February 3, 2016, at http://ec.europa.eu/justice/data-protection/article-29/press-material/press-release/art29_press_material/2016/20160203_statement_consequences_schrems_judgement_en.pdf.

[§] GDPR. Wong, "The Data Protection Directive 95/46/EC: Idealisms and Realisms," *International Review of Law, Computers & Technology* (2012) (26) 229.

[¶] Wong, "The Data Protection Directive 95/46/EC: Idealisms and Realisms," *International Review of Law, Computers & Technology* (2012) (26) 229.

EU Commission

The EU Commission recognizes the need for modern update. The EU Commission states* that the policy in reviewing the data protection regime seeks to

- Modernize the EU legal system for the protection of personal data, in particular to meet the challenges resulting from globalization and the use of new technologies.
- Strengthen individuals' rights and at the same time reduce administrative formalities to ensure a free flow of personal data within the EU and beyond.
- Improve the clarity and coherence of the EU rules for personal data protection and achieve a consistent and effective implementation and application of the fundamental right to the protection of personal data in all areas of the EU's activities.†

It aims to enhance consumer confidence in eCommerce.‡ In addition, it aims to bring comprehensive savings to organizations, as the obligations of complying with somewhat differing member state data protection regimes will be reduced, if not eliminated.§ The EU Commissioner dealing with data protection issues further summarizes the need for new data protection rules as follows:

> The current EU data protection rules date from 1995. Back then, the Internet was virtually unknown to most people. Today, 250 million people use the Internet daily in Europe.
>
> Think how that has changed our personal data landscape through the explosion of ecommerce, social networks, online games and cloud computing.
>
> The [EU] Commission has therefore adopted proposals for updating data protection rules to meet the challenges of the digital age. In

---

* Reform of Data Protection Legal Framework, Commission, Justice Directorate, at http://ec.europa.eu/justice/data-protection/review/index_en.htm.
† ibid.
‡ In Brief, *Communications Law* (2012) (17) 3.
§ ibid. See details of some of the steps and consultations at http://ec.europa.eu/justice/data-protection/review/actions/index_en.htm.

particular, the proposals will strengthen protection of … personal data online.*

The GDPR also seems to ensure an element of future proofing to deal with further upcoming issues. One EU Minister for Justice states:

> A minority of EU citizens had access to personal computers, mobile phones and Internet when the Data Protection Directive was adopted in 1995. The opposite is now the case … developments have in some instances led to … "commoditisation of human beings," whereby personal information is bundled and sold to commercial entities for financial gain. This is done without the knowledge or express permission of the individual.
>
> The [new] data protection [regime] … will not only serve to protect the [data protection] of all European citizens but, in doing so, will also increase the confidence and trust consumers have in online transactions and encourage their greater use.
>
> … [the expanded right to be forgotten] seeks to address the possible reputational, financial and psychological risks associated with social networking and other Internet-based sites. Those who fail to comply could face [significant] fines.†

The EU Commission's press statement notes that the GDPR "will enable people to better control their personal data. At the same time modernised and unified rules will allow businesses to make the most of the opportunities of the [EU] Digital Single Market by cutting red tape and benefiting from reinforced consumer trust."‡

---

* See Commission, "Why Do We Need New Data Protection Rules Now?," at http://ec.europa.eu/justice/data-protection/minisite/index.html.

† Minister for Justice, Equality and Defence, Alan Shatter, TD, "Data Protection is Key Focus for European Presidency, New Safeguards Are Essential in order for the Digital Economy to Thrive," *Sunday Business Post*, January 13, 2013.

‡ European Commission: Press release, "Agreement on Commission's EU Data Protection Reform Will Boost Digital Single Market," Brussels (December 15, 2015), at http://europa.eu/rapid/press-release_IP-15-6321_en.htm.

The EU Commission also refers to the benefits of the changes. It states:

> The reform will allow people to regain control of their personal data. Two-thirds of Europeans (67%), according to a recent Eurobarometer survey, stated they are concerned about not having complete control over the information they provide online. Seven Europeans out of ten worry about the potential use that companies may make of the information disclosed. The data protection reform will strengthen the right to data protection, which is a fundamental right in the EU, and allow them to have trust when they give their personal data.
>
> The new rules address these concerns by strengthening the existing rights and empowering individuals with more control over their personal data.*

These include "[m]ost notably," according to the EU Commission

- *Easier Access to Your Own Data*: Individuals will have more information on how their data is processed and this information should be available in a clear and understandable way.
- *A Right to Data Portability*: It will be easier to transfer your personal data between service providers.
- *A Clarified "Right to Be Forgotten"*: When you no longer want your data to be processed, and provided that there are no legitimate grounds for retaining it, the data will be deleted.
- *The Right to Know When Your Data Has Been Hacked*: For example, companies and organizations must notify the national [data protection] supervisory authority of serious data breaches as soon as possible so that users can take appropriate measures.†

The EU Commission also refers to

---

* ibid.
† ibid. Note format amended.

Clear Modern Rules for Businesses

In today's digital economy, personal data has acquired enormous economic significance, in particular in the area of big data. By unifying Europe's rules on data protection, lawmakers are creating a business opportunity and encouraging innovation.

One Continent, One Law

The [GDPR] will establish one single set of rules that will make it simpler and cheaper for companies to do business in the EU.

One-Stop-Shop

Businesses will only have to deal with one single [data protection] supervisory authority. This is estimated to save €2.3 billion per year.

European Rules on European Soil

Companies based outside of Europe will have to apply the same rules when offering services in the EU.

Risk-Based Approach

The rules will avoid a burdensome one-size-fits-all obligation and rather tailor them to the respective risks.

Rules Fit for Innovation

The [GDPR] will guarantee that data protection safeguards are built into products and services from the earliest stage of development (data protection by design). [Data protection]–friendly techniques such as pseudonymization will be encouraged, to reap the benefits of big data innovation while protecting [data protection].

Benefits for Big and Small Alike

The data protection reform will stimulate economic growth by cutting costs and red tape for European business, especially for small and medium enterprises (SMEs). The EU's data protection reform will help SMEs break into new markets. Under the new rules, SMEs will benefit from four reductions in red tape.*

---

* European Commission: Press release, "Agreement on Commission's EU Data Protection Reform Will Boost Digital Single Market," Brussels (December 15, 2015), at http://europa.eu/rapid/press-release_IP-15-6321_en.htm. Note format amended.

The four red tape reductions are

No More Notifications
Notifications to [data protection] supervisory authorities are a formality that represents a cost for business of €130 million every year. The reform will scrap these entirely.

Every Penny Counts
Where requests to access data are manifestly unfounded or excessive, SMEs will be able to charge a fee for providing access.

Data Protection Officers
SMEs are exempt from the obligation to appoint a data protection officer insofar as data processing is not their core business activity.

Impact Assessments
SMEs will have no obligation to carry out an impact assessment unless there is a high risk.*

The EU Commission also refers to

Better Protection of Citizens' Data
Individuals' personal data will be better protected, when processed for any law enforcement purpose including prevention of crime. It will protect everyone—regardless of whether they are a victim, criminal or witness. All law enforcement processing in the EU must comply with the principles of necessity, proportionality and legality, with appropriate safeguards for the individuals. Supervision is ensured by independent national data protection authorities, and effective judicial remedies must be provided.

The Data Protection Directive for Police and Criminal Justice Authorities provides clear rules for the transfer of personal data by law enforcement authorities outside the EU, to ensure that the level of protection of individuals guaranteed in the EU is not undermined.[†]

---

* ibid. Note format amended.
† ibid. Note format amended.

In one survey, 72% of Internet users are concerned that they give away too much personal data.* However, red tape reduction and economic growth are also commercial issues considered under the new regime. New technological changes are also recognized and encompassed. European harmonization issues are also a central consideration.

Update and New and Enhanced Provisions

The key changes are referred to in the following list. In some respects, these could also be seen as advantages of the new GDPR data protection regime

- Administrative costs are to be reduced with a single EU-wide set of rules and obligations.
- There may be less need to interact with the data protection supervisory authority as more responsibility and accountability are passed to the organizational level.
- The consent requirement has been clarified to mean explicit consent (previously there were references to different categories of consent).
- Rights are improved with easier access to personal data as well as its transferability.
- The enhanced right to be forgotten will improve the position of individual data subjects and the ability to delete data.
- The EU data protection regime will apply to non-EU entities operating with regard to EU personal data and EU citizens.
- The national authorities will be able to impose significant new fines including millions of euros or a percentage of global turnover.†

The GDPR "strengthens the position of individuals, recognises important concepts such as [data protection] by design and [data protection] impact assessments and requires organizations to be able

---

* Eurobarometer, "Attitudes on Data Protection and Electronic Identity in the EU" (June 2011).
† In Brief, *Communications Law* (2012) (17) 3.

to demonstrate that they have measures in place to ensure personal information is properly protected."*

The GDPR recognizes the need for updating the rules and that there is a need for updating the data protection regime. In particular, it refers to the following

- *Technology and Increased Data Collection*: Rapid technological developments and globalization have brought new challenges for the protection of personal data. The scale of the collection and sharing of personal data has increased significantly. Technology allows both private companies and public authorities to make use of personal data on an unprecedented scale to pursue their activities. Natural persons increasingly make personal information available publicly and globally. Technology has transformed both the economy and social life, and should further facilitate the free flow of personal data within the EU and the transfer to third countries and international organizations, while ensuring a high level of protection of personal data.†

- *Need for Stronger Data Protection and Control*: These developments require a strong and more coherent data protection framework in the EU, backed by strong enforcement, given the importance of creating the trust that will allow the digital economy to develop across the internal market. Natural persons should have control of their own personal data. Legal and practical certainty for natural persons, economic operators, and public authorities should be enhanced.‡

- *Freedoms and Specific Issues*: To ensure a consistent and high level of protection of natural persons and to remove the obstacles to flows of personal data within the EU, the level of

---

* Ibid; reference to statement of UK data protection supervisory authority (ICO). Commentators also describe the GDPR as "ambitious"; De Hert and Papakonstantinou, "The Proposed Data Protection Regulation Replacing Directive 95/46/EC: A Sound System for the Protection of Individuals," *Computer Law & Security Review* (2012) (28) 130. Note also Walden and Savage, "Data Protection and Privacy Laws: Should Organizations be Protected?" *International and Comparative Law Quarterly* (1988) (37) 337.
† GDPR Recital 6.
‡ GDPR Recital 7.

protection of the rights of natural persons with regard to the processing of such data should be equivalent in all member states. Consistent and homogeneous application of the rules for the protection of the fundamental rights of natural persons with regard to the processing of personal data should be ensured throughout the EU. Regarding the processing of personal data for compliance with a legal obligation, for the performance of a task carried out in the public interest, or in the exercise of official authority vested in the controller, member states should be allowed to maintain or introduce national provisions to further specify the application of the rules of the GDPR. In conjunction with the general and horizontal law on data protection implementing DPD95, member states have several sector-specific laws in areas that need more specific provisions. The GDPR also provides a margin of maneuver for member states to specify its rules, including for the processing of special categories of personal data ("sensitive data"). To that extent, the GDPR does not exclude member state law that sets out the circumstances for specific processing situations, including determining more precisely the conditions under which the processing of personal data is lawful.*

- *Rights and Obligations*: The effective protection of personal data throughout the EU requires the strengthening and setting out in detail of the rights of individual data subjects and the obligations of those who process and determine the processing of personal data, as well as equivalent powers for monitoring and ensuring compliance with the rules for the protection of personal data and equivalent sanctions for infringements in the member states.†

- *Data Flows*: The economic and social integration resulting from the functioning of the internal market has led to a substantial increase in cross-border flows of personal data. The exchange of personal data between public and private actors, including natural persons, associations, and organizations, across the EU has increased. National authorities in the

---

* GDPR Recital 10.
† GDPR Recital 11.

member states are being called on by EU law to cooperate and exchange personal data so as to be able to perform their duties or carry out tasks on behalf of an authority in another member state.*

- *Freedoms, Transfers, Fragmentation, Update Needed*: The objectives and principles of DPD95 remain sound, but it has not prevented fragmentation in the implementation of data protection across the EU, legal uncertainty, or a widespread public perception that there are significant risks to the protection of natural persons, in particular with regard to online activity. Differences in the level of protection of the rights of natural persons, in particular the right to the protection of personal data, with regard to the processing of personal data in the member states may prevent the free flow of personal data throughout the EU. Those differences may therefore constitute an obstacle to the pursuit of economic activities at the level of the EU, distort competition, and impede authorities in the discharge of their responsibilities under EU law. Such a difference in levels of protection is due to the existence of differences in the implementation and application of DPD95.†

  To ensure a consistent and high level of protection of natural persons and to remove the obstacles to flows of personal data within the EU, the level of protection of the rights of natural persons with regard to the processing of such data should be equivalent in all member states.‡

- *Protection of Natural Living Persons*: The GDPR protects *natural persons*, of whatever nationality or residence, regarding personal data. The GDPR cannot be claimed by legal persons and organizations.§ Protection must be technologically neutral and not depend on the techniques used; otherwise, this

---

* GDPR Recital 5.
† GDPR Recital 9.
‡ GDPR Recital 10. The GDPR also provides a margin of maneuver for member states to specify its rules, including for sensitive data. The GDPR does not exclude member state law that defines the circumstances of specific processing situations, including determining more precisely the conditions for processing personal data; ibid.
§ GDPR Recital 14.

would create a serious risk of circumvention. Protection must apply to personal data processing by automated and manual means, if the data are contained or are *intended to be* contained in a filing system.*

The GDPR should not apply to personal data processing by a natural person in the course of a purely personal or household activity and thus without a connection with a professional or commercial activity. However, the GDPR applies to controllers or processors that provide the means for processing personal data for such personal or household activities.†
The GDPR does *not* apply to data of *deceased persons*.‡

- *Identifiers*: The background Recitals refer to identifiers and the increasing possibility of identifying individuals through linking different data sets together. Natural persons may be associated with online identifiers provided by their devices, applications, tools, and protocols, such as Internet protocol addresses, cookie identifiers, or other identifiers such as radio frequency identification tags. This may leave traces that, in particular when combined with unique identifiers and other information received by the servers, may be used to create profiles of the natural persons and identify them.§

- *Combining Data*: If the personal data processed by a controller do not permit the controller to identify a natural person, the data controller should not be obliged to acquire additional information to identify the individual data subject for the sole purpose of complying with any provision of the GDPR. However, the controller should not refuse to take additional information provided by the individual data subject to support the exercise of their rights. Identification should include the digital identification of an individual data subject, for example

---

* GDPR Recital 18. Files that are not structured according to specific criteria should not fall within the GDPR; ibid.

† GDPR Recital 18. Personal and household activities could include correspondence and the holding of addresses, or social networking and online activity undertaken within the context of such personal and household activities; ibid.

‡ GDPR Recital 27. Member states may provide rules regarding the processing of data of deceased persons; ibid.

§ GDPR Recital 30.

through authentication mechanisms such as the same creden-
tials used by the individual data subject to log in to the online
service offered by the data controller.*

- *Coupling*: By coupling information from registries, researchers can obtain new knowledge of great value with regard to
  widespread medical conditions such as cardiovascular disease,
  cancer, and depression. On the basis of registries, research
  results can be enhanced, as they draw on a larger population. Within social science, research on the basis of registries enables researchers to obtain essential knowledge about
  the long-term correlation of a number of social conditions,
  such as unemployment and education, with other life conditions. Research results obtained through registries provide
  solid, high-quality knowledge, which can provide the basis
  for the formulation and implementation of knowledge-based
  policy, improve the quality of life for a number of people, and
  improve the efficiency of social services. To facilitate scientific
  research, personal data can be processed for scientific research
  purposes, subject to appropriate conditions and safeguards set
  out in EU or member state law.†

- *Cloud*: The popularity of cloud computing and virtualization
  services with users, enterprise, and official organizations is
  ever-increasing. However, there are real concerns in relation
  to data protection, data security,‡ continuity, discovery, liability, record-keeping, and so on.§ One commentator refers to

---

* GDPR Recital 57.

† GDPR Recital 157.

‡ See, for example, Soghoian, "Caught in the Cloud: Privacy, Encryption, and
Government Back Doors in the Web 2.0 Era," *Journal of Telecommunications & High
Technology Law* (2010) (8) 359.

§ *Guidance on the Use of Cloud Computing*, ICO; *Opinion 05/2012 on Cloud Computing*,
Article 29 Working Party, WP 196; Lanois, "Caught in the Clouds: The Web 2.0,
Cloud Computing, and Privacy?" *Northwestern Journal of Technology and Intellectual
Property* (2010) (9) 29; Pinguelo and Muller, "Avoid the Rainy Day: Survey of US
Cloud Computing Caselaw," *Boston College Intellectual Property & Technology Forum*
(2011) 1; Kattan, "Cloudy Privacy Protections: Why the Stored Communications Act
Fails to Protect the Privacy of Communications Stored in the Cloud," *Vandenburg
Journal of Entertainment and Technology Law* (2010–2011) (3) 617.

cloud computing as the data protection storm on the horizon.* Any organization considering cloud services needs to
carefully consider the advantages, disadvantages, assessments,
and contract assurances that will be required. Such organizations, as well as the service operators, also need to assure
themselves as to how they ensure data protection compliance.

• *Need for Consent*: The background Recitals refer to the important issue of the consent of individual data subjects. Consent
should be given by a clear affirmative act establishing a *freely
given, specific, informed, and unambiguous indication* of the
individual data subject's agreement to the processing of personal data relating to them, such as by a written statement,
including by electronic means, or an oral statement. This
could include ticking a box when visiting an Internet website,
choosing technical settings for information society services,
or another statement or conduct that clearly indicates in this
context the individual data subject's acceptance of the proposed processing of their personal data. Silence, pre-ticked
boxes, or inactivity should not, therefore, constitute consent.
Consent should cover all processing activities carried out for
the same purpose or purposes.†

When the processing has *multiple purposes*, consent should
be given for all of them. If the individual data subject's consent is to be given following a request by electronic means, the
request must be clear, concise, and not unnecessarily disrup-
tive to the use of the service for which it is provided.‡

Where processing is based on the individual data subject's consent, the controller should be able to demonstrate
that the individual data subject has given consent to the processing operation. In particular in the context of a written
declaration on another matter, safeguards should ensure that
the individual data subject is aware of the fact that, and the
extent to which, consent is given. A declaration of consent

---

* DeVere, "Cloud Computing: Privacy Storm on the Horizon?" *Albany Law Journal*
  (2010) (20) 365.
† GDPR Recital 32.
‡ GDPR Recital 32.

pre-formulated by the controller should be provided in an intelligible and easily accessible form, using clear and plain language, and it should not contain unfair terms.*

For consent to be informed, the individual data subject should be aware at least of the identity of the controller and the purposes of the processing for which the personal data are intended. Consent should not be regarded as freely given if the individual data subject has no genuine or free choice or is unable to refuse or withdraw consent without detriment.[†]

To ensure that consent is freely given, consent should not provide a valid legal ground for the processing of personal data in a specific case where there is a clear imbalance between the individual data subject and the controller, in particular where the controller is a public authority and it is therefore unlikely that consent was freely given in all the circumstances of that specific situation. Consent is presumed not to be freely given if it does not allow separate consent to be given to different personal data processing operations, despite its being appropriate in the individual case, or if the performance of a contract, including the provision of a service, is dependent on the consent despite such consent not being necessary for such performance.[‡]

For processing to be lawful, personal data should be processed on the basis of the consent of the individual data subject concerned or some other legitimate basis, laid down by law, either in the GDPR or in other EU or member state law as referred to in the GDPR, including the necessity for compliance with the legal obligation to which the controller is subject or the necessity for the performance of a contract to which the individual data subject is party or to take steps at

---

* GDPR Recital 42. In line with Directive 93/13/EEC, a declaration of consent pre-formulated by the controller should be provided in an intelligible and easily accessible form, using clear and plain language, and it should not contain unfair terms; ibid.
† ibid.
‡ GDPR Recital 43.

the request of the individual data subject prior to entering into a contract.*

- *Consent*: Broader parameters are contained in the GDPR in relation to consent. The definition and conditions are broader than previously. The inclusion of the words "freely given," "specific," and "unambiguous indication" in Article 4(11) is more specific than the previous "unambiguously" consented.

- *Consent and Scientific Research Purposes*: It is often not possible to fully identify the purpose of personal data processing for scientific research purposes at the time of data collection. Therefore, individual data subjects should be allowed to give their consent to certain areas of scientific research when in keeping with recognized ethical standards for scientific research. Individual data subjects should have the opportunity to give their consent only to certain areas of research or parts of research projects to the extent allowed by the intended purpose.†

- *Pseudonymization and Anonymization*: The background Recitals refer to the need for pseudonymization and anonymization. Personal data that have undergone pseudonymization but that could be attributed to a natural person by the use of additional information should be considered to be information on an identifiable natural person. To determine whether a natural person is identifiable, account should be taken of all the means reasonably likely to be used, such as singling out, either by the controller or by another person to identify the natural person directly or indirectly. To ascertain whether means are reasonably likely to be used to identify the natural person, account should be taken of all objective factors, such as the costs of, and the amount of time required for, identification, taking into consideration the available technology at the time of the processing and technological developments. The principles of data protection should therefore not apply to anonymous information—that is, information that does not relate to an identified or identifiable natural person—or

---

* GDPR Recital 40.
† GDPR Recital 33.

to personal data rendered anonymous in such a manner that the individual data subject is not or is no longer identifiable. The GDPR *does not* therefore concern the processing of such anonymous information, including for statistical or research purposes.*

The application of pseudonymization to personal data can reduce the risks to the individual data subjects concerned and help controllers and processors to meet their data protection obligations. The explicit introduction of "pseudonymization" in the GDPR is not intended to preclude any other measures of data protection† to create incentives to apply pseudonymization when processing personal data; measures of pseudonymization should, while allowing general analysis, be possible within the same controller when that controller has taken the technical and organizational measures necessary to ensure, for the processing concerned, that the GDPR is implemented and that additional information for attributing the personal data to a specific individual data subject is kept separately. The controller processing the personal data should indicate the authorized persons within the same controller.‡

- *Added Innovative Measures*: Commentators have indicated that parts of the GDPR contain particular "legislative innovation."§ Some examples of this innovation are indicated to be the
  - Data protection principles
  - Individual data subjects' rights
  - Controllers' and processors' obligations
  - Regulation issues regarding technologies¶

It has been noted that while the DPD95 emphasizes protection for the fundamental rights of individuals "and in particular their right to [data protection]," the GDPR in Articles 1 and 2 stresses the need to protect the fundamental rights of

---

* GDPR Recital 26.
† GDPR Recital 28.
‡ GDPR Recital 29.
§ Costa and Poullet, "Privacy and the Regulation of 2012," (2012)(28) *Computer Law & Security Review*, 254.
¶ ibid.

individuals "and in particular their right to the protection of personal data."* Further references also emphasize data protection as a stand-alone concept from data protection, such as data protection assessments and data protection by design.

- *Consistency*: There is a new consistency mechanism whereby the national data protection authorities are obliged to cooperate with each other and with the EU Commission.† Two examples given include data protection assessments and also obligation in terms of notifying individual data subjects in relation to data breaches.‡

- *Data Portability*: Data portability is a newly expressed right. It implies the right of data subjects to obtain from the [data] controller a copy of their personal data in a structured and commonly used format (Article 18.1) ... data portability is a kind of right to backup and use personal information under the management of the controller. Second, data portability grants the right to transmit personal data and other information provided by the data subject from one automated processing system to another one (Article 18.2) ... therefore the right to take personal data and leave.§

- *Proportionality and Excessive Processing*: The DPD95 requires that the controller must not process personal data excessively. However, this is now more limited. The GDPR states that data collection and processing must be limited to the minimum.

- *Automated Decisions*: The DPD95 Article 15 protection in relation to automated individual decisions "is considerably enlarged"¶ regarding profiling in GDPR Articles 21 and 22. The use of, *inter alia*, the word "measure" in the GDPR as opposed to "decision" in the DPD95 makes the category of activity encompassed within the obligation now much wider.** There is greater individual data subject protection. While there

---

* ibid. at 255.
† Chapter VII, Section 10. Costa and Poullet, above, at 255.
‡ ibid.
§ Costa and Poullet, above, at 15. The portability right is referred to in GDPR art. 20.
¶ Costa and Poullet, above, at 258. Also see Council of Europe Recommendation regarding profiling, November 25, 2010.
** ibid at 258–259.

were previously two exemptions, in terms of contract and also a specific law, the GDPR adds a third in terms of consent from the individual data subject. However, controllers will need to ensure a stand-alone consent for profiling separate from any consent for data collection and processing per se.*

- *Policies and Procedures*: The GDPR also moves significantly further than the DPD95 in terms of creating obligations, responsibility, and liability on controllers.† Appropriate policies must be implemented by controllers, as well as compliant data processing, secure data processing, the undertaking of data protection impact assessments, liability as between joint controllers, appointing representatives within the EU where the controllers are located elsewhere, and provisions regarding processors.‡

- *Controllers/Processors*: While the DPD95 imposed compensation obligations on controllers in the case of harm to individual data subjects, the GDPR extends liability to processors. In addition, where harm is suffered by individual data subjects, any joint controller and/or processors are "jointly and severally liable for the entire amount of the damage."§

- *Data Protection by Design, Data Protection by Default, and Impact Assessments*: The concepts of data protection by design, data protection by default, and impact assessments all emphasize the ability of the data protection regime to become involved in standards setting and the regulation of particular technologies and technical solutions.¶ The Ontario Data Protection Commissioner, Anne Cavoukian, refers to data protection and privacy by design (a form of data protection by design).** The GDPR describes it as follows in GDPR Article 25, indicating that

---

* ibid at 259.
† ibid.
‡ Costa and Poullet, above.
§ ibid.
¶ ibid.
** For example, Anne Cavoukian (DPC Ontario, Privacy Guidelines for RFID Information Systems, at www.ipc.on.ca) indicates that the privacy and security must be built into the solution from the outset, at the design stage. Referred to ibid.

[t]aking into account the state of the art, the cost of imple-mentation and the nature, scope, context and purposes of processing as well as the risks of varying likelihood and severity for rights and freedoms of natural persons posed by the processing, the controller shall, both at the time of the determination of the means for processing and at the time of the processing itself, implement appropriate technical and organisational measures, such as pseudonymisation, which are designed to implement data-protection principles, such as data minimisation, in an effective manner and to integrate the necessary safeguards into the processing in order to meet the requirements of [the GDPR] and protect the rights of data subjects.

Data protection by default is referred to and defined in Article 25(2) as follows:

The controller shall implement appropriate technical and organisational measures for ensuring that, by default, only personal data which are necessary for each specific purpose of the processing are processed. That obligation applies to the amount of personal data collected, the extent of their pro-cessing, the period of their storage and their accessibility. In particular, such measures shall ensure that by default personal data are not made accessible without the individual's inter-vention to an indefinite number of natural persons.

The concept of data protection by design and data protec-tion by default as provided in the GDPR are predicted to soon impact on organizational contracts and contracting practices relating to data processing activities.*

• *Certification*: The new Article 25(3) provides that an approved certification mechanism pursuant to Article 42 may be used as an element to demonstrate compliance with the require-ments set out in paragraphs 1 and 2 of this Article.

These accord with the general principle of data minimi-zation, whereby non-personal data should be processed first, and where the collection and processing of personal data are required, it must be the minimum data as opposed to the

---

* ibid. at 260.

maximum data that are so processed. This is referred to in Article 5(1)(c).

Individual data subjects have more control over their personal data. In the context of social networks, individual profiles should be kept private from others by default.*

As mentioned earlier, one of the new areas is the obligation to engage in data protection impact assessments. Article 35(1) provides that

[w]here a type of processing in particular using new technologies, and taking into account the nature, scope, context and purposes of the processing, is likely to result in a high risk to the rights and freedoms of natural persons, the controller shall, prior to the processing, carry out an assessment of the impact of the envisaged processing operations on the protection of personal data. A single assessment may address a set of similar processing operations that present similar high risks.

This is particularly the case where the envisaged processing could give rise to specific risks.

- *Group Claims/Class Actions*: One further addition is the possibility of mass group claims or claims through representative organizations. This is referred to as "collective redress" and allows data protection non-governmental organizations to complain both to the data protection supervisory authority and to the courts (see Article 80).† "Civil procedure rules"‡ may also need to be introduced.

The regime as regards cross-border data flows will be "significantly altered."§ These are included in Articles 40 and 41.

---

* Costa and Poullet, above, at 260, and referring to European Data Protection Supervisor on the Communications from Commission to the European Parliament, the Council, the Economic and Social Committee and the Committee of the Regions, "A Comprehensive Approach on Personal Data Protection in the European Union," at 23.

† See also Commission on a Common Framework for Collective Redress, http://ec.europa.eu/consumers/redress_cons/collective_redress_en.htm.

‡ Costa and Poullet, above, at 261.

§ ibid.

- *Data Protection Supervisory Authorities*: The GDPR also enhances and expands the various powers of the national authorities, such as the data protection supervisory authority.*

  One of the data protection supervisory authorities' annual reports notes the following:

  the data protection landscape is changing. We are now seeing a definite shift in the nature and type of complaints received by the Office from the traditional complaint related to inappropriate or unfair use of personal data to a clearer technology focus with individuals concerned about the security of their personal data and the uses made of that data by software and technology applications. Last year for the first time the number of data breach notifications outstripped the number of complaints opened for investigation (by six). The need to deal with the reality of the potential impact on individual ... data protection rights which can be caused by poorly thought out technology is in many respects the backdrop to the [EU] Commission's proposals for a new uniform [GDPR] that will apply across all EU member states.†

- *Free Movement*: The new GDPR should not be viewed simply as merely promoting rights of individual data subjects. In addition, it recognizes the need for the free movement of data and commercial imperatives.

  To ensure a consistent level of protection for natural persons throughout the EU and to prevent divergences hampering the free movement of personal data within the internal market, a Regulation is necessary to provide legal certainty and transparency for economic operators, including micro, small, and medium-sized enterprises, and to provide natural persons in all member states with the same level of legally enforceable rights and obligations and responsibilities for controllers and processors, to ensure consistent monitoring of the processing of personal data, and equivalent sanctions in all member states as well as effective cooperation between the data protection supervisory authorities of different

---

* ibid., at 260.
† Irish data protection supervisory authority (DPC), Annual Report 2011, at 6.

member states. The proper functioning of the internal market requires that the free movement of personal data within the EU is not restricted or prohibited for reasons connected with the protection of natural persons with regard to the processing of personal data. To take account of the specific situation of micro, small, and medium-sized enterprises, the GDPR includes a derogation for organizations with fewer than 250 employees with regard to record keeping. In addition, the EU institutions and bodies, and member states and their data protection supervisory authorities, are encouraged to take account of the specific needs of micro, small, and medium-sized enterprises[*] in the application of the GDPR.[†]

DPD95 Repealed

Given the update to the data protection regime with the new GDPR, the GDPR repeals the DPD95. Processing already under way on the date of application of the GDPR must be brought into conformity with the GDPR within the period of *two years*, after which the GDPR enters into force. Where processing is based on consent pursuant to DPD95, it is not necessary for the individual data subject to give consent again if the way the consent has been given is in line with the conditions of the GDPR.[‡]

EU Commission decisions adopted and authorizations by data protection supervisory authorities based on DPD95 remain in force until amended, replaced, or repealed.[§]

Conclusion

Data protection compliance is never a one-size-fits-all or a single one-time policy document. The nature of what amounts to personal data and the activities for which such data can be processed are ever

---

[*] The notion of micro, small, and medium-sized enterprises should draw from Article 2 of the Annex to Commission Recommendation 2003/361/EC.

[†] GDPR Recital 13.

[‡] GDPR Recital 134.

[§] GDPR Recital 134.

changing. Those within an organization, therefore, need to be constantly alert to compliance issues and changes. Organizations also need to be constantly alert to new issues and dangers.

All organizations need to become very familiar with the new GDPR. It reflects the shape of the new and expanded EU data protection regime. While in some instances the current compliance mechanisms are continued, there are many new requirements for compliance. Organizations need to start now in terms of ensuring compliance. Indeed, the most prudent organizations will continually adopt best practice, and data protection compliance is an area where best practice has positive benefits above and beyond mere compliance.

KEY CONCEPTS

The imperative for change and update has been growing for some time, and the new GDPR addresses many of the developing problem issues. The implementation of these will affect many organizations for years to come.

KEY WORDS

- Update needed.
- Changes.
- Stronger protection.
- Data flows and transfers.
- Consent.
- Pseudonymization and anonymization.
- Portability.
- Automated decisions.

FURTHER READING

- Buffington, *Data Protection for Virtual Data Centers* (Wiley, 2010).
- Clarke, "How Reliable is Cloudsourcing? A Review of Articles in the Technical Media 2005–11," *Computer Law & Security Review* (2012) (28) 90.
- Cohen, "The Regulatory State in the Information Age," *Theoretical Inquiries in Law* (2016) (17:2) 369.
- Custers and Uršič, Big Data and Data Reuse: A Taxonomy of Data Reuse for Balancing Big Data Benefits and Personal Data Protection, *International Data Privacy Law* (2016) 28.
- Datta and Datta, *Face Detection and Recognition: Theory and Practice* (CRC Press, 2015).
- Diffie and Landau, *Privacy on the Line: The Politics of Wiretapping and Encryption* (MIT, 2007).
- *First Report on the Implementation of the Data Protection Directive* (95/46/EC) (i.e. DPD95).
- Gutwirth and Leenes, *Data Protection on the Move: Current Developments in ICT and Privacy/Data Protection* (Springer, 2015).
- Gutwirth and Leenes, *Reforming European Data Protection Law* (Law, Governance and Technology Series / Issues in Privacy and Data Protection) (Springer, 2014).
- Hess, *Protecting Privacy in Private International and Procedural Law and by Data Protection: European and American Developments* (Ashgate, 2015).
- King and Raja, "Protecting the Privacy and Security of Sensitive Customer Data in the Cloud," *Computer Law & Security Review* (2012) (28) 308.
- Lambert, *International Handbook of Social Media Laws* (Bloomsbury, 2015).
- Lambert, *Social Networking: Law, Rights and Policy* (Clarus, 2014).
- O'Brien, "The Internet of Things," *Journal of Internet Law* (2016) (19:12) 3.

- Peng, "A New Model of Data Protection on Cloud Storage," *Journal of Networks* (03/2014) (9:3) 666.

- Roethlisberger, "Someone is Watching: The Need for Enhanced Data Protection," *Hastings Law Journal* (2011) (62:6) 1793.
- Schmidt and Payton, *Privacy in the Age of Big Data: Recognizing Threats, Defending Your Rights, and Protecting Your Family* (Rowman, 2015).
- Ticher, *Data Protection and the Cloud: Are the Risks Too Great?* (Ticher, 2015).
- UK supervisory authority (ICO), *Guidance on the Use of Cloud Computing*; WP29, *Opinion 05/2012 on Cloud Computing*, WP 196.
- UK supervisory authority (ICO) in relation to privacy by design (PbD), and the report *Privacy by Design*, at https://ico.org.uk.
- Varella, "When It Rains, It Pours: Protecting Student Data Stored in the Cloud," *Rutgers Computer & Technology Law Journal* (2016) (42:1) 94.
- Webster, *Effective Data Protection: Managing Information in an Era of Change* (ICSA Information & Training, 2011).

5

EU DATA PROTECTION CONCEPTS

Introduction

Everyone is concerned with personal data. Organizations are concerned to know personal data for certain commercial activities and also in relation to their legal obligations. These obligations are increased with the new data protection regime under the new General Data Protection Regulation (GDPR). Individuals are concerned with information relating to them that is in the hands of third-party organizations. This can often be legitimate. However, there are increasing instances where it is not legitimate and information has been collected without the individual knowing that it would be collected or what it would be used for. In addition, there are increasing instances of organizations legitimately collecting personal data relating to individuals, but which the organization then seeks to use in an unlawful manner; for example, a charity selling its database of donors to a bank or marketing company without permission or transparency.

Personal Data

What is personal information or personal data? The new GDPR defines personal data as *any information relating to an identified or identifiable natural person* ("data subject").*

---

* Personal data in the United States are referred to as personally identifiable information (PII).

PERSONAL DATA

Any information relating to an identified or identifiable natural person ("data subject"); an identifiable natural person is one who can be identified, directly or indirectly, in particular by reference to an identifier such as a name, an identification number, location data, or an online identifier or to one or more factors specific to the physical, physiological, genetic, mental, economic, cultural, or social identity of that natural person.

This means that the net of personal data is much wider than those individuals for whom data are immediately transparently identified, as it includes not only currently identified data but also particular data that may become identified or linked to a living individual. An identifiable person is a person who can be identified, whether directly or indirectly, in particular by reference to an identification number or factors specific to their physical, physiological, mental, economic, cultural, or social identity. The net is wide. The GDPR also recognizes that data sets are becoming easier to couple, link, and cross reference; thus, data that might not have identified anyone become capable of identifying an individual through amalgamation of different data from different sources. Coupling, Big Data, and so on make this an important issue.

The Parties

Data protection involves a number of key parties:

Individuals: Individuals are referred to as "data subjects." It is their personal information and personal data that are being protected.

Organizations: Organizations are referred to as "controllers" that wish to collect, use, and process individuals' personal data.

Outsource organizations: Outsource organizations are referred to as "processors." The main controller organization has outsourced or delegated some of its processing activities to a third-party organization; for example, payroll processing regarding employees; marketing or market research regarding customers or prospective customers.

In addition, organizations need to consider the following roles in relation to data protection compliance and data protection issues that arise:

Data protection officer: The data protection officer is the individual office holder in the organization tasked with ensuring data protection compliance, education, and so on. He or she is the general point of contact within organizations for queries regarding personal data.

Board member: Organizations should ensure that data protection compliance is prioritized at organizational board level. The data protection officer should regularly report to this board member.

IT Manager: Given the importance of security for personal data enshrined in the data protection regime, the IT Manager needs to be appraised and involved in assisting compliance.

Data protection supervisory authority: The official agency in each EU member state responsible for data protection compliance.

European Data Protection Board: The EU body made up of representatives of each national data protection supervisory authority, which investigates issues and provides guidance and reports on data protection issues. (Previously, the Article 29 Data Protection Working Party [WP29] under the 1995 data protection directive [DPD95] undertook similar tasks.)

Personal Data Use and Compliance

Appreciation of and compliance with the data protection regime in relation to personal data are important. Everyone has personal data relating to them. Every organization and entity collects and processes personal data of individuals. Sometimes this is on a small scale. Sometimes it is on a massive scale. Data protection compliance obligations apply to all organizations, whether small, large, commercial enterprises, government organizations, or even charities. Obligations also apply to the primary organization involved (the "controller" organization) as well as to outsource entities such as agents, consultants, processors, and so on. Arguably, the extent varies between the United States and the EU.

Furthermore, the instances where personal data are used are ever-increasing. Every reservation, booking, transaction, or journey, and every organization that one deals with, whether governmental, enterprise, non-profit, or other, uses or creates data in relation to the person. The volume of such personal data collection and processing is now even more prevalent with the advent of digitization, the Internet, social media, and eCommerce. Big Data, coupling, and increasing aggregation and linking capabilities also have implications in relation to personal data and what may become personal data. Commercial organizations realize the value in personal data. Increasingly, new business models are relying on personal data. Regardless, the data still remain the personal data of the individual data subject.*

The default position is that organizations must inform individuals that they intend to collect and use their personal data, and for what purposes, and obtain consent to do so. Frequently, tensions arise when organizations do not do so, or seek to do so in a manner that does not fully or transparently respect the rights of individuals. While compliance is always possible, there are many instances of organizations getting it wrong and facing the consequences of audit, fine, penalty, prosecution, investigation, and/or litigation.

Describing Data Protection

Data protection laws protect the personal information of individuals; that is, the personal data of and in relation to individuals. The data protection regime provides a regulatory protection regime around personal informational and personal data. Personal data are data or information that relates to or identifies, directly or indirectly, an individual. Data protection is in many respects wider than data protection and confidentiality. Personal data is defined in the previous EU DPD95 and now the new GDPR. It is also an express fundamental right.

---

* On the general topic, see Rees, "Who Owns Our Data?" *Computer Law and Security Report* (2014) (30:1) 75. On Big Data, note, for example, Sampson, "Rights of Individuation: The Need for Greater Protection of Individual Rights in Big Data," *2014 IEEE/ACM 7th International Conference on Utility and Cloud Computing* (2014).

The data protection legal regime governs whether, when, and how organizations may collect and process personal data, and, when permitted, for how long.

This applies to all sorts of personal information, from general to highly confidential and sensitive. Examples of the latter include sensitive health data, sexuality data, and details of criminal offenses.

The data protection regime is twofold in the sense of

- Providing obligations (both inward-facing and outward-facing) that organizations must comply with.
- Providing individuals (or individual data subjects, as they are technically known) with various data protection *rights* that they, representative organizations, and/or the data protection supervisory authority can invoke or enforce, as appropriate. Significantly, the ability to invoke the data protection rights on behalf of individuals by data protection groups and collective non-governmental type organizations is new.*

Previously, organizations, as part of their compliance obligations, had to register or notify the data protection supervisory authority in relation to their data processing activities (unless exempted). This compliance obligation in the national data protection laws and the DPD95 is changed in the new GDPR. Now, there is no need for general registration, unless they come within special categories of data protection risk activities (which can include frequency and volume as factors).†

Certain specific sections of industry and certain specific activities (e.g., data transfers abroad, direct marketing, etc.) also have additional data protection compliance rules.

In terms of individuals, they can invoke their rights directly with organizations; with the data protection supervisory authority; and also with the courts in legal proceedings. Now, particular requests may also be made by representative organizations on behalf of groups of individuals. Compensation can also be awarded. Injunction relief

---

* See GDPR, replacing the DPD95. The GDPR brings "comprehensive reform" to the EU and Irish data protection regime. In brief, *Communications Law* (2012) (17) 3.

† Gellert, "Understanding Data Protection as Risk Regulation," *Journal of Internet Law* (2015) (18:11) 3. These changes potentially require specific amendment to the data protection laws in EU member states to reflect the new GDPR.

can also arise.* In addition, criminal offenses can be prosecuted.† Data protection compliance is therefore very important. Indeed, fines and penalties are significantly increased under the new GDPR in the event of breach or non-compliance.

As regards implementing compliance frameworks, organizations must have defined structures, policies, and teams in place to ensure that they know what personal data they have and for what purposes, and that it is held fairly, lawfully, and in compliance with the data protection regime and is safely secured against damage, loss, and unauthorized access. A significant new measure is the obligation to designate a data protection officer. Data protection aims in part to reduce or eliminate data breach incidents, in particular in various security-related rule requirements.

The cost of loss, and of security breach, can be significant financially, brand-wise, and publicity-wise. An IBM study in 2015 estimates the cost of data breach study as averaging $3.8 million per data breach incident. The TalkTalk mobile company data breach (2015) is estimated as costing £35 million. The One Target (a US retail chain) data breach is estimated as costing $162 million plus a 5.3% drop in sales. Breaches can also give rise to criminal offenses, which can be prosecuted. In addition, personal liability can attach to organizational personnel separately and in addition to the organization itself.

The Data Protection Regime

Personal data protection is enshrined in national data protection laws and the new GDPR.‡ The definitions, or building blocks, of data protection are referred to in this section. The GDPR significantly enhances the data protection regime. The new GDPR is directly effective in EU

---

* Such as, for example, *Sunderland Housing*; *Kordowski* and *Microsoft v McDonald (t/s Bizards)*. *Sunderland Housing Company v Baines* [2006] EWHC 2359; *Law Society v Kordowski* [2011] EWHC 3185; *Microsoft Corp v McDonald (t/s Bizads)* [2006] EWHC 3410.

† Note also Erdos, "Data Protection and the Right to Reputation: Filling the 'Gaps' after the Defamation Act 2013," *Cambridge Law Journal* (2014) (73:3) 536.

‡ The Data Protection Acts in the United Kingdom and Ireland, respectively, implement the DPD95, as does respective national legislation in the other EU member states; ibid.

member states. However, it may require parts of the data protection rules to be amended and equivalent national laws updated.

Outward-Facing Data Protection Compliance

The data protection regime, as implemented in the data protection laws and the new GDPR, creates legal obligations organizations must comply with when collecting and processing the personal data of individuals: "if someone can be distinguished from other people, data protection legislation is applicable."* This applies to customers and prospective customers. Hence, these are *outward-facing* obligations. It can also apply to non-customers, who may be using a particular website but are not registered customers, if their personal data is being collected.

Customers, and indeed users who may not be customers but whose data is collected by the organization, all have rights in relation to their personal data. These rights may be used and enforced by customers against controllers. Controllers need to prepare for respecting these rights and also for preparing to deal with rights issues in advance of requests being made. Some of these are referred to later (e.g., Chapter 14).

Beyond the inward-facing employee-related sphere, organizations also need to consider the outward-facing sphere. For many organizations, the outward-facing data protection issues frequently seem to dominate more. They can also be the most contentious. These issues raise significant data protection concerns and compliance issues to be dealt with.

Some of the queries that can arise include

- New designated data protection officers.
- The forms of outward-facing personal data to consider.
- How organizations can comply with the data protection regime when dealing with existing customers.
- Organizations contacting potential customers yet seeking to remain data protection compliant.
- Organizations engaging in direct marketing.

---

* Costa and Poullet, "Privacy and the Regulation of 2012," *Computer Law & Security Review* (2012) (28) 254, at 256.

- Whether profiling is possible generally, or even in more limited circumstances.
- Additional issues with users who are not customers.
- Security considerations arising.
- Whether there are even more new security issues to consider.
- Whether there are higher security obligations for customers and users.
- How the deletion and right to be forgotten regime work.
- What the new risk assessment and impact assessment provisions mean.
- Information where data is collected from the individual data subject.
- Information provided where data is not obtained from the individual data subject.
- Right of access.
- Right to rectification.
- Right to be forgotten.
- Right to restriction of processing.
- Notification obligation regarding rectification, erasure, or restriction.
- Right to data portability.
- Right to object.
- Automated individual decision-making, including profiling.

The general increase in data, data collection capabilities, Internet usage, profiling, advertising, marketing, and social media is also an important issue to consider. Abuse, whether online or via social media or related websites, is increasingly recognized as a problem to be dealt with. There is likely to be an increase in the instances where civil sanctions and actions may need to be invoked. In some instances and in some jurisdictions, organizations may also need to consider criminal law sanctions.

How can an organization focus on the elements that will ensure data protection compliance when dealing with the personal data of customers, prospects, and/or users? In terms of personal data collected and processed relating to these categories, the following must be considered and complied with

- Data protection principles.
- Legitimate processing conditions.

- Sensitive personal data legitimate processing conditions.
- Prior information requirements.
- Security requirements.
- Data protection impact assessments.
- Data protection by design and by default.
- Notification requirements (note potential changes in this regard).
- Risk and risk assessments, particularly as regards new processes and activities.
- Security requirements.
- Direct marketing.
- Consequences of non-compliance.
- Users versus customers.

Particular considerations can arise in relation to users who may not be customers in the normal and contractual sense.

When organizations begin to look outwards, a separate range of data collection possibilities will arise. The avenues for data collection are more diverse. In addition, the intended uses of this type of personal data will be potentially more numerous. The data protection principles and legitimate processing conditions require particular consideration and configuration to the intended data processing activities of customers' personal data. Different security and enforcement risks can arise, and it is necessary to protect against these. It cannot be assumed that everyone from whom the organization may wish to collect personal data will be an actual customer. Therefore, organizations need to consider how to ensure separate consent and notifications to this category of person. An example of this may be cookies that can obtain personal data. There are significant new issues for organizations to consider and to comply with under the new data protection regime.

Inward-Facing Data Protection Compliance

The data protection regime applies to an organization in its dealings regarding the personal data of its employees. Equally, where the organization is engaging third-party independent contractors but is collecting, processing, and using their personal data, the data protection regime will also apply. Hence, the data protection regime in relation to organizations is *inward-facing*.

This refers to employees. Organizations will also be considering other persons in addition to actual employees, such as employee family members, retirees, contractors, and so on. Organizations sometimes focus on their customer-relations data compliance issues. It is important for new and existing organizations to look inwards. There are important inward-facing data protection obligations. Personal data include the personal data of employees also. In addition, the employees of the organization also have individual data subject rights that must be respected. Data protection compliance is also an inward-facing requirement.

The variety of inward-facing data protection issues that organizations need to deal with on a daily basis is ever-increasing. Some of these include whether to allow employees to bring their own devices (bring your own devices [BYOD]) into the organization and whether to permit them to place organizational data onto such devices. If this is permitted, a particular BYOD policy needs to be considered and implemented. If employee's own devices are not permitted, it should be expressly specified in a transparent manner that is permitted.

The ability for organizations to track their employees off-site is also a new consideration. This can include technologies on board vehicles as well as satellite and location technologies. It also includes the organization's (and employee's) smartphone (and other) devices.

Clearly, there are many more means by which new and/or expanded sets of personal data may be collected and used by an organization. However, it is equally necessary to consider the data protection compliance issues, and which collections are permissible and which are not, at the earliest opportunity.

Who is covered by the inward-facing organizational data protection obligations? Organizations should be aware that while this section refers to "employees," it really includes employees and related parties. While full-time employees are the most obvious example, they are not the only ones. Organizations must consider the inward-facing personal data of

- Full-time employees.
- Part-time employees.

- Other workers such as temps and casual staff.
- Agency staff.
- Contractors.
- Ex-employees.
- Retired employees.
- Job applicants, including unsuccessful applicants.
- Volunteers.
- Apprentices and trainees.
- Work experience staff.
- Suppliers.*
- Indirectly engaged persons, such as actors (e.g., the massive data breach incident related to the Sony film *The Interview*, after which the online publication of internal disparaging emails regarding certain actors caused significant reputational damage and potential lawsuits. It also cost key personnel their jobs).

It can also include

- Family members of these individuals.

Universities and schools might also consider that some or all inward-facing data protection issues also include

- Students and prospective students.

Where an organization engages with any of these categories, it will have to ensure that the data protection regime is complied with.

Organizations need to have actively considered data protection compliance issues. Compliance issues arise even before an employee is engaged. Data protection and personal data are gathered at recruitment, selection, and interview stages. Personal data and issues of notifying relevant policies are important issues for organizations to deal with systematically. Unless data protection issues and policy issues are properly incorporated into the employment relationship, the organization may be non-compliant. In addition, it may not be able to enforce and rely on particular contract terms, policies, employee obligations, disciplinary rules, and suchlike. The advent of the new data

---

* MacDonald, *Data Protection: Legal Compliance and Good Practice for Employers* (Tottel, 2008) 41.

protection officer obligations in relation to employee inward-facing issues will understandably take some bedding-in time for organizations. It clearly creates a new dynamic. Organizations need to be aware of the data protection rights of employees.*

One of the more contentious areas of employee data protection issues relates to the nature of the monitoring of employee usage of email, Internet, and so on. This issue has also been highlighted in a recent controversial case. Unfortunately, there has been significant misreporting in relation to the case, which may cause certain organizations to misunderstand the position in relation to monitoring and the data protection regime.†

A large number of issues arise in terms of dealing with employee personal data in terms of audits, planning, and compliance.‡ Note

---

* The rights of employees include: right to transparency; right to prior information: directly obtained data; right to prior information: indirectly obtained data; right of confirmation and *Right of Access*; right to be informed of third-country safeguards; right to rectification; right to erasure (right to be forgotten) (RtbF); right to restriction of processing; notifications re rectification, erasure, or restriction; right to data portability; right to object; rights re automated individual decision-making, including profiling; data protection by design; security rights; data protection impact assessment and prior consultation; and communicating data breach to individual data subjects. Also note the data protection officer obligations and employee remedies, liability, and sanctions.

† More generally, and apart from the above case, employers may not be familiar enough with their obligations under the data protection regime. The most common reason for this is that employers are concerned about certain risks that can arise as result of the activities of employees in the workplace. In addition, the new data protection changes are only just finalized, and organizations may not be immediately familiar with them.

‡ Some examples of the legal issues and concerns that can arise for employers and organizations as a result of the actions of their employees include vicarious liability; defamation; copyright infringement; confidentiality breaches and leaks; data protection; inadvertent contract formation; discrimination; computer crime; interception offenses; criminal damage; data loss; data damage; computer crime; criminal damage; eCommerce law; arms and dual use good export restrictions; non-fatal offenses against the person; child pornography; data protection policy; Internet usage policy; social media usage mobile and device usage policies; vehicle use policy; location; evidence; enforceability; data breach; notification of employee data breaches; employee data organizations; employee misuse of email, Internet, and so on; online abuse; offline abuse; contract; employment equality; harassment; dealing with the employee risks; employee–corporate communications usage policies; focus of organizational communications usage policies; data protection and employee monitoring; human rights; application of data protection regime; ILO code; Article 29 and

also guidance on the issue of vetting employees* and background checks on potential employees;† monitoring and employee guidance‡ (see the European Court of Human Rights [ECHR] case of *Bărbulescu v Romania* (January 2016),§ which refers to monitoring in the employment context); official guidance on monitoring issues;¶ guidance in relation to whether an organization can access employee email or Internet usage;** enforced access offense (it is an offense for an employer to require a prospective or current employee to provide their police records in conjunction with applying for a job or continuing to hold their job); general compliance checklists.†† The Canadian Supreme Court also held that employees have data protection interests in work-related activities.‡‡

A Rights-Based Regime

As well as creating legal compliance obligations for organizations, the data protection regime enshrines rights or data protection rights for individuals in terms of ensuring their ability to know what personal data is being collected, to consent—or not consent—to the collection of their personal data, and to control the uses to which their personal data may be put. There is also a mechanism through which individuals can complain to controllers holding their personal data, to the data protection supervisory authority, and to the courts directly. Data protection and data protection rights are fundamental legal rights.

---

employment processing; WP29: electronic communications; employment contracts, terms, policies; processing compliance rules; suggested guidelines. These are examples of an expanding list of concerns for organizations. Obviously, some of these will be recalibrated in importance depending on the type of organization, the business sector, and what its activities are. Confidentiality, for example, may be critically important for certain organizations, but less important for others.

* See Irish data protection supervisory authority (DPC), at www.dataprotection.ie.
† See ibid.
‡ See ibid.
§ *Bărbulescu v Romania*, ECHR, Case No 61496/08, January 12, 2016.
¶ ibid.
**See DPC, at www.dataprotection.ie.
††See DPC, *Guide Data Controllers*.
‡‡*R v Cole*, Canadian Supreme Court, at http://scc.lexum.org/decisia-scc-csc/scc-csc/scc-csc/en/item/12615/index.do.

National Data Protection Supervisory Authorities

To ensure that the duties are complied with and the rights of individuals vindicated, official data protection supervisory authorities are established in EU member states to monitor and act as appropriate in relation to the efficient operation of the data protection regime. The importance of EU member state data protection authorities is enhanced in the new GDPR.

Data Protection Rules Introduced

Controllers (i.e., the organizations that collect and process personal data; see definitions section) must comply with a number of data protection issues, perhaps the foremost of which relate to

- Fairness.
- Consent.
- Transparency.
- Accuracy.
- Security.
- Proper and transparent purposes for processing.
- Proportionality of the need and use of personal data.
- Risk assessments.
- Correction and deletion.

The collection, use, and onward transfer of personal data must be fair, legitimate, and transparent. There are particular definitions and provisions as regards the "processing" of personal data. There are also restrictions in relation to the ability of organizations to transfer personal data both to third-party organizations generally and also to third-party organizations outside of the EU/ European Economic Area (EEA). Transfers were referred to as trans-border data flows under the old data protection regime, and are now referred to as cross-border transfers under the new GDPR regime.

The personal data must be correct and accurate. The reason is that damage or harm to the individual data subject can be a consequence of inaccurately held personal data. For example, a credit rating could be adversely affected through incorrect or wrong personal data records being recorded regarding personal payment histories.

There is a general obligation in terms of safeguarding personal data. Organizations must assess and implement security measures to protect personal data. Increasingly, this is also being considered in relation to the developing cloud environment and the increasing use of processors and third parties.*

There can also be an obligation on controllers to register or notify the data protection supervisory authority as regards their high-risk data processing activities.

If EU personal data are permitted to be transferred to third countries, they must first qualify under a specific exemption, as well as the general security conditions. No such transfer is permitted from the EU unless explicitly exempted. The issue of the EU–US Safe Harbor Arrangement exemption mechanism is a matter of particular contention and import at this time, given that the EU Court of Justice has invalidated this mechanism.† The EU and the US have therefore negotiated a new arrangement, entitled the EU–US Privacy Shield. The application, changes, and any challenges will need careful attention from organizations and data protection officers.

Organizations have a duty of care to individuals as regards their personal data being processed by the organization, particularly if loss or damage arises. Injunctive relief is also possible in appropriate circumstances.

Controllers and processors have obligations to have legal contracts in place between them. Processors process and deal with personal

---

* In relation to cloud generally, see Kuan Hon and Millard, "Data Export Cloud Computing: How Can Personal Data be Transferred Outside the EEA? The Cloud of Unknowing," *SCRIPTed (2012) (9:1)*; Singh and Mishra, "Cloud Computing Security and Data Protection: A Review," *International Journal of Computers & Technology* (2015) (14:7) 5887; Pfarr, Buckel, and Winkelmann, "Cloud Computing Data Protection: A Literature Review and Analysis," *2014 47th Hawaii International Conference on System Sciences* (2014) 5018.

† *Schrems v Commissioner*, Court of Justice, Case C-362/14, October 6, 2015, at http://curia.europa.eu/juris/document/document.jsf?text=&docid=169195&pageIndex=0&doclang=en&mode=req&dir=&occ=first&part=1&cid=113326. The case technically related to Prism and Facebook Europe and transfers to the United States. However, the wider import turned out to be the entire EU-US Safe Harbor Agreement and data transfers to the United States. As such, this is one of the most important cases, if not the most important, decided by the Court of Justice to date. Note, for example, Ni Loidean, "The End of Safe Harbor: Implications for EU Digital Privacy and Data Protection Law," *Journal of Internet Law* (2016) (19:8) 1.

data for and on behalf of a controller in relation to specific, defined tasks; for example, activities such as outsourced payroll, personnel, marketing, market research, customer satisfaction surveys, and so on. Additional issues and considerations arise for cloud services and data protection compliance.*

Data Protection Concepts

The previous DPD95 and the new GDPR set out a number of structures, obligations, rights, and implementing criteria that are together the basis of the legal data protection regime.

The main criteria and obligations to be followed, respected, and complied with so as to be able to legally collect and process personal data include

- The definitions of personal data and the data protection regime (the building blocks of data protection).
- The data protection principles, also known as the "data quality principles."
- The legitimate processing conditions.
- The requirement that processing of personal data be "legitimate" under at least one of the legitimate processing conditions.
- Transparency and the prior information requirements.
- Recognition of the two categories of personal data covered by the data protection regime: namely, sensitive personal data and non-sensitive or general personal data.
- In the case of sensitive personal data, compliance with the additional sensitive personal data legitimate processing conditions.
- Ensuring that all personal data collected and processed is obtained fairly.

---

* From an organizational perspective, it is sometimes considered that organizational customers have less opportunity to negotiate clauses in cloud service provider contracts, including processor and security-related issues. There is, therefore, a greater obligation to be satisfied with the cloud service provider, where data is located, and the security measures and security documentation available.

- Appropriate security measures in relation to all processing activities.
- Implementation of formal legal contracts when engaging or dealing with third-party processors (e.g., outsourcing data processing tasks or activities).
- Compliance with the separate criteria in relation to automated decisions.
- Compliance with the legal criteria for direct marketing.
- A duty of care exists in relation to the individual data subjects whose personal data the organization is collecting and processing.
- Transfer of personal data outside of the EU is strictly controlled. Personal data may not be transferred outside of the EU unless specifically permitted under the data protection regime.*
- Compliance with access requests, or requests by individuals for copies of their personal data held by the organization (unless excepted).
- Compliance with registration obligations by organizations.
- Implementation of internal data protection policies and terms.
- Implementation of outward-facing data protection policies for customers, etc.
- Implementation of outward-facing website data protection statements (generally, a data protection policy covers organization-wide activities. A website data protection statement† governs only the online collection and processing of personal data).
- Implementation of device, mobile, computer, and Internet usage policies.
- Implementation of data loss, data breach, incident handling, and incident reporting policies and associated reaction plans.‡

---

* The EEA is wider than the EU member states and includes Iceland, Liechtenstein, and Norway. Switzerland has a similar arrangement with the EU. EU data protection law frequently refers to the EEA, generally meaning the EU member states plus the EEA countries.

† Also known as a privacy statement.

‡ Note, for example, the UK data protection supervisory authority (ICO) PECR (privacy and electronic communications regulations) security breach notifications—guidance for service providers, at https://ico.org.uk.

- Reporting of data incidents, losses, and breaches to the data protection supervisory authority (unless exempted).
- Keeping abreast of the increasing trend toward sector/issue specific rules, for example spam; direct marketing.
- Industry codes of conduct* in relation to personal data.
- Children and personal data issues.
- Children, consent, and social media.
- Data protection impact assessments and privacy consultations.
- Data protection by design and by default.
- Compliance with new legal developments.

General Criteria for Data Processing

Generally, to lawfully collect and process personal data, an organization should be aware that

- The individual data subject must consent to the collection and processing of their personal data.
- The data subject may object to processing or continued processing.
- Legal data protection requirements must be complied with.
- The prior information requirements, transparency, data protection principles, legitimate processing conditions, sensitive personal data legitimate processing conditions (in the case of sensitive personal data), and security obligations must be complied with.
- and so on; risk assessment; risk minimization; data protection by design; and data protection by default.

The interests of the controller can sometimes be relevant in particular instances in deciding what data processing is necessary and permitted.

---

* The EU national data protection laws and the EU data protection regime provide for codes of conduct being agreed with national data protection authorities in relation to specific industry sectors.

Legitimate Processing

There is a prohibition on the collection and processing of personal data and sensitive personal data unless

- The processing complies with the data protection principles.
- The processing comes with one of a limited number of specified conditions (the legitimate processing conditions or sensitive personal data legitimate processing conditions, as appropriate).
- The processing also complies with the security requirements.

Definitions

The data protection rules and new GDPR contain a number of key definitions. These are central to understanding the data protection regime and complying with it. These are essentially the building blocks of the data protection regime. While these can be "complex concepts,"* organizations need to fully understand them. Some examples of the matters defined include

- Individual data subject.
- Controller.
- Processor.
- Personal data.
- Processing.
- Sensitive personal data.

The definitions are found in greater detail later (e.g., Chapter 8).

KEY CONCEPTS

All organizations collect and process personal data, and hence all organizations need to be cognizant and compliant with the data protection rules.

---

* Hallinan, Friedewald, and McCarthy, "Citizens' Perceptions of Data Protection and Privacy in Europe," *Computer Law & Security Review* (2012) (28) 263.

KEYWORDS

- Data protection.
- Personal data.
- Parties involved.
- Data protection rules and regime.
- Inward-facing data protection issues.
- Outward-facing data protection issues.
- Rights and obligations.
- Definitions.

FURTHER READING

- Bygrave, *Data Protection Law: Approaching Its Rationale, Logic and Limits* (Kluwer, 2002).
- Carey, *Data Protection: A Practical Guide to Irish and EU Law* (Thomson Round Hall, 2010).
- Carey, *Data Protection: A Practical Guide to UK and EU Law* (Oxford University Press, 2015).
- Clark, *Data Protection Law in Ireland* (Round Hall Press, 1990).
- Delany, Carolan and Murphy, *The Right to Privacy: A Doctrinal and Comparative Analysis* (Thomson Round Hall, 2008).
- *First Report on the Implementation of the Data Protection Directive* (95/46/EC) (i.e., DPD95).
- Fuster, *The Emergence of Personal Data Protection as a Fundamental Right of the EU* (Springer, 2014).
- Goodbody, *A Practical Guide to Data Protection Law in Ireland* (Thomson Round Hall, 2003).
- Gutwirth and Leenes, *Reforming European Data Protection Law* (Law, Governance and Technology Series / Issues in Privacy and Data Protection) (2014).
- Jay, *Data Protection: Law and Practice* (Sweet and Maxwell, 2012).
- Jay, *Data Protection Law and Practice* First Supplement (2014).

- Jay and Clarke, *Data Protection Compliance in the UK: A Pocket Guide* (IT Governance Publishing, 2008).
- Jay and Hamilton, *Data Protection Law and Practice* (Sweet and Maxwell, 2007).
- Bainbridge, *Data Protection Law* (XPL, 2005).
- Kelleher, *Privacy and Data Protection Law in Ireland* (Bloomsbury, 2015).
- Kuner, *European Data Protection Law: Corporate Regulation and Compliance* (Oxford University Press, 2007).
- Lambert, *A Users Guide to Data Protection*, second edition (Bloomsbury, 2016).
- Lambert, *Data Protection Law in Ireland*, second edition (Clarus Press, 2016).
- Lynskey, *The Foundations of EU Data Protection Law* (OUP, 2015).
- Purtova, *Property Rights in Personal Data: A European Perspective* (Kluwer, 2012).
- "In Brief," *Communications Law* (2012) (17) 3.

6

THE INSTRUMENTS

Introduction

What are the legal instruments of data protection? Primarily, they are the national data protection laws, the new General Data Protection Regulation (GDPR) and the previous 1995 data protection directive (DPD95).

Data Protection Laws

The national data protection laws implement the provisions of the DPD95 on the protection of individuals with regard to the processing of personal data and on the free movement of such data. The DPD95 applies data protection to EU, and indirectly to EEA, member states.

The data protection laws have important implications for businesses and organizations that collect, process, and deal in information relating to living individuals—in particular, customers and employees. They contain stringent data protection measures to safeguard personal and informational privacy and to ensure that personal data are not misused or used for purposes that are incompatible with data protection legislation.

Legal Instruments

The introductions or Recitals to the European legal rules are not legally binding, unlike the main legal text-related Article provisions. However, the Recitals are still very influential in terms of interpreting the focus of the data protection rules, and they also highlight some of the history, purpose, and policy behind particular data protection rules.

General Provisions in the DPD95

The DPD95 provides the overarching framework for data protection in the EU and the European Economic Area (EEA). The Directive provides the data protection principles, legitimate processing conditions, security requirements, individual data subject rights, fair collection and processing, and restriction of trans-border data flows or transfers of personal data and sensitive personal data. The DPD95 at a headline level also provides for

- Privacy and data protection
- Harmonization of such measures throughout the EU

Some of the pertinent background Recitals to the DPD95 include the following themes, which are also illustrative of the aims and intentions of the DPD95: harmonization;[*] privacy/data protection/fundamental rights/sectors;[†] technology/increased processing;[‡] barriers;[§] automated processing;[¶] member states/jurisdiction;[**] third-party controllers and EU data subjects;[††] balance;[‡‡] security and technical security;[§§] access right to personal data;[¶¶] right to object to processing;[***] security;[†††] transmission;[‡‡‡] specific processing risks;[§§§] court and judicial remedy;[¶¶¶] trans-border data flows;[****] and consent.[††††]

---

[*] DPD 95 Recital 1.
[†] DPD 95 Recitals 2, 3, 22, 23, 26, 27, 28, 30, 31, 33, 38, 39, and 68.
[‡] DPD 95 Recitals 4, 6, and 10.
[§] DPD 95 Recitals 7, 8, 9.
[¶] DPD 95 Recital 11.
[**] DPD 95 Recitals 18 and 19.
[††] DPD 95 Recital 20.
[‡‡] DPD 95 Recital 25.
[§§] DPD 95 Recital 25.
[¶¶] DPD 95 Recital 41.
[***] DPD 95 Recital 45.
[†††] DPD 95 Recital 46.
[‡‡‡] DPD 95 Recital 47.
[§§§] DPD 95 Recital 53.
[¶¶¶] DPD 95 Recital 55.
[****] DPD 95 Recitals 56, 57, 59, 60 and 66.
[††††] DPD 95 Recital 58.

Chapter I of DPD95 contains the general legal provisions of the Directive. Article 1 refers to the object of the Directive. In particular, Article 1(1) states that member states must protect the fundamental rights of natural persons and in particular their right to data protection with respect to the processing of personal data. Article 1(2) provides that member states must neither restrict nor prohibit the free flow of personal data between member states for reasons connected with the protection afforded.

General Provisions in the GDPR

Chapter I of the new GDPR contains the general provisions. Article 1 refers to the subject matter and objectives. Particularly, it states that the GDPR lays down rules relating to the protection of natural persons with regard to the processing of personal data and rules relating to the free movement of personal data.

It states that the GDPR protects fundamental rights of natural persons and in particular their right to the protection of personal data. The free movement of personal data within the EU must be neither restricted nor prohibited for reasons connected with the protection of natural persons with regard to the processing of personal data.

Article 2 relates to material scope. The GDPR applies to the processing of personal data wholly or partly by automated means and to the processing other than by automated means of personal data that form part of a filing system or are intended to form part of a filing system. However, it makes clear that the GDPR does not apply to the processing of personal data

- In the course of an activity that falls outside the scope of EU law.
- By the member states when carrying out activities that fall within the scope of Chapter 2 of Title V of the EU Treaty.
- By a natural person in the course of a purely personal or household activity.
- By competent authorities for the purposes of the prevention, investigation, detection, or prosecution of criminal offenses or the execution of criminal penalties, including the safeguarding against and the prevention of threats to public security.

In addition, the GDPR is without prejudice to the application of the eCommerce Directive,* in particular of limited liability defense rules for internet service providers (ISPs) of caching, hosting, and mere conduit.†

Article 3 relates to territorial scope. The GDPR applies to the processing of personal data in the context of the activities of an establishment of a controller or a processor in the EU, regardless of whether the processing takes place in the EU or not.

Further, the GDPR applies to the processing of personal data of individual data subjects who are in the EU by a controller or processor not established in the EU, where the processing activities are related to (a) the offering of goods or services, irrespective of whether a payment of the individual data subject is required, to such individual data subjects in the EU; or (b) the monitoring of their behavior as far as their behavior takes place within the EU.

The GDPR applies to the processing of personal data by a controller not established in the EU, but in a place where member state law applies by virtue of public international law.

Data Protection Principles

Chapter II of the GDPR refers to the data protection principles. Article 5 relates to principles relating to personal data processing. Personal data must be

- Processed lawfully, fairly, and in a transparent manner in relation to the individual data subject ("lawfulness, fairness and transparency").
- Collected for specified, explicit, and legitimate purposes and not further processed in a manner that is incompatible with

---

* Directive 2000/31/EC of the European Parliament and of the Council of June 8, 2000 on certain legal aspects of information society services, in particular electronic commerce, in the Internal Market (Directive on eCommerce). Article 12 relates to mere conduit; Article 13 relates to caching; and Article 14 relates to hosting. Note also UNCITRAL Model Law on Electronic Commerce; "UNCITRAL model law on electronic commerce," *Tulane Journal of International and Comparative Law* (1999) (7) 237–250.

† The three limited liability rules of certain activities of website intermediary service providers (ISPs) are set out in Articles 12 to 15 of the eCommerce Directive.

those purposes; further processing for archiving purposes in the public interest, for scientific or historical research purposes, or for statistical purposes must, in accordance with Article 89(1), not be considered to be incompatible with the initial purposes ("purpose limitation").

- Adequate, relevant, and limited to what is necessary in relation to the purposes for which they are processed ("data minimization").
- Accurate and, where necessary, kept up to date; every reasonable step must be taken to ensure that personal data that are inaccurate, having regard to the purposes for which they are processed, are erased or rectified without delay ("accuracy").
- Kept in a form that permits identification of individual data subjects for no longer than is necessary for the purposes for which the personal data are processed; personal data may be stored for longer periods insofar as the personal data will be processed solely for archiving purposes in the public interest, for scientific or historical research purposes, or for statistical purposes in accordance with Article 89(1) subject to implementation of the appropriate technical and organizational measures required by the GDPR to safeguard the rights and freedoms of the individual data subject ("storage limitation").
- Processed in a manner that ensures appropriate security of the personal data, including protection against unauthorized or unlawful processing and against accidental loss, destruction, or damage, using appropriate technical or organizational measures ("integrity and confidentiality").

The controller must be responsible for, and be able to demonstrate compliance with, these principles ("accountability"). This will obviously require records and proofs of compliance to be kept.*

---

* The DPD95 also provided for the data protection principles. See DPD95 Article 6(2).

Legitimate Data Processing Conditions for Lawfulness of Processing

Article 6 of the GDPR refers to the lawfulness of processing. Processing must be lawful only if and to the extent that at least one of the following applies

1. The individual data subject has given consent to the processing of their personal data for one or more specific purposes.
2. Processing is necessary for the performance of a contract to which the individual data subject is party or to take steps at the request of the individual data subject prior to entering into a contract.
3. Processing is necessary for compliance with a legal obligation to which the controller is subject.
4. Processing is necessary to protect the vital interests of the individual data subject or of another natural person.
5. Processing is necessary for the performance of a task carried out in the public interest or in the exercise of official authority vested in the controller.
6. Processing is necessary for the purposes of the legitimate interests pursued by the controller or by a third party, except where such interests are overridden by the interests or fundamental rights of the individual data subject, which require protection of personal data, in particular where the individual data subject is a child.*

The purpose of the processing must be determined in that legal basis or, as regards the processing referred to in paragraph 1(e), must be necessary for the performance of a task carried out in the public interest or in the exercise of official authority vested in the controller. That legal basis may contain specific provisions to adapt the application of rules of the GDPR, *inter alia*: the general conditions governing the lawfulness of processing by the controller; the types of data that are subject to the processing; the individual data subjects concerned; the entities to, and the purposes for which, the personal data may be disclosed; the purpose limitation; storage periods; and processing operations and processing procedures, including measures to ensure

---

* 2. Section II of the DPD95 referred to the criteria for making data processing legitimate.

lawful and fair processing such as those for other specific processing situations.* The EU or the member state law must meet an objective of public interest and be proportionate to the legitimate aim pursued.

Where the processing for a purpose other than that for which the personal data have been collected is not based on the individual data subject's consent or on an EU or member state law that constitutes a necessary and proportionate measure in a democratic society to safeguard the societal objectives,[†] the controller must, to ascertain whether processing for another purpose is compatible with the purpose for which the personal data are initially collected, take into account, *inter alia*

- Any link between the purposes for which the personal data have been collected and the purposes of the intended further processing.
- The context in which the personal data have been collected, in particular regarding the relationship between individual data subjects and the controller.
- The nature of the personal data, in particular whether special categories of personal data are processed,[‡] or whether personal data related to criminal convictions and offenses are processed.[§]
- The possible consequences of the intended further processing for individual data subjects.
- The existence of appropriate safeguards, which may include encryption or pseudonymization.

GDPR Background Recitals

The guidance Recitals of the GDPR provide some of the context and intention behind the GDPR, including the following

---

* As provided for in Chapter IX.
[†] The societal objectives referred to in Article 23(1).
[‡] Pursuant to GDPR Article 9.
[§] Pursuant to GDPR Article 10.

- *DPD95 Repealed:* The DPD95 is repealed; EU Commission decisions based on DPD95 remain until replaced;* and Directive 2002/58[†] is to be updated on the foot of GDPR (Recital 173).
- *WP29/EDPB:* The establishment of the European Data Protection Board (EDPB), which is the effective equivalent of the Article 29 Data Protection Working Party (WP29) under the DPD95, is referred to.[‡]
- *Background and Rationale:* Personal data protection is a fundamental right;[§] Article 8(1) of the EU Charter and Article 16(1) of the EU Treaty;[¶] data processing should be designed to serve mankind; balanced with other fundamental rights; principle of proportionality;[**] internal market and cross-border transfers;[††] rapid technological developments and challenges;[‡‡] developments require a strong and more coherent data protection framework;[§§] the DPD95 has not prevented fragmentation in how data protection is implemented;[¶¶] need to ensure consistent and high level of protection and to remove obstacles to data flows;[***] need for a consistent level of protection through-

---

* GDPR Recital 171.

[†] Directive 2002/58/EC of the European Parliament and of the Council of July 12, 2002 concerning the processing of personal data and the protection of privacy in the electronic communications sector (Directive on privacy and electronic communications).

[‡] GDPR Recitals 72, 77, 105, 119, 124, 136, 139, 140, 143, 168.

[§] In relation to data protection as a fundamental right, see, for example, Rodata, "Data Protection as a Fundamental Right," in Gutwirth, Poullet, de Hert, de Terwangne, and Nouwt, *Reinventing Data Protection?* (Springer, 2009) 77. It is necessary to reinforce data protection to make it effective and not conditioned by the asymmetries that characterize the relationship between data subject and data controllers. Also note Richards, "Why Data Privacy Law is Constitutional," *William and Mary Law Review* (2015) (56:4) 1501; Clark, "The Constitutional Protection of Information in a Digital Age," *Suffolk University Law Review* (2014) (47:2) 267.

[¶] GDPR Recital 1.

[**] GDPR Recital 4.

[††] GDPR Recital 5.

[‡‡] GDPR Recital 6.

[§§] GDPR Recital 7.

[¶¶] GDPR Recital 9.

[***] GDPR Recital 10.

out the EU;* the GDPR protects natural persons and their personal data;† protections should be technologically neutral.‡

- *Obligations:* Data processing must be lawful and fair;§ processing necessary for a contract;¶ processing for a legal obligation;** processing necessary to protect life;†† the legitimate interests of the controller.‡‡
- *Security:* Network and information security, Computer Emergency Response Teams (CERTs) and Computer Security Incident Response Teams (CSIRTs);§§ guidance for appropriate measures;¶¶ appropriate technical protection and organizational measures;*** breach, security, and risk evaluation;††† high risk and impact assessments;‡‡‡ and impact assessments;§§§ and large-scale processing operations;¶¶¶ consultations with data protection supervisory authorities; data breach and data breach notification;**** EU Commission delegated acts.
- *Processing:* Processing; pseudonymized data;†††† online identifiers;‡‡‡‡ consent;§§§§ lawful processing and consent;¶¶¶¶ principle of transparency;***** children;††††† processing for (additional)

---

* GDPR Recital 13.
† GDPR Recital 14.
‡ GDPR Recital 15.
§ GDPR Recital 39.
¶ GDPR Recital 40.
** GDPR Recital 40.
††GDPR Recital 46.
‡‡GDPR Recital 47.
§§ GDPR Recital 49.
¶¶ GDPR Recital 77.
*** GDPR Recitals 78, 88.
††† GDPR Recital 88.
‡‡‡ GDPR Recital 90.
§§§ GDPR Recitals 90, 91, 92, 93, 94, 95.
¶¶¶ GDPR Recital 71.
**** GDPR Recitals 73, 85, 86.
†††† GDPR Recitals 26, 28, 29, 78, 85, 156.
‡‡‡‡ GDPR Recitals 30, 64.
§§§§ GDPR Recitals 32, 33, 38, 40, 42, 43, 50, 51, 54, 65, 68, 71, 111, 112, 155, 161, 171.
¶¶¶¶ GDPR Recital 40.
***** GDPR Recital 39.
††††† GDPR Recitals 38, 58, 65, 71, 75.

other purposes;* genetic data;† health data;‡ sensitive personal data§ and special categories of personal data;¶ additional
identifying information;** processing and electoral activities;††
religious associations;‡‡ processing and direct marketing;§§
right not to be subject to a decision; automated processing;¶¶
profiling;*** registry data and coupling data;††† restrictions
on principles and rights;‡‡‡ responsibility and liability of
controllers;§§§ risks;¶¶¶ processors and controllers;**** Codes of
Conduct;††††transparency and certification mechanisms;‡‡‡‡pen-
alties and fines;§§§§other rights, issues, derogations;¶¶¶¶employee
data;***** public authorities; processing in the public interest
or official authority;††††† processing and public interest, scientific and historical research purposes, statistical purposes,
safeguards;‡‡‡‡‡ professional and secrecy obligations.§§§§§

---

* GDPR Recital 32.
† GDPR Recital 34.
‡ GDPR Recital 35.
§ GDPR Recitals 10, 51.
¶ GDPR Recitals 10, 51, 52, 53, 54, 71, 80, 91, 97.
** GDPR Recitals 26, 29.
†† GDPR Recital 56.
‡‡ GDPR Recitals 55, 71.
§§ GDPR Recitals 38, 47, 70.
¶¶ GDPR Recital 71.
*** GDPR Recitals 24, 60, 63, 70, 71, 72, 73, 91.
††† GDPR Recital 127.
‡‡‡ GDPR Recital 73.
§§§ GDPR Recital 74.
¶¶¶ GDPR Recitals 9, 28, 38, 39, 51, 65, 71, 83, 122.
**** GDPR Recitals 13, 18, 28, 78, 79, 81, 98, 99, 101, 109, 132, 146, 168.
†††† GDPR Recitals 77, 98, 168.
‡‡‡‡ GDPR Recitals 77, 81, 100.
§§§§ GDPR Recitals 19, 50, 73, 75, 80, 91, 97, 104, 149, 151, 152.
¶¶¶¶ GDPR Recitals 13, 51, 52, 107, 112, 153, 156.
***** GDPR Recitals 48, 127, 155.
††††† GDPR Recital 45.
‡‡‡‡‡ GDPR Recitals 50, 52, 53, 62, 65, 113, 156, 160.
§§§§§ GDPR Recitals 50, 53, 75, 85, 165.

- *Rights:* Data subject rights;* principles of fair and transparent processing;† prior information requirements;‡ right of access;§ right of rectification and right to be forgotten;¶ right to complain to single data protection supervisory authority;** automated processing.††
- *Proceedings:* Proceedings against controllers, processors, and jurisdiction;‡‡ damages and compensation;§§ the prevention, investigation, detection, or prosecution of criminal offenses or the execution of criminal penalties, including public security.¶¶
- *Establishment:* Establishment;*** groups of organizations;††† establishment.‡‡‡
- *Transfers:* Cross-border data transfers.§§§
- *Data Protection Supervisory Authorities, etc.*; Data protection supervisory authorities and their independence.¶¶¶
- *New Bodies*: Data protection of non-profit bodies, organizations, and associations.****
- *Notification/Registration Replaced:* Replacement of "general" notification/registration requirement.††††
- *Exceptions/Exemptions:* The GDPR does not address national security;‡‡‡‡ the GDPR should not apply to data processing by a natural person in the course of a purely personal or household activity and thus without a connection with a professional

---

* GDPR Recitals 1, 11, 38, 39, 50.
† GDPR Recitals 39, 60.
‡ GDPR Recital 61.
§ GDPR Recitals 63–64.
¶ GDPR Recitals 65–67.
** GDPR Recital 141.
†† GDPR Recitals 67, 68.
‡‡ GDPR Recital 145.
§§ GDPR Recitals 146, 147.
¶¶ GDPR Recital 19.
*** GDPR Recitals 22–24, 36.
††† GDPR Recitals 37.
‡‡‡ GDPR Recital 80.
§§§ GDPR Recitals 53, 116.
¶¶¶ GDPR Recitals 104, 117, 118, 121, 153.
**** GDPR Recital 143.
†††† GDPR Recital 89.
‡‡‡‡ GDPR Recital 16.

or commercial activity;[*] without prejudice to eCommerce Directive,[†] in particular eCommerce defenses of Articles 12–15;[‡] the GDPR does not apply to the data of the deceased.[§]

- *Lawful Processing and Consent:* Lawful processing and consent.[¶]
- *Online Identifiers:* Online identifiers.[**]
- *Sensitive Personal Data*: Sensitive personal data[††] and special categories of personal data.[‡‡]
- *Children:* Processing of children's personal data.[§§]
- *Health Data:* Health data processing.[¶¶]

Consent Conditions

Article 7 of the GDPR relates to the conditions for consent. Where processing is based on consent, the controller must be able to demonstrate that the individual data subject has consented to processing of their personal data.

If the individual data subject's consent is given in the context of a written declaration that also concerns other matters, the request for consent must be presented in a manner that is clearly distinguishable from the other matters, in an intelligible and easily accessible form, using clear and plain language. Any part of such a declaration that constitutes an infringement of the GDPR must not be binding.

Freely Given Consent

When assessing whether consent is freely given, utmost account must be taken of whether, *inter alia*, the performance of a contract, including the provision of a service, is conditional on consent to the

---

[*] GDPR Recital 18.
[†] Directive 2000/31/EC.
[‡] GDPR Recital 21.
[§] GDPR Recital 27.
[¶] GDPR Recital 40.
[**] GDPR Recital 30.
[††] GDPR Recitals 10, 51.
[‡‡] GDPR Recitals 10, 51, 52, 53, 54.
[§§] GDPR Recital 38.
[¶¶] GDPR Recital 35.

processing of personal data that is not necessary for the performance of that contract. It is unclear what interpretation will be given to "freely given" and "utmost account." Obviously, other factors may also be relevant. There may be some contention as to what is and is not actually "necessary." Quite often, also, consent may be conditional in practical terms, but may not be expressly specified as being conditional. It is also worth noting that the EU Commission original proposed version stated that consent must not provide a legal basis for processing where there is a significant imbalance between the position of the individual data subject and that of the controller.*

Consent for Processing: Conditions for Consent

Consent is an important issue under the new GDPR.† Lawful processing and consent are referred to in Recital 39. The WP29 also refers to consent issues.‡

Article 7 of the GDPR refers to conditions for consent as follows. Where processing is based on consent, the controller must be able to demonstrate that consent was given by the individual data subject to the processing of their personal data.§

If the individual data subject's consent is given in the context of a written declaration that also concerns other matters, the request for consent must be presented in a manner that is clearly distinguishable from the other matters, in an intelligible and easily accessible form, using clear and plain language. Any part of the declaration that constitutes an infringement of the GDPR must not be binding.¶

The individual data subject must have the right to withdraw their consent at any time. The withdrawal of consent must not affect the lawfulness of processing based on consent before its withdrawal.

---

* EU Commission's original proposal for the GDPR, Article 7(4).
† Vandenbroucke and Olsen, "Informed Consent and the New EU Regulation on Data Protection," *International Journal of Epidemiology* (2013) (42:6) 1891.
‡ WP29 Opinion 15/2011 Consent; Working Document 02/2013 providing guidance on obtaining consent for cookies, 201; Opinion 04/2012 on Cookie Consent Exemption.
§ GDPR Article 7(1).
¶ GDPR Article 7(2).

Prior to giving consent, the individual data subject must be informed thereof. It must be as easy to withdraw consent as to give consent.[*]

When assessing whether consent is freely given, utmost account must be taken of whether, among other things, the performance of a contract, including the provision of a service, is made conditional on the consent to the processing of personal data that is not necessary for the performance of this contract.[†]

Withdrawing Consent

The individual data subject must have the right to withdraw their consent at any time. However, the withdrawal of consent must not affect the lawfulness of processing based on consent before its withdrawal. Prior to giving consent, the individual data subject must be informed thereof. It must be as easy to withdraw as to give consent.

Conclusion

Data protection is evolving as technology changes how personal data are collected, used, and processed. The current data protection legal regime is viewed as requiring updating. The DPD95 was enacted in 1995, prior to social media, cloud computing, mass data storage, data mining, electronic profiling, Web 2.0, and the threats to the security surrounding personal data. Data protection needs to evolve to deal with these issues. This is partly the reason for the GDPR. This is important for the issues it addresses as well as the current legal provisions it will enhance. As a legal regulation, as opposed to a legal directive, it means that it is directly applicable in EU member states without the need for a directive or member state implementing legislation. Law and practice will be changed, as will many of the obligations of organizations. This will also differ more for organizations in particular sectors. Areas that are being highlighted include better awareness and more hands-on board management responsibility, planning, and data protection assessment, and including risk assessment, data protection impact assessments, risk consultations, in

---

[*] GDPR Article 7(3).
[†] GDPR Article 7(4).

advance of product or service launch via the data protection by design and default concept, and explicit recognition of children under the data protection regime for the first time.

KEY CONCEPTS

The new data protection regime under the GDPR imposes and expands the conditions for organizations to be able to collect, use, and process personal data. The new principles and legitimate processing conditions and amendments to consent issues all need to be considered.

KEY WORDS

- Compliance to collect and process personal data.
- Data protection principles.
- Legitimate processing conditions.
- Background context and Recitals.
- Consent.
- Consent for processing.
- Consent conditions.
- When consent freely given.
- Mere conduit.
- Caching.
- Hosting.

7

THE NEW RULES

Introduction

The EU data protection regime is being fundamentally updated and expanded.* Many things have changed since the introduction of the 1995 data protection directive (DPD95). Data processing activities have changed as well as increased in scale and complexity. The EU undertook a review of the current effectiveness of the data protection regime. Partly on the foot of the review, the EU Commission proposed a new legal update to the data protection regime. This culminated in the proposals for the new General Data Protection Regulation (GDPR). Indeed, the Council of Europe is also proposing to update the Data Protection Convention.† The Article 29 Data Protection Working Party (WP29) also refers to the need for future data protection measures in *The Future of Privacy*.‡ There have also been calls for greater political activism in relation to particular data protection issues.§ Others¶ have also highlighted new problematic developments in relation to such issues as location data and location-based services,

---

* Graham, "Prepare for European Data Protection Reform," *Computer and Law* (November 30, 2011).
† Data Protection Convention, at http://conventions.coe.int/Treaty/en/Treaties/Html/108.htm. The Convention pre-dated the DPD95 and was incorporated into the national law of many EU and other states prior to the DPD95. See Kierkegaard et al., "30 Years on: The Review of the Council of Europe Data Protection Convention 108," *Computer Law & Security Review* (2011) (27) 223.
‡ *The Future of Privacy*, WP29, referred to in Wong, "Data Protection: The Future of Privacy," *Computer Law & Security Review* (2011) (27) 53.
§ Ripoll Servent and MacKenzie, "Is the EP Still a Data Protection Champion? The Case of SWIFT," *Perspectives on European Politics & Society* (2011) (12) 390.
¶ Cuijpers and Pekarek, "The Regulation of Location-Based Services: Challenges to the European Union Data Protection Regime," *Journal of Location Based Services* (2011) (5) 223.

which need to be dealt with. Online and offline abuse issues are yet other matters needing to be addressed.

The new processing rules as set out in the new GDPR regime are listed here.*

Detailed core rules, known as the principles or data protection principles, must be complied with. These refer to

- Prior information requirements.
- Lawfulness, fairness, and transparency.
- Purpose limitation.
- Data minimization.
- Accuracy.
- Storage limitation.
- Integrity and confidentiality.
- Accountability.

There are also detailed rules relating to

- Lawfulness of processing and legitimate processing conditions.
- Consent for processing and conditions for consent.

Repeal of DPD95

The DPD of 1995 is repealed with effect from May 25, 2018 (Article 94(1)). References to the repealed DPD95 will be construed as references to the GDPR (Article 94(2)).

Context of GDPR

The initial provisions refer to the context of the GDPR: namely, the subject matter and objectives (Article 1); material scope (Article 2); and territorial scope (Article 3).

---

* The Recitals refer to the following: data processing must be lawful and fair (Recitals 10, 39); processing necessary for a contract (Recital 40); processing for a legal obligation (Recital 40); processing necessary to protect life (Recital 46); the legitimate interests of the controller (Recital 47).

Fundamental Right

Personal data protection is now recognized as a fundamental legal right for individuals in the new GDPR and the EU Charter of Fundamental Rights of 2000, the Lisbon Treaty (Treaty on the Functioning of the European Union), and the Data Protection Convention.

EU CHARTER

Article 8(1)
Protection of Personal Data
Everyone has the right to the protection of personal data concerning them.

EU LISBON TREATY

Article 16(1)
Everyone has the right to the protection of personal data concerning them.

Formal Nature of Regulations and Directives

The GDPR is now agreed, and organizations will, in some instances, have two years to fully comply with the new data protection regime. However, it is important to note that an EU Regulation differs from a Directive under formal EU law.* A Regulation is immediately directly effective in all EU member states, without the need for member states implementing laws. Once the Regulation is passed, it will apply throughout the EU. It will also change the data protection regime in Europe and beyond. The reform is "comprehensive."†

---

* Generally see, for example, Biondi and Eeckhout (eds), *EU Law after Lisbon* (Oxford University Press, 2012); Foster, *Foster on EU Law* (Oxford University Press, 2011); O'Neill, *EU Law for UK Lawyers* (Hart, 2011); Steiner and Woods, *EU Law* (Oxford University Press, 2011).
† In brief, *Communications Law* (2012)(17) 3.

Introducing the New GDPR Changes

There are a large number of new issues for organizations to consider. Some of the new headline changes include

- New and updated fundamental principles, such as fairness and legality, processing conditions, prior information, consent, transparency, accuracy, lawfulness of processing, and definitions.
- Data protection officers.
- Special rules concerning children in relation to information society services.
- Expanded rights, including subject access rights.
- New enforcement and sanctions provisions.
- Right to be forgotten.
- Right to data portability.
- New security and breach provisions.
- Provisions regarding single data protection supervisory authority or one-stop-shop.
- Risk-based approach, risk minimization, consultations, and reporting.

Some of the new detailed changes include

• Repeal of DPD95	• Right to prior information: directly obtained data
• WP29 and European Data Protection Board	
• Background and rationale	• Right to prior information: indirectly obtained data
• Context objectives, scope of GDPR	
• New and expanded obligations	• Right of confirmation and *right of access*
• Security	• Right to be informed of third-country safeguards
• Processing	
• Rights	• Rectification and erasure
• Proceedings	• Right to rectification
• Establishment	• Right to erasure (right to be forgotten)
• Transfers	• Right to restriction of processing
• Data protection supervisory authority	• Notifications re rectification, erasure, or restriction
• New bodies	
• Notification/registration replaced	• Right to data portability
• Exceptions/exemptions	• Right to object
• Lawful processing and consent	• Rights against automated individual decision-making, including profiling
• Online identifiers	
• Sensitive personal data	• Data protection by design and by default
• Children	

(Continued)

(Continued)

- Health data
- New and updated definitions
- New processing rules: obligations
- New (data protection) principles
- Lawfulness of processing: legitimate processing conditions
- Child's consent: conditions for information society services
- Processing special categories of personal data
- Processing re criminal convictions and offenses data
- Processing not requiring identification
- Controllers and processors
- Responsibility of the controller
- Joint controllers
- Processor
- Processing under authority of controller and processor
- Records of processing activities
- Representatives of controllers not established in EU
- Cooperation with data protection supervisory authority
- Security
- Security of processing
- Notifying data breach to data protection supervisory authority
- Communicating data breach to individual data subject
- Data protection impact assessment and prior consultation
- Data protection impact assessment
- Prior consultation
- New data protection officer
- Position and tasks of new data protection officer
- General principle for transfers
- Transfers via adequacy decision
- Transfers via appropriate safeguards
- Transfers via binding corporate rules
- Transfers or disclosures not authorized by EU law
- Derogations for specific situations
- New processing rules: individual data subject rights
- Right to transparency
- Data access rights
- Security rights
- Data protection impact assessment and prior consultation
- Communicating data breach to individual data subjects
- Data protection officer (contact)
- Remedies, liability, and sanctions
- Right to lodge complaint with the data protection supervisory authority
- Right to judicial remedy against the data protection supervisory authority
- Right to effective judicial remedy against controller or processor
- Representation of individual data subjects
- Suspension of proceedings
- Right to compensation and liability
- Codes of conduct and certification
- International cooperation on personal data
- Data protection supervisory authorities
- General conditions for imposing administrative fines
- Penalties
- Specific data processing situations
- Processing and freedom of expression and information
- Processing and public access to official documents
- Processing national identification numbers
- Processing in employment context
- Safeguards and derogations: public interest/scientific/historical research/statistical archiving processing
- Obligations of secrecy
- Churches and religious associations
- Delegated acts and implementing acts
- Exercise of the delegation
- Relationship to Directive 2002/58
- Relationship to previously concluded agreements
- Review of other EU data protection instruments
- Restrictions

Processing of Criminal Convictions and Offenses Data

Article 10 refers to processing of data relating to criminal convictions and offenses. The processing of personal data relating to criminal convictions and offenses or related security measures based on Article 6(1) must be carried out only under the control of official authority or when the processing is authorized by EU or member state law providing for appropriate safeguards for the rights of data subjects. Any comprehensive register of criminal convictions must be kept only under the control of official authority.

Processing Not Requiring Identification

Article 11 refers to processing not requiring identification. If the purposes for which a controller processes personal data do not or do no longer require the identification of a data subject by the controller, the controller must not be obliged to maintain, acquire, or process additional information to identify the data subject for the sole purpose of complying with the GDPR.*

Where, in cases referred to in the preceding paragraph, the controller is able to demonstrate that it is not in a position to identify the data subject, the controller must inform the data subject accordingly, if possible. In such cases, Articles 15–20 must not apply except where the data subject, for the purpose of exercising their rights under those articles, provides additional information enabling their identification.†

Controllers and Processors

Chapter IV of the GDPR refers to controllers and processors. Chapter IV, Section 1 refers to general obligations. The WP29 also refers to controller and processor issues.‡ Article 24 refers to the responsibility of the controller.

---

* GDPR Article 11(1).
† GDPR Article 11(2).
‡ WP29 Opinion 1/2010 on the concepts of "controller" and "processor."

Responsibility of the Controller

Taking into account the nature, scope, context, and purposes of processing as well as the risks of varying likelihood and severity for the rights of natural persons, the controller must implement appropriate technical and organizational measures to ensure and to be able to demonstrate that processing is performed in accordance with the GDPR. Those measures must be reviewed and updated where necessary.[*]

Where proportionate in relation to processing activities, these measures must include the implementation of appropriate data protection policies by the controller.[†]

Adherence to approved codes of conduct[‡] or approved certification mechanisms[§] may be used as an element by which to demonstrate compliance with the obligations of the controller.[¶]

Joint Controllers

Where two or more controllers jointly determine the purposes and means of processing, they will be joint controllers. They must in a transparent manner determine their respective responsibilities for compliance with the obligations under the GDPR, in particular as regards the exercising of the rights of the data subject and their respective duties to provide the information required by the prior information requirements (referred to in Articles 13 and 14), by means of an arrangement between them unless the respective responsibilities of the controllers are determined by EU or member state law to which the controllers are subject. The arrangement may designate a contact point for data subjects.[**]

This arrangement must duly reflect the respective roles and relationships of the joint controllers *vis*-à-*vis* the data subjects. The essence of the arrangement must be made available to the data subject.[††]

---

[*] GDPR Article 24(1).
[†] GDPR Article 24(2).
[‡] As referred to in GDPR Article 40.
[§] As referred to in GDPR Article 42.
[¶] GDPR Article 24(3).
[**] GDPR Article 26(1).
[††] GDPR Article 26(2).

Irrespective of the terms of the arrangement, the data subject may exercise their rights under the GDPR in respect of and against each of the controllers.*

Processor

Organizations that are processors also should appreciate that while they may indeed be processors, they can also at the same time be controllers in relation to different sets of personal data.

Processing under Authority of Controller and Processor

The processor, and any person acting under the authority of the controller or of the processor who has access to personal data, must not process those data except on instructions from the controller, unless required to do so by EU or member state law.†

Processing Not Allowing Identification

Article 10 refers to processing not allowing identification, and provides that if the purposes for which a controller processes personal data do not or do no longer require the identification of an individual data subject by the controller, the controller must not be obliged to maintain, acquire, or process additional information to identify the individual data subject for the sole purpose of complying with the GDPR.

Exemptions

In considering compliance obligation, it is also important to consider the exemptions that may apply.‡ The new GDPR Recitals refer to

---

* GDPR Article 26(3). Generally see Mäkinen, "Data Quality, Sensitive Data and Joint Controllership as Examples of Grey Areas in the Existing Data Protection Framework for the Internet of Things," *Information & Communications Technology Law* (2015) (24:3) 262.
† GDPR Article 29.
‡ Provided for in Articles 6(1), 10, 11(1), 12 and 21.

exemption issues: the GDPR does not address national security;* the GDPR should not apply to data processing by a natural person in the course of a purely personal or household activity and thus without a connection with a professional or commercial activity;† the GDPR is without prejudice to the eCommerce Directive,‡ in particular eCommerce defenses of Articles 12–15;§ the GDPR does not apply to the data of the deceased.¶ One of the most important exemptions is perhaps that the GDPR applies to the personal data of living individuals, thus excluding data of deceased persons and organizations.

The GDPR does not apply to the processing of personal data

- In the course of an activity that falls outside the scope of EU law.
- By the member states when carrying out activities that fall within the scope of Chapter 2 of Title V of the Treaty on European Union.
- By a natural person in the course of a purely personal or household activity.
- By competent authorities for the purposes of prevention, investigation, detection, or prosecution of criminal offenses or the execution of criminal penalties, including the safeguarding against and the prevention of threats to public security.**

For the processing of personal data by the EU institutions, bodies, offices, and agencies, a different Regulation applies. Regulation (EC) No 45/2001 and other EU legal instruments applicable to such processing of personal data must be adapted to the principles and rules of the GDPR.††

---

* GDPR background Recital 16.
† GDPR background Recital 18.
‡ Directive 2000/31/EC.
§ GDPR background Recital 21.
¶ GDPR background Recital 27.
** GDPR Articles 2(2). Article 13 of the DPD95, under the heading of *Exemptions and Restrictions*, provides that member states may adopt legislative measures to restrict the scope of the obligations and rights.
††GDPR Articles 2(3).

The GDPR is without prejudice to the application of the eCommerce Directive, in particular of the liability rules of intermediary service providers in Articles 12–15 of the eCommerce Directive.*

Certain exemptions can be enacted nationally, particularly processing of personal data carried out for journalistic purposes or the purpose of academic artistic or literary expression, if necessary.† It remains to be seen whether this will occur.

Conclusion

The exemptions are important when and where they are applicable. They will often be more relevant to particular sectors. Generally, the exemptions appear to be less litigated than other areas of data protection. Particular organizations will also need to consider any national amending measures that may also occur.

KEY CONCEPTS

The previous DPD95 is being repealed and replaced by the GDPR. The new rules are significant for all individuals and organizations to consider. Those who must comply must overhaul their compliance frameworks. Individuals have important new rights to aid them in enforcing and protecting their personal data, enhancing the fundamental right to personal data and data protection.

KEYWORDS

- Personal data.
- Fundamental right.
- DPD95.
- GDPR.

---

* The eCommerce Directive is Directive 2000/31/EC. GDPR Article 2(3).
† GDPR Article 85.

- EU Charter
- Lisbon Treaty
- Many new changes in GDPR

FURTHER READING

- Gutwirth and Leenes, *Data Protection on the Move: Current Developments in ICT and Privacy/Data Protection* (Springer, 2015).
- Gutwirth and Leenes, *Reforming European Data Protection Law* (Law, Governance and Technology Series/Issues in Privacy and Data Protection) (Springer, 2014).
- "In Brief," *Communications Law* (2012) (17) 3.

8
DEFINITIONS

Introduction

What are the definitions central to data protection? It is critical to understanding the data protection regime to know and appreciate the definitions of the key terms that underpin the legal measures implementing the data protection regime. The definitions are the building blocks for the data protection regime. They are contained in the data protection laws, the DPD95 and now the new GDPR. The new definitions in the GDPR should be considered in particular, as these expand and enhance the EU data protection legal regime. The GDPR will be the central EU data protection legal measure for many years to come. The various categories and definitions are referred to in this chapter.

Categories of Personal Data

Organizations need to be familiar with two separate categories of personal data in relation to their data protection actions and compliance obligations. These also affect what personal data they may collect in the first instance. The categories of personal data are *general personal data* and *sensitive personal data*. (Note: in the United States, personal data are often generally referred to as personally identifiable information [PII].)

The first general category is general personal data. The second general category is sensitive personal data. The importance of sensitive personal data is that they trigger additional and more onerous obligations of compliance and initial collection conditions. Unless they fall within the definition of sensitive personal data, all personal data fall into the general personal data category.

Why is there a distinction? Certain types of personal data are more important and sensitive to individuals than other categories of personal data. This is recognized in the data protection regime. Additional rules are put in place. First, sensitive personal data are defined differently. Second, to collect and process sensitive personal data, an organization must satisfy additional processing conditions, in addition to the data protection principles and the general legitimate processing conditions; namely, it must comply with the sensitive personal data legitimate processing conditions.

General Personal Data

(General) personal data are data relating to a living individual who is (or can be) identified either from the data or from the data in conjunction with other information that is in, or is likely to come into, the possession of the controller.*

Sensitive Personal Data

Sensitive personal data contain higher compliance obligations and conditions. Sensitive personal data are personal data relating to any of the following: (a) racial or ethnic origin; (b) political opinions; (c) religious or philosophical beliefs; (d) trade union membership; (e) physical or mental health or condition or sexual life; (f) the commission or alleged commission of any offense; or (g) any proceedings for an offense committed or alleged to have been committed, the disposal of such proceedings or the sentence of any court in such proceedings, by the individual data subject.

This can be summarized as personal data relating to

- Racial or ethnic origin.
- Political opinions.
- Religious or philosophical beliefs.
- Trade union membership.

---

* However, there are calls to ensure that some or all data protection rights and protections are extended to entities other than just individuals. Indeed, organizations have certain rights under the data protection regime as regards electronic and related commercial communications (e.g., anti-spam rights). Generally see, for example, van der Sloot, "Do Privacy and Data Protection Rules Apply to Legal Persons and Should They? A Proposal for a Two-Tiered System," *Computer Law and Security Review* (2015) (31:1) 26.

- Physical or mental health or condition or sexual life.
- Commission of offense.
- Proceedings for an offense.

Article 8 of the DPD95 refers to the processing of special categories of data. It states that member states must prohibit the processing of personal data revealing racial or ethnic origin, political opinions, religious or philosophical beliefs, or trade union membership, and the processing of data concerning health or sex life.*

Article 9 of the GDPR relates to the processing of special categories of personal data. The processing of personal data revealing racial or ethnic origin, political opinions, religious or philosophical beliefs, or trade union membership, and the processing of genetic data, biometric data to uniquely identify a person, or data concerning health or sex life and sexual orientation must be prohibited.† Article 9(2) of the GDPR provides that the processing prohibitions above must not apply where

- The individual data subject has given explicit consent to the processing of those personal data for one or more specified purposes, except where EU law or member state law provides that the prohibition referred to above may not be lifted by the individual data subject; or
- Processing is necessary for the purposes of carrying out the obligations and exercising specific rights of the controller or of the individual data subject in the field of employment and social security and social protection law insofar as it is authorized by EU law or member state law or a collective agreement pursuant to member state law providing for adequate safeguards for the fundamental rights and the interests of the individual data subject; or
- Processing is necessary to protect the vital interests of the individual data subject or of another person where the individual

---

* Member states shall determine the conditions under which a national identification number or any other identifier of general application may be processed; DPD95 Article 8.
† GDPR Article 9(1).

data subject is physically or legally incapable of giving consent; or

- Processing is carried out in the course of its legitimate activities with appropriate safeguards by a foundation, association, or any other non-profit-seeking body with a political, philosophical, religious, or trade union aim and on condition that the processing relates solely to the members or to former members of the body or to persons who have regular contact with it in connection with its purposes and that the data are not disclosed outside that body without the consent of the individual data subjects; or

- Processing relates to personal data that are manifestly made public by the individual data subject; or

- Processing is necessary for the establishment, exercise, or defense of legal claims or whenever courts are acting in their judicial capacity; or

- Processing is necessary for reasons of substantial public interest, on the basis of EU or member state law, which must be proportionate to the aim pursued, respect the essence of the right to data protection, and provide for suitable and specific measures to safeguard the fundamental rights and the interests of the individual data subject; or

- Processing is necessary for the purposes of preventive or occupational medicine, for the assessment of the working capacity of the employee, medical diagnosis, the provision of health or social care or treatment or the management of health or social care systems and services on the basis of EU law or member state law or pursuant to contract with a health professional and subject to the conditions and safeguards referred to in Article 9(4) [Article 9(2)(h)]; or

- Processing is necessary for reasons of public interest in the area of public health, such as protecting against serious cross-border threats to health or ensuring high standards of quality and safety of health care and of medicinal products or medical devices, on the basis of EU law or member state law that provides for suitable and specific measures to safeguard the rights of the individual data subject, in particular professional secrecy; or

- Processing is necessary for archiving purposes in the public interest or scientific and historical research purposes or statistical purposes in accordance with Article 83(1) based on EU or member state law, which must be proportionate to the aim pursued, respect the essence of the right to data protection, and provide for suitable and specific measures to safeguard the fundamental rights and the interests of the individual data subject.

Personal data referred to in Article 9(1) may be processed for the purposes referred to in Article 9(2)(h) when those data are processed by or under the responsibility of a professional subject to the obligation of professional secrecy under EU or member state law or rules established by national competent bodies or by another person also subject to an obligation of secrecy under EU or member state law or rules established by national competent bodies.

Member states remain free to maintain or introduce further conditions, including limitations, with regard to the processing of genetic data, biometric data, or health data.*

Data Protection Definitions

There are various definitions in relation to personal data. These are the building blocks of the data protection regime and the respective obligations and rights as regards organizations and individuals.

New Definitions in GDPR

The GDPR introduces certain new definitions, such as the following.

Restriction of Processing

"Restriction of processing" means the marking of stored personal data with the aim of limiting their processing in the future.

---

* GDPR Article 9(5).

Profiling

"Profiling" means any form of automated processing of personal data consisting of the use of personal data to evaluate certain personal aspects relating to a natural person, in particular to analyze or predict aspects concerning that natural person's performance at work, economic situation, health, personal preferences, interests, reliability, behavior, location, or movements.

Pseudonymization

"Pseudonymization" means the processing of personal data in such a manner that the personal data can no longer be attributed to a specific data subject without the use of additional information, provided that such additional information is kept separately and is subject to technical and organizational measures to ensure that the personal data are not attributed to an identified or identifiable natural person.

Personal Data Breach

"Personal data breach" means a breach of security leading to the accidental or unlawful destruction, loss, alteration, or unauthorized disclosure of, or access to, personal data transmitted, stored, or otherwise processed.

Genetic Data

"Genetic data" means personal data relating to the inherited or acquired genetic characteristics of a natural person that give unique information about the physiology or the health of that natural person and that result, in particular, from an analysis of a biological sample from the natural person in question.

Biometric Data

"Biometric data" means personal data resulting from specific technical processing relating to the physical, physiological, or behavioral characteristics of a natural person, which allow or confirm the unique identification of that natural person, such as facial images or dactylo-scopic data.

Data Concerning Health

"Data concerning health" means personal data related to the physical or mental health of a natural person, including the provision of health care services, which reveal information about their health status.

Main Establishment

"Main establishment" as regards a controller with establishments in more than one member state, the place of its central administration in the EU, unless the decisions on the purposes and means of the processing of personal data are taken in another establishment of the controller in the EU and the latter establishment has the power to have such decisions implemented, in which case the establishment having taken such decisions is to be considered to be the main establishment; and as regards a processor with establishments in more than one member state, the place of its central administration in the EU, or, if the processor has no central administration in the EU, the establishment of the processor in the EU where the main processing activities in the context of the activities of an establishment of the processor take place to the extent that the processor is subject to specific obligations under the GDPR.

Enterprise

"Enterprise" means a natural or legal person engaged in an economic activity, irrespective of its legal form, including partnerships or associations regularly engaged in an economic activity.

Group of Undertakings

"Group of undertakings" means a controlling undertaking and its controlled undertakings.

Binding Corporate Rules

"Binding corporate rules" means personal data protection policies that are adhered to by a controller or processor established on the territory of a member state for transfers or a set of transfers of personal data to a controller or processor in one or more third countries within a group of undertakings, or group of enterprises engaged in a joint economic activity.

Data Protection Supervisory Authority

Data protection "supervisory authority" means an independent public authority that is established by a member state pursuant to Article 51.

Supervisory Authority Concerned

"Supervisory authority concerned" means a data protection supervisory authority that is concerned by the processing of personal data because

- The controller or processor is established on the territory of the member state of that data protection supervisory authority.
- Individual data subjects residing in the member state of that data protection supervisory authority are substantially affected or likely to be substantially affected by the processing.

or

- A complaint has been lodged with that data protection supervisory authority.

Data Protection Supervisory Authority

Article 4 of the GDPR sets out the following definition of data protection "supervisory authority": an independent public authority that is established by a member state. This emphasizes the independence necessary for national data protection supervisory authorities.

Cross-Border Processing of Personal Data

"Cross-border processing of personal data" means either

- Processing of personal data that takes place in the context of the activities of establishments in more than one member state of a controller or processor in the EU where the controller or processor is established in more than one member state.

or

- Processing of personal data that takes place in the context of the activities of a single establishment of a controller or processor in the EU but that substantially affects or is likely to substantially affect individual data subjects in more than one member state.

Relevant and Reasoned Objection

"Relevant and reasoned objection" means an objection to a draft decision as to whether there is an infringement of the GDPR or whether envisaged action in relation to the controller or processor complies with the GDPR, which clearly demonstrates the significance of the risks posed by the draft decision as regards the fundamental rights of individual data subjects and, where applicable, the free flow of personal data within the EU.

Information Society Service

"Information Society service" means a service as defined in point (b) of Article 1(1) of Directive (EU) 2015/1535 of the European Parliament and of the Council.

International Organization

"International organization" means an organization and its subordinate bodies governed by public international law, or any other body that is set up by, or on the basis of, an agreement between two or more countries.

Child

The original EU Commission proposed version for the GDPR defines "child" as any person below the age of 18 years. This is not contained in the agreed version of December 2015. The final version in Article 8 refers to a child in relation to the offer of information society services directly to a child; the processing of the personal data of a child will be lawful where the child is at least 16 years old. (Note final provisions below specifically relating to children and online services.)

Updated Definitions in the GDPR

The GDPR introduces certain updated and enhanced definitions from those in the DPD95, referred to as follows.

Personal Data

"Personal data" means any information relating to an identified or identifiable natural person ("data subject"); an identifiable natural person is one who can be identified, directly or indirectly, in particular by reference to an identifier such as a name, an identification number, location data, or an online identifier or to one or more factors specific to the physical, physiological, genetic, mental, economic, cultural, or social identity of that natural person.*

Sensitive Personal Data

The new GDPR refers to processing of special categories of personal data. It refers to personal data revealing racial or ethnic origin, political opinions, religious or philosophical beliefs, or trade union membership, and the processing of genetic data, biometric data for the purpose of uniquely identifying a natural person, data concerning

---

* The DPD95 provided the following definition of "personal data": any information relating to an identified or identifiable natural person ("data subject"). An identifiable person is one who can be identified, directly or indirectly, in particular by reference to an identification number or to one or more factors specific to their physical, physiological, mental, economic, cultural, or social identity.

health, or data concerning a natural person's sex life or sexual orientation, the processing of which is prohibited.

Background Guidance

Sensitive personal data are referred to in Recitals 10 and 51, and special categories of personal data are referred to in Recitals 10, 51 and 52.

Personal data that are, by their nature, particularly sensitive in relation to fundamental rights merit specific protection, as the context of their processing could create significant risks to the fundamental rights. Those personal data should include personal data revealing racial or ethnic origin, whereby the use of the term "racial origin" in the GDPR does not imply an acceptance by the EU of theories that attempt to determine the existence of separate human races. The processing of photographs should not systematically be considered to be processing of special categories of personal data, as they are covered by the definition of biometric data only when processed through a specific technical means allowing the unique identification or authentication of a natural person. Such personal data should not be processed, unless processing is allowed in specific cases set out in the GDPR, taking into account that member states' law may lay down specific provisions on data protection to adapt the application of the rules of the GDPR for compliance with a legal obligation or for the performance of a task carried out in the public interest or in the exercise of official authority vested in the controller.*

In addition to the specific requirements for such processing, the general principles and other rules of the GDPR should apply, in particular as regards the conditions for lawful processing. Derogations from the general prohibition for processing such special categories of personal data should be explicitly provided, *inter alia*, where the individual data subject gives their explicit consent or in respect of specific needs, in particular where the processing is carried out in the course of legitimate activities by certain associations or foundations, the purpose of which is to permit the exercise of fundamental freedoms.† Special

---

* GDPR Recital 53.
† GDPR Recital 51.

categories of personal data that deserve higher protection may only be processed for health-related purposes and subject to conditions.*

The processing of special categories of personal data may be necessary for reasons of public interest in the areas of public health without consent of the individual data subject. Such processing should be subject to suitable and specific measures so as to protect the rights of natural persons. In that context, "public health" should be interpreted as defined in Regulation 1338/2008: all elements related to health, namely health status, including morbidity and disability, the determinants having an effect on that health status, health care needs, resources allocated to health care, the provision of, and universal access to, health care as well as health care expenditure and financing, and the causes of mortality. Such processing of data concerning health for reasons of public interest should not result in personal data being processed for other purposes by third parties such as employers or insurance and banking companies.†

Legal Rule

Article 9 refers to processing of special categories of personal data. The processing of personal data, revealing racial or ethnic origin, political opinions, religious or philosophical beliefs, or trade union membership, and the processing of genetic data, biometric data for the purpose of uniquely identifying a natural person, data concerning health, or data concerning a natural person's sex life or sexual orientation must be prohibited.‡

This must not apply if one of the following applies

- The individual data subject has given explicit consent to the processing of those personal data for one or more specified purposes, except where EU or member state law provides

---

* GDPR Recital 53.
† GDPR Recital 54.
‡ GDPR Article 9(1). In relation to genetic data generally, see, for example, Hallinan, de Hert, and Friedewald, "Genetic Data and the Data Protection Regulation: Anonymity, Multiple Subjects, Sensitivity and a Prohibitionary Logic Regarding Genetic Data?" *Computer Law and Security Review* (2013) (29:4) 317.

that the prohibition referred to above may not be lifted by the individual data subject.

- Processing is necessary for the purposes of carrying out the obligations and exercising specific rights of the controller or of the individual data subject in the field of employment and social security and social protection law insofar as it is authorized by EU or member state law or a collective agreement pursuant to member state law providing for appropriate safeguards for the fundamental rights and the interests of the individual data subject.
- Processing is necessary to protect the vital interests of the individual data subject or of another natural person where the individual data subject is physically or legally incapable of giving consent.
- Processing is carried out in the course of its legitimate activities with appropriate safeguards by a foundation, association, or any other not-for-profit body with a political, philosophical, religious, or trade union aim and on condition that the processing relates solely to the members or to former members of the body or to persons who have regular contact with it in connection with its purposes and that the personal data are not disclosed outside that body without the consent of the individual data subjects.
- Processing relates to personal data that are manifestly made public by the individual data subject.
- Processing is necessary for the establishment, exercise, or defense of legal claims or whenever courts are acting in their judicial capacity.
- Processing is necessary for reasons of substantial public interest, on the basis of EU or member state law, which must be proportionate to the aim pursued, respect the essence of the right to data protection, and provide for suitable and specific measures to safeguard the fundamental rights and the interests of the individual data subject.
- Processing is necessary for the purposes of preventive or occupational medicine, for the assessment of the working capacity of the employee, medical diagnosis, the provision of health or social care or treatment, or the management of health or

social care systems and services on the basis of EU or member state law or pursuant to contract with a health professional and subject to the conditions and safeguards referred to in paragraph 3; [h]

• Processing is necessary for reasons of public interest in the area of public health, such as protecting against serious cross-border threats to health or ensuring high standards of quality and safety of health care and of medicinal products or medical devices, on the basis of EU or member state law that provides for suitable and specific measures to safeguard the rights of the individual data subject, in particular professional secrecy.

• Processing is necessary for archiving purposes in the public interest, scientific or historical research purposes, or statistical purposes in accordance with Article 89(1) based on EU or member state law, which must be proportionate to the aim pursued, respect the essence of the right to data protection, and provide for suitable and specific measures to safeguard the fundamental rights and the interests of the individual data subject.*

The personal data referred to here may be processed for the purposes referred to in point (h) of paragraph 2 when those data are processed by or under the responsibility of a professional subject to the obligation of professional secrecy under EU or member state law or rules established by national competent bodies or by another person also subject to an obligation of secrecy under EU or member state law or rules established by national competent bodies.†

Member states may maintain or introduce further conditions, including limitations, with regard to the processing of genetic data, biometric data, or data concerning health.‡

Data Subject

The GDPR§ indirectly refers to a definition of "data subject," not as a stand-alone definition but rather, within the definition of personal

---

* GDPR Article 9(2).
† GDPR Article 9(3).
‡ GDPR Article 9(4).
§ GDPR Article 4.

data. It refers to an individual data subject as "an identified or *identifiable* natural person."

Processing

"Processing" means any operation or set of operations that is performed on personal data or on sets of personal data, whether or not by automated means, such as collection, recording, organization, structuring, storage, adaptation or alteration, retrieval, consultation, use, disclosure by transmission, dissemination or otherwise making available, alignment or combination, restriction, erasure, or destruction.[*]

Filing System

"Filing system" means any structured set of personal data that are accessible according to specific criteria, whether centralized, decentralized, or dispersed on a functional or geographical basis.

Controller

"Controller" (previously referred to as "data controller") means the natural or legal person, public authority, agency or other body that, alone or jointly with others, determines the purposes and means of the processing of personal data, where the purposes and means of such processing are determined by EU or member state law, the controller or the specific criteria for its nomination may be provided for by EU or member state law.[†]

---

[*] The DPD95 provided the following definition of "processing of personal data" ("processing"): any operation or set of operations that is performed on personal data, whether or not by automatic means, such as collection, recording, organization, storage, adaptation or alteration, retrieval, consultation, use, disclosure by transmission, dissemination or otherwise making available, alignment or combination, blocking, erasure, or destruction of the personal data.

[†] The DPD95 provided the following definition of data "controller." It means the natural or legal person, public authority, agency or any other body that alone or jointly with others, decides the purposes and means of the processing of personal data. Where the purposes and means of processing are determined by member state or EU laws, the controller or the specific criteria for their nomination may be designated by member state or EU law.

Processor

"Processor" (previously referred to as "data processor") means a natural or legal person, public authority, agency, or other body that processes personal data on behalf of the controller.*

Recipient

"Recipient" means a natural or legal person, public authority, agency, or another body to which the personal data are disclosed, whether a third party or not. However, public authorities that may receive personal data in the framework of a particular inquiry in accordance with EU or member state law must not be regarded as recipients; the processing of those data by those public authorities must be in compliance with the applicable data protection rules according to the purposes of the processing.†

Third Party

"Third party" means a natural or legal person, public authority, agency, or body other than the individual data subject, controller, processor, and persons who, under the direct authority of the controller or processor, are authorized to process personal data.

Data Subject's Consent

The individual data subject's "consent" means any freely given, specific, informed, and unambiguous indication of the individual data subject's wishes by which they, by a statement or by a clear affirmative

---

* The DPD95 provided the following definition of "processor" as a natural or legal person, public authority, agency or any other body that processes personal data on behalf of the controller.

† The DPD95 provided that "recipient" means a natural or legal person, public authority, agency or any other body to whom data are disclosed, whether a third party or not. However, authorities that may receive data in the framework of a particular inquiry shall not be regarded as recipients.

action, signify agreement to the processing of personal data relating to them.*

Representative

The GDPR sets out the following definition of "representative": a natural or legal person established in the EU who, designated by the controller or processor in writing, represents the controller or processor with regard to their respective obligations under the GDPR.

Relevant Filing System

In addition, the DPD95 and GDPR provide the following definition of "personal data filing system"/"filing system": any structured set of personal data accessible according to specific criteria, whether centralized, decentralized, or dispersed on a functional or geographical basis.

Conclusion

It is important for organizations to distinguish, in advance of collecting personal data, whether the proposed data collection relates to general personal data or sensitive personal data. They also need to be able to confirm compliance procedures in advance of collecting and maintaining personal data, and particularly sensitive personal data. The organization could be asked to demonstrate at a future date that it obtained consent and how it maintains general compliance. If it cannot, it may have to delete the data. It may have committed breaches and offenses. It may potentially face prosecution, fines, and/or being sued by the individual data subjects. Depending on the circumstances, personal liability can also arise. The new GDPR risk assessments, data protection impact assessments, risk consultations, and data protection by design and by default obligations now require more nuanced policies, records, and methodologies.

---

* The DPD95 provides that "the data subject's consent" means any freely given specific and informed indication of their wishes by which the individual data subject signifies their agreement to personal data relating to them being processed.

KEY CONCEPTS

The definitions are the bricks and mortar building blocks on which the data protection rules rest, and no proper understanding of data protection and personal data can suffice without appreciating what the definitions contain and what they do.

KEYWORDS

• General personal data.
• Sensitive personal data.
• Definitions.
• New and updated definitions.
• New breach definitions.
• New health data definitions.
• Profiling.

FURTHER READING

• Harrell and Rothstein, "Biobanking Research and Privacy Laws in the United States," *Journal of Law, Medicine & Ethics* (2016) (44:1) 106.
• Jasserand, "Avoiding Terminological Confusion between the Notions of 'Biometrics' and 'Biometric Data': An Investigation into the Meanings of the Terms from a European Data Protection and a Scientific Perspective," *International Data Privacy Law* (2015) (6:1) 63.
• King and Raja, "Protecting the Privacy and Security of Sensitive Customer Data in the Cloud," *Computer Law & Security Review* (2012) (28) 308.
• Schropp, "Biometric Data Collection and RFID Tracking in Schools: A Reasoned Approach to Reasonable

Expectations of Privacy," *North Carolina Law Review* (2016) (94:3) 1068.

- Townend, "EU Laws on Privacy in Genomic Databases and Biobanking," *Journal of Law, Medicine & Ethics* (2016) (44:1) 128.

9
PRINCIPLES

Introduction

All organizations that collect and process personal data must comply with the obligations of the data protection regime. The data protection regime provides details as to what constitutes fair processing and identifies the information that must be given to individual data subjects not only where the personal data are obtained directly from the individual data subjects but also if they are obtained indirectly. It also refers to the times at which this information needs to be given. These can serve as preconditions to lawful data processing of personal data.

Organizations cannot collect and process personal data unless they

- Comply with the registration requirements (to the extent that some or all of these will be maintained after the General Data Protection Regulation (GDPR), given that the GDPR emphasizes a more industry-sensitive approach of moving away from a formal registration requirement unless specific risks arise).
- Comply with the data protection principles (also known as the data quality principles).
- Ensure the processing is carried out in accordance with the legitimate processing conditions (and the sensitive personal data legitimate processing conditions in the case of sensitive personal data).
- Provide specific information to individual data subjects in advance of the collection and processing of personal data, known as the prior information requirements.
- Comply with the security requirements, including breach notifications.

- Undertake risk assessments and data protection impact assessments, and implement data protection by design and by default.
- Implement compliance procedures to ensure the individual data subject's rights.
- Respect the data transfer restrictions and legitimizing mechanisms if appropriate.

Background Guidance on Lawful, Fair, Transparent

Background Recital 2 indicates that the principles and rules on the protection of natural persons with regard to the processing of their personal data should, whatever their nationality or residence, respect their fundamental rights, in particular their right to the protection of personal data. The GDPR is intended to contribute to the accomplishment of an area of freedom, security, and justice and of an economic union, to economic and social progress, to the strengthening and the convergence of the economies within the internal market, and to the well-being of natural persons.

Background Recital 26 states that the principles of data protection should apply to any information concerning an identified or identifiable natural person. Personal data that have undergone pseudonymization but that could be attributed to a natural person by the use of additional information should be considered to be information on an identifiable natural person.*

To determine whether a natural person is identifiable, account should be taken of all the means reasonably likely to be used, such as singling out, either by the controller or by another person, to identify the natural person directly or indirectly. To ascertain whether means are reasonably likely to be used to identify the natural person, account should be taken of all objective factors, such as the costs of and the amount of time required for identification, taking into consideration the available technology at the time of the processing and technological developments. The principles of data protection should therefore not apply to anonymous information; that is, information that does not relate to an identified or identifiable natural person or to personal

---

* GDPR Recital 39.

data rendered anonymous in such a manner that the individual data subject is not or no longer identifiable. The GDPR does not therefore concern the processing of such anonymous information, including for statistical or research purposes.*

The background Recitals refer to the context of requirements for lawful, fair, and transparent data processing. Any processing of personal data should be lawful and fair. It should be transparent to natural persons that personal data concerning them are collected, used, consulted, or otherwise processed and to what extent the personal data are or will be processed. The principle of transparency requires that any information and communication relating to the processing of those personal data be easily accessible and easy to understand, and that clear and plain language be used. That principle concerns, in particular, information to the individual data subjects on the identity of the controller and the purposes of the processing and further information to ensure fair and transparent processing in respect of the natural persons concerned and their right to obtain confirmation and communication of personal data concerning them that are being processed.†

Natural persons should be made aware of risks, rules, safeguards, and rights in relation to the processing of personal data and how to exercise their rights in relation to such processing. In particular, the specific purposes for which personal data are processed should be explicit and legitimate and determined at the time of the collection of the personal data. The personal data should be adequate, relevant, and limited to what is necessary for the purposes for which they are processed. This requires, in particular, ensuring that the period for which the personal data are stored is limited to a strict minimum.‡

Personal data should be processed only if the purpose of the processing could not reasonably be fulfilled by other means. To ensure that the personal data are not kept longer than necessary, time limits should be established by the controller for erasure or for a periodic review. Every reasonable step should be taken to ensure that personal data that are inaccurate are rectified or deleted. Personal data should

---

* GDPR Recital 39.
† GDPR Recital 39.
‡ GDPR Recital 39.

be processed in a manner that ensures appropriate security and confidentiality of the personal data, including for preventing unauthorized access to or use of personal data and the equipment used for the
processing.[*]

For processing to be lawful, personal data should be processed on
the basis of the consent of the data subject concerned or some other
legitimate basis, laid down by law, either in the GDPR or in other EU
or member state law as referred to in the GDPR, including the necessity for compliance with the legal obligation to which the controller is
subject or the necessity for the performance of a contract to which the
individual data subject is party or to take steps at the request of the
individual data subject prior to entering into a contract.[†]

There is specific reference and requirements to processing necessary
for the performance of a task carried out in the public interest or in the
exercise of an official authority, including for health purposes.[‡]

There is also reference to processing necessary to protect an interest
that is essential for the individual data subject's life or that of another
person (vital interests, e.g., humanitarian purposes, monitoring epi-
demics, or humanitarian emergencies and disasters).[§] The legitimate
interests of a controller and processing are also referred to.[¶]

Controllers that are part of a group of undertakings and internal
administrative purpose transfers are referred to.[**]

The processing of personal data to the extent strictly necessary and
proportionate for the purposes of ensuring network and information
security, that is, the ability of a network or an information system
to resist, at a given level of confidence, accidental events or unlawful or malicious actions that compromise the availability, authenticity,
integrity, and confidentiality of stored or transmitted personal data,
and the security of the related services offered by, or accessible via,
those networks and systems, by public authorities, by computer emergency response teams (CERTs), computer security incident response
teams (CSIRTs), by providers of electronic communications networks

---

[*] GDPR Recital 39.
[†] GDPR Recital 40.
[‡] GDPR Recital 45.
[§] GDPR Recital 46.
[¶] GDPR Recital 47.
[**] GDPR Recital 48.

and services, and by providers of security technologies and services, constitutes a legitimate interest of the data controller concerned. This could, for example, include preventing unauthorized access to electronic communications networks and malicious code distribution and stopping "denial of service" attacks and damage to computer and electronic communication systems.*

The processing of personal data for purposes other than those for which the personal data were initially collected should be allowed only where the processing is compatible with the purposes for which the personal data were initially collected. In such a case, no legal basis separate from that which allowed the collection of the personal data is required. If the processing is necessary for the performance of a task carried out in the public interest or in the exercise of official authority vested in the controller, EU or member state law may determine and specify the tasks and purposes for which the further processing should be regarded as compatible and lawful. Further processing for archiving purposes in the public interest, scientific or historical research purposes, or statistical purposes should be considered to be compatible lawful processing operations. The legal basis provided by EU or member state law for the processing of personal data may also provide a legal basis for further processing.[†]

To ascertain whether a purpose of further processing is compatible with the purpose for which the personal data are initially collected, the controller, after having met all the requirements for the lawfulness of the original processing, should take into account, *inter alia*: any link between those purposes and the purposes of the intended further processing; the context in which the personal data have been collected, in particular the reasonable expectations of individual data subjects based on their relationship with the controller as to their further use; the nature of the personal data; the consequences of the intended further processing for individual data subjects; and the existence of appropriate safeguards in both the original and intended further processing operations.[‡]

---

* GDPR Recital 49.
† GDPR Recital 40.
‡ GDPR Recital 40.

Where the individual data subject has given consent, or the processing is based on EU or member state law, which constitutes a necessary and proportionate measure in a democratic society to safeguard, in particular, important objectives of general public interest, the controller should be allowed to further process the personal data irrespective of the compatibility of the purposes. In any case, the application of the principles set out in the GDPR, and in particular the information of the individual data subject on those other purposes and on their rights, including the right to object, should be ensured. Indicating possible criminal acts or threats to public security by the controller and transmitting the relevant personal data in individual cases or in several cases relating to the same criminal act or threats to public security to a competent authority should be regarded as being in the legitimate interest pursued by the controller. However, such transmission in the legitimate interest of the controller or further processing of personal data should be prohibited if the processing is not compatible with a legal, professional, or other binding obligation of secrecy.*

Data Protection Principles

The principles or data protection principles are also known as the data quality principles. The background Recitals refer to context for the principles. The data protection principles apply to *any* information concerning an identified or *identifiable* natural person.†

The data protection principles are also known as the data quality principles. Personal data must be processed fairly and lawfully. In particular, personal data must not be processed unless at least one of the specified conditions is met, and in the case of sensitive personal data, the additional sensitive conditions are also met.

Hence, the *general* personal data legitimate-processing-conditions, and the *sensitive* personal data legitimate-processing-conditions.

The GDPR does not apply to the personal data of deceased persons. Member states may provide for rules regarding the processing of data of deceased persons.‡

---

* GDPR Recital 40.
† GDPR Recital 26.
‡ GDPR Recital 27.

Article 5 GDPR sets out the new Principles relating to data protection. All organizations with personal data must comply with the following data protection principles. The data protection principles state that data must be

- Processed lawfully, fairly, and in a transparent manner in relation to the individual data subject ("lawfulness, fairness and transparency").
- Collected for specified, explicit, and legitimate purposes and not further processed in a manner that is incompatible with those purposes; further processing for archiving purposes in the public interest, scientific or historical research purposes, or statistical purposes must, in accordance with Article 89(1), not be considered to be incompatible with the initial purposes ("purpose limitation").
- Adequate, relevant, and limited to what is necessary in relation to the purposes for which they are processed ("data minimization").
- Accurate and, where necessary, kept up to date; every reasonable step must be taken to ensure that personal data that are inaccurate, having regard to the purposes for which they are processed, are erased or rectified without delay ("accuracy").
- Kept in a form that permits identification of individual data subjects for no longer than is necessary for the purposes for which the personal data are processed; personal data may be stored for longer periods insofar as the personal data will be processed solely for archiving purposes in the public interest, scientific or historical research purposes, or statistical purposes in accordance with Article 89(1) subject to implementation of the appropriate technical and organizational measures required by the GDPR to safeguard the rights and freedoms of the individual data subject ("storage limitation").
- Processed in a manner that ensures appropriate security of the personal data, including protection against unauthorized or unlawful processing and against accidental loss, destruction, or damage, using appropriate technical or organizational measures ("integrity and confidentiality").

The controller must be responsible for, and be able to demonstrate, compliance with the above ("accountability"). This will require that records be kept and available in the case that they are requested by the data protection supervisory authority.

Controllers must also give a copy of personal data to any individual on request (known as a data access request). As one national data protection law states, a "controller shall, as respects personal data kept ... comply with" the data protection principles.

The following table sets out a comparison of the data protection principles under the DPD95 and the new GDPR.

PRINCIPLES COMPARED	
DPD95	GDPR16
PRINCIPLES RELATING TO DATA QUALITY Article 6 Member states must provide that personal data must be	PRINCIPLES Article 5 Principles relating to personal data processing Personal data must be
Processed fairly and lawfully	Processed lawfully, fairly, and in a *transparent* manner in relation to the data subject ("Lawfulness, Fairness, and Transparency" Principle)
Collected for specified, explicit, and legitimate purposes and not further processed in a way incompatible with those purposes. Further processing of data for historical, statistical, or scientific purposes must not be considered as incompatible provided that member states provide appropriate safeguards	Collected for specified, explicit, and legitimate purposes and not further processed in a manner that is incompatible with those purposes; further processing for archiving purposes in the public interest, scientific or historical research purposes, or statistical purposes must, in accordance with Article 89(1), not be considered to be incompatible with the initial purposes ("Purpose Limitation" Principle)
Adequate, relevant, and not excessive in relation to the purposes for which they are collected and/or further processed	Adequate, relevant, and limited to what is necessary in relation to the purposes for which they are processed ("Data Minimization" Principle)
Accurate and, where necessary, kept up to date; every reasonable step must be taken to ensure that data that are inaccurate or incomplete, having regard to the purposes for which they were collected or for which they are further processed, are erased or rectified	Accurate and, where necessary, kept up to date; every reasonable step must be taken to ensure that personal data that are inaccurate, having regard to the purposes for which they are processed, are erased or rectified without delay ("Accuracy" Principle)

(Continued)

(Continued)

PRINCIPLES COMPARED	
DPD95	GDPR16
Kept in a form that permits identification of data subjects for no longer than is necessary for the purposes for which the data were collected or for which they are further processed. Member states must lay down appropriate safeguards for personal data stored for longer periods for historical, statistical, or scientific use	Kept in a form that permits identification of data subjects for no longer than is necessary for the purposes for which the personal data are processed; personal data may be stored for longer periods insofar as the personal data will be processed solely for archiving purposes in the public interest, scientific or historical research purposes, or statistical purposes in accordance with Article 89(1) subject to implementation of the appropriate technical and organizational measures required by the GDPR to safeguard the rights and freedoms of the data subject ("Storage Limitation" Principle)
	Processed in a manner that ensures appropriate security of the personal data, including protection against unauthorized or unlawful processing and against accidental loss, destruction, or damage, using appropriate technical or organizational measures ("Integrity and Confidentiality" Principle)
	The controller must be responsible for, and be able to demonstrate compliance with, the above("Accountability" Principle).

Note that the EU–US Safe Harbor data transfer regime needs to be replaced, given that the EU Court of Justice in the *Schrems* case* struck down the original EU–US Safe Harbor regime as invalid. Longstanding negotiations between the EU and the United States have recently resulted in the EU–US Privacy Shield arrangement being agreed to facilitate data transfers. This will require particular attention by organizations and data protection officers as it is rolled out, quite apart from the GDPR and new data protection regime.

---

* *Schrems v Commissioner*, Court of Justice, Case C-362/14, October 6, 2015. The case technically related to Prism and Facebook Europe and transfers to the United States. However, the wider import turned out to be the entire EU-US Safe Harbor Agreement and data transfers to the United States. Note WP29 statement on the case, "Statement on the Implementation of the Judgement of the Court of Justice of the European Union of 6 October 2015 in the *Maximilian Schrems v Data Protection Commissioner* case (C-362-14)".

Processor

As one of the national data protection laws states, a "processor shall, as respects personal data processed … comply with paragraph (d) of subsection (1) of this section"—that is the security principle. It also states that "[p]ersonal data processed by a data processor shall not be disclosed by [it] or by an employee or agent of [it], without the prior authority of the controller on behalf of whom the data are processed." If the processor contravenes this obligation, an offense is committed.

How to Collect and Process Personal Data

Organizations need to comply with these principles, but in addition need to comply with the prior information requirements and the legitimate processing conditions.

COMPLIANCE AND LAWFUL PROCESSING

Principles

↓

Prior information requirements

↓

Lawful processing conditions

Conclusion

One of the most important requirements of the data protection regime is the data protection principles. These are now enhanced under the new data protection regime, and organizations, and their data protection officers, need to take careful cognizance for their particular organization of the changes that will be required.

KEY CONCEPTS

Personal data must be lawful, fair, and transparent; for a specified, explicit, and legitimate purpose (and not further processed); adequate, relevant, limited (necessary) to the purpose; accurate, kept up to date with inaccurate data erased or rectified; kept no longer than necessary; protected by appropriate security; and compliance with these points must be demonstrated. Controllers must also give a copy of personal data to any individual on request (i.e., a data access request).

KEY WORDS

- Lawfulness, fairness, and transparency principle.
- Purpose limitation principle.
- Data minimization principle.
- Accuracy principle.
- Storage limitation principle.
- Integrity and confidentiality principle.
- Accountability principle.
- Individual data subjects.
- Principles.
- Prior information.
- Legitimate processing conditions.

10

PRIOR INFORMATION CONDITIONS

Introduction

In addition to the principles, organizations must also be compliant with the prior information requirements. Even prior to obtaining and processing personal data, organizations are obliged to provide certain information to individual data subjects. This is so that individual data subjects can be properly informed and can decide whether or not to consent to the proposed data processing.

An individual may consent to processing for a given transaction, but may be less willing to consent if they are informed that their details may then be sold on to unknown third parties. There are also many recent examples of organizations being criticized for changing their data protection policies (and other terms) and what they may do with existing and new personal data.

The General Data Protection Regulation (GDPR) Changes

The GDPR also refers to these obligations. GDPR Chapter III (rights of individual data subjects), Section 1 refers to transparency and modalities. Article 12 is headed "[t]ransparent information, communication and modalities for the exercise of the rights of the data subject." The controller must take appropriate measures to provide any information referred to in Articles 13 and 14 and any communication under Articles 15–22 and 34 relating to processing to the individual data subject in a concise, transparent, intelligible, and easily accessible form, using clear and plain language, in particular for any information addressed specifically to a child. The information must be provided in writing, or by other means, including, where appropriate, by electronic means. When requested by the individual data subject, the information may be provided orally, provided that the identity of the individual data subject is proved by other means.

The controller must facilitate the exercise of individual data subject rights under Articles 15–22. In the cases referred to in Article 11(2), the controller must not refuse to act on the request of the individual data subject for exercising their rights under Articles 15–22, unless the controller demonstrates that it is not in a position to identify the individual data subject.

The controller must provide information on action taken on a request under Articles 15–22 to the individual data subject without undue delay and in any event within one month of receipt of the request. That period may be extended by two further months where necessary, taking into account the complexity and number of the requests. The controller must inform the individual data subject of any such extension within one month of receipt of the request, together with the reasons for the delay. Where the individual data subject makes the request by means of electronic form, the information must be provided by electronic means where possible, unless otherwise requested by the individual data subject.

If the controller does not take action on the request of the individual data subject, the controller must inform the individual data subject without delay and at the latest within one month of receipt of the request of the reasons for not taking action and on the possibility of lodging a complaint with a data protection supervisory authority and seeking a judicial remedy.

Information provided under Articles 13 and 14 and any communication and any actions taken under Articles 15–22 and 34 must be provided free of charge. Where requests from an individual data subject are manifestly unfounded or excessive, in particular because of their repetitive character, the controller may either charge a reasonable fee, taking into account the administrative costs of providing the information or communication or taking the action requested, or refuse to act on the request. The controller must bear the burden of demonstrating the manifestly unfounded or excessive character of the request.

Prior Information Requirements: Directly Obtained Data

The GDPR refers to information and access to data, beginning with Article 13. Article 13 of the GDPR relates to the prior information requirements and information to be provided where the data are collected from the individual data subject. Where personal data relating to an individual data subject are collected from the individual data subject, the controller must, at the time when personal data are obtained, provide the individual data subject with all of the following information

- The identity and the contact details of the controller and, where applicable, of the controller's representative.
- The contact details of the data protection officer, where applicable.
- The purposes of the processing for which the personal data are intended as well as the legal basis for the processing.
- Where the processing is based on Article 6(1)(f), the legitimate interests pursued by the controller or by a third party.
- The recipients or categories of recipients of the personal data, if any.
- Where applicable, the fact that the controller intends to transfer personal data to a third country or international organization and the existence or absence of an adequacy decision by the EU Commission, or in the case of transfers referred to in Article 46 or 47, or the second subparagraph of Article 49(1), reference to the appropriate or suitable safeguards and the means by which to obtain a copy of them or where they have been made available.*

---

* Article 10 of the DPD95 provided for information in cases of collection of personal data from the individual data subject. It states that member states shall provide that the controller, or its representative, must provide an individual data subject from whom personal data are collected with at least the following information, except where they already have it: the identity of the controller and its representative, if any; the purposes of the processing; any further information, such as the recipients or categories of recipients of the data; whether replies to the questions are obligatory or voluntary, as well as the possible consequences of failure to reply; the existence of the right of access to and the right to rectify the data concerning them, in so far as such further information is necessary, having regard to the specific circumstances in which the data are collected, to guarantee fair processing in respect of the individual data subject.

In addition to this information, the controller must, at the time when personal data are obtained, provide the individual data subject with the following further information necessary to ensure fair and transparent processing

- The period for which the personal data will be stored, or if that is not possible, the criteria used to determine that period.
- The existence of the right to request from the controller access to and rectification or erasure of personal data or restriction of processing concerning the individual data subject or to object to processing as well as the right to data portability.
- Where the processing is based on Article 6(1)(a) or Article 9(2)(a), the existence of the right to withdraw consent at any time without affecting the lawfulness of processing based on consent before its withdrawal.
- The right to lodge a complaint with a data protection supervisory authority.
- Whether the provision of personal data is a statutory or contractual requirement, or a requirement necessary to enter into a contract, as well as whether the individual data subject is obliged to provide the personal data and the possible consequences of failure to provide such data.
- The existence of automated decision-making, including profiling, referred to in Article 22(1) and (4) and, at least in those cases, meaningful information about the logic involved, as well as the significance and the envisaged consequences of such processing for the individual data subject.

Where the controller intends to further process the personal data for a purpose other than that for which the personal data were collected, the controller must provide the individual data subject prior to that further processing with information on that other purpose and with any relevant further information as referred to in the two preceding lists.

However, this must not apply where and insofar as the individual data subject already has the information.

Prior Information Requirements: Indirectly Obtained Data

Article 14 of the GDPR refers to information to be provided where the data have not been obtained from the individual data subject.

Where personal data have not been obtained from the individual data subject, the controller must provide the individual data subject with the following information

- The identity and the contact details of the controller and, where applicable, of the controller's representative.
- The contact details of the data protection officer, where applicable.
- The purposes of the processing for which the personal data are intended as well as the legal basis for the processing.
- The categories of personal data concerned.
- The recipients or categories of recipients of the personal data, if any.
- Where applicable, that the controller intends to transfer personal data to a recipient in a third country or international organization and the existence or absence of an adequacy decision by the EU Commission, or in the case of transfers referred to in Article 46 or 47, or the second subparagraph of Article 49(1), reference to the appropriate or suitable safeguards and the means to obtain a copy of them or where they have been made available.*

In addition to this information, the controller must provide the individual data subject with the following information necessary to

---

* Article 11 of the DPD95 provided and distinguished information where the data have not been obtained from the individual data subject. In this case, where the personal data have not been obtained from the individual data subject, the controller or their representative must at the time of obtaining personal data or if a disclosure to a third party is envisaged, no later than the time when the data are first disclosed, provide the individual data subject with at least the following information, except where they already have it: the identity of the controller and of their representative, if any; the purposes of the processing; any further information, such as the categories of data concerned; the recipients or categories of recipients; and the existence of the right of access to and the right to rectify the data concerning them, in so far as such further information is necessary, having regard to the specific circumstances in which the data are processed, to guarantee fair processing in respect of the individual data subject. Article 11(2) of DPD95 provides that Article 11(1) shall not apply where, for processing for statistical, historical, or scientific research purposes, the provision of such information proves impossible or would involve a disproportionate effort or if recording or disclosure is expressly laid down by law. In these cases, member states shall provide appropriate safeguards.

ensure fair and transparent processing in respect of the individual data subject

- The period for which the personal data will be stored, or if that is not possible, the criteria used to determine that period.
- Where the processing is based on Article 6(1)(f), the legitimate interests pursued by the controller or by a third party.
- The existence of the right to request from the controller access to and rectification or erasure of personal data or restriction of processing concerning the individual data subject and to object to processing as well as the right to data portability.
- Where processing is based on Article 6(1)(a) or Article 9(2)(a), the existence of the right to withdraw consent at any time without affecting the lawfulness of processing based on consent before its withdrawal.
- The right to lodge a complaint with a data protection supervisory authority.
- From which source the personal data originate, and if applicable, whether they came from publicly accessible sources.
- The existence of automated decision-making, including profiling, referred to in Article 22(1) and (4) and, at least in those cases, meaningful information about the logic involved, as well as the significance and the envisaged consequences of such processing for the individual data subject.

Timing of Information

The controller must provide this prior information (in the case of indirectly obtained data)

- Within a reasonable period after obtaining the personal data, but at the latest within one month, having regard to the specific circumstances in which the personal data are processed.
- If the personal data are to be used for communication with the individual data subject, at the latest at the time of the first communication to that individual data subject.

or

- If a disclosure to another recipient is envisaged, at the latest when the personal data are first disclosed.

Where the controller intends to further process the personal data for a purpose other than that for which the personal data were obtained, the controller must provide the individual data subject prior to that further processing with information on that other purpose and with any relevant further information as referred to in the preceding lists.

The above rules will not apply where and insofar as

- The individual data subject already has the information.
- The provision of such information proves impossible or would involve a disproportionate effort, in particular for processing for archiving purposes in the public interest, scientific or historical research purposes, or statistical purposes, subject to the conditions and safeguards referred to in Article 89(1) or insofar as the obligation referred to in paragraph 1 of this Article is likely to render impossible or seriously impair the achievement of the objectives of that processing. In such cases, the controller must take appropriate measures to protect the individual data subject's rights and freedoms and legitimate interests, including making the information publicly available.
- Obtaining or disclosure is expressly laid down by EU or member state law, to which the controller is subject and which provides appropriate measures to protect the individual data subject's legitimate interests

or

- Where the personal data must remain confidential subject to an obligation of professional secrecy regulated by EU or member state law, including a statutory obligation of secrecy.

Conclusion

Unless the prior information conditions are complied with, there may remain a question as to the fairness and legality of the personal data collection and processing. These issues may not be able to be rectified retrospectively. Compliance from the date of initial collection, and even in advance of such collection, is required by organizations.

KEY CONCEPTS

In addition to the principles, organizations must provide certain prior information to individual data subjects so as to be able to collect, use, and process personal data.

KEY WORDS

- Prior information processing conditions.
- Direct data.
- Indirect data.
- Timing.
- Details of prior information.

11

LEGITIMATE PROCESSING CONDITIONS

Introduction

In addition to complying with (1) the principles and (2) the prior information requirements, organizations must also comply with the legitimate processing conditions. These legitimate processing conditions are separated in relation to general personal data and also sensitive personal data.

Companies and organizations, so as to function, generally collect and maintain data on a variety of individual data subjects, be they employees, customers, prospective customers, and so on. However, organizations must not mislead individual data subjects when obtaining and processing personal data and must also provide a number of prior information requirements to the individual data subjects. Without these, it would be deemed that there is unfair obtaining and processing. The new GDPR enhances this obligation by requiring greater transparency. For example, an organization may have obtained consent for processing and has informed individuals that their personal data will only be used in relation to activity or purpose A. However, if it really uses the personal data in relation to activities or purposes A, B, C, and D, this will not be fair and transparent obtaining and processing in accordance with the data protection principles. The data protection principles will have been breached, in particular the first principle. The organization has not fairly informed individual data subjects and has not obtained fair and informed consent.

In addition to the data protection principles, organizations must satisfy and meet one of the legitimate processing conditions. These are divided in relation to ordinary or general personal data and sensitive personal data.

Lawfulness of Processing: General Legitimate Processing Conditions

The legitimate processing conditions must be complied with in addition to the data protection principles. To collect and process personal data, in addition to complying with the data protection principles, organizations must comply with or fall within *one* of the following general or ordinary personal data legitimate processing conditions.

Personal data must not be processed by a controller unless the controller complies with the principles and at least *one* of the following conditions is satisfied. Article 6 of the GDPR sets out the new provisions in relation to the lawfulness of processing. Processing of personal data must be lawful only if and to the extent that at least one of the following applies

- The individual data subject has given consent to the processing of their personal data for one or more specific purposes (see following section and also Article 7).
- Processing is necessary for the performance of a contract to which the individual data subject is party or to take steps at the request of the individual data subject prior to entering into a contract.
- Processing is necessary for compliance with a legal obligation to which the controller is subject [c].
- Processing is necessary to protect the vital interests of the individual data subject or of another natural person.
- Processing is necessary for the performance of a task carried out in the public interest or in the exercise of official authority vested in the controller [e].
- Processing is necessary for the purposes of the legitimate interests pursued by the controller or by a third party, except where such interests are overridden by the interests or fundamental rights and freedoms of the individual data subject, which require protection of personal data, in particular where the individual data subject is a child. This must not apply to processing carried out by public authorities in the performance of their tasks.*

---

* GDPR Article 6(1).

Member states may maintain or introduce more specific provisions to adapt the application of the rules of the GDPR with regard to the processing of personal data for compliance with Article 6(1)(c) and (e) by determining more precisely specific requirements for the processing and other measures to ensure lawful and fair processing, including for other specific processing situations as provided for in GDPR Chapter IX.*

The basis for the processing referred to in Article 6(1)(c) and (e) must be laid down by EU law or member state law to which the controller is subject. The purpose of the processing must be determined in that legal basis or, as regards the processing referred to in point (e), must be necessary for the performance of a task carried out in the public interest or in the exercise of official authority vested in the controller. That legal basis may contain specific provisions to adapt the application of rules of the GDPR, *inter alia*: the general conditions governing the lawfulness of processing by the controller; the types of data that are subject to the processing; the individual data subjects concerned; the entities to, and the purposes for which, the personal data may be disclosed; the purpose limitation; storage periods; and processing operations and processing procedures, including measures to ensure lawful and fair processing, such as those for other specific processing situations as provided for in GDPR Chapter IX. The EU or member state law must meet an objective of public interest and be proportionate to the legitimate aim pursued.†

Where the processing for a purpose other than that for which the personal data have been collected is not based on the individual data subject's consent or on an EU or member state law that constitutes a necessary and proportionate measure in a democratic society to safeguard the objectives referred to in Article 23(1), the controller must, to ascertain whether processing for another purpose is compatible with the purpose for which the personal data are initially collected, take into account, *inter alia*

- Any link between the purposes for which the personal data have been collected and the purposes of the intended further processing.

---

* GDPR Article 6(2).
† GDPR Article 6(3).

- The context in which the personal data have been collected, in particular regarding the relationship between individual data subjects and the controller.
- The nature of the personal data, in particular whether special categories of personal data are processed,* or whether personal data related to criminal convictions and offenses are processed.†
- The possible consequences of the intended further processing for individual data subjects.
- The existence of appropriate safeguards, which may include encryption or pseudonymization.‡

Lawfulness of Processing: Sensitive Personal Data Legitimate Processing Conditions

In the case of sensitive personal data, an organization must, *in addition* to complying with the data protection principles, be able to comply with or fall within one of the sensitive personal data legitimate processing conditions.

Sensitive or special categories of personal data must not be processed by a controller unless meeting one of the following conditions

- The data subject has given explicit consent to the processing of those personal data for one or more specified purposes, except where EU or member state law provides that the prohibition referred to may not be lifted by the data subject.
- Processing is necessary for the purposes of carrying out the obligations and exercising specific rights of the controller or of the data subject in the field of employment and social security and social protection law insofar as it is authorized by EU or member state law or a collective agreement pursuant to member state law providing for appropriate safeguards for the fundamental rights and the interests of the data subject.

---

* Pursuant to GDPR Article 9.
† Pursuant to GDPR Article 10.
‡ GDPR Article 6(4).

- Processing is necessary to protect the vital interests of the data subject or of another natural person where the data subject is physically or legally incapable of giving consent.
- Processing is carried out in the course of its legitimate activities with appropriate safeguards by a foundation, association, or any other not-for-profit body with a political, philosophical, religious, or trade union aim and on condition that the processing relates solely to the members or to former members of the body or to persons who have regular contact with it in connection with its purposes and that the personal data are not disclosed outside that body without the consent of the data subjects.
- Processing relates to personal data that are manifestly made public by the data subject.
- Processing is necessary for the establishment, exercise, or defense of legal claims or whenever courts are acting in their judicial capacity.
- Processing is necessary for reasons of substantial public interest, on the basis of EU or member state law, which shall be proportionate to the aim pursued, respect the essence of the right to data protection, and provide for suitable and specific measures to safeguard the fundamental rights and the interests of the data subject.
- Processing is necessary for the purposes of preventive or occupational medicine, for the assessment of the working capacity of the employee, medical diagnosis, the provision of health or social care or treatment or the management of health or social care systems and services on the basis of EU or member state law or pursuant to contract with a health professional and subject to the conditions and safeguards referred to in paragraph 3 [h].
- Processing is necessary for reasons of public interest in the area of public health, such as protecting against serious cross-border threats to health or ensuring high standards of quality and safety of health care and of medicinal products or medical devices, on the basis of EU or member state law that provides for suitable and specific measures to safeguard the rights and freedoms of the data subject, in particular professional secrecy.

- Processing is necessary for archiving purposes in the public interest, scientific or historical research purposes, or statistical purposes* based on Union or member state law that shall be proportionate to the aim pursued, respect the essence of the right to data protection, and provide for suitable and specific measures to safeguard the fundamental rights and the interests of the data subject.†

The personal data referred to in the preceding list may be processed for the purposes referred to in Point (h) above (third last bullet) when those data are processed by or under the responsibility of a professional subject to the obligation of professional secrecy under EU or member state law or rules established by national competent bodies or by another person also subject to an obligation of secrecy under EU or member state law or rules established by national competent bodies.

Member states may maintain or introduce further conditions, including limitations, with regard to the processing of

- Genetic data.
- Biometric data.
- Data concerning health.

Conclusion

It is important for organizations to fully understand the different legitimate processing grounds and which are most applicable to the circumstances of the different processing activities that the organization would propose to engage in.

KEY CONCEPTS

In addition to the principles and prior information conditions, organizations must also fall within one of the legitimate processing conditions to be able to lawfully collect, use, and process personal data.

---

* In accordance with GDPR Article 89(1).
† GDPR Article 9.

KEYWORDS

- Legitimate processing conditions.
- General personal data.
- Sensitive personal data.
- Legitimate interest processing.
- Consent.
- Transparency.

12
KEEPING RECORDS

Introduction

There are new express requirements on organizations to keep and maintain records of their processing activities in the new GDPR.

Liability and Measures to Demonstrate Compliance

The responsibility and liability of the controller for any processing of personal data carried out by the controller or on the controller's behalf should be established. In particular, the controller should be obliged to implement appropriate and effective measures and be able to demonstrate the compliance of processing activities with the GDPR, including the effectiveness of the measures. Those measures should take into account the nature, scope, context, and purposes of the processing and the risk to the rights of natural persons.[*]

Maintaining Records

Article 30 refers to documentation issues and is headed "Records of Processing Activities." Each controller and, where applicable, the controller's representative, must maintain a record of processing activities under its responsibility. That record must contain all of the following information

- The name and contact details of the controller and, where applicable, the joint controller, the controller's representative, and the data protection officer.
- The purposes of the processing.

---

[*] GDPR Recital 74.

- A description of the categories of individual data subjects and of the categories of personal data.
- The categories of recipients to whom the personal data have been or will be disclosed, including recipients in third countries or international organizations.
- Where applicable, transfers of personal data to a third country or an international organization, including the identification of that third country or international organization and, in the case of transfers,[*] the documentation of suitable safeguards.
- Where possible, the envisaged time limits for erasure of the different categories of data.
- Where possible, a general description of the technical and organizational security measures.[†]

Each processor and, where applicable, the processor's representative must maintain a record of all categories of processing activities carried out on behalf of a controller, containing

- The name and contact details of the processor or processors and of each controller on behalf of which the processor is acting, and, where applicable, of the controller's or the processor's representative, and the data protection officer.
- The categories of processing carried out on behalf of each controller.
- Where applicable, transfers of personal data to a third country or an international organization, including the identification of that third country or international organization and, in the case of transfers,[‡] the documentation of suitable safeguards.
- Where possible, a general description of the technical and organizational security measures.[§]

These records must be in writing, including in electronic form.[¶] The controller or the processor and, where applicable, the controller's or the processor's representative must make the record available to

---

[*] Transfers referred to in the second subparagraph of Article 49(1).
[†] Security measures referred to in GDPR Article 32(1). GDPR Article 30(1).
[‡] Referred to in the second subparagraph of GDPR Article 49(1).
[§] Security measures referred to in GDPR Article 32(1). GDPR Article 30(2).
[¶] GDPR Article 30(3).

the data protection supervisory authority on request.* The obligations referred to must not apply to an enterprise or an organization employing fewer than 250 persons unless the processing it carries out is likely to result in a risk to the rights of individual data subjects, the processing is not occasional, or the processing includes special categories of data† or personal data relating to criminal convictions and offenses.‡

Records Requirement

Each controller and, where applicable, the controller's representative must maintain a record of processing activities under its responsibility. That record must contain all of the following information

- The name and contact details of the controller and, where applicable, the joint controller, the controller's representative, and the data protection officer.
- The purposes of the processing.
- A description of the categories of data subjects and of the categories of personal data.
- The categories of recipients to whom the personal data have been or will be disclosed, including recipients in third countries or international organizations.
- Where applicable, transfers of personal data to a third country or an international organization, including the identification of that third country or international organization and, in the case of transfers,§ the documentation of suitable safeguards.
- Where possible, the envisaged time limits for erasure of the different categories of data.
- Where possible, a general description of the technical and organizational security measures.¶

Each processor and, where applicable, the processor's representative must maintain a record of all categories of processing activities carried out on behalf of a controller, containing

---

* GDPR Article 30(4).
† GDPR as referred to in GDPR Article 9(1).
‡ Referred to in Article 10. GDPR Article 30(5).
§ Transfers referred to in the second subparagraph of Article 49(1).
¶ Security measures referred to in GDPR Article 32(1). GDPR Article 30(1).

- The name and contact details of the processor or processors and of each controller on behalf of which the processor is acting, and, where applicable, of the controller's or the processor's representative, and the data protection officer.
- The categories of processing carried out on behalf of each controller.
- Where applicable, transfers of personal data to a third country or an international organization, including the identification of that third country or international organization and, in the case of transfers referred to in the second subparagraph of Article 49(1), the documentation of suitable safeguards.
- Where possible, a general description of the technical and organizational security measures referred to in Article 32(1).*

The records referred to above must be in writing, including in electronic form.†

The controller or the processor and, where applicable, the controller's or the processor's representative must make the record available to the data protection supervisory authority on request.‡

The obligations referred to must not apply to an enterprise or an organization employing fewer than 250 persons unless the processing it carries out is likely to result in a risk to the rights of data subjects, the processing is not occasional, or the processing includes special categories of data§ or personal data relating to criminal convictions and offenses.¶

The Principles' Record Requirements

The new principles also impose record-keeping requirements. The Accountability Principle expressly provides that the controller must be responsible for, and be able to demonstrate, compliance with the principles. To do so, records must be available to demonstrate such compliance.

---

* GDPR Article 30(2).
† GDPR Article 30(3).
‡ GDPR Article 30(4).
§ As referred to in GDPR Article 9(1).
¶ Referred to in GDPR Article 10. GDPR Article 30(5).

Cooperation with the Data Protection Supervisory Authority

Article 31 refers to cooperation with the data protection supervisory authority. The controller and the processor and, where applicable, their representatives must cooperate, on request, with the data protection supervisory authority in the performance of its tasks.

Conclusion

Record-keeping is important for a large variety of reasons. However, in this instance, record-keeping is an express requirement in relation to data collection, data usage, and data deletion under the new data protection regime. The data protection regime has become more specific in the record-keeping obligations, as well as more specific on the details of what the records must contain.

KEY CONCEPTS

- Record-keeping is required by the principles.
- Record-keeping is required by Article 30 of the GDPR.
- The data protection supervisory authorities can seek records and documentation.
- Records and documentation can be needed to demonstrate compliance and to defend complaints and legal cases.

KEY WORDS

- Must demonstrate compliance with the principles.
- Records of processing activities.
- Controller.
- Controller's representative.
- Must maintain records of its processing activities.
- Data protection officer.

13

REPRESENTATIVES OF CONTROLLERS NOT ESTABLISHED IN EU

Introduction

Organizations in the United States need to consider the new obligation to have a representative designated in the EU.

Representatives/Non-EU Controllers

Background Guidance

Where a controller or a processor not established in the EU is processing personal data of individual data subjects who are in the EU, and the processing activities are related to the offering of goods or services, irrespective of whether payment is required to the individual data subject or to such individual data subjects in the EU, or to the monitoring of their behavior as far as their behavior takes place within the EU, the controller or the processor should designate a representative, unless the processing is occasional, does not include processing on a large scale of special categories of personal data or the processing of personal data relating to criminal convictions and offenses, and is unlikely to result in a risk to the rights of natural persons, taking into account the nature, context, scope and purposes of the processing or if the controller is a public authority or body. The representative should act on behalf of the controller or the processor and may be addressed by any data protection supervisory authority.*

The representative should be explicitly designated by a written mandate of the controller or of the processor to act on its behalf with regard to its obligations under the General Data Protection Regulation

---

* GDPR Recital 80.

(GDPR). The designation of such a representative does not affect the responsibility or liability of the controller or of the processor under the GDPR. Such a representative should perform its tasks according to the mandate received from the controller or processor, including cooperating with the competent data protection supervisory authorities with regard to any action taken to ensure compliance with the GDPR. The designated representative should be subject to enforcement proceedings in the event of non-compliance by the controller or processor.[*]

Article Requirement

The GDPR refers to representatives of controllers not established in the EU. Article 27(1) provides that "[w]here Article 3(2) applies, the controller or the processor must designate in writing a representative in the [EU]."

This obligation will not apply to

- Processing that is occasional, does not include, on a large scale, processing of special categories of data[†] or processing of personal data relating to criminal convictions and offenses,[‡] and is unlikely to result in a risk to the rights of natural persons, taking into account the nature, context, scope, and purposes of the processing, or
- A public authority or body.[§]

The representative must be established in one of the member states where the data subjects are whose personal data are processed in relation to the offering of goods or services to them, or whose behavior is monitored.[¶]

The representative must be mandated by the controller or processor to be addressed in addition to or instead of the controller or the processor by, in particular, data protection supervisory authorities and

---

[*] GDPR Recital 80.
[†] As referred to in GDPR Article 9(1).
[‡] Referred to in GDPR Article 10.
[§] GDPR Article 27(2).
[¶] GDPR Article 27(3).

data subjects, on all issues related to processing, for the purposes of ensuring compliance with the GDPR.*

The designation of a representative by the controller or processor must be without prejudice to legal actions that could be initiated against the controller or the processor themselves.†

Conclusion

Organizations seeking to target or otherwise deal with EU personal data must ensure that they have a designated representative to deal with issues, particularly where they are located outside of the EU. This is a separate obligation from that of appointing a data protection officer.

KEY CONCEPTS

Organizations must appoint a representative in the EU when the organization is outside of the EU and is dealing with EU personal data.

KEYWORDS

- Controllers not established in the EU.
- Controllers.
- Processors.
- Must designate in writing a representative in the EU.

---

* GDPR Article 27(4).
† GDPR Article 27(5).

14

RIGHTS OF INDIVIDUAL DATA SUBJECTS

Introduction

The data protection regime provides, or enshrines, a number of key rights for individuals in relation to their informational personal data. These are important because organizations must respect these procedural and fundamental rights.* They are also important because the individuals themselves can enforce their rights where, for example, they feel an organization is abusing their rights and obligations. Some of these rights also apply regardless of any suspicion of a breach or non-compliance by an organization. Additionally, there are increasing instances of groups of individual data subjects cooperating together against organizations. This possibility is further facilitated under the new General Data Protection Regulation (GDPR), whereby individual data subject representative organizations are permitted.

The new GDPR background Recitals refer to individual data subject rights;† principles of fair and transparent processing;‡ prior information requirements;§ right of access right of rectification and right to be forgotten;¶ right to complain to single data protection supervisory authority;** *and* automated processing,†† which set the context of the processes and procedures that organizations need to consider.

---

* See Article 8(1) Charter of Fundamental Rights of the EU and Article 16(1) of the Treaty.
† GDPR Recitals 1, 38, 39, 50, 63, 65, 66, 68, 69, 70, 71.
‡ GDPR Recitals 39, 60.
§ GDPR Recitals 39, 58, 60, 61.
¶ GDPR Recital 65.
**GDPR Recital 141.
††GDPR Recital 71.

Recipients of Rights

When considering the respective rights, organizations should not forget to consider the potential recipients of the various data protection rights. The data protection rights apply generally in relation to any individuals whose personal data are being collected and processed. Specifically, they can include

- Employees.
- Other workers such as contractors, temps, and casual staff.
- Agency staff.
- Ex-employees and retired employees.
- Job applicants, including unsuccessful applicants.
- Volunteers.
- Apprentices and trainees.
- Customers and clients.
- Prospective customers and clients.
- Users of services provided without monetary remuneration.
- Suppliers.
- Related family members.

The list is also expanding.

Issues

Court and civil tortious remedies are available to individual data subjects in addition to enforcing compliance with the prior information requirements, data protection principles, legitimate processing conditions, and security requirements. The data protection rules contain a number of further important rights for individuals in respect of their personal data. The data protection rights enshrined in the data protection regime for individuals are set out in the data protection principles. They include the details in the paragraphs following.

Individuals have a right to be informed by an organization as to their identity and details when it is collecting and processing the individual's personal data.

The organization must disclose to the individual the purpose for which it is collecting and processing the individual's personal data.

If the organization is forwarding or transferring the personal data to third-party recipients, it must disclose this to the individual as well as identify the third-party recipients. If it is permitted to transfer the personal data outside of the country, the organization must then also identify which third-party country will be receiving the personal data.

Possibly the most important right relates to the right of individual data subjects to access or obtain a copy of their personal data as held by organizations. Organizations must reply to requests from the individual in relation to their data protection rights. This includes requests for access to a copy of the personal data held in relation to the individual. This is known as a personal data access request. Every individual about whom a controller keeps personal information has a number of other rights under the data protection laws, in addition to the right of access. These include the rights to have any inaccurate information rectified or erased and to have personal data taken off a direct marketing or direct mailing list.

The individual data subject has a right to prevent processing likely to cause damage or distress. A further right relates to automated decision taking. Importantly, individual data subjects have specific rights in relation to rectification, blocking, erasure, and destruction. This is being further calibrated as encompassing the right to oblivion/right to be forgotten in the GDPR.

Individual data subjects are also entitled to compensation, as well as being entitled to complain to the data protection supervisory authority and to file actions in the courts to obtain judicial remedies. The 1995 data protection directive (DPD95) noted, for example, that data protection laws must not result in any lessening of the protection but must, on the contrary, seek to ensure a high level of protection in the EU.*

These individual rights are enhanced and expanded under the new GDPR. Transparency and consent are very important aspects of respecting and enabling the fundamental rights to be vindicated, used, and enforced by individual data subjects. Individual data subjects have a right of access to personal data. Certain fees may be charged for access copies—although they are minimal. There are also time limits to be complied with by the organization in relation to replying

* DPD95 Recital (10).

to individual data subjects' access requests (i.e., a request to access or obtain a copy of their personal data that the organization holds).

Individuals also have a right to prevent data processing for direct marketing purposes.

The individual data subject has a right to prevent processing likely to cause damage or distress.

A further right relates to automated computer decision-making, which relates to automated decisions being taken without human oversight or intervention. The traditional example often used is adverse credit decisions being taken automatically without human intervention.*

There has been a lot of publicity in relation to the deletion and right to be forgotten rights of individuals. Importantly, individual data subjects have specific rights in relation to rectification, blocking, erasure, and destruction and what is becoming known as the right to be forgotten. This has gained significance and attention given the EU Court of Justice decision in a "right to be forgotten" takedown case.†

Individual data subjects are also entitled to compensation, as well as being entitled to complain to the data protection supervisory authority and to the courts to obtain judicial remedies.

Background Guidance

Background Recital 1 provides guidance and states that the protection of natural persons in relation to the processing of personal data is a fundamental right. Article 8(1) of the Charter‡ and Article 16(1) of the EU Treaty§ provide that everyone has the right to the protection of personal data concerning them. The Recitals also refer to individual

---

* However, it can equally encompass such adverse decisions and activities as so-called neutral algorithmic processing and arranging of information and result outputs. Examples include search rankings and priorities; search suggestions; search prompts; autosuggest; autocomplete; and so on. Other examples could arise in relation to profiling and advertising-related activities.
† *Google Spain SL, Google Inc. v Agencia Española de Protección de Datos (AEPD), Mario Costeja González*, Court of Justice (Grand Chamber), Case C131/12, May 13, 2014. This relates to outdated search engine result listings.
‡ Charter of Fundamental Rights of the European Union (EU Charter).
§ Treaty on the Functioning of the European Union (TFEU).

data subject rights;* principles of fair and transparent processing;†
prior information requirements;‡ right of access;§ right of rectification
and right to be forgotten;¶ right to complain to single data protection
supervisory authority;** and automated processing issues.††

Procedures or modalities need to be provided for facilitating the
exercise of the individual data subject's rights under the GDPR,
including mechanisms to request and, if applicable, obtain, free of
charge, access to and rectification or erasure of personal data and the
exercise of the right to object. The controller should also provide means
for requests to be made electronically, especially where personal data
are processed by electronic means. The controller should be obliged to
respond to requests from the individual data subject without undue
delay and at the latest *within one month*. The organization must give
reasons where it does not intend to comply with any such requests.‡‡
The main proactive rights for individual data subjects are referred to
in the following section.

Legal Rules and Rights

Chapter III of the GDPR refers to the rights of individual data subjects. Some rights refer to compliance-type rights. The others refer to
proactive rights exercisable directly by individual data subjects. These
categories can interact with each other depending on individual circumstances. Some of the rights are also exercisable regardless of any
wrongdoing or breach by the controller.

These rights include

- *Right to Transparency*: The GDPR provides that individual
  data subjects are entitled to transparency in relation to the
  collection and processing of their personal data. There are also

---

* GDPR Recital 59.
† GDPR Recital 60.
‡ GDPR Recital 61.
§ GDPR Recital 63.
¶ GDPR Recitals 65, 66.
** GDPR Recital 141.
††GDPR Recital 71.
‡‡GDPR Recital 59.

consequent obligations on organizations seeking to use such data.* See Chapter 35 for more details.

- *Right to Prior Information: Directly Obtained Data*: The GDPR sets out various prior information requirements or conditions for directly obtained data that must be satisfied prior to collecting and using personal data from individuals. Individual data subjects have a right to be informed of certain required criteria in relation to *directly* obtained data.† See Chapter 10 for more details.

- *Right to Prior Information: Indirectly Obtained Data*: The GDPR sets out various prior information requirements or conditions for indirectly obtained data that must be satisfied prior to collecting and using personal data from individuals. Individual data subjects have a right to be informed of certain required criteria in relation to indirectly obtained data.‡ See Chapter 10 for more details.

- *Right of Confirmation and Right of Access*: Individual data subjects have a right to know or have confirmed whether a given organization is holding any of their personal data. Individual data subjects also have a right to obtain access to their personal data, which generally means obtaining a copy of the data from the organization.§ See Chapter 15 for more details.

- *Right to Be Informed of Third-Country Safeguards*: Individual data subjects have the right to be informed, where personal data are transferred to a third country or to an international organization, of the appropriate safeguards¶ relating to the transfer of data.** This has added relevance as part of the potential ripples from the *Schrems* EU Court of Justice case.†† See Chapter 34 for more details.

---

* GDPR Articles 5, 12.
† GDPR Article 13.
‡ GDPR Article 14.
§ GDPR Article 15.
¶ Pursuant to GDPR Article 46.
** GDPR Article 15(2).
††See GDPR Articles 13, 6, 15(2).

- *Right to Rectification*: Individuals have a right to rectification or correction of their personal data held by organizations.[*] See Chapter 16 for more details.
- *Right to Erasure and Right to be Forgotten*: Individuals have a right to have personal data erased or deleted.[†] See Chapter 17 for more details.
- *Right to Restriction of Processing*: Individuals have a right to restrict the processing of their personal data.[‡] See Chapter 18 for more details.
- *Notifications re Rectification, Erasure, or Restriction*: Individuals have a right to notification regarding rectification, erasure, or restriction of personal data.[§] See Chapter 20 for more details.
- *Right to Data Portability*: Individuals have a right to be able to move their personal data from one service provider to another service provider, essentially to port or have their data that are essential for the continuation or replacement of the service transferred; hence the reference to the data portability right.[¶] See Chapter 23 for more details.
- *Right to Object*: Individuals have a right to object to processing.[**] See Chapter 19 for more details.
- *Right to Object to Marketing and Direct Marketing*: Individuals have a right to object to processing of their personal data in marketing and direct marketing.[††] See Chapter 19 for more details.
- *Rights re Automated Individual Decision-Making, Including Profiling*: Individuals have a right in relation to automated individual decisions or automated individual decision-making processes, including in relation to their profiling by organizations.[‡‡] See Chapter 21 for more details.

---

[*] GDPR Article 16.
[†] GDPR Article 17.
[‡] GDPR Article 18.
[§] GDPR Article 19.
[¶] GDPR Article 20.
[**] GDPR Article 21.
[††] GDPR Article 21.
[‡‡] GDPR Article 22.

- *Data Protection by Design and Default*: Organizations are obliged to adopt the policy of data protection by design and by default, and individual data subjects are entitled to expect such procedures to be adopted.* See Chapters 31 and 32 for more details.
- *Security Rights*: Organizations are obliged to ensure that personal data are protected, and individuals expect that their data will be properly protected. See Chapter 28 for more details.
- *Impact Assessment and Prior Consultation*: Organizations are obliged to provide, and individual data subjects expect, appropriate new impact design protections and prior consultation protections. See Chapter 30 for more details.
- *Communicating Data Breach to Individual Data Subjects*: Data subjects have rights to be informed in the event of data breaches involving their data at organizations. See Chapter 29 for more details.
- *Data Protection Officer*: Organizations can be obliged to appoint data protection officers, and there are certain obligations thereby owed to data subjects, such as the ability to contact the data protection officer with data queries. See Chapter 41 for more details.
- *Remedies, Liability, and Sanctions*: Chapter VIII of the GDPR refers to remedies, liability issues, and sanctions regarding data protection. Organizations have compliance obligations and duties, including to data subjects, in relation to remedies, liability, and sanctions. These include, for example, right to effective judicial remedy against the controller or processor; representation of individual data subjects; right to compensation and liability; right to lodge complaint with data protection supervisory authority; right to judicial remedy against a data protection supervisory authority. See Chapters 38 and 26 for more details.

Organizations, in dealing with individuals and in considering the rights of individual data subjects, must be fully aware that the data

---

* GDPR Article 25.

protection principles must also be complied with as regards the individual data subject. Personal data must be

- Lawful, fair, and transparent.
- For a specified, explicit, and legitimate purpose (and not further processed).
- Adequate, relevant, limited (necessary) to the purpose.
- Accurate, kept up to date, with inaccurate data erased or rectified.
- Kept no longer than necessary.
- Protected by appropriate security.
- And organizations must demonstrate compliance with these points.

Organizations must also give a copy of personal data to any individual on request (i.e., a data access request) and ensure adequate security of personal data.

Conclusion

These rights are very important for organizations to recognize and protect. They need to be incorporated into the organization from day one, as it may not always be possible to become compliant retrospectively if the initial collection and processing were illegitimate. This is increasingly significant as data protection authorities become more proactive and as the levels of fines and penalties increase. The rights are expanding, more explicit, and more nuanced in the GDPR. It is important that organizations keep abreast of the expanding rights and obligations.

KEY CONCEPTS

Organizations need to consider each of the various rights of individual data subjects, as each right refers to a separate issue, and therefore separate procedural mechanisms need to be configured. In addition, procedures, records, and so on need to be established to demonstrate compliance to the data protection supervisory authority in the event of query, audit, or complaint. Compliance procedures and contentious related procedures need to be implemented so as to have advance preparation in the event of individual data subject or group data subject complaints or litigation arising.

KEYWORDS

* Right of confirmation.
* Right of access.
* Erasure and right to be forgotten.
* Right to restriction of processing.
* Right to object to processing.
* Right against automated individual decision-making, including profiling.
* Notification obligation regarding rectification, erasure, or restriction.
* Right to prevent processing for direct marketing.
* Rectification and erasure right.
* Portability right.
* Outsourcing to third-party data processors.
* Children's rights issues.
* Increased penalties, fines, and enforcement.
* Codes of conduct and certification.
* Security of personal data.
* Data breaches.

FURTHER READING

* Lambert, *International Handbook of Social Media Laws* (Bloomsbury, 2015).
* Lambert, *Social Networking: Law, Rights and Policy* (Clarus, 2014).
* Spanish EU Court of Justice "right to be forgotten" case.*

---

* *Google Spain SL, Google Inc. v Agencia Española de Protección de Datos (AEPD), Mario Costeja González*, Court of Justice (Grand Chamber), Case C131/12, 13 May 2014.

15

RIGHTS OF CONFIRMATION AND RIGHT OF ACCESS

Introduction

The data protection regime recognizes that individuals are hindered in their ability to decide what happens with their personal data if they are not able to know that organizations are seeking to collect, use, and process their personal data. Therefore, individual data subjects should be able to have a given organization confirm whether or not they are holding their data, and if it is affirmative and they wish to do so, the right to be able to obtain a copy of such data.

Right of Confirmation

Individual data subjects have a right to establish the existence of personal data. An individual who believes that an organization keeps personal data must, when requested in writing, have a right

- To be informed by the organization whether it keeps any such data; and
- If it does, to be given by the organization a description of the data and the purposes for which the data are kept.

This must be given as soon as possible and in any event not more than a specified number of days after the request has been given or sent to the organization. The new General Data Protection Regulation (GDPR) refers to a maximum of one month, but this may be extended in particular circumstances.*

---

* GDPR Article 12.

179

Background Guidance

The principles of fair and transparent processing require that the individual data subject be informed of the existence of the processing operation and its purposes. The controller should provide the individual data subject with any further information necessary to ensure fair and transparent processing, taking into account the specific circumstances and context in which the personal data are processed. Furthermore, the individual data subject should be informed of the existence of profiling and the consequences of such profiling. Where the personal data are collected from the individual data subject, the individual data subject should also be informed whether he or she is obliged to provide the personal data and of the consequences if he or she does not provide such data. This information may be provided in combination with standardized icons to give, in an easily visible, intelligible, and clearly legible manner, a meaningful overview of the intended processing. Where the icons are presented electronically, they should be machine-readable.*

The information in relation to the processing of personal data relating to the individual data subject should be given to them at the time of collection from the individual data subject, or, where the personal data are obtained from another source, within a reasonable period, depending on the circumstances of the case. Where personal data can be legitimately disclosed to another recipient, the individual data subject should be informed when the personal data are first disclosed to the recipient. Where the controller intends to process the personal data for a purpose other than that for which they were collected, the controller should provide the individual data subject prior to that further processing with information on that other purpose and other necessary information. Where the origin of the personal data cannot be provided to the individual data subject because various sources have been used, general information should be provided.†

However, it is not necessary to impose the obligation to provide information where the individual data subject already possesses the information, where the recording or disclosure of the personal data is expressly laid down by law, or where the provision of information to

---

* GDPR Recital 60.
† GDPR Recital 61.

the individual data subject proves to be impossible or would involve a disproportionate effort. The last in particular could be the case where processing is carried out for archiving purposes in the public interest, scientific or historical research purposes, or statistical purposes. In that regard, the number of individual data subjects, the age of the data, and any appropriate safeguards adopted should be taken into consideration.*

Legal Rule

The access right is also referred to in Article 15 of the GDPR. It refers to the right of access for individual data subjects. The individual data subject must have the right to obtain from the controller confirmation as to whether or not personal data concerning them are being processed and where such personal data are being processed, access to the data, and the following information

- The purposes of the processing.
- The categories of personal data concerned.
- The recipients or categories of recipients to whom the personal data have been or will be disclosed, in particular to recipients in third countries or international organizations.
- Where possible, the envisaged period for which the personal data will be stored, or if this is not possible, the criteria used to determine this period.
- The existence of the right to request from the controller rectification or erasure of personal data or restriction of the processing of personal data concerning the individual data subject or to object to the processing of such personal data.
- The right to lodge a complaint to a data protection supervisory authority.
- Where the personal data are not collected from the individual data subject, any available information as to their source.
- The existence of automated decision-making, including profiling,† and at least in those cases, meaningful information

---

* GDPR Recital 62.
† Referred to in GDPR Article 22(1) and (4).

about the logic involved as well as the significance and the envisaged consequences of such processing for the individual data subject.

Article 15(3) provides that the controller must provide a copy of the personal data undergoing processing. For any further copies requested by the individual data subject, the controller may charge a reasonable fee based on administrative costs. Where the individual data subject makes the request in electronic form, and unless otherwise requested by the individual data subject, the *information must be provided in a commonly used electronic form.*

It should be noted that it may no longer be possible to charge for the initial copy of the personal data furnished to the individual data subject.

Where personal data are transferred to a third country or to an international organization, the individual data subject must have the right to be informed of the appropriate safeguards pursuant to Article 46 relating to the transfer.*

The controller must provide a copy of the personal data undergoing processing.

The right to obtain a copy of the personal data must not adversely affect the rights of others.†

Right of Access

One of the rights that individual data subjects have is a *right of access* to personal data. This applies to individual data subjects. It is an individual data subject's right. Certain fees may be charged for obtaining copies of personal data held by an organization. These are minimal, however. There are also time limits to be complied with by controllers in relation to replying to an individual data subject access request. It is

---

* GDPR Article 15(2).
† GDPR Articles 15(4). Prior to the new GDPR, the UK data protection supervisory authority (Information Commissioner's Office [ICO]) has issued recommendations in relation to data access issues, namely: Access to Information Held in Complaint Files; Enforced Subject Access; How to Disclose Information Safely—Removing Personal Data from Information Requests and Datasets; Regulatory Activity Exemption; Subject Access: Code of Practice; Subject Access: Responding to a Request Checklist. These now need to be read in light of the GDPR changes.

also important to note that certain rights, including the access right, can be invoked by individuals at any time and for any reason. They do not have to wait for an apparent breach by an organization.

Background Guidance

An individual data subject should have the right of access to personal data that have been collected concerning them, and to exercise that right easily and at reasonable intervals, so as to be aware of, and verify, the lawfulness of the processing. This includes the right for individual data subjects to have access to data concerning their health; for example, the data in their medical records containing information such as diagnoses, examination results, assessments by treating physicians, and any treatment or interventions provided. Every individual data subject should therefore have the right to know and obtain communication in particular with regard to the purposes for which the personal data are processed, where possible the period for which the personal data are processed, the recipients of the personal data, the logic involved in any automatic personal data processing and, at least when based on profiling, the consequences of such processing. Where possible, the controller should be able to provide remote access to a secure system, which would provide the individual data subject with direct access to their personal data. That right should not adversely affect the rights or freedoms of others, including trade secrets or intellectual property and in particular the copyright protecting the software.*

However, the result of those considerations should not be a refusal to provide all information to the individual data subject. Where the controller processes a large quantity of information concerning the individual data subject, the controller should be able to request that, before the information is delivered, the individual data subject specify the information or processing activities to which the request relates. The controller should use all reasonable measures to verify the identity of an individual data subject who requests access, in particular in the context of online services and online identifiers. A controller should

---

* GDPR Recital 63; GDPR Recital 64.

not retain personal data for the sole purpose of being able to react to potential requests.*

Legal Rule

Chapter III, Section 2 of the GDPR refers to data access. It should be noted that the prior information requirements might have previously been viewed as controller compliance obligations. However, they are now reformulated as part of the individual data subject rights. This is therefore a change in emphasis.

Article 12 of the DPD95 also provides for the right of access. It provides that member states must guarantee every data subject the right to obtain from the controller without constraint, at reasonable intervals and without excessive delay or expense

- Confirmation as to whether or not data relating to them are being processed and information at least as to the purposes of the processing, the categories of data concerned, and the recipients or categories of recipients to whom the data are disclosed.
- Communication to them in an intelligible form of the data undergoing processing and of any available information as to their source.
- Knowledge of the logic involved in any automatic processing of data concerning them, at least in the case of automated decisions.†
- As appropriate, the rectification, erasure, or blocking of data the processing of which does not comply with the provisions of the Directive, in particular because of the incomplete or inaccurate nature of the data.‡
- Notification to third parties to whom the data have been disclosed of any rectification, erasure, or blocking carried out, unless this proves impossible or involves a disproportionate effort.

---

* GDPR Recital 63; GDPR Recital 64.
† Referred to in Article 15(1).
‡ Article 12(b).

Access: What Must Be Supplied

An individual must, if they so request a controller by notice in writing, be informed by the controller whether the data processed by or on behalf of the controller include personal data relating to the individual. If the individual data subject requests, they must be supplied by the controller with a description of

- The categories of data being processed by or on behalf of the controller.
- The personal data constituting the data of which that individual is the individual data subject.
- The purpose or purposes of the processing.
- The recipients or categories of recipients to whom the data are or may be disclosed.

Time Limits for Access

The individual data subject must have communicated to them in intelligible form

- The information constituting any personal data of which that individual is the individual data subject.
- Any information known or available to the controller as to the source of those data, unless the communication of that information is contrary to the public interest.
- Where the processing by automatic means of the data of which the individual is the individual data subject has constituted or is likely to constitute the sole basis for any decision significantly affecting them, information free of charge by the controller on the logic involved in the processing.

Making Request for Access

To make an access request, the individual data subject must

- Apply in writing (which can include email [or other electronic form]).
- Give any details that might be needed to help the organization identify them and locate all the information the organization

may keep about them; for example, previous addresses, customer account numbers.

- Pay the organization an access fee if the organization charges one. Such a fee is nominal.

Dealing with Access Requests

One commentary* refers to the advisability of having a process flow chart in place. The main components referred to include

- Individual data subject asks for personal data.
- Individual data subject access request form issued.
- Individual data subject access request form returned plus appropriate fee (if requested).
- Personal data located by legal department, data protection personnel, or other.
- Data examined in relation to any third-party information, health data, or exempt data.
- Data reviewed by legal department.
- Personal data copy issued to individual data subject.

On making an access request, any individual about whom personal data is kept is entitled to

- A copy of the personal data being held about them.
- Know the categories of their personal data and the purpose/s for processing it.
- Know the identity of those to whom the controller discloses the personal data.
- Know the source of the personal data, unless it is contrary to public interest.
- Know the logic involved in automated decisions.
- Data held in the form of opinions, except where such opinions were given in confidence, and in such cases, where the person's fundamental rights suggest that they should access the personal data in question.

---

* Morgan and Boardman, *Data Protection Strategy* (Sweet & Maxwell, 2003) 252.

It is important that organizations have clear and *documented* procedures in place to ensure that all relevant manual files and computers are checked for personal data in respect of which the access request is being made.

Response to Access Requests

In response to an access request an organization must

- Supply the information to the individual data subject promptly and within a specified number of days of receiving the request.
- Provide the information in a form that will be clear to the ordinary person; for example, any codes must be explained.*

If the organization does not keep any information about the individual making the request, the organization should inform the individual within a specified number of days.† An organization is not obliged to refund any fee charged for dealing with the access request should it not, in fact, keep any personal data.‡ However, the fee must be refunded if the organization does not comply with the request or if the organization has to rectify, supplement, or erase the personal data concerned.

If the organization restricts the individual's right of access in accordance with one of the very limited restrictions set down in the national data protection laws, the organization must notify the individual data subject in writing within a specified number of days, and it must include a statement of the reasons for refusal. The organization must also inform the individual of their entitlement to complain to the data protection supervisory authority about the refusal.

There are certain modifications to the basic right to access granted by the data protection laws, which include the following

- Access to health and social work data.
- Modifications to the right of access in the interest of the individual data subject or the public interest, designed to protect the individual from hearing anything about them that might

---

* Morgan and Boardman, *Data Protection Strategy* (Sweet & Maxwell, 2003) 252.
† ibid.
‡ ibid.

cause serious harm to their physical or mental health or emotional well-being.
- Examinations data.

In the case of examinations data, there is an increased time limit for responding to an access request from 40 to 60 days, and an access request is deemed to be made at the date of the first publication of the results or at the date of the request, whichever is the later.

Possible Access Exceptions and Issues

This must be done as soon as possible and in any event not more than a specified number of days after compliance by the individual with the provisions, and where any of the information is expressed in terms that are not intelligible to the average person without explanation, the information must be accompanied by an explanation of those terms.

Where personal data relating to an individual data subject consist of an expression of opinion about the individual data subject by another person, the data may be disclosed to the individual data subject without obtaining the consent of that person to the disclosure.

The obligations imposed to communicate to the individual data subject the personal data and details as to the source of the personal data can be complied with by supplying the individual data subject with a copy of the information concerned in permanent form, unless

- The supply of such a copy is not possible or would involve disproportionate effort, or
- The individual data subject agrees otherwise.

Where a controller has previously complied with an access request, the controller is not obliged to comply with a subsequent identical or similar request under that subsection by the same individual unless, in the opinion of the controller, a reasonable interval has elapsed between compliance with the previous request and the making of the current request. In determining whether such reasonable interval has elapsed, regard must be given to the nature of the data, the purpose for which the data are processed, and the frequency with which the data are altered.

The provision regarding automated data is not to be regarded as requiring the provision of information as to the logic involved in the taking of a decision if and to the extent only that such provision would adversely affect trade secrets or intellectual property (in particular any copyright protecting computer software).

Conclusion

Two of the earliest rights that organizations may have to interact with individual data subject queries will be the right of confirmation of whether there is personal data held in relation to the requestor, and also the right to provide access or copies of the personal data held, once so requested. This requires advance processes and procedures to be put in place within the organization, as well as associated records and designations of responsibility.

KEY CONCEPTS

Two of the most commonly used rights by data subjects are the confirmation and access rights in relation to personal data. Organizations must comply with the new GDPR confirmation and access rights. This includes preparing policies and procedures in advance, such as designing sets of standard reply correspondence and sets of internal requests to departments, guidance, and so on.

KEYWORDS

- Confirmation right; that is, right to have confirmed whether personal data are being held.
- Reply to confirmation request.
- Access right; that is, right to copy of personal data being held.
- Reply to access request.
- Advance processes and procedures.
- Search process.

- Reply process.
- Records.
- Representative.
- Data protection officer.

FURTHER READING

- Birkinshaw and Varney, *Government and Information: The Law Relating to Access, Disclosure and Their Regulation* (Bloomsbury, 2012).
- Lambert, *A Users' Guide to Data Protection* (Bloomsbury, 2016).
- Morgan and Boardman, *Data Protection Strategy* (Sweet & Maxwell, 2003).
- Spiller, "Experiences of Accessing CCTV Data: The Urban Topologies of Subject Access Requests," *Urban Studies* (2016) (53:13).

16

RIGHT TO RECTIFICATION

Introduction

Chapter III, Section 3 of the General Data Protection Regulation (GDPR) refers to rectification and erasure. The individual data subject must have the right to obtain from the controller without undue delay the rectification of inaccurate personal data concerning them. Taking into account the purposes of the processing, the data subject must have the right to have incomplete personal data completed, including by means of providing a supplementary statement.[*]

Background Guidance

Background Recital 59 states that modalities should be provided for facilitating the exercise of the data subject's rights under the GDPR, including mechanisms to request and, if applicable, obtain, free of charge, in particular, access to and rectification or erasure of personal data and the exercise of the right to object. The controller should also provide means for requests to be made electronically, especially where personal data are processed by electronic means. The controller should be obliged to respond to requests from the data subject without undue delay and at the latest within one month and to give reasons where the controller does not intend to comply with any such requests.

Background Recital 73 adds that restrictions concerning specific principles and the rights of information, access to, and rectification or erasure of personal data; the right to data portability; the right to object; decisions based on profiling; as well as the communication of a personal data breach to a data subject and certain related obligations of the controllers may be imposed by EU or member state law, as far

---

[*] GDPR Article 16.

as necessary and proportionate in a democratic society to safeguard public security, including the protection of human life, especially in response to natural or manmade disasters; the prevention, investigation, and prosecution of criminal offenses or the execution of criminal penalties, including the safeguarding against and the prevention of threats to public security, or of breaches of ethics for regulated professions; other important objectives of general public interest of the EU or of a member state, in particular an important economic or financial interest of the EU or of a member state; the keeping of public registers for reasons of general public interest; further processing of archived personal data to provide specific information related to the political behavior under former totalitarian state regimes or the protection of the data subject or the rights of others, including social protection, public health, and humanitarian purposes. Those restrictions should be in accordance with the requirements set out in the EU Charter and in the Human Rights Convention.

Background Recital 156 states that the processing of personal data for archiving purposes in the public interest, scientific or historical research purposes, or statistical purposes should be subject to appropriate safeguards for the rights of the data subject pursuant to the GDPR. Those safeguards should ensure that technical and organizational measures are in place to ensure, in particular, the principle of data minimization. The further processing of personal data for archiving purposes in the public interest, scientific or historical research purposes, or statistical purposes is to be carried out when the controller has assessed the feasibility of fulfilling those purposes by processing data that do not permit or no longer permit the identification of data subjects, provided that appropriate safeguards exist (such as, e.g., pseudonymization of the data). Member states should provide appropriate safeguards for the processing of personal data for archiving purposes in the public interest, scientific or historical research purposes, or statistical purposes. Member states should be authorized to provide, under specific conditions and subject to appropriate safeguards for data subjects, specifications and derogations with regard to the information requirements and rights to rectification, to erasure, to be forgotten, to restriction of processing, to data portability, and to object when processing personal data for archiving

purposes in the public interest, scientific or historical research purposes, or statistical purposes. The conditions and safeguards in question may entail specific procedures for data subjects to exercise those
rights if this is appropriate in the light of the purposes sought by the
specific processing along with technical and organizational measures
aimed at minimizing the processing of personal data in pursuance of
the proportionality and necessity principles. The processing of personal data for scientific purposes should also comply with other relevant legislation, such as on clinical trials.

Legal Rule

Individual data subjects have a right of rectification, blocking, and
erasure. The 1995 data protection directive (DPD95) provided for the
right of rectification, erasure, or blocking. Article 12 states that member states must guarantee every individual data subject the right to
obtain from the controller

- As appropriate, the rectification, erasure, or blocking of data
  the processing of which does not comply with the provisions
  of the Directive, in particular because of the incomplete or
  inaccurate nature of the data.
- Notification to third parties to whom the data have been disclosed of any rectification, erasure, or blocking carried out in
  compliance, unless this proves impossible or involves a disproportionate effort.

Chapter III, Section 3 of the GDPR refers to rectification and erasure. This was already an important and topical issue and is now even
more important on the foot of the *Google Spain* case and also issues
such as online abuse. The GDPR contains important new rectification
rights, known as the right of rectification and erasure. In particular,
Article 16 provides that the individual data subject must have the right
to obtain from the controller without undue delay the rectification of
inaccurate personal data concerning them. Taking into account the
purposes of the processing, the individual data subject must have the
right to have incomplete personal data completed, including by means
of providing a supplementary statement.

Conclusion

The explosion in electronically held data means that there is increased potential for inaccurate or incomplete data relating to individuals. Recognizing this issue, the GDPR provides a right of rectification to individuals, which organizations must comply with.

KEY CONCEPTS

The rectification right addresses two specific issues. The first is personal data that is incorrect. The second is personal data that is incomplete. Individual data subjects have a right as regards each situation.

KEY WORDS

- Data right.
- Right.
- Controller.
- Without undue delay.
- Rectification of inaccurate personal data.
- Purposes of the processing.
- Right to have incomplete personal data completed.
- Including a supplementary statement.

FURTHER READING

- Lambert, *International Handbook of Social Media Laws* (Bloomsbury, 2014).
- Lambert, *Social Networking: Law, Rights and Policy* (Clarus Press, 2014).
- Lynskey, "Control over Personal Data in a Digital Age: *Google Spain v AEPD and Mario Costeja Gonzalez*," *Modern Law Review* (2015) (78:3) 522.

- Mantelero, "Competitive Value of Data Protection: The Impact of Data Protection Regulation on Online Behaviour," *International Data Privacy Law* (2013) (3:4) 229.
- Mayer-Schönberger, *Delete: The Virtue of Forgetting in the Digital Age* (Princeton, 2009).
- Sartor, "The Right to be Forgotten in the Draft Data Protection Regulation," *International Data Privacy Law* (2015) (5:1) 64.
- Spanish EU Court of Justice "right to be forgotten" case.*
- WP29 Guidelines on the implementation of the Court of Justice of the European Union judgment on "*Google Spain andInc. v Agencia Española de Protección de Datos (AEPD) and Mario Costeja González*" c-131/121.
- WP29 Opinion 8/2010 on applicable law.

---

* *Google Spain SL, Google Inc. v Agencia Española de Protección de Datos (AEPD), Mario Costeja González*, Court of Justice (Grand Chamber), Case C-131/12, May 13, 2014.

17

RIGHT TO ERASURE AND RIGHT TO BE FORGOTTEN

Introduction

The damage that perpetual retention of personal data can cause for individuals has been increasing. There are numerous examples of individuals being harmed. This has resulted in the enhanced argument for the ability of individual data subjects to have personal data erased. This is sometimes referred to as the right, or a right, to be forgotten. This is particularly referenced recently in terms of personal data online. It is also sometimes abbreviated to RtbF.

Chapter III, Section 3 of the General Data Protection Regulation (GDPR) refers to rectification and erasure. This was already an important and topical issue and is now even more important on the foot of the *Google Spain* case and also issues such as online abuse, age, when data may be placed online, age of data, and so on.

Background Guidance

An individual data subject should have the right to have personal data concerning them rectified and a "right to be forgotten" where the retention of such data infringes the GDPR or EU or member state law to which the controller is subject. In particular, an individual data subject should have the right to have their personal data erased and no longer processed where the personal data are no longer necessary in relation to the purposes for which they were collected or otherwise processed, where an individual data subject has withdrawn their consent or objects to the processing of personal data concerning them, or where the processing of their personal data does not otherwise comply with the GDPR. That right is relevant in particular where the individual data subject had given their consent as a child and was not fully aware of the risks involved by the processing, and later wants to remove such personal data, especially on the Internet. The individual data subject should be able to exercise that right notwithstanding the fact that he or she is no longer a child. However, the further retention of the personal data should be lawful where it is necessary for exercising the right of freedom of expression and information, for compliance with a legal obligation, for the performance of a task carried out in the public interest or in the exercise of official authority vested in the controller, on the grounds of public interest in the area of public health, for archiving purposes in the public interest, scientific or historical research purposes, or statistical purposes, or for the establishment, exercise, or defense of legal claims.* To strengthen the right to be forgotten in the online environment, the right to erasure should also be extended in such a way that a controller who has made the personal data public should be obliged to inform the controllers that are processing such personal data to erase any links to, or copies or replications of, those personal data. In doing so, that controller should take reasonable steps, taking into account available technology and the means available to the controller, including technical measures, to inform the controllers that are processing the personal data of the individual data subject's request.†

One of the more important extensions and enhancements in the new data protection regime relates to the right to be forgotten: the "right to be forgotten and to erasure, which consists of securing from the [data] controller the erasure of personal data as well as prevention of any further dissemination of [their] data."‡ (It is also said to interface with the new right to data portability.§)

The right to be forgotten is even more enhanced in instances where the personal data was originally disclosed when the individual data

---

* GDPR Recital 65. However, the further retention of the data should be lawful where it is necessary for exercising the right of freedom of expression and information, for compliance with a legal obligation, for the performance of a task carried out in the public interest or in the exercise of official authority vested in the Controller, for reasons of public interest in the area of public health, for archiving purposes in the public interest, or scientific and historical research purposes, or statistical purposes, or for the establishment, exercise, or defense of legal claims; ibid.

† GDPR Recital 66.

‡ Costa and Poullet, "Privacy and the Regulation of 2012," (2012)(28) *Computer Law & Security Review*, 256.

§ ibid.

subject was a child. Some commentators refer to the option of an entire "clean slate."*

Costa states

> The use of data from social networks in employment contexts is a representative example. Personal data such as photos taken in private contexts have been used to refuse job positions and fire people. But forgetfulness is larger. It is one dimension of how people deal with their own history, being related not only to leaving the past behind but also to living in the present without the threat of a kind of "Miranda" warning, where whatever you say can be used against you in the future. In this sense the right to be forgotten is closely related to entitlements of dignity and self-development. Once again, privacy appears as the pre-requisite of our liberties, assuring the possibility to freely express ourselves and move freely on the street.†

The right to be forgotten is most clearly associated with and related to the following in particular

- Where the personal data are no longer necessary in relation to the purposes for which they were originally collected and processed (and the associated finality principle).
- Where the individual data subject has withdrawn their consent for processing.
- Where individual data subjects object to the processing of the personal data concerning them.
- Where the processing of the personal data does not comply with the GDPR.‡

The GDPR, and the right to be forgotten, "amplifies the effectiveness of data protection principles and rules."§

Individual data subjects can have their data erased under the right to be forgotten when there is no compliance as well as where they simply withdraw their consent.¶ User control and individual data subject control are, therefore, enhanced.

---

* ibid., at 257.
† ibid.
‡ ibid.
§ ibid.
¶ ibid.

The GDPR and right to be forgotten create the following compliance obligations

- Erasing personal data and not processing it further.
- Informing third parties that the individual data subject has requested the deletion of the personal data.
- Taking responsibility for publication by third parties under the controller's authority.*

Legal Rule

Article 17(1) of the GDPR provides for the enhanced right to be forgotten and to erasure. This is known as the right to erasure and or right to be forgotten. It provides that the individual data subject must have the right to obtain from the controller the erasure of personal data concerning them without undue delay, and the controller must have the obligation to erase personal data without undue delay where one of the following grounds applies

- The personal data are no longer necessary in relation to the purposes for which they were collected or otherwise processed.
- The individual data subject withdraws consent on which the processing is based,† and where there is no other legal ground for the processing.
- The individual data subject objects to the processing‡ and there are no overriding legitimate grounds for the processing, or the individual data subject objects to the processing.§
- The personal data have been unlawfully processed.
- The personal data have to be erased for compliance with a legal obligation in EU or member state law to which the controller is subject.
- The personal data have been collected in relation to the offer of information society services.¶

---

* ibid., Articles 17, 2, and 8.
† According to Article 6(1)(a), or Article 9(2)(a).
‡ Pursuant to Article 21(1).
§ Pursuant to Article 21(2).
¶ Referred to in Article 8(1).

The GDPR provides that where the controller has made the personal data public and is obliged to erase the personal data, the controller, taking account of available technology and the cost of implementation, must take reasonable steps, including technical measures, to inform controllers that are processing the personal data that the individual data subject has requested the erasure by such controllers of any links to, or copy or replication of, those personal data.

Article 17(3) of the GDPR provides that Article 17(1) and (2) will not apply to the extent that processing is necessary

- For exercising the right of freedom of expression and information.
- For compliance with a legal obligation that requires processing by EU or member state law to which the controller is subject or for the performance of a task carried out in the public interest or in the exercise of official authority vested in the controller.
- For reasons of public interest in the area of public health.*
- For archiving purposes in the public interest, scientific or historical research purposes, or statistical purposes† insofar as the right referred to is likely to render impossible or seriously impair the achievement of the objectives of that processing or.
- For the establishment, exercise, or defense of legal claims.

There were obviously various amendments, and it must be agreed that the right to be forgotten is, or has been portrayed as, contentious, which would have been an issue during the process of negotiating the finalization of the GDPR.

The data subject has the right to obtain from the controller the erasure of personal data concerning them without undue delay, and the controller must have the obligation to erase personal data without undue delay, where one of the following grounds applies

- The personal data are no longer necessary in relation to the purposes for which they were collected or otherwise processed.

---

* In accordance with Article 9(2)(h) and (i) as well as Article 9(3).
† In accordance with Article 89(1).

- The data subject withdraws consent on which the processing is based,* and where there is no other legal ground for the processing.
- The data subject objects to the processing† and there are no overriding legitimate grounds for the processing, or the data subject objects to the processing.‡
- The personal data have been unlawfully processed.
- The personal data have to be erased for compliance with a legal obligation in EU or member state law to which the controller is subject.
- The personal data have been collected in relation to the offer of information society services.§

Where the controller has made the personal data public and is obliged pursuant to the above to erase the personal data, the controller, taking account of available technology and the cost of implementation, must take reasonable steps, including technical measures, to inform controllers that are processing the personal data that the data subject has requested the erasure by such controllers of any links to, or copy or replication of, those personal data.¶

The above does not apply to the extent that processing is necessary

- For exercising the right of freedom of expression and information.
- For compliance with a legal obligation that requires processing by EU or member state law to which the controller is subject or for the performance of a task carried out in the public interest or in the exercise of official authority vested in the controller.
- For reasons of public interest in the area of public health.**

---

* According to Article 6(1)(a) or Article 9(2)(a).
† Pursuant to Article 21(1).
‡ Pursuant to Article 21(2).
§ Referred to in Article 8(1). GDPR Article 17(1).
¶ GDPR Article 17(2).
** In accordance with Article 9(2)(h) and (i) as well as Article 9(3).

- For archiving purposes in the public interest, scientific or historical research purposes, or statistical purposes* insofar as the right referred to is likely to render impossible or seriously impair the achievement of the objectives of that processing.
- For the establishment, exercise, or defense of legal claims.[†]

In the *Google Spain* case, the EU Court of Justice held that

Article 2(b) and (d) of [the DPD] ... are to be interpreted as meaning that, first, the activity of a search engine consisting in finding information published or placed on the internet by third parties, indexing it automatically, storing it temporarily and, finally, making it available to internet users according to a particular order of preference must be classified as "processing of personal data" within the meaning of Article 2(b) when that information contains personal data and, second, the operator of the search engine must be regarded as the "controller" in respect of that processing, within the meaning of Article 2(d).

Article 4(1)(a) of [the DPD] is to be interpreted as meaning that processing of personal data is carried out in the context of the activities of an establishment of the controller on the territory of a member state, within the meaning of that provision, when the operator of a search engine sets up in a member state a branch or subsidiary that is intended to promote and sell advertising space offered by that engine and that orientates its activity towards the inhabitants of that member state.[‡]

---

* In accordance with Article 89(1).

† GDPR Article 17(3). In relation to the original draft, and so on, see, for example, Sartor, "The Right to Be Forgotten in the Draft Data Protection Regulation," *International Data Privacy Law* (2015) (5:1) 64. Also, Mantelero, "Competitive Value of Data Protection: The Impact of Data Protection Regulation on Online Behaviour," *International Data Privacy Law* (2013) (3:4) 229.

‡ *Google Spain SL and Google Inc v Agencia Española de Protección de Datos (AEPD) and Mario Costeja González,* Case C-131/12, May 13, 2014. Lynskey, "Control Over Personal Data in a Digital Age: *Google Spain v AEPD and Mario Costeja Gonzalez,*" *Modern Law Review* (2015) (78:3) 522. Also see, for example, Lambert, *International Handbook of Social Media Laws* (Bloomsbury, 2014); Lambert, *Social Networking: Law, Rights and Policy* (Clarus Press, 2014); Mayer-Schönberger, *Delete: The Virtue of Forgetting in the Digital Age* (Princeton, 2009).

The Article 29 Data Protection Working Party (WP29) also refers to RtbF issues as well as the Google Spain case.* This includes WP29 "Guidelines on the implementation of the EU Court of Justice of the European Union judgment on '*Google Spain and Inc. v Agencia Española de Protección de Datos (AEPD) and Mario Costeja González.*'" No doubt the European Data Protection Board (EDPB) will comment on these issues further in due course. Google has also issued a report on some of the issues following on from various consultations in a number of different locations with interested parties.

Synodinou[†] refers to the "right to oblivion" and notes in relation to her research that media interests are not immune to the right to be forgotten. Examples are given where cases have been successful in preventing particular media stories dragging up past events long after they had occurred, including court cases.[‡] Indeed, many countries, such as Germany, Austria, Greece, Finland, Belgium, Hungary, the Netherlands, Poland, and Portugal, already anonymize party names from decisions and judgments.[§] The right to be forgotten has also been recognized in France, Belgium, and elsewhere[¶] It is also important to bear in mind that the GDPR introduces enhanced rights as regards deletion and being forgotten, and does not introduce such provisions *de novo.*

---

[*] WP29 Guidelines on the implementation of the Court of Justice of the European Union judgment on "*Google Spain and Inc v Agencia Española de Protección de Datos (AEPD) and Mario Costeja González*" c-131/121; Opinion 8/2010 on applicable law (WP29 adds as follows: "In its judgment in Google Spain the Court of Justice of the European Union decided upon certain matters relating to the territorial scope of Directive 95/46/EC. The WP29 commenced an internal analysis of the potential implications of this judgment on applicable law and may provide further guidance on this issue during the course of 2015, including, possibly, additional examples.")

[†] Synodinou, "The Media Coverage of Court Proceedings in Europe: Striking a Balance between Freedom of Expression and Fair Process," *Computer Law & Security Review* (2012) (28) 208 at 217.

[‡] ibid. at 218.

[§] ibid. at 218 and fn 106.

[¶] ibid., 217.

Conclusion

One of the most important rights for organizations to be aware of and to provide compliance mechanisms for is the expanded right to erasure and right to be forgotten. Partly due to the parties involved, there has been a lot of media and public attention on this issue. This in turn has led to some contention. However, the issues involved and the concerns sought to be addressed are real. Arguably, this issue should not be as surprising or contentious as it sometimes appears.

KEY CONCEPTS

The right to be forgotten has received substantial commercial and media attention following on from the *Google Spain* case. However, the right has existed from some time and is included in the previous DPD95. Various national laws also refer to deletion and right to be forgotten entitlements. The new GDPR enhances and makes the right more explicit. Organizations need to consider this issue in detail and must provide for compliance—and processes and procedures—as appropriate to the organization, its activities, its services, and its business partners, and most importantly, the types of data and data interests that can be affected.

KEY WORDS

- Enhanced right.
- Right to erasure.
- Right to be forgotten.
- Right to obtain and have organization erase personal data.
- Must erase without undue delay.
- Detailed rules and grounds apply.
- Rights and interests to be protected.
- Consider different interests and different rights to be forgotten.
- Consider child's right to be forgotten.
- Consider adults' right to be forgotten.

- Consider general personal data and right to be forgotten.
- Consider sensitive personal data and right to be forgotten.
- Consider sexual personal data and right to be forgotten.
- Consider hacked sexual personal data and right to be forgotten.
- Consider blackmail, threats, and extortion revenge porn.
- Consider graduated urgency issues.

FURTHER READING

- Cooper, "The Right to Be Virtually Clothed," *Washington Law Review* (2016) (91:2) 817.
- Google report in relation to its right to be forgotten consultations, See http://docs.dpaq.de/8527-report_of_the_advisory_committee_to_google_on_the_right_to_be_forgotten.pdf.
- Lambert, *International Handbook of Social Media Laws* (Bloomsbury, 2014).
- Lambert, *Social Networking: Law, Rights and Policy* (Clarus Press, 2014).
- Lynskey, "Control over Personal Data in a Digital Age: *Google Spain v AEPD and Mario Costeja Gonzalez*," *Modern Law Review* (2015) (78:3) 522.
- Mantelero, "Competitive Value of Data Protection: The Impact of Data Protection Regulation on Online Behaviour," *International Data Privacy Law* (2013) (3:4) 229.
- Mayer-Schönberger, *Delete: The Virtue of Forgetting in the Digital Age* (Princeton, 2009).
- McGoldrick, "Developments in the Right to Be Forgotten," *Human Rights Law Review* (2013) (13:4) 761.
- Sartor, "The Right to be Forgotten in the Draft Data Protection Regulation," *International Data Privacy Law* (2015) (5:1) 64.
- Spanish EU Court of Justice "right to be forgotten" case.*
- Voss, "The Right to Be Forgotten in the European Union: Enforcement in the Court of Justice and Amendment to the

---

* *Google Spain SL, Google Inc v Agencia Española de Protección de Datos (AEPD), Mario Costeja González*, Court of Justice (Grand Chamber), Case C-131/12, 13 May 2014.

Proposed General Data Protection Regulation," *Journal of Internet Law* (2014) (18:1) 3.
- WP29 Guidelines on the implementation of the Court of Justice of the European Union judgment on "*Google Spain and Inc v Agencia Española de Protección de Datos (AEPD) and Mario Costeja González*" c-131/121.
- WP29 Opinion 8/2010 on applicable law.

18

RIGHT TO RESTRICTION OF PROCESSING

Introduction

Individual data subjects have a right to restrict the processing of personal data by organizations relating to them. Individuals have a right not to be subject to processing about them.

Background Guidance

The individual data subject should have the right not to be subject to a decision, which may include a measure, evaluating personal aspects relating to them, which is based solely on automated processing and which produces legal effects concerning them or similarly significantly affects them, such as automatic refusal of an online credit application or e-recruiting practices without any human intervention. Such processing includes "profiling" that consists of any form of automated processing of personal data evaluating the personal aspects relating to a natural person, in particular to analyze or predict aspects concerning the individual data subject's performance at work, economic situation, health, personal preferences or interests, reliability or behavior, location, or movements, where it produces legal effects concerning them or similarly significantly affects them.*

However, decision-making based on such processing, including profiling, should be allowed where expressly authorized by EU or member state law to which the controller is subject, including for fraud and tax-evasion monitoring and prevention purposes conducted in accordance with the regulations, standards, and recommendations of EU institutions or national oversight bodies and to ensure the security and reliability of a service provided by the controller, or necessary for

---

* GDPR Recital 71.

the entering or performance of a contract between the individual data subject and a controller, or when the individual data subject has given their explicit consent. In any case, such processing should be subject to suitable safeguards, which should include specific information to the individual data subject and the right to obtain human intervention, to express their point of view, to obtain an explanation of the decision reached after such assessment, and to challenge the decision.*

Such measures should not concern a child. To ensure fair and transparent processing in respect of the individual data subject, taking into account the specific circumstances and context in which the personal data are processed, the controller should use appropriate mathematical or statistical procedures for the profiling; implement technical and organizational measures appropriate to ensure, in particular, that factors that result in inaccuracies in personal data are corrected and the risk of errors is minimized; and secure personal data in a manner that takes account of the potential risks involved for the interests and rights of the individual data subject and that prevents, *inter alia*, discriminatory effects on natural persons on the basis of racial or ethnic origin, political opinion, religion or beliefs, trade union membership, genetic or health status, or sexual orientation, or that results in measures having such an effect. Automated decision-making and profiling based on special categories of personal data should be allowed only under specific conditions.†

Background Guidance on Methods to Restrict Processing

Methods by which to restrict the processing of personal data could include, *inter alia*, temporarily moving the selected data to another processing system, making the selected personal data unavailable to users, or temporarily removing published data from a website. In automated filing systems, the restriction of processing should in principle be ensured by technical means in such a manner that the personal data are not subject to further processing operations and cannot be changed. The fact that the processing of personal data is restricted should be clearly indicated in the system.‡

---

* GDPR Recital 71.
† GDPR Recital 71.
‡ GDPR Recital 67.

Legal Rule

Article 18 of the new GDPR includes a new section on the right to restriction of processing. The individual data subject must have the right to obtain from the controller restriction of processing where one of the following applies

- The accuracy of the personal data is contested by the individual data subject, for a period enabling the controller to verify the accuracy of the personal data.
- The processing is unlawful, and the individual data subject opposes the erasure of the personal data and requests the restriction of their use instead.
- The controller no longer needs the personal data for the purposes of the processing, but they are required by the individual data subject for the establishment, exercise, or defense of legal claims.
- The individual data subject has objected to processing* pending the verification of whether the legitimate grounds of the controller override those of the individual data subject.

Where processing has been restricted under one of these conditions, such personal data must, with the exception of storage, only be processed with the individual data subject's consent, or for the establishment, exercise, or defense of legal claims, or for the protection of the rights of another natural or legal person, or for reasons of important public interest of the EU or of a member state.

An individual data subject who has obtained restriction of processing pursuant to the above must be informed by the controller before the restriction of processing is lifted.

Conclusion

Perhaps more important from a practical perspective for organizations is not the right to be forgotten, but the right of the individual data subject to have data processing in relation to them restricted. This is wider in ambit, both potentially and in practice, than the right

---

* Pursuant to Article 21(1).

to be forgotten. Separate processes and procedures must be in place to deal with objections and requests as regards restricted processing issues.

KEY CONCEPTS

There may be instances where, apart from erasure and right to be forgotten, an individual data subject may prefer that the processing of their personal data is confined or restricted. They may enforce a right to have such restriction apply.

KEY WORDS

• New provision.
• Right to restriction of processing.
• Right to have organizations restrict processing.
• Contested accuracy of personal data.
• Verifying accuracy of personal data.
• Unlawful processing.
• Data subject opposes erasure but requests restriction of processing instead.
• Organization no longer needs the personal data, but individual data subject needs them for establishment, exercise, or defense of legal claims.
• Individual data subject has objected to processing.
• Verification of legitimate grounds versus right of individual data subject.
• Restricted personal data must, excepting storage, only be processed with the individual data subject's consent, or for the establishment, exercise, or defense of legal claims, or for the protection of the rights.
• Once data are restricted, individual data subject must be informed by organization before the restriction is lifted.

19

RIGHT TO OBJECT TO PROCESSING

Introduction

Individuals can object to processing relating to them. This is also something that individual data subjects were entitled to under the prior data protection regime.

Background Guidance

Background Recital 50 states that where the data subject has given consent or the processing is based on EU or member state law that constitutes a necessary and proportionate measure in a democratic society to safeguard, in particular, important objectives of general public interest, the controller should be allowed to further process the personal data irrespective of the compatibility of the purposes. In any case, the application of the principles set out in the General Data Protection Regulation (GDPR), and in particular the information of the data subject on those other purposes and on their rights, including the right to object, should be ensured. Indicating possible criminal acts or threats to public security by the controller and transmitting the relevant personal data in individual cases or in several cases relating to the same criminal act or threats to public security to a competent authority should be regarded as being in the legitimate interest pursued by the controller. However, such transmission in the legitimate interest of the controller or further processing of personal data should be prohibited if the processing is not compatible with a legal, professional, or other binding obligation of secrecy.

Background Recital 59 states that modalities should be provided for facilitating the exercise of the data subject's rights under the GDPR, including mechanisms to request and, if applicable, obtain, free of charge, in particular, access to and rectification or erasure of personal data and the exercise of the right to object. The controller should also provide means for requests to be made electronically, especially where personal data are processed by electronic means. The controller should be obliged to respond to requests from the data subject without undue delay and at the latest within one month and to give reasons where the controller does not intend to comply with any such requests.

Background Recital 65 states that a data subject should have the right to have personal data concerning them rectified and a "right to be forgotten" where the retention of such data infringes this GDPR or EU or member state law to which the controller is subject. In particular, a data subject should have the right to have their personal data erased and no longer processed where the personal data are no longer necessary in relation to the purposes for which they are collected or otherwise processed, where a data subject has withdrawn their consent or objects to the processing of personal data concerning them, or where the processing of their personal data does not otherwise comply with the GDPR. That right is relevant in particular where the data subject had given their consent as a child and was not fully aware of the risks involved by the processing, and later wants to remove such personal data, especially on the Internet. The data subject should be able to exercise that right notwithstanding the fact that he or she is no longer a child. However, the further retention of the personal data should be lawful where it is necessary for exercising the right of freedom of expression and information, for compliance with a legal obligation, for the performance of a task carried out in the public interest or in the exercise of official authority vested in the controller, on the grounds of public interest in the area of public health, for archiving purposes in the public interest, scientific or historical research purposes, or statistical purposes, or for the establishment, exercise, or defense of legal claims.

Background Recital 69 states that where personal data might lawfully be processed because processing is necessary for the performance of a task carried out in the public interest or in the exercise of official authority vested in the controller, or on grounds of the legitimate interests of a controller or a third party, a data subject should, nevertheless, be entitled to object to the processing of any personal data relating to their particular situation. It should be for the controller to demonstrate that its compelling legitimate interest overrides the interests or the fundamental rights of the data subject.

Background Recital 70 states that where personal data are processed for the purposes of direct marketing, the data subject should have the right to object to such processing, including profiling to the extent that it is related to such direct marketing, whether with regard to initial or further processing, at any time and free of charge. That right should be explicitly brought to the attention of the data subject and presented clearly and separately from any other information.

Background Recital 73 states that restrictions concerning specific principles and the rights of information, access to, and rectification or erasure of personal data; the right to data portability; the right to object; decisions based on profiling; as well as the communication of a personal data breach to a data subject and certain related obligations of the controllers may be imposed by EU or member state law, as far as necessary and proportionate in a democratic society to safeguard public security, including the protection of human life, especially in response to natural or manmade disasters; the prevention, investigation, and prosecution of criminal offenses or the execution of criminal penalties, including the safeguarding against and the prevention of threats to public security, or of breaches of ethics for regulated professions; other important objectives of general public interest of the EU or of a member state, in particular an important economic or financial interest of the EU or of a member state; the keeping of public registers for reasons of general public interest; further processing of archived personal data to provide specific information related to the political behavior under former totalitarian state regimes or the protection of the data subject or the rights of others, including social protection, public health, and humanitarian purposes. Those restrictions should be in accordance with the requirements set out in the Charter and in the Human Rights Convention.

Legal Rule

Article 21 of the GDPR refers to the right to object. The individual data subject must have the right to object, on grounds relating to their particular situation, at any time to processing of personal data

concerning them that is based on Article 6(1)(e) or (f), including profiling based on those provisions. The controller must no longer process the personal data unless the controller demonstrates compelling
legitimate grounds for the processing that override the interests or
rights of the individual data subject or for the establishment, exercise,
or defense of legal claims.*

Where personal data are processed for direct marketing purposes,
the individual data subject must have the right to object at any time
to processing of personal data concerning them for such marketing,
which includes profiling to the extent that it is related to such direct
marketing.† Where the individual data subject objects to processing
for direct marketing purposes, the personal data must no longer be
processed for such purposes.‡ At the latest at the time of the first communication with the individual data subject, this right must be explicitly brought to the attention of the individual data subject and must be
presented clearly and separately from any other information.§

In the context of the use of information society services, and notwithstanding the ePrivacy Directive, the individual data subject may
exercise their right to object by automated means using technical
specifications.¶

Where personal data are processed for scientific or historical
research purposes or statistical purposes pursuant to Article 89(1), the
individual data subject, on grounds relating to their particular situation, must have the right to object to processing of personal data concerning them, unless the processing is necessary for the performance
of a task carried out for reasons of public interest.**

---

* GDPR Article 21(1). The DPD95 referred to the individual data subject's right to
  object in Article 14.
† GDPR Article 21(2).
‡ GDPR Article 21(3).
§ GDPR Article 21(4).
¶ GDPR Article 21(5).
**GDPR Article 21(6).

Conclusion

Organizations need to assess and implement procedures for the right to object by individual data subjects. This requires nuanced assessment and appropriate processes and procedures in advance.

KEY CONCEPTS

Individuals have a right to object to data processing, and organizations must prepare for and comply with these detailed provisions.

KEY WORDS

- Right to object to processing on grounds relating to individual situation.
- At any time.
- Article 6(1)(e) or (f).
- Profiling.
- Organization must stop unless there are compelling legitimate grounds for the processing that override the interests or rights of the individual data subject.
- Or for the establishment, exercise, or defense of legal claims.

20

Notification Obligation regarding Rectification, Erasure, or Restriction

Introduction

There is also a right dealing with those instances where changes and correction may have been made, and where the data may be in the possession of more than one organization.

One organization may have corrected or erased particular data, but the second organization may not, unless there is a mechanism for the second organization to become aware of the need to update its database also.

Legal Rule

Article 19 of the new GDPR includes a new section regarding notification obligation regarding rectification, erasure, or restriction. The controller must communicate any rectification or erasure of personal data or restriction of processing carried out in accordance with Article 16 (i.e., right to rectification), Article 17(1) (i.e., right to erasure, right to be forgotten) and Article 18 (i.e., right to restriction of processing) to each recipient to whom the personal data have been disclosed, unless this proves impossible or involves disproportionate effort. The controller must inform the individual data subject about those recipients if the individual data subject requests it.

Conclusion

Where rectification, erasure, or a restriction applies, it may be that the relevant data are also held, having been transferred onwards by the organization, in a secondary organization. In those instances there is, therefore, a corresponding or complementary right or obligation to have the third-party organization also notified of the change in status of the data.

KEY CONCEPTS

There is a right to rectification, erasure, and restriction of personal data. This applied to the original personal data held by the organization. There is, therefore, a corresponding notification obligation to ensure that third-party recipients of the data are made aware of the changes and the need for them to make the corresponding changes also. In addition, the organization must provide details regarding the third parties to the individual data subject once so requested.

KEY WORDS

- Notification obligation regarding rectification, erasure, or restriction.
- Organization must communicate any rectification or erasure of personal data or processing restriction to each data recipient.
- Unless impossible or disproportionate effort.
- Organization must inform individual data subject about recipients if requested.

21

RIGHT AGAINST AUTOMATED INDIVIDUAL DECISIONS AND PROFILING

Introduction

Increasingly, organizations rely on automation and automated decision-making (including profiling). However, there is a concern when this brings the potential for decisions to be made using automated decisions regarding individuals. One of the concerns is that adverse decisions can arise, which may or may not be correct, and there is no human oversight or input to the decision, and no ability to find and correct incorrect automated decisions. There is also wide concern over the data protection impact of increased profiling techniques.*

This is essentially a right to object to automated individual decision-making (including profiling). Individual data subjects have a right not to be subjected to automated decision-taking processes. This refers to decisions taken in relation to and affecting individuals but that are computer-based and automated, and that occur without human intervention. An example would be a financial institution making a credit application decision by automated computer without oversight by personnel of the institution. This is not the only instance of such automated decisions, however. Indeed, such instances may be increasing.† (Also note comments on the right to be forgotten.)

Chapter III, Section 4 of the new General Data Protection Regulation (GDPR) refers to the right to object to automated individual decision-making.

---

* This is in the EU as well as the United States (and elsewhere). From a US perspective, see Roethlisberger, "Someone Is Watching: The Need for Enhanced Data Protection," *Hastings Law Journal* (2011) (62:6) 1793.

† The 1995 data protection directive (DPD95) also referred to automated individual decisions. DPD95 Articles 15.

Background Guidance on Profiling

Profiling is subject to the rules of the GDPR governing the processing of personal data, such as the legal grounds for processing or data protection principles. The European Data Protection Board (EDPB), established by the GDPR, should be able to issue guidance in that context.* Restrictions concerning specific principles and the rights of information, access to, and rectification or erasure of personal data; the right to data portability; the right to object; decisions based on profiling; as well as the communication of a personal data breach to a data subject and certain related obligations of the controllers may be imposed by EU or member state law, as far as necessary and proportionate in a democratic society to safeguard public security, including the protection of human life, especially in response to natural or manmade disasters; the prevention, investigation, and prosecution of criminal offenses or the execution of criminal penalties, including the safeguarding against and the prevention of threats to public security, or of breaches of ethics for regulated professions; other important objectives of general public interest of the EU or of a member state, in particular an important economic or financial interest of the EU or of a member state; the keeping of public registers for reasons of general public interest; further processing of archived personal data to provide specific information related to the political behavior under former totalitarian state regimes or the protection of the data subject or the rights of others, including social protection, public health, and humanitarian purposes. Those restrictions should be in accordance with the requirements set out in the EU Charter and in the Human Rights Convention.†

Legal Rule

The new GDPR provides that the individual data subject must have the right not to be subject to a decision based solely on automated

---

* GDPR Recital 72.
† GDPR Recital 73. Charter of Fundamental Rights of the European Union and by the Human Rights Convention.

processing, including profiling, that produces legal effects concerning them or similarly significantly affects them.[*]

Article 20(1) must not apply if the decision

- Is necessary for entering into, or performance of, a contract between the individual data subject and a data controller [a]

or

- Is authorized by EU or member state law to which the controller is subject and that also lays down suitable measures to safeguard the individual data subject's rights and legitimate interests

or

- Is based on the individual data subject's explicit consent (Article 22(c)) [c]

In cases referred to in Article 22(2)(a) and (c), the controller must implement suitable measures to safeguard the individual data subject's rights and legitimate interests, at least the right to obtain human intervention on the part of the controller, to express their point of view, and to contest the decision.[†]

Decisions referred to in paragraph 2 must not be based on special categories of personal data,[‡] unless Article 9(2)(a) or (g) applies and suitable measures to safeguard the individual data subject's rights and legitimate interests are in place.[§]

Conclusion

An increasing number of data decisions in relation to individuals occur in an automated manner. Where there is potential for adverse decision as a result, rights exist for individuals to check these decisions and processes. Organizations should assess where such potential decisions or processes may occur within the organization. Arguably, this could be one of the more difficult issues for organizations to deal with.

---

[*] GDPR Article 22(1).
[†] GDPR Article 22(3).
[‡] Referred to in Article 9(1).
[§] GDPR Article 22(4).

KEY CONCEPTS

There is an increase in automated computer decisions and processes. The concern that some of these, which involve individuals and their personal data, may occur in an adverse manner or create an adverse impact is recognized in the GDPR. Individuals have a right not to be subject to such automated decisions. How this works in practice, given the increased reliance on such processes and the recent advent of Big Data processes, remains to be fully seen.

KEY WORDS

- Right not to be subject to a decision based solely on automated processing.
- Including profiling.
- Producing legal effects concerning or similarly significantly affecting the individual data subject.

22

RIGHT TO PREVENT DIRECT MARKETING PROCESSING

Introduction

Individual data subjects have a right to prevent processing for direct marketing purposes. Where personal data are kept for the purpose of direct marketing, the individual data subject concerned can request the controller in writing

- Not to process the data for that purpose; or
- To cease processing the data for that purpose.

If requested to cease processing, the controller, not more than a specified number of days after the request, must erase the data; and where the data are kept for that purpose and other purposes, cease processing the data for that purpose. The controller must notify the individual data subject in writing and, where appropriate, inform them of those other purposes.

Where a controller anticipates that personal data, including personal data that are required by law to be made available to the public, will be processed for the purposes of direct marketing, the controller must inform the persons to whom the data relates that they may object, by means of a request in writing to the controller and free of charge, to such processing.

Background Guidance

Where personal data are processed for the purposes of direct marketing, the individual data subject should have the right to object to such processing, including profiling to the extent that it is related to such direct marketing, whether with regard to initial or further processing, at any time and free of charge. That right should be explicitly brought to the attention of the individual data subject and presented clearly and separately from any other information.*

Legal Rule

Article 21 of the GDPR refers as follows. Where personal data are processed for direct marketing purposes, the data subject must have the right to object at any time to processing of personal data concerning them for such marketing, which includes profiling to the extent that it is related to such direct marketing.

Where the data subject objects to processing for direct marketing purposes, the personal data must no longer be processed for such purposes.

This has significant consequence, given that marketing is so central to many organizations.

Conclusion

Marketing and direct marketing are very important for many organizations. However, the ability to engage in marketing to known individuals is not unlimited. For example, industry codes may apply. In addition, the data protection regime provides that individual data subjects have a right to object (in advance) to and not be subject to direct marketing.

KEY CONCEPTS

Direct marketing is a concern for the public, consumer bodies, and regulators. There are restrictions or controls on the extent to which organizations operate marketing data. In terms of data protection, the rule is that individual data subjects have a right to object to data protection for use in direct marketing activities.

---

* GDPR Recital 70.

KEYWORDS

- Personal data for marketing.
- Right to object to processing of personal data for direct marketing.
- Includes profiling for direct marketing.
- Can object at any time.

23
PORTABILITY

Introduction

The GDPR includes a new right to data portability for individual data subjects. The difficulties experienced by individuals seeking to move from one (technology) service provider to another when the first organization may be unable or unwilling to transfer the necessary customer personal data to the alternative service provider are recognized. This is referred to as *porting* or *portability*.

Background Guidance on Automated Processing and Portability

To further strengthen the control over their own data, where the processing of personal data is carried out by automated means, the individual data subject should also be allowed to receive personal data concerning them, which they have provided to a controller, in a structured, commonly used, machine-readable and interoperable format, and to transmit them to another controller. Controllers should be encouraged to develop interoperable formats that enable data portability. That right should apply where the individual data subject provided the personal data on the basis of their consent, or the processing is necessary for the performance of a contract. It should not apply where processing is based on a legal ground other than consent or contract. By its very nature, that right should not be exercised against controllers processing personal data in the exercise of their public duties. It should therefore not apply where the processing of the personal data is necessary for compliance with a legal obligation to which the controller is subject or for the performance of a task carried out in the public interest or in the exercise of an official authority vested in the controller. The individual data subject's right to transmit or receive personal data concerning them should not create an obligation for the controllers to adopt or maintain processing systems that are technically compatible. Where, in a certain set of personal data, more than one individual data subject is concerned, the right to receive the personal data should be without prejudice to the rights of other individual data subjects in accordance with the General Data Protection Regulation (GDPR). Furthermore, that right should not prejudice the right of the individual data subject to obtain the erasure of personal data and the limitations of that right as set out in the GDPR and should, in particular, not imply the erasure of personal data concerning the individual data subject that have been provided by them for the performance of a contract to the extent that and for as long as the personal data are necessary for the performance of that contract. Where technically feasible, the individual data subject should have the right to have the personal data transmitted directly from one controller to another.[*]

Legal Rule

Article 20 of the new GDPR refers to the right to data portability. The individual data subject must have the right to receive the personal data concerning them, which they have provided to a controller, in a structured, commonly used, and machine-readable format and have the right to transmit those data to another controller without hindrance from the controller to which the personal data have been provided, where

- The processing is based on consent pursuant to Article 6(1) (a) or Article 9(2)(a) or on a contract pursuant to Article 6(1) (b); and
- The processing is carried out by automated means.

In exercising their right to data portability pursuant to the above, the individual data subject must have the right to have the personal data transmitted directly from one controller to another where technically feasible.[†] It remains to be seen how this will apply in practice, and also more nuanced issues, such as how it may apply differently across different industries.

---

[*] GDPR Recital 68.
[†] GDPR Article 20(2).

The exercise of this right must be without prejudice to Article 17. That right must not apply to processing necessary for the performance of a task carried out in the public interest or in the exercise of official authority vested in the controller.* The portability right referred to must not adversely affect the rights of others.†

Conclusion

Organizations, particularly those in service sectors, need to accommodate competitors and individuals when they wish to change service providers by allowing the transfer of customer histories and personal data to the new service provider. Otherwise, the blocking of such data portability can mean that the new provider does not have enough information to actually provide the service, thus blocking the change-over. Portability and the portability right will become ever more important as telephone (fixed and mobile), technology, and other services continue to advance.

KEY CONCEPTS

Across all industries, especially service industries, competition means that customers will move from one provider organization to another over time. However, a difficulty can arise where certain historical personal data of the customer in the possession of the original service provider organization are not made available or transferred to the new service provider. The new provider may need these data to provide the service. The move to the new provider can be prevented if the original provider refuses or otherwise does not facilitate the data transfer. A right to the transfer, portability, or porting of the personal data to the new provider is granted to the individual data subject.

---

* GDPR Article 20(3).
† GDPR Article 20(4).

KEYWORDS

- Portability.
- Portability of data.
- Transfer from one service provider to another.
- Right to transfer of associated personal data from first provider to second provider.
- Technical necessity for service supply.

24

OUTSOURCING TO THIRD-PARTY DATA PROCESSORS

Introduction

While many organizations may feel that they do not engage third parties to deal with their personal data, processes, and databases, closer inspection often indicates that this assumption is not correct. Many organizations, across all sectors of activity, engage third parties or outsource certain of their internal activities.*

One example is where an organization may find it more convenient to outsource its payroll functions to another organization specializing in such activities. It is necessary, therefore, that the employee personal data, or certain of them, are transferred to the third-party organization for processing. This third party is a processor acting for the organization. A contract must be in place and appropriate security standards implemented.

Sometimes, organizations outsource other activities, such as marketing, recruitment, or employment of consultants or agents or part-time employees. Organizations increasingly outsource market research and customer satisfaction surveys to third parties. These are all processors for which personal data are involved.

If an organization must transfer or export personal data outside of the EU and lawfully permit transfers outside of the restriction ban, it must satisfy the following, as appropriate

- An export to one of the safe permitted countries; or
- An export to the United States under the new Safe Harbor program; or

---

* See generally Van Alsenoy, "Allocating Responsibility among Controllers, Processors, and 'Everything in between': The Definition of Actors and Roles in Directive 95/46/EC," *Computer Law & Security Review* (2012) (28) 25; Morgan, "Data Controllers, Data Processors and Data Sharers," *Computers and Law* (March 4, 2011).

- An export pursuant to the accepted standard contractual clauses; or
- An export pursuant to the accepted binding corporate rules.

Background Guidance

To ensure compliance with the requirements of the GDPR in respect of the processing to be carried out by the processor on behalf of the controller, when entrusting a processor with processing activities, the controller should use only processors providing sufficient guarantees, in particular in terms of expert knowledge, reliability, and resources, to implement technical and organizational measures that will meet the requirements of the GDPR, including for the security of processing. The adherence of the processor to an approved code of conduct or an approved certification mechanism may be used as an element to demonstrate compliance with the obligations of the controller. The carrying-out of processing by a processor should be governed by a contract or other legal act under EU or member state law, binding the processor to the controller and setting out the subject matter and duration of the processing, the nature and purposes of the processing, the type of personal data, and categories of individual data subjects, taking into account the specific tasks and responsibilities of the processor in the context of the processing to be carried out and the risk to the rights of the individual data subject. The controller and processor may choose to use an individual contract or standard contractual clauses that are adopted either directly by the EU Commission or by a data protection supervisory authority in accordance with the consistency mechanism and then adopted by the EU Commission. After the completion of the processing on behalf of the controller, the processor should, at the choice of the controller, return or delete the personal data, unless there is a requirement to store the personal data under EU or member state law to which the processor is subject.*

Where processing is to be carried out on behalf of a controller, the controller must use only processors providing sufficient guarantees to implement appropriate technical and organizational measures in such a manner that processing will meet the requirements of the General

---

* GDPR Recital 81.

Data Protection Regulation (GDPR) and ensure the protection of the rights of the individual data subject.*

The processor must not engage another processor without the prior specific or general written authorization of the controller. In the case of general written authorization, the processor must inform the controller of any intended changes concerning the addition or replacement of other processors, thereby giving the controller the opportunity to object to such changes.†

Processing by a processor must be governed by a contract or other legal act under EU or member state law, which is binding on the processor with regard to the controller and which sets out the subject matter and duration of the processing, the nature and purpose of the processing, the type of personal data and categories of individual data subjects, and the obligations and rights of the controller. That contract or other legal act must stipulate, in particular, that the processor

- Processes the personal data only on documented instructions from the controller, including with regard to transfers of personal data to a third country or an international organization, unless required to do so by EU or member state law to which the processor is subject; in such a case, the processor must inform the controller of that legal requirement before processing, unless that law prohibits such information on important grounds of public interest.
- Ensures that persons authorized to process the personal data have committed themselves to confidentiality or are under an appropriate statutory obligation of confidentiality.
- Takes all measures required pursuant to Article 32.
- Respects the conditions referred to in paragraphs 2 and 4 for engaging another processor.
- Taking into account the nature of the processing, assists the controller by appropriate technical and organizational measures, insofar as this is possible, for the fulfillment of the controller's obligation to respond to requests for exercising the individual data subject's rights laid down in GDPR Chapter III.

---

* GDPR Article 28(1).
† GDPR Article 28(2).

- Assists the controller in ensuring compliance with the obligations pursuant to Articles 32 to 36 taking into account the nature of processing and the information available to the processor.
- At the choice of the controller, deletes or returns all the personal data to the controller after the end of the provision of services relating to processing, and deletes existing copies unless EU or member state law requires storage of the personal data.
- Makes available to the controller all information necessary to demonstrate compliance with the obligations laid down in this Article and allow for and contribute to audits, including inspections, conducted by the controller or another auditor mandated by the controller. (The processor must immediately inform the controller if, in its opinion, an instruction infringes the GDPR or other EU or member state data protection provisions).*

Legal Rule

Where a processor engages another processor for carrying out specific processing activities on behalf of the controller, the same data protection obligations as set out in the contract or other legal act between the controller and the processor as referred to in paragraph 3 must be imposed on that other processor by way of a contract or other legal act under EU or member state law, in particular providing sufficient guarantees to implement appropriate technical and organizational measures in such a manner that the processing will meet the requirements of the GDPR. Where that other processor fails to fulfill its data protection obligations, the initial processor must remain fully liable to the controller for the performance of that other processor's obligations.†

---

* GDPR Article 28(3).
† GDPR Article 28(4).

Adherence of a processor to an approved code of conduct* or an approved certification mechanism[†] may be used as an element by which to demonstrate sufficient guarantees as referred to in paragraphs 1 and 4 of this Article.[‡]

Without prejudice to an individual contract between the controller and the processor, the contract or the other legal act referred to in paragraphs 3 and 4 of this Article may be based, in whole or in part, on standard contractual clauses referred to in paragraphs 7 and 8 of this Article, including when they are part of a certification granted to the controller or processor.[§]

The EU Commission may lay down standard contractual clauses for the matters referred to in paragraph 3 and 4 of this Article and in accordance with the examination procedure referred to in Article 93(2).[¶]

A data protection supervisory authority may adopt standard contractual clauses for the matters referred to in paragraph 3 and 4 of this Article and in accordance with the consistency mechanism referred to in Article 63.[**]

The contract or the other legal act referred to in paragraphs 3 and 4 must be in writing, including in electronic form.[††]

Without prejudice to Articles 82, 83 and 84, if a processor infringes the GDPR by determining the purposes and means of processing, the processor must be considered to be a controller in respect of that processing.[‡‡]

Processing under Authority

Article 27 refers to processing under the authority of the controller and processor and provides that the processor and any person acting under the authority of the controller or of the processor who has access

---

* As referred to in GDPR Article 40.
[†] As referred to in GDPR Article 42.
[‡] GDPR Article 28(5).
[§] Pursuant to Articles 42 and 43. GDPR Article 28(6).
[¶] GDPR Article 28(7).
[**] GDPR Article 28(8).
[††] GDPR Article 28(9).
[‡‡] GDPR Article 28(10).

to personal data must not process them except on instructions from the controller, unless required to do so by EU or member state law.

Processors and Security

Processors also have obligations in relation to processing personal data and security. Where the processing of personal data is carried out by a processor on behalf of a controller, then the controller must have a contract in writing in place with the processor, containing certain clauses and obligations. The contracts with processors must address the following

- The processing must be carried out in pursuance of a contract in writing or another equivalent form.
- The contract must provide that the processor carries out the processing only on, and subject to, the instructions of the controller.
- The processor must comply with the "security" requirements.

There are also certain other requirements. The controller

- Must ensure that the processor provides sufficient guarantees in respect of the technical security measures and organizational measures governing the processing.
- Must take reasonable steps to ensure compliance with these measures.

Processors also have compliance obligations under the new GDPR.

New Processor Requirements

The new GDPR explicitly refers to processors. Chapter IV of the new GDPR is headed "Controller and processor." Processors from outside of the EU may have to designate a representative in the EU.* Article 26 of the GDPR is headed as referring to processors. It provides that where processing is to be carried out on behalf of a controller, the controller shall use only processors providing sufficient guarantees to implement appropriate technical and organizational measures in such

---

* GDPR Article 27.

a manner that processing will meet the requirements of the GDPR and ensure the protection of the rights of the individual data subject.*

It should be noted, therefore, that there is no discretion left for organizations. They "shall" or must comply as regards the new requirements. The data controller organization must ensure that there is proper compliance. It follows also that the controller is responsible when there is non-compliance, or indeed, insufficient compliance.

The processor organization (or individual, e.g., outsource contractor) must also comply with the data protection regime. Security is the most obvious example. However, there are other obligations.

Controller Records

Each controller and, where applicable, the controller's representative shall maintain a record of processing activities under its responsibility. That record shall contain all of the following information

- The name and contact details of the controller and, where applicable, the joint controller, the controller's representative, and the data protection officer.
- The purposes of the processing.
- A description of the categories of individual data subjects and of the categories of personal data.
- The categories of recipients to whom the personal data have been or will be disclosed, including recipients in third countries or international organizations.
- Where applicable, transfers of personal data to a third country or an international organization, including the identification of that third country or international organization and, in the case of transfers referred to in the second subparagraph of Article 49(1), the documentation of suitable safeguards.
- Where possible, the envisaged time limits for erasure of the different categories of data.
- Where possible, a general description of the technical and organizational security measures.†

---

* GDPR Article 28(1).
† Referred to in Article 32(1). GDPR Article 30(1).

Processor Records

Each processor and, where applicable, the processor's representative shall maintain a record of all categories of processing activities carried out on behalf of a controller, containing

- The name and contact details of the processor or processors and of each controller on behalf of which the processor is acting, and, where applicable, of the controller's or the processor's representative and the data protection officer.
- The categories of processing carried out on behalf of each controller.
- Where applicable, transfers of personal data to a third country or an international organization, including the identification of that third country or international organization and, in the case of transfers referred to in the second subparagraph of Article 49(1), the documentation of suitable safeguards.
- Where possible, a general description of the technical and organizational security measures.*

These records must be in writing, including in electronic form.†

The controller or the processor and, where applicable, the controller's or the processor's representative must make the record available to the data protection supervisory authority on request.‡

The obligations referred to in paragraphs 1 and 2 must not apply to an enterprise or an organization employing fewer than 250 persons unless the processing it carries out is likely to result in a risk to the rights of individual data subjects, the processing is not occasional, or the processing includes special categories of data§ or personal data relating to criminal convictions and offenses.¶

In terms of security, the processor (as controller) should consult technical standards-setting organizations, which sometimes have guidelines and standards in terms of technical security. Examples include

---

* Security measures referred to in Article 32(1). GDPR Article 30(2).
† GDPR Article 30(3).
‡ GDPR Article 30(4).
§ As referred to in Article 9(1).
¶ Referred to in Article 10. GDPR Article 30(5).

- ISO 27001 relating to data security.
- ISO 31000.
- ISO TC262.
- ISO 15408.
- BS10012:2009.

Conclusion

It is also important that the organization undertakes ongoing assessments and checks regarding the operation of the data processing undertaken by the processor. This should also include the security and compliance measures. This will be an increasing issue as personal data continues to expand in the online environment.

KEY CONCEPTS

Organizations need to be aware that they need to be responsible about what data they transfer to third-party organizations on their behalf. While this is permitted, appropriate contractual documentation must be in place. Safeguards must be in place also. Records must be maintained. Organizations should consider that they need to be alerted by the third-party processor if and when problems arise, such as a data breach. Another consideration is whether there are limits on the transfer to ensure that only the data that are necessary for the particular task or activity are transferred; that is, that there is no over-sharing or disclosure of too much data. The respective tasks should be clearly understood and delineated in writing. Escalation points and contact points should be clearly known.

KEY WORDS

- Controller.
- Processor.
- Outsource tasks and activities.
- Contracts, schedules, documentation, specification.

- Escalation.
- Reporting.
- Problem issues.
- Contacts.
- Data protection supervisory authority.
- Data protection officer.
- Representatives.
- Rights carry-through issues.
- Records.

FURTHER READING

- Burnett, *Outsourcing IT: The Legal Aspects: Planning, Contracting, Managing and the Law* (Gower, 2009).
- Burnett, *Outsourcing: The Legal Contract* (Faculty of Information Technology of the Institute of Chartered Accountants, 2005).
- Room, *Butterworths Data and Cyber Security Law and Practice* (Butterworths, 2009).
- Room, *Butterworths Data Security Law and Practice by Stewart Room* (Butterworths, 2014).

25

CHILDREN

Introduction

The issue of children in the data protection regime has been steadily rising. The increased use of social media and Web 2.0 services enhances the exposures and risks for children and the uninitiated.* These concerns are expressed by children's groups, regulators, and also the Article 29 Data Protection Working Party (WP29) (now replaced by the European Data Protection Board [EDPB]). WP29 issued "Opinion on the Protection of Children's Personal Data (General Guidelines and the Special Case of Schools)"† and also "Working Document on the Protection of Children's Personal Data (General Guidelines and the Special Case of Schools)."‡ Schools are being encouraged to be proactive and to have appropriate codes and policies for children's social media and Internet usage.§

There is now going to be an explicit acknowledgement of children's interest in the EU data protection regime, unlike with the 1995 data protection directive (DPD95), which contained no explicit reference. The General Data Protection Regulation (GDPR) originally defined a child as any person below the age of 16 years. This is significant, among other things, in relation to consent, contracting, and so on.

---

* See, for example, Gourlay and Gallagher, "Collecting and Using Children's Information Online: The UK/US Dichotomy," *Computers and Law* (December 12, 2011).

† WP19 Opinion 2/2009.

‡ WP29 Working Document 1/2008.

§ Note generally, for example, Groppe, "A Child's Playground or a Predator's Hunting Ground?: How to Protect Children on Internet Social Networking Sites," *CommLaw Conspectus* (2007) (16) 215; Steadman, "MySpace, but Whose Responsibility? Liability of Social Networking Websites When Offline Sexual Assault of Minors Follows Online Interaction," *Villanova Sports and Entertainment Law Journal* (2007) (14) 363; Beckstrom, "Who's Looking at Your Facebook Profile? The Use of Student Conduct Codes to Censor College Students' Online Speech," *Willamette Law Review* (2008) 261.

It is also significant for social networks that have significant numbers of children. Up until now it has been common for certain social networks to aim to accept users only over the age of 13. Now that a child has been defined in the first version of the GDPR as up to 16 (but later reduced), this may require careful assessment in relation to social media contracts, terms, processes, sign ups, and so on.

The issue of children in the data protection regime has been steadily rising. The increased use of social media and Web 2.0 services enhances the exposures and risks for children and the uninitiated.* Children merit specific protection with regard to their personal data, as they may be less aware of the risks, consequences, and safeguards concerned and their rights in relation to the processing of personal data. Such specific protection should, in particular, apply to the use of personal data of children for the purposes of marketing or creating personality or user profiles and the collection of personal data with regard to children when using services offered directly to a child. The consent of the holder of parental responsibility should not be necessary in the context of preventive or counseling services offered directly to a child.† Given that children merit specific protection, any information and communication, where processing is addressed to a child, should be in such clear and plain language that the child can easily understand it.‡ The GDPR makes new provisions in relation to conditions for children's consent for information society services.

Background Guidance

The background Recitals refer to the increasing concerns over children and personal data and provide background context.

Children Merit Specific Protection

Children merit specific protection with regard to their personal data, as they may be less aware of the risks, consequences, and safeguards

---

* Gourlay and Gallagher, "Collecting and Using Children's Information Online: The UK/US Dichotomy," *Computers and Law* (December 12, 2011).
† GDPR Recital 38.
‡ GDPR Recital 58.

concerned and their rights in relation to the processing of personal data. Such specific protection should, in particular, apply to the use of the personal data of children for the purposes of marketing or creating personality or user profiles and the collection of personal data with regard to children when using services offered directly to a child. The consent of the holder of parental responsibility should not be necessary in the context of preventive or counseling services offered directly to a child.*

Transparency and Children

Given that children merit specific protection, any information and communication, where processing is addressed to a child, should be in such clear and plain language that the child can easily understand it.[†]

Legal Rules

It is important for organizations to note the definition of "child" in the GDPR. This will have implications for how organizations

- Consider the interaction with children and what personal data may be collected and processed
- Ensure that there is appropriate compliance for such collection and processing for children as distinct from adults

Age

Article 6, referring to the lawfulness of processing or the legitimate processing conditions, provides that processing is necessary for the purposes of the legitimate interests pursued by the controller or by a third party, except where such interests are overridden by the interests or fundamental rights of the individual data subject, which require protection of personal data, "in particular where the data subject is a child."[‡]

---

* GDPR Recital 38.
[†] GDPR Recital 58.
[‡] GDPR Article 6(1)(f).

The original EU Commission proposal for the GDPR defined a "child" as any person below the age of 18 years. This is significant in relation to consent, contracting, and so on. It is significant for social networks that have significant numbers of children. Up until now it has been common for certain social networks to accept users only over the age of 13. Defining a child as up to 18 necessitated careful assessment in relation to social media contracts, terms, processes, registrations, sign ups, and so on. However, the final agreed version of the GDPR refers instead to a child "below the age of 16 years" with the option for member states to refer to 13 years. This is in Article 8, which is an Article other than the definitions section.*

Article 8 of the final version of the GDPR contains particular provisions in relation to the processing of the personal data of a child. Article 8(1) provides that

> where the individual data subject must have the right to obtain from the controller restriction of processing where one of the following applies

- The accuracy of the personal data is contested by the individual data subject, for a period enabling the controller to verify the accuracy of the personal data.
- The processing is unlawful, and the individual data subject opposes the erasure of the personal data and requests the restriction of their use instead.
- The controller no longer needs the personal data for the purposes of the processing, but they are required by the individual data subject for the establishment, exercise, or defense of legal claims.
- The individual data subject has objected to processing pursuant to Article 21(1) pending the verification of whether the legitimate grounds of the controller override those of the individual data subject.

---

* Note general commentary at Jasmontaite and De Hert, "The EU, Children under 13 Years, and Parental Consent: A Human Rights Analysis of a New, Age-Based Bright-Line for the Protection of Children on the Internet," *International Data Privacy Law* (2014) (5:1) 20.

Where processing has been restricted under this rule, such personal data must, with the exception of storage, only be processed with the individual data subject's consent, or for the establishment, exercise, or defense of legal claims, or for the protection of the rights of another natural or legal person, or for reasons of important public interest of the EU or of a member state.*

An individual data subject who has obtained restriction of processing must be informed by the controller before the restriction of processing is lifted.†

No Legitimate Interest Processing of Personal Data of Child

Article 6 refers to lawfulness of processing or the legitimate processing conditions. This is relevant, as it refers to children. One of the legitimate processing conditions, which many organizations may seek to rely on, or fall within, is

> processing ... necessary for the purposes of the legitimate interests pursued by the controller.

However, there is a caveat, which means that this cannot be relied on by organizations where the processing relates to the personal data of a child. It states:

> except where such interests are overridden by the interests or fundamental rights and freedoms of the data subject ... in particular where the data subject is a child.

Therefore, organizations cannot seek to lawfully process the personal data of a child by referring to their own "legitimate interests." The legitimate interest ground cannot be relied on, and one of the other grounds must be looked at.‡

Child's Consent and Conditions for Information Society Services

The processing of children's personal data is referred to in Recital 389. Article 8 of the GDPR makes new provisions in relation to conditions

---

* GDPR Article 18(2).
† GDPR Article 18(3).
‡ GDPR Article 6(1)(f).

for children's consent for information society services. Where Article 6(1)(a) (i.e., consent) applies, in relation to the offering of information society services directly to a child, the processing of personal data of a child below the age of 16 years, or, if provided for by member state law, a lower age, which shall not be below 13 years, shall only be lawful if and to the extent that such consent is given or authorized by the holder of parental responsibility over the child.*

Note that member states may provide for an age of 13 years.

The controller must make reasonable efforts to verify in such cases that consent is given or authorized by the holder of parental responsibility over the child, taking into consideration available technology.†️ This must not affect the general contract law of member states, such as the rules on the validity, formation, or effect of a contract in relation to a child.‡

Transparency and Children

Article 12 of the GDPR provides that the controller must take appropriate measures to provide any information referred to in Articles 13 and 14 and any communication under Articles 15 to 22 and 34 relating to processing to the data subject in a concise, transparent, intelligible, and easily accessible form, using clear and plain language, "in particular for any information addressed specifically to a child." The information must be provided in writing or by other means, including, where appropriate, by electronic means. When requested by the data subject, the information may be provided orally, provided that the identity of the data subject is proved by other means.

Codes of Conduct and Certification

Article 40(2)(g) of the GDPR refers to bodies being able to provide codes of conduct with regard to "the information provided to, and the protection of, children, and the manner in which the consent of the holders of parental responsibility over children is to be obtained."

---

* GDPR Article 8(1).
† GDPR Article 8(3).
‡ GDPR Article 8(3).

Data Protection Supervisory Authority

The tasks of the data protection supervisory authority include having to "promote public awareness and understanding of the risks, rules, safeguards and rights in relation to processing. *Activities addressed specifically to children shall receive specific attention.*"*

Conclusion

The explicit reference to children is new and, some would argue, overdue. Increasingly, the activities of children on the Internet and on social media are posing risks and concerns.[†] This has been further emphasized of late with tragic events involving online abuse, in particular cyber-bullying. Risks obviously arise from children's activities online (e.g., inappropriate content, cyber-bullying, but also from the collection and use of their personal data online and collected online, sometimes without their knowledge or consent). Their personal data and privacy are more vulnerable than those of older people.

The issues and concerns in relation to children's personal data are continually increasing. This has increased as children's activity has increased online and on new communications technologies. The new GDPR is just one example of rules in the United States and the EU that seek to protect the interests of children. Organizations should seek to differentiate considerations for children's personal data from adults' personal data in relation to the organization's activities.

KEY CONCEPTS

It is important for organizations to note the indirect definition of "child" in the GDPR. A child was defined in the original EU Commission proposal for the GDPR to mean any person below the age of 18 years. Ultimately, the final agreed version of the GDPR has been amended to 13 years.

---

* GDPR Article 57(1)(b). Emphasis added.
† See, for example, McDermott, "Legal Issues Associated with Minors and Their Use of Social Networking Sites," *Communications Law* (2012) (17) 19.

KEYWORDS

- Children.
- Children's issues and concerns.
- Children's personal data.
- Consent.
- Internet and information society services.
- Prior information.
- Restriction of processing.

FURTHER READING

- Gourlay and Gallagher, "Collecting and Using Children's Information Online: The UK/US Dichotomy," *Computers and Law* (December 12, 2011).
- Lambert, *Social Networking: Law, Rights and Policy* (Clarus, 2014).
- Lambert, *International Handbook of Social Media Laws* (Bloomsbury, 2015).

26

INCREASED PENALTIES AND FINES

Introduction

US organizations need to be particularly mindful of EU data protection rules given the new fines and penalties regime, the increase in fines, and the express inclusion of worldwide turnover as a factor.

Background Guidance

To strengthen the enforcement of the rules of the General Data Protection Regulation (GDPR), penalties including administrative fines should be imposed for any infringement of the GDPR in addition to, or instead of, appropriate measures imposed by the data protection supervisory authority pursuant to the GDPR. In the case of a minor infringement, or if the fine likely to be imposed would constitute a disproportionate burden to a natural person, a reprimand may be issued instead of a fine. Due regard should, however, be given to

- The nature, gravity, and duration of the infringement.
- The intentional character of the infringement.
- Actions taken to mitigate the damage suffered.
- Degree of responsibility.
- Any relevant previous infringements.
- The manner in which the infringement became known to the data protection supervisory authority.
- Compliance with measures ordered against the controller or processor.
- Adherence to a code of conduct.
- Any other aggravating or mitigating factor.*

---

* GDPR Recital 148.

The imposition of penalties including administrative fines should be subject to appropriate procedural safeguards in accordance with the general principles of EU law and the EU Charter, including effective judicial protection and due process.*

To strengthen and harmonize administrative penalties for infringements of the GDPR, each data protection supervisory authority should have the power to impose administrative fines. The GDPR should indicate infringements and the upper limit and criteria for setting the related administrative fines, which should be determined by the competent data protection supervisory authority in each individual case, taking into account all relevant circumstances of the specific situation, with due regard in particular to

- The nature, gravity, and duration of the infringement.
- Its consequences.
- The measures taken to ensure compliance with the obligations under the GDPR and to prevent or mitigate the consequences of the infringement.†

Where administrative fines are imposed on an organization, an organization should be understood to be an undertaking in accordance with Articles 101 and 102 of the Treaty on the Functioning of the European Union (TFEU) for those purposes. Where administrative fines are imposed on persons that are not an undertaking, the data protection supervisory authority should take account of the general level of income in the member state as well as the economic situation of the person in considering the appropriate amount of the fine. The consistency mechanism may also be used to promote a consistent application of administrative fines. It should be for the member states to determine whether and to what extent public authorities should be subject to administrative fines. Imposing an administrative fine or giving a warning does not affect the application of other powers of the data protection supervisory authorities or of other penalties under the GDPR.‡

---

* GDPR Recital 148.
† GDPR Recital 150.
‡ GDPR Recital 150.

Fines of Ten Million

Infringements of the following provisions must be subject to administrative fines up to €10,000,000 or in the case of an organization, up to 2% of the total worldwide annual turnover of the preceding financial year, whichever is higher

- The obligations of the controller and the processor pursuant to Articles 8, 11, 25–39, 42 and 43.
- The obligations of the certification body.*
- The obligations of the monitoring body.†

Articles 8, 11, 25–39, 42 and 43, respectively, refer to

Article 8: Conditions applicable to child's consent in relation to information society services

Article 11: Processing that does not require identification

Article 25: Data protection by design and by default

Article 26: Joint controllers

Article 27: Representatives of controllers or processors not established in the EU

Article 28: Processor

Article 29: Processing under the authority of the controller or processor

Article 30: Records of processing activities

Article 31: Cooperation with the supervisory authority

Article 32: Security of processing

Article 33: Notification of a personal data breach to the supervisory authority

Article 34: Communication of a personal data breach to the data subject

Article 35: Data protection impact assessment

Article 36: Prior consultation

Article 37: Designation of the data protection officer

Article 38: Position of the data protection officer

Article 39: Tasks of the data protection officer

Article 42: Certification

Article 43: Certification bodies

---

* Pursuant to Articles 42 and 43.
† GDPR Article 83(4). That is, a monitoring body pursuant to Article 41(4).

Fines of Twenty Million

Infringements of the following provisions must, in accordance with paragraph 2, be subject to administrative fines up to €20,000,000 or in the case of an organization, up to 4% of the total worldwide annual turnover of the preceding financial year, whichever is higher

- The basic principles for processing, including conditions for consent, pursuant to Articles 5, 6, 7, and 9.
- The data subjects' rights.*
- The transfers of personal data to a recipient in a third country or an international organization.†
- Any obligations pursuant to member state law.‡
- Non-compliance with an order or a temporary or definitive limitation on processing or the suspension of data flows by the data protection supervisory authority§ or failure to provide access in violation of Article 58(1).¶

Articles 5, 6, 7, and 9, and Article 58(1), respectively, refer to

Article 5: Principles relating to processing of personal data
Article 6: Lawfulness of processing
Article 7: Conditions for consent
Article 9: Processing of special categories of personal data
Article 58(1): Investigative powers of the data protection supervisory authority

Fines for Non-Compliance with Data Protection
Supervisory Authority Order

Non-compliance with an order by the data protection supervisory authority as referred to in Article 58(2) must, in accordance with paragraph 2 of this Article, be subject to administrative fines up to €20,000,000, or in the case of an organization, up to 4% of the total

---

* Pursuant to GDPR Articles 12 to 22.
† Pursuant to GDPR Articles 44 to 49.
‡ Adopted under GDPR Chapter IX.
§ Pursuant to GDPR Article 58(2).
¶ GDPR Article 83(5).

worldwide annual turnover of the preceding financial year, whichever is higher.*

Without prejudice to the corrective powers of data protection supervisory authorities pursuant to Article 58(2), each member state may lay down the rules on whether and to what extent administrative fines may be imposed on public authorities and bodies established in that member state.†

The exercise by the data protection supervisory authority of its powers under this Article must be subject to appropriate procedural safeguards in accordance with EU and member state law, including effective judicial remedy and due process.‡

Where the legal system of the member state does not provide for administrative fines, this Article may be applied in such a manner that the fine is initiated by the competent data protection supervisory authority and imposed by competent national courts, while ensuring that those legal remedies are effective and have an equivalent effect to the administrative fines imposed by data protection supervisory authorities. In any event, the fines imposed must be effective, proportionate, and dissuasive.§

Without prejudice to the corrective powers of data protection supervisory authorities pursuant to Article 58(2), each member state may lay down the rules on whether and to what extent administrative fines may be imposed on public authorities and bodies established in that member state.¶ So, there is some potential for non-compliance and breaches for the public sector being graduated somewhat from the commercial sector, if particular national laws were to attempt to set double standards. One should bear in mind that there are many data breaches reported in terms of the public sector, so the concerns are not limited to the private sector.

The exercise by the data protection supervisory authority of its powers under this Article must be subject to appropriate procedural

---

* GDPR Article 83(6).
† GDPR Article 84(7).
‡ GDPR Article 84(8).
§ GDPR Article 83(9). Those member states must notify to the EU Commission the provisions of their laws that they adopt pursuant to this paragraph by May 25, 2018 and, without delay, any subsequent amendment law or amendment affecting them.
¶ GDPR Article 83(7).

safeguards in accordance with EU and member state law, including effective judicial remedy and due process.*

Where the legal system of the member state does not provide for administrative fines, this Article may be applied in such a manner that the fine is initiated by the competent data protection supervisory authority and imposed by competent national courts, while ensuring that those legal remedies are effective and have an equivalent effect to the administrative fines imposed by data protection supervisory authorities. In any event, the fines imposed must be effective, proportionate, and dissuasive.†

Impact

Organizations might consider that Sony was fined £250,000 in relation to specific hacking data breaches of the PlayStation Network (PSN) (which occurred in 2011) by the UK data protection supervisory authority (Information Commissioner's Office [ICO]). The breaches were described as negligent and preventable.

Sony sales for the third quarter 2015 are reported as $21.4 billion,‡ which if multiplied for four quarters could be $85.6 billion (while acknowledging that this might not be a full annual reflection, as certain quarters can be better than others). So, a contemporary fine for a security data breach post the GDPR could be up to €10,000,000 or 2% of $85.6 billion, whichever is higher.

Other breaches could be even higher. Consider an organization with an annual turnover of $100 billion facing a fine of 4%, which would amount to $4 billion.

This emphasizes the significantly enhanced importance of data protection compliance by organizations. The cost of non-compliance is vastly increased by the new GDPR.

---

* GDPR Article 83(8).
† GDPR Article 83(9). Those member states must notify to the EU Commission the provisions of their laws that they adopt pursuant to this paragraph by May 25, 2018 and, without delay, any subsequent amendment law or amendment affecting them.
‡ Referred to in "Sony Reports a Jump in Fiscal Third Quarter Profit on PS4," *Economic Times*, January 29, 2016.

General Conditions for Imposing Administrative Fines

Article 83 of the new GDPR refers to general conditions for imposing administrative fines. Each data protection supervisory authority
must ensure that the imposition of administrative fines pursuant to
this Article in respect of infringements of the GDPR referred to in
paragraphs 4, 5, and 6 must in each individual case be *effective, proportionate, and dissuasive.**

Administrative fines must, depending on the circumstances of each
individual case, be imposed *in addition* to, or instead of, measures
referred to in Article 58(2)(a) to (h) and (j). When deciding whether
to impose an administrative fine and deciding on the amount of the
administrative fine in each individual case, due regard must be given
to the following

- The *nature*, *gravity*, and *duration* of the infringement, taking
  into account the nature, scope, or purpose of the processing
  concerned as well as the *number of data subjects* affected and
  the *level of damage* suffered by them.
- The *intentional or negligent* character of the infringement (consider, e.g., the Target and Sony data breach examples, where
  it is understood that particular risks were known in advance
  and documented but were not addressed. It could perhaps be
  argued that that this provision is wider in some respects than
  the Target and Sony examples, where particular risks were
  known).
- Any *action taken* by the controller or processor to mitigate the
  damage suffered by data subjects (actions before the breach
  and actions after the breach can arise).
- The *degree of responsibility* of the controller or processor, taking
  into account technical and organizational measures implemented by them pursuant to Articles 25 and 32.
- Any relevant *previous infringements* by the controller or
  processor.
- The degree of *cooperation* with the data protection supervisory
  authority to remedy the infringement and mitigate the possible adverse effects of the infringement.

---

* GDPR Article 83(1).

- The *categories* of personal data affected by the infringement.
- The manner in which the infringement became known to the data protection supervisory authority, in particular whether, and if so to what extent, the controller or processor *notified* the infringement.
- Where measures referred to in Article 58(2) have *previously* been *ordered* against the controller or processor concerned with regard to the same subject matter, compliance with those measures.
- Adherence to approved *codes* of conduct* or approved *certification* mechanisms.†
- *Any other* aggravating or mitigating *factor* applicable to the circumstances of the case, such as financial benefits gained, or losses avoided, directly or indirectly, from the infringement.‡ (Obviously, each case will vary; and it will also take some time to flesh out what these additional factors may be, both generally and specifically.)

If a controller or processor intentionally or negligently, for the same or linked processing operations, infringes several provisions of the GDPR, the total amount of the administrative fine must not exceed the amount specified for the gravest infringement.§ One can envisage that this potential aggregation capping provision may be contested in particular cases. The nuances of this provision will take some time to fully appreciate. It will be interesting to see whether it contrasts with provisions in certain US statutes that provide for penalties per spam communication, which therefore can add up to significant total fines even where only a sample of the breaches are taken into account.

Without prejudice to the corrective powers of data protection supervisory authorities pursuant to Article 58(2), each member state may lay down the rules on whether and to what extent administrative fines may be imposed on public authorities and bodies established in that member state.¶

---

* GDPR Article 40.
† GDPR Article 42.
‡ GDPR Article 83(2).
§ GDPR Article 83(3).
¶ GDPR Article 83(7).

The exercise by the data protection supervisory authority of its powers under this Article must be subject to appropriate procedural safeguards in accordance with EU and member state law, including effective judicial remedy and due process.*

Where the legal system of the member state does not provide for administrative fines, this Article may be applied in such a manner that the fine is initiated by the competent data protection supervisory authority and imposed by competent national courts, while ensuring that those legal remedies are effective and have an equivalent effect to the administrative fines imposed by data protection supervisory authorities. In any event, the fines imposed must be effective, proportionate, and dissuasive.†

Penalties

Article 84 of the new GDPR refers to penalties. Member states must lay down the rules on other penalties applicable to infringements of the GDPR in particular for infringements that are not subject to administrative fines pursuant to Article 83, and must take all measures necessary to ensure that they are implemented. Such penalties must be *effective, proportionate, and dissuasive*.‡

Therefore, in addition to the fines regime described, organizations need to be aware of the potential for additional penalties arising.

Member states must lay down the rules on other penalties applicable to infringements of the GDPR in particular for infringements that are not subject to administrative fines pursuant to Article 83, and must take all measures necessary to ensure that they are implemented. Such penalties must be effective, proportionate, and dissuasive.§

---

* GDPR Article 83(8).

† Those member states must notify to the EU Commission the provisions of their laws that they adopt pursuant to this paragraph by May 25, 2018 and, without delay, any subsequent amendment law or amendment affecting them. GDPR Article 83(9).

‡ GDPR Article 84(1). Each member state must notify to the EU Commission the provisions of its law that it adopts pursuant to paragraph 1, by May 25, 2018 and, without delay, any subsequent amendment affecting them. GDPR Article 84(2).

§ GDPR Article 84(1). Each member state must notify to the EU Commission the provisions of its law that it adopts pursuant to paragraph 1 by May 25, 2018 and, without delay, any subsequent amendment affecting them; see GDPR Article 84(2).

Organizations will need to review these separate issues in particular detail, as well as any changes that may occur or be introduced over time.

Enforcement

The data protection supervisory authority may investigate, or cause to be investigated, whether any of the provisions of the data protection rules have been, are being, or are likely to be contravened in relation to an individual, either where the individual complains to them of a contravention of any of those provisions *or* the data protection supervisory authority is otherwise of the opinion that there may be such a contravention. It is clear that the data protection supervisory authority need not wait for the receipt of an actual complaint.

Conclusion

As noted previously, the new GDPR sets out significant amendments to the prosecution and fines regime. The creation of new, significantly enhanced penalties in the new data protection regime will be a significant spur for many organizations to seriously consider data protection compliance. While the Federal Trade Commission (as well as competition law rules) in the US had imposed, and also consensually agreed, significant fines in relation to data protection issues, the increase in fines and penalties in the EU—including on a percentage of worldwide turnover level—raises the stakes for getting compliance wrong.

While it is important to get compliance right, it is also important to ensure compliance, and compliance with orders, in a prompt and timely manner. If not, this also opens up potential for penalties.

KEY CONCEPTS

Organizations can now be fined millions of euros or a percentage of turnover on a worldwide basis if they get data protection compliance wrong. The fines and penalties can vary depending on the type of breach involved

KEYWORDS

- Fines.
- Penalties.
- €10,000,000.
- 2% of the total worldwide annual turnover.
- €20,000,000.
- 4% of the total worldwide annual turnover.
- Breaches.
- Non-compliance.
- Additional penalty rules.

27

CODES OF CONDUCT AND CERTIFICATION

Introduction

Many commercial sectors have entered into various forms of industry codes and codes of conduct. The new General Data Protection Regulation (GDPR) refers to the possibility of codes of conduct and certification in relation to data protection.

Background Guidance: Codes of Conduct

Associations or other bodies representing categories of controllers or processors are encouraged to draw up codes of conduct so as to facilitate the effective application of the GDPR, taking account of the specific characteristics of the processing carried out in certain sectors and the specific needs of micro, small, and medium enterprises. In particular, such codes of conduct could calibrate the obligations of controllers and processors, taking into account the risk likely to result from the processing for the rights of natural persons.*

Codes of Conduct

Chapter IV, Section 5 of the GDPR refers to and is headed "Codes of Conduct and Certification." Article 40 refers to codes of conduct and provides that the member states, the data protection supervisory authorities, the European Data Protection Board (EDPB), and the EU Commission must encourage the drawing up of codes of conduct intended to contribute to the proper application of the GDPR, taking

---

* GDPR Recital 98.

account of the specific features of the various processing sectors and the specific needs of micro, small, and medium-sized enterprises.*

A code of conduct must contain mechanisms that enable the responsible body† to carry out the mandatory monitoring of compliance with its provisions by the controllers or processors that undertake to apply it, without prejudice to the tasks and powers of data protection supervisory authorities.‡

Associations and other bodies that intend to prepare a code of conduct or to amend or extend an existing code must submit the draft code, amendment, or extension to the data protection supervisory authority, which is competent pursuant to Article 55. The data protection supervisory authority must provide an opinion on whether the draft code, amendment, or extension complies with the GDPR and must approve that draft code, amendment, or extension if it finds that it provides sufficient appropriate safeguards.§

Where the draft code, amendment, or extension is approved, and where the code of conduct does not relate to processing activities in several member states, the data protection supervisory authority must register and publish the code.¶

Where a draft code of conduct relates to processing activities in several member states, the competent data protection supervisory authority must, before approving the draft code, amendment, or extension, submit it to the EDPB, which must provide an opinion on whether the draft code, amendment, or extension complies with the GDPR or provides appropriate safeguards.**

Where the opinion referred to confirms that the draft code, amendment, or extension complies with the GDPR or provides appropriate safeguards, the EDPB must submit its opinion to the EU Commission.††

---

* GDPR Article 40(1). The 1995 data protection directive (DPD95) also referred to codes of conduct. Chapter V, DPD95 Article27(1).

† Referred to in GDPR Article 41(1).

‡ GDPR Article 40(4).

§ GDPR Article 40(5).

¶ GDPR Article 40(6).

**GDPR Article 40(7).

††GDPR Article 40(8).

The EU Commission may, by way of implementing acts, decide that the approved code of conduct, amendment, or extension has general validity within the EU. Those implementing acts must be adopted in accordance with the examination procedure set out in Article 93(2).*

The EU Commission must ensure appropriate publicity for the approved codes that have been decided as having general validity in accordance with paragraph 9.† It must collate all approved codes of conduct, amendments, and extensions in a register and must make them publicly available by way of appropriate means.‡

Monitoring Approved Codes of Conduct

The new Article 41 refers to the monitoring of approved codes of conduct. Without prejudice to the tasks and powers of the competent data protection supervisory authority, the monitoring of compliance with a code of conduct may be carried out by a body that has an appropriate level of expertise in relation to the subject matter of the code and is accredited for that purpose by the competent data protection supervisory authority.§

A body as referred to in this section may be accredited to monitor compliance with a code of conduct where that body has

- Demonstrated its independence and expertise in relation to the subject matter of the code to the satisfaction of the competent data protection supervisory authority.
- Established procedures that allow it to assess the eligibility of controllers and processors concerned to apply the code, to monitor their compliance with its provisions, and to periodically review its operation.
- Established procedures and structures to handle complaints about infringements of the code or the manner in which the code has been, or is being, implemented by a controller or processor, and to make those procedures and structures transparent to individual data subjects and the public.

---

* GDPR Article 40(9).
† GDPR Article 40(10).
‡ GDPR Article 40(11).
§ GDPR Article 41(1).

- Demonstrated to the satisfaction of the competent data protection supervisory authority that its tasks and duties do not result in a conflict of interests.*

The competent data protection supervisory authority must submit the draft criteria for accreditation of a body as referred to in this section to the EDPB pursuant to the consistency mechanism referred to in Article 63.†

Without prejudice to the tasks and powers of the competent data protection supervisory authority and the provisions of GDPR Chapter VIII, a body as referred to in this section must, subject to appropriate safeguards, take appropriate action in cases of infringement of the code by a controller or processor, including suspension or exclusion of the controller or processor concerned from the code. It must inform the competent data protection supervisory authority of such actions and the reasons for taking them.‡

The competent data protection supervisory authority must revoke the accreditation of a body as referred to in this section if the conditions for accreditation are not, or are no longer, met or where actions taken by the body infringe the GDPR.§

However, these rules may not apply to processing carried out by public authorities and bodies.¶

Details of Codes of Conduct

The member states, the data protection supervisory authorities, the EDPB, and the EU Commission must encourage the drawing up of codes of conduct intended to contribute to the proper application of the GDPR, taking account of the specific features of the various processing sectors and the specific needs of micro, small, and medium-sized enterprises.**

---

* GDPR Article 41(2).
† GDPR Article 41(3).
‡ GDPR Article 41(4).
§ GDPR Article 41(5).
¶ GDPR Article 41(6).
**GDPR Article 40(1).

Associations and other bodies representing categories of controllers or processors may prepare codes of conduct, or amend or extend such codes, for the purpose of specifying the application of the GDPR, such as with regard to

- Fair and transparent processing.
- The legitimate interests pursued by controllers in specific contexts.
- The collection of personal data.
- The pseudonymization of personal data.
- The information provided to the public and to data subjects.
- The exercise of the rights of data subjects.
- The information provided to, and the protection of, children, and the manner in which the consent of the holders of parental responsibility over children is to be obtained.
- The measures and procedures referred to in Articles 24 and 25 and the measures to ensure security of processing referred to in Article 32.
- The notification of personal data breaches to data protection supervisory authorities and the communication of such personal data breaches to data subjects.
- The transfer of personal data to third countries or international organizations.
- Out-of-court proceedings and other dispute resolution procedures for resolving disputes between controllers and data subjects with regard to processing, without prejudice to the rights* of data subjects.†

In addition to adherence by controllers or processors subject to the GDPR, codes of conduct approved pursuant to paragraph 5 of this Article and having general validity pursuant to paragraph 9 of this Article may also be adhered to by controllers or processors that are not subject to the GDPR pursuant to Article 3 so as to provide appropriate safeguards within the framework of personal data transfers to third countries or international organizations under the terms referred to in Article 46(2)(e). Such controllers or processors must

---

* Pursuant to GDPR Articles 77 and 79.
† GDPR Article 40(2).

make binding and enforceable commitments, via contractual or other legally binding instruments, to apply those appropriate safeguards, including with regard to the rights of data subjects.*

The body will carry out mandatory monitoring of compliance by the controllers or processors.† There are also provisions in relation to the monitoring of approved codes of conduct.‡

Certification Seals and Marks

Background Guidance

To enhance transparency and compliance with the GDPR, the establishment of certification mechanisms and data protection seals and marks should be encouraged, allowing individual data subjects to quickly assess the level of data protection of relevant products and services.§

Legal Rule

Article 39 refers to certification. The member states, the data protection supervisory authorities, the EDPB, and the EU Commission must encourage, in particular at EU level, the establishment of data protection certification mechanisms and of data protection seals and marks for the purpose of demonstrating compliance with the GDPR of processing operations carried out by controllers and processors. The specific needs of micro, small, and medium-sized enterprises must be taken into account.¶

In addition to adherence by controllers or processors subject to the GDPR, approved data protection certification mechanisms, seals, or marks may be established for the purpose of demonstrating the existence of appropriate safeguards provided by controllers or processors that are not subject to the GDPR pursuant to Article 3 within the framework of personal data transfers to third countries

---

* GDPR Article 40(3).
† GDPR Article 40(4).
‡ GDPR Article 40(4)–40(11); 41.
§ GDPR Recital 100.
¶ GDPR Article 42(1).

or international organizations.* Such controllers or processors shall make binding and enforceable commitments, via contractual or other legally binding instruments, to apply those appropriate safeguards, including with regard to the rights of data subjects.†

The certification must be voluntary and available via a process that is transparent.‡

A certification pursuant to this Article does not reduce the responsibility of the controller or the processor for compliance with the GDPR and is without prejudice to the tasks and powers of the data protection supervisory authority.§

A certification shall be issued by the certification bodies or by the competent supervisory authority on the basis of criteria approved by that competent supervisory authority or by the EDPB. Where the criteria are approved by the EDPB, this may result in a common certification, the European Data Protection Seal.¶

The certification must be issued to a controller or processor for a maximum period of 3 years and may be renewed under the same conditions as long as the relevant requirements continue to be met. It shall be withdrawn, where applicable, by the certification bodies or by the competent data protection supervisory authority where the requirements for the certification are not or no longer met.**

The controller or processor that submits its processing to the certification mechanism must provide the certification body or, where applicable, the competent data protection supervisory authority with all the information and access to its processing activities that are necessary to conduct the certification procedure.††

The EDPB must collate all certification mechanisms and data protection seals and marks in a register and must make them publicly available by any appropriate means.‡‡

---

* Under the terms referred to in GDPR Article 46(2)(f).
† GDPR Article 42(2).
‡ GDPR Article 42(3).
§ GDPR Article 43(4).
¶ GDPR Article 42(5).
**GDPR Article 42(7).
††GDPR Article 42(6).
‡‡GDPR Article 42(8).

Conclusion

As with other areas of industry, it is now recognized that industry codes and certification mechanisms can assist organizations within designated sectors in compliance with data protection. As these are developed, organizations should monitor them to assess the applicability and benefits to their organizations of these codes and certification mechanisms.

KEY CONCEPTS

Organizations can assist in establishing, maintaining, and demonstrating compliance by adherence to appropriate industry codes of conduct and/or certification mechanisms. These can relate to one or more aspects of data processing and compliance.

KEY WORDS

- Organizations.
- Demonstrating compliance.
- Codes of conduct.
- Certification.

FURTHER READING

- Myers, "Cross-Border Commerce without Constraint: Shifting from Territorial-Based Regulation to an Industry-Based Code of Conduct for the Online Payment Processing Industry," *Computer & Internet Lawyer* (2016) (33:7) 11.
- Rodrigues, Barnard-Wills, De Hert, and Papakonstantinou, "The Future of Privacy Certification in Europe: An Exploration of Options under Article 42 of the GDPR," *International Review of Law, Computers & Technology* (2016) (30:3) 248.

28

SECURITY OF PERSONAL DATA

Introduction

"[Personal data] has become the prime target of hackers and cyber-criminals. It can be exploited in many ways, from identity theft, spamming and phishing right through to cyber-espionage."* Various types of blackmail in relation to personal data are also increasing among adults, teenagers, and children. The data protection regime sets information and data security obligations on all controllers as well as processors. These procedural, information technology (IT), and personal data security requirements must be complied with. While security risks have increased with the Internet,† security issues are not just limited to the organization's Internet.

The increasing instances of data security breach, including through inadequate security, as well as Internet usage and social media, cloud computing, and online abuse, will all increase attention to security and data protection. Sony, for example, was fined £250,000 in relation to a hacking data breach incident. Recently, telco TalkTalk and children's electronic toy manufacturer VTech were hacked. The MD of TalkTalk has said that "cyber criminals are becoming increasingly sophisticated and attacks against companies which do business online are becoming more frequent."

Directors and other executives can also face official as well as internal sanctions. Data protection officers must be appointed, and they have significant independence and authority in carrying out their functions. Risks, in particular security risks to personal data, must be

---

* Rozenberg, "Challenges in PII Data Protection," *Computer Fraud & Security* (2012) (6) 5–9.
† "Security of the Internet and the Known Unknowns," *Communications of the ACM* (2012) (55) 35.

assessed and appropriate procedures put in place. The significant new level of the penalties regime, amounting to millions of euros, is a significant incentive for organizations to raise their level of compliance.

In addition, quite apart from the new general data protection regulation (GDPR), there is also a new Directive coming that deals specifically with security issues, in addition to the security obligations in the GDPR. The Network and Information Security Directive was proposed in 2013 and was significantly advanced by the time of writing.* Once it is finalized, organizations will need to take on board the relevant obligations of this new Directive also.

Background Guidance

The background Recitals refer to network and information security, Computer Emergency Response Teams (CERTs), and Computer Security Incident Response Teams (CSIRTs);[†] issues and measures;[‡] appropriate technical and organizational measures;[§] security and risk evaluation;[¶] high risk and impact assessments;[**] impact assessments;[††] large-scale processing operations;[‡‡] consultations;[§§] data breach and data breach notification;[¶¶] and EU Commission delegated acts.

Risk and Damage

There is increasing opportunity for risk and damage to both individuals and organizations in relation to personal data. There is thus a need for updating new rules in this regard.

The risk to the rights of natural persons, of varying likelihood and severity, may result from personal data processing, which could lead

---

* See generally, James, "The Network and Information Security Directive" ("Cybersecurity" Directive), SCL, at www.scl.org/site.aspx?i=ed46506.
[†] GDPR Recital 49.
[‡] GDPR Recitals 71, 77.
[§] GDPR Recitals 77, 78.
[¶] GDPR Recitals 51, 74, 76, 83.
[**] GDPR Recitals 76, 77, 84.
[††] GDPR Recitals 76, 77, 84, 89, 90, 91, 92, 93, 94, 95.
[‡‡] GDPR Recitals 80, 91, 97.
[§§] GDPR Recitals 84, 94, 95.
[¶¶] GDPR Recitals 85, 87, 88.

to physical, material, or non-material damage, in particular where the processing may give rise to discrimination, identity theft or fraud, financial loss, damage to the reputation, loss of confidentiality of personal data protected by professional secrecy, unauthorized reversal of pseudonymization, or any other significant economic or social disadvantage; where individual data subjects might be deprived of their rights or prevented from exercising control over their personal data; where personal data are processed that reveal racial or ethnic origin, political opinions, religion or philosophical beliefs, trade union membership; the processing of genetic data, data concerning health, or data concerning sex life or criminal convictions and offenses or related security measures; where personal aspects are evaluated, in particular analyzing or predicting aspects concerning performance at work, economic situation, health, personal preferences or interests, reliability or behavior, or location or movements, to create or use personal profiles; where the personal data of vulnerable natural persons, in particular of children, are processed; or where processing involves a large amount of personal data and affects a large number of individual data subjects.*

The likelihood and severity of the risk to the rights of the individual data subject should be determined by reference to the nature, scope, context, and purposes of the processing. Risk should be evaluated on the basis of an objective assessment, by which it is established whether data processing operations involve a risk or a high risk.†

Guidance on the implementation of appropriate measures and on the demonstration of compliance by the controller or the processor, especially as regards the identification of the risk related to the processing, its assessment in terms of origin, nature, likelihood, and severity, and the identification of best practices to mitigate the risk, could be provided in particular by means of approved codes of conduct, approved certifications, guidelines provided by the European Data Protection Board (EDPB), or indications provided by a data protection officer. The EDPB may also issue guidelines on processing operations that are considered to be unlikely to result in a high risk to

---

* GDPR Recital 75.
† GDPR Recital 76.

the rights of natural persons and indicate what measures may be sufficient in such cases to address such risk.*

The protection of the rights of natural persons with regard to the processing of personal data requires that appropriate technical and organizational measures be taken to ensure that the requirements of the GDPR are met. To be able to demonstrate compliance with the GDPR, the controller should adopt internal policies and implement measures that meet in particular the principles of data protection by design and data protection by default. Such measures could consist, *inter alia*, of minimizing the processing of personal data, pseudonymizing personal data as soon as possible, transparency with regard to the functions and processing of personal data, enabling the individual data subject to monitor the data processing, and enabling the controller to create and improve security features. When developing, designing, selecting, and using applications, services, and products that are based on the processing of personal data or process personal data to fulfill their task, the producers of the products, services, and applications should be encouraged to take into account the right to data protection when developing and designing such products, services, and applications and, with due regard to the state of the art, to make sure that controllers and processors are able to fulfill their data protection obligations. The principles of data protection by design and by default should also be taken into consideration in the context of public tenders.†

Breaches

The obligations in terms of insufficient security and data breaches are more detailed in the GDPR than previously.‡ The obligations are now more detailed than the obligation in relation to telcos and ISPs in the ePrivacy Directive.§ Data breaches are referred to in Articles 4 and 9 of the GDPR. In the event of a data breach, the controller must notify

---

* GDPR Recital 77.
† GDPR Recital 78.
‡ Costa and Poullet, "Privacy and the Regulation of 2012," (2012)(28) *Computer Law & Security Review*, at 256.
§ ibid.

the data protection supervisory authority.* In addition, the controller must communicate to the individual data subjects if there is a risk of harm to their privacy or personal data.†

Risk Evaluation

To maintain security and to prevent processing in infringement of the GDPR, the controller or processor should evaluate the risks inherent in the processing and implement measures to mitigate those risks, such as encryption. Those measures should ensure an appropriate level of security, including confidentiality, taking into account the state of the art and the costs of implementation in relation to the risks and the nature of the personal data to be protected. In assessing data security risk, consideration should be given to the risks that are presented by personal data processing, such as accidental or unlawful destruction, loss, alteration, unauthorized disclosure of, or access to, personal data transmitted, stored, or otherwise processed that may in particular lead to physical, material, or non-material damage.‡

High Risks

To enhance compliance with the GDPR where processing operations are likely to result in a high risk to the rights of natural persons, the controller should be responsible for the carrying-out of a data protection impact assessment to evaluate, in particular, the origin, nature, particularity, and severity of that risk. The outcome of the assessment should be taken into account when determining the appropriate measures to be taken to demonstrate that the processing of personal data complies with the GDPR. Where a data protection impact assessment indicates that processing operations involve a high risk that the controller cannot mitigate by appropriate measures in terms of available technology and costs of implementation, a consultation of the data protection supervisory authority should take place prior to the processing.§

---

* GDPR Article 33.
† GDPR Article 34.
‡ GDPR Recital 83.
§ GDPR Recital 84.

Risk and Damage

There is increasing opportunity for risk and damage to both individuals and organizations in relation to personal data. There is thus a need for updating the rules in this regard.

The risk to the rights of natural persons, of varying likelihood and severity, may result from personal data processing that could lead to physical, material, or non-material damage, in particular where the processing may give rise to discrimination, identity theft or fraud, financial loss, damage to the reputation, loss of confidentiality of personal data protected by professional secrecy, unauthorized reversal of pseudonymization, or any other significant economic or social disadvantage; where individual data subjects might be deprived of their rights or prevented from exercising control over their personal data; where personal data are processed that reveal racial or ethnic origin, political opinions, religion or philosophical beliefs, or trade union membership; the processing of genetic data, data concerning health, or data concerning sex life or criminal convictions and offenses or related security measures; where personal aspects are evaluated, in particular analyzing or predicting aspects concerning performance at work, economic situation, health, personal preferences or interests, reliability or behavior, or location or movements, to create or use personal profiles; where personal data of vulnerable natural persons, in particular of children, are processed; or where processing involves a large amount of personal data and affects a large number of individual data subjects.*

The likelihood and severity of the risk to the rights of the individual data subject should be determined by reference to the nature, scope, context, and purposes of the processing. Risk should be evaluated on the basis of an objective assessment, by which it is established whether data processing operations involve a risk or a high risk.†

Guidance on the implementation of appropriate measures and on the demonstration of compliance by the controller or the processor, especially as regards the identification of the risk related to the processing, its assessment in terms of origin, nature, likelihood, and severity, and the identification of best practices to mitigate the risk,

---

* GDPR Recital 75.
† GDPR Recital 76.

could be provided in particular by means of approved codes of conduct, approved certifications, guidelines provided by the EDPB, or indications provided by a data protection officer. The EDPB may also issue guidelines on processing operations that are considered to be unlikely to result in a high risk to the rights of natural persons and indicate what measures may be sufficient in such cases to address such risk.*

The protection of the rights of natural persons with regard to the processing of personal data requires that appropriate technical and organizational measures be taken to ensure that the requirements of the GDPR are met. To be able to demonstrate compliance with the GDPR, the controller should adopt internal policies and implement measures that meet in particular the principles of data protection by design and data protection by default. Such measures could consist, *inter alia*, of minimizing the processing of personal data, pseudonymizing personal data as soon as possible, transparency with regard to the functions and processing of personal data, enabling the individual data subject to monitor the data processing, and enabling the controller to create and improve security features. When developing, designing, selecting, and using applications, services, and products that are based on the processing of personal data or process personal data to fulfill their task, the producers of the products, services, and applications should be encouraged to take into account the right to data protection when developing and designing such products, services, and applications and, with due regard to the state of the art, to make sure that controllers and processors are able to fulfill their data protection obligations. The principles of data protection by design and by default should also be taken into consideration in the context of public tenders.†

Legal Rule: Appropriate Security Measures

There are specific requirements with regard to the security measures that need to be implemented under the data protection laws.

---

* GDPR Recital 77.
† GDPR Recital 78.

There is greater emphasis on security in the new GDPR. It is a separate distinct section in the GDPR. Previously, the DPD95 highlighted security as part of the data protection principles.

Organizations and controllers must take appropriate security measures against unauthorized access to, or unauthorized alteration, disclosure, or destruction of, the data, in particular where the processing involves the transmission of data over a network, and against all other unlawful forms of processing. As these risks grow,* so too must the efforts of organizations to address the risks appropriately in compliance with the data protection regime and satisfy the expectations of customers, users, employees, and regulators. However, it is not the case that one solution on one occasion will be sufficient.

The requirements regarding security of processing were originally contained in the data protection principles and are now more expressly expanded in the new GDPR. The controller must take appropriate technical and organizational measures against the unauthorized or unlawful processing of personal data and against the accidental loss or destruction of, or damage to, personal data. The controller must ensure the following:

> Taking into account the state of the art, the costs of implementation, and the nature, scope, context, and purposes of processing as well as the risk of varying likelihood and severity for the rights and freedoms of natural persons, the controller and the processor shall implement appropriate technical and organizational measures to ensure a level of security appropriate to the risk, including *inter alia* as appropriate
>
> - The pseudonymization and encryption of personal data.
> - The ability to ensure the ongoing confidentiality, integrity, availability, and resilience of processing systems and services.
> - The ability to restore the availability and access to personal data in a timely manner in the event of a physical or technical incident.
> - A process for regularly testing, assessing, and evaluating the effectiveness of technical and organizational measures for ensuring the security of the processing.†

---

* See, for example, "The Cybersecurity Risk," *Communications of the ACM* (2012) (55) 29.
† GDPR Article 32(1).

In assessing the appropriate level of security, account must be taken in particular of the risks that are presented by processing, in particular from accidental or unlawful destruction, loss, alteration, or unauthorized disclosure of, or access to, personal data transmitted, stored, or otherwise processed.*

Adherence to an approved code of conduct[†] or an approved certification mechanism[‡] may be used as an element by which to demonstrate compliance with these requirements.[§]

The controller and processor must take steps to ensure that any natural person acting under the authority of the controller or the processor who has access to personal data does not process them except on instructions from the controller, unless he or she is required to do so by EU or member state law.[¶]

The different elements and requirements, therefore, include

- Not just security measures, but security measures that are appropriate. This means that the security measures will vary from organization to organization and sector to sector, as well as depending on the history of risk in the individual organization.
- Preventing unauthorized access.
- Preventing unauthorized alteration.
- Preventing unauthorized disclosure; or
- Preventing unauthorized destruction; and
- Especially where there is a network involved, preventing all other unlawful forms of processing.

The security obligations are therefore serious and demanding.

The new GDPR places significantly greater emphasis on risk and risk assessment, in addition to security. Organizations need to be compliant with these obligations. It is also a somewhat complex clause given the different parts.

Chapter IV, Section 2 of the new GDPR relates to data security. Article 32 specifically refers to security of processing. It obliges

---

* GDPR Article 32(2).
[†] As referred to in Article 40.
[‡] As referred to in Article 42.
[§] GDPR Article 32(3).
[¶] GDPR Article 32(4).

controllers and processors to implement appropriate technical and organizational measures to ensure a level of security appropriate to the risk. The Article refers to having regard to the state of the art and the costs of implementation and taking into account the nature, scope, context, and purposes of the processing as well as the risk of varying likelihood and severity for the rights of individuals. After the primary obligation is set out in the clause, it then also refers explicitly to examples of technical and organizational measures. It is clear that these are examples only and not a fixed closed list of such measures to be taken, as it indicates "including *inter alia*" before listing the measures.*

Section 2 refers to security in detail. Taking into account the state of the art, the costs of implementation, and the nature, scope, context, and purposes of processing as well as the risk of varying likelihood and severity for the rights of natural persons, the controller and the processor must implement appropriate technical and organizational measures to ensure a level of security appropriate to the risk, including *inter alia* as appropriate

- The pseudonymization and encryption of personal data.
- The ability to ensure the ongoing confidentiality, integrity, availability, and resilience of processing systems and services.
- The ability to restore the availability and access to personal data in a timely manner in the event of a physical or technical incident.
- A process for regularly testing, assessing, and evaluating the effectiveness of technical and organizational measures for ensuring the security of the processing.†

In assessing the appropriate level of security, account must be taken in particular of the risks that are presented by processing, in particular from accidental or unlawful destruction, loss, alteration, or unauthorized disclosure of, or access to, personal data transmitted, stored, or otherwise processed.‡

---

* Article 17 of the DPD95 referred to security of processing.
† GDPR Article 32(1).
‡ GDPR Article 32(2).

Adherence to an approved code of conduct* or an approved certi-fication mechanism† may be used as an element by which to demon-strate compliance with these requirements.‡

The controller and processor must take steps to ensure that any natural person acting under the authority of the controller or the pro-cessor who has access to personal data does not process them except on instructions from the controller, unless they are required to do so by EU or member state law.§

Article 32(1) provides that "[t]aking into account the state of the art, the costs of implementation and the nature, scope, context and purposes of processing as well as the risk of varying likelihood and severity for the rights and freedoms of natural persons, the controller and the processor shall implement appropriate technical and organ-isational measures to ensure a level of security appropriate to the risk, including *inter alia* as appropriate." The emphasis here is on risk over costs.

It is most important for controllers, and processors, to fully consider this obligation. They should also note that the list is noted as being "including," and is therefore not a final fixed list. Controllers and pro-cessors need to go even further than these expressed requirements.

Adherence to an approved code of conduct or an approved certifi-cation mechanism may be used as *an element* to demonstrate compli-ance. Adopting a minimalistic approach could expose the organization both technically and in compliance terms.

The controller and processor must take steps to ensure that any natural person acting under the authority of the controller or the pro-cessor who has access to personal data does not process them except on instructions from the controller, unless he or she is required to do so by EU or member state law.¶ Liability issues therefore arise for organizations, even if they are unaware of the breach issues until the event happens. As an example, an errant employee, partner, pro-cessor, or outsource party may do something that they are not sup-posed to do and that the organization is wholly unaware of, yet the

---

* GDPR Article 40.
† GDPR Article 42.
‡ GDPR Article 32(3).
§ GDPR Article 32(4).
¶ GDPR Article 32(4).

controller organization will be held responsible. There are examples of this occurring even under the previous 1995 data protection directive (DPD95) data protection regime, such as when Irish Life was liable as controller when a previous agent continued to contact the Irish Life client list.

Notification of Data Breach to Data Protection Supervisory Authority

Article 33 of the GDPR provides that in the case of a personal data breach, the controller must without undue delay and, where feasible, not later than 72 hours after having become aware of it, notify the personal data breach to the competent data protection supervisory authority,[*] unless the personal data breach is unlikely to result in a risk to the rights of natural persons. There is an additional requirement if the notification is late. Article 33 requires that where the notification to the data protection supervisory authority is not made within 72 hours, it must be accompanied by reasons for the delay.

The processor must notify the controller without undue delay after becoming aware of a personal data breach.[†]

There is also guidance in relation to what the notice in Article 31(1) should contain. Article 33(3) provides that the notification must *at least*

- Describe the nature of the personal data breach including, where possible, the categories and approximate number of individual data subjects concerned and the categories and approximate number of personal data records concerned.
- Communicate the name and contact details of the data protection officer or other contact point from which more information can be obtained.
- Describe the likely consequences of the personal data breach.
- Describe the measures taken or proposed to be taken by the controller to address the personal data breach, including, where appropriate, measures to mitigate its possible adverse effects.

---

[*] In accordance with GDPR Article 55.
[†] GDPR Article 33(2).

Where, and insofar as, it is not possible to provide the information at the same time, the information may be provided in phases without undue further delay.*

The controller *shall document* any personal data breaches, comprising the facts relating to the personal data breach, its effects, and the remedial action taken.† That documentation must enable the data protection supervisory authority to verify compliance.‡

Communication of Personal Data Breach to Data Subject

The new GDPR also sets out obligations to notify individual data subjects of data breaches. Article 34 of the GDPR refers to the communication of a personal data breach§ to the individual data subject. When the personal data breach is likely to result in a high risk to the rights of natural persons, the controller must communicate the personal data breach to the individual data subject without undue delay.¶ The communication to the individual data subject referred to in paragraph 1 of this Article must describe in clear and plain language the nature of the personal data breach and contain at least the information and measures referred to in Article 33(3)(b), (c) and (d).** The communication to the individual data subject referred to in paragraph 1 must not be required if any of the following conditions are met

- The controller has implemented appropriate technical and organizational protection measures, and those measures were applied to the personal data affected by the personal data breach, in particular those that render the personal data unintelligible to any person who is not authorized to access it, such as encryption.

---

* GDPR Article 33(4).
† GDPR Article 33(5).
‡ Ibid.
§ Note, for example, Wainman, "Data Protection Breaches: Today and Tomorrow," *Computers and Law* (June 30, 2012). Also see Dekker, Christoffer Karsberg, and Daskala, *Cyber Incident Reporting in the EU* (European Network and Information Security Agency, 2012).
¶ GDPR Article 34(1).
**GDPR Article 34(2).

- The controller has taken subsequent measures that ensure that the high risk to the rights of individual data subjects referred to in paragraph 1 is no longer likely to materialize.
- It would involve disproportionate effort. In such a case, there must instead be a public communication or similar measure whereby the individual data subjects are informed in an equally effective manner.*

If the controller has not already communicated the personal data breach to the individual data subject, the data protection supervisory authority, having considered the likelihood of the personal data breach resulting in a high risk, may require it to do so or may decide that any of the conditions referred to in paragraph 3 are met.† It remains to be seen how this provision will be interpreted in practice.

Data Protection Impact Assessment

Chapter IV, Section 3 of the GDPR refers to *data protection impact assessments* and *prior consultations*. These are new requirements. This is a new provision. Where a type of processing in particular using new technologies, and taking into account the nature, scope, context, and purposes of the processing, is likely to result in a *high risk* to the rights of natural persons, the controller *shall, prior* to the processing, carry out an assessment of the impact of the envisaged processing operations on the protection of personal data. A single assessment may address a set of similar processing operations that present similar high risks.‡

The controller must seek the advice of the data protection officer, where designated, when carrying out a data protection impact assessment.§

A data protection impact assessment must in particular be required in the case of

- A systematic and extensive evaluation of personal aspects relating to natural persons that is based on automated processing, including profiling, and on which decisions are based

---

* GDPR Article 34(3).
† GDPR Article 34(4).
‡ GDPR Article 35(1).
§ GDPR Article 35(2).

that produce legal effects concerning the natural person or similarly significantly affect the natural person.

- Processing on a large scale of special categories of data referred to in Article 9(1) or of personal data relating to criminal convictions and offenses referred to in Article 10; or.
- Systematic monitoring of a publicly accessible area on a large scale.*

The data protection supervisory authority must establish and make public a list of the kinds of processing operations that are subject to the requirement for a data protection impact assessment. The data protection supervisory authority must communicate those lists to the EDPB.†

The data protection supervisory authority may also establish and make public a list of the kind of processing operations for which no data protection impact assessment is required. The data protection supervisory authority must communicate those lists to the EDPB.‡

Prior to the adoption of these lists, the competent data protection supervisory authority must apply the consistency mechanism referred to in Article 63 where such lists involve processing activities that are related to the offering of goods or services to individual data subjects or to the monitoring of their behavior in several member states, or may substantially affect the free movement of personal data within the EU.§

The assessment must contain at least

- A systematic description of the envisaged processing operations and the purposes of the processing, including, where applicable, the legitimate interest pursued by the controller.
- An assessment of the necessity and proportionality of the processing operations in relation to the purposes.
- An assessment of the risks to the rights of individual data subjects referred to in paragraph 1.
- The measures envisaged to address the risks, including safeguards, security measures, and mechanisms to ensure the

---

* GDPR Article 35(3).
† GDPR Article 35(4).
‡ GDPR Article 35(5).
§ GDPR Article 35(6).

protection of personal data and to demonstrate compliance with the GDPR, taking into account the rights and legitimate interests of individual data subjects and other persons concerned.*

Compliance with approved codes of conduct by the relevant controllers or processors must be taken into due account in assessing the impact of the processing operations performed by such controllers or processors, in particular for the purposes of a data protection impact assessment.†

Where appropriate, the controller must seek the views of individual data subjects or their representatives on the intended processing, without prejudice to the protection of commercial or public interests or the security of processing operations.‡

Where processing pursuant to Article 6(1)(c) or (e) has a legal basis in EU law or in the law of the member state to which the controller is subject, that law regulates the specific processing operation or set of operations in question, and a data protection impact assessment has already been carried out as part of a general impact assessment in the context of the adoption of that legal basis, paragraphs 1 to 7 must not apply unless member states deem it to be necessary to carry out such an assessment prior to processing activities.§

Where necessary, the controller must carry out a review to assess whether processing is performed in accordance with the data protection impact assessment, at least when there is a change of the risk represented by processing operations.¶

Prior Consultation

Prior consultations are also a new requirement. The controller must consult the data protection supervisory authority prior to processing where a data protection impact assessment under Article 35 indicates that the processing would result in a high risk in the absence of measures taken by the controller to mitigate the risk.**

---

* GDPR Article 35(7).
† GDPR Article 35(8).
‡ GDPR Article 35(9).
§ GDPR Article 35(10).
¶ GDPR Article 35(11).
** GDPR Article 36(1).

Where the data protection supervisory authority is of the opinion that the intended processing referred to in paragraph 1 would infringe the GDPR, in particular where the controller has *insufficiently identified* or *mitigated* the risk, the data protection supervisory authority must, within a period of up to 8 weeks of receipt of the request for consultation, provide written advice to the controller and, where applicable, to the processor, and may use any of its powers referred to in Article 58. That period may be extended by 6 weeks, taking into account the complexity of the intended processing. The data protection supervisory authority must inform the controller and, where applicable, the processor of any such extension within 1 month of receipt of the request for consultation together with the reasons for the delay. Those periods may be suspended until the data protection supervisory authority has obtained information it has requested for the purposes of the consultation.*

When consulting the data protection supervisory authority, the controller must provide the data protection supervisory authority with

- Where applicable, the respective responsibilities of the controller, joint controllers, and processors involved in the processing, in particular for processing within a group of undertakings.
- The purposes and means of the intended processing.
- The measures and safeguards provided to protect the rights of individual data subjects pursuant to the GDPR.
- Where applicable, the contact details of the data protection officer.
- The data protection impact assessment.[†]
- Any other information requested by the data protection supervisory authority.[‡]

Ensuring Appropriate Security Measures

Controllers must have an adequate level of protection and security as regards their storage, and so on, of personal data. What are security

---

* GDPR Article 36(2).
[†] GDPR Article 35.
[‡] GDPR Article 36(3).

and "appropriate security measures"? What must the organization do? The data protection principles refer to security obligations. In determining appropriate technical and organizational measures, a controller may have regard to a number of factors.

In determining appropriate security measures, in particular (but without prejudice to the generality of that provision) where the processing involves the transmission of data over a network, a controller

- May have regard to the state of technological development and the cost of implementing the measures.
- Must ensure that the measures provide a level of security appropriate to
  - The harm that might result from unauthorized or unlawful processing, accidental or unlawful destruction, or accidental loss of, or damage to, the data concerned
  - The nature of the data concerned.
- May have regard to the state of technological development and the cost of implementing the measures.

A controller or processor must take all reasonable steps to ensure that

- Persons employed by it; and
- Other persons at the place of work concerned

are aware of and comply with the relevant security measures.

Where processing of personal data is carried out by a processor on behalf of a controller, the controller must

- Ensure that the processing is carried out in pursuance of a *contract* in writing or in another equivalent form between the controller and the processor and that the contract provides that the processor carries out the processing only on and subject to the instructions of the controller and that the processor complies with obligations equivalent to those imposed on the controller.
- Ensure that the processor provides sufficient *guarantees* in respect of the technical security measures, and organizational measures, governing the processing.
- Take reasonable steps to ensure compliance with those measures.

Employees and Security

Organizations need to appraise employees and involve them in addressing security concerns. Employees need to be made aware of the overall need for security and also of the security obligations and protocols with which they are required to comply. Employees are also integral to the organization's efforts to deal with security issues appropriately. They must be aware of the issues and their role in implementing and adhering to relevant policies and procedures.

Engaging Processors and Security Issues

Processors* also have obligations in relation to processing personal data and security. Where the processing of personal data is carried out by a processor on behalf of a controller, the controller must, to comply with the seventh principle

- Ensure that the processing is carried out in pursuance of a contract in writing or in another equivalent form between the controller and the processor and that the contract provides that the processor carries out the processing only on and subject to the instructions of the controller and that the processor complies with obligations equivalent to those imposed on the controller.
- Ensure that the processor provides sufficient guarantees in respect of the technical security measures, and organizational measures, governing the processing.
- Take reasonable steps to ensure compliance with those measures.

Where processing of personal data is carried out by a processor on behalf of a controller, the controller must have a contract in writing with the processor containing certain clauses and obligations. Contracts with processors must address the following

- That processing must be carried out in pursuance of a contract in writing.
- That the processor carries out the processing only on and subject to the instructions of the controller.
- That the processor must comply with the *security* requirements.

---

* Note generally, for example, Morgan, "Data Controllers, Data Processors and Data Sharers," *Computers and Law* (4 March 2011).

There are specific requirements where processors are engaged and relied on. Where controllers engage processors, the controller must

- Have a contract in writing or other equipment form that provides that the processor will act only on the instructions of the controller and will comply with the data security measures to which the controller is subject.
- Ensure that the processor provides sufficient guarantees in respect of the technical security measures and organizational measures it implements.
- Takes reasonable steps to ensure compliance with such matters.

What actions should an organization take if third parties process its data? The following may assist

- Ideally, an organization should have advance procedures and policies in place to cater for such an eventuality; for example, ensuring that an appropriate senior manager/board member has an assigned role and takes responsibility for data protection compliance, including dealing with breaches, and also having a documented IT security incident handling procedure policy in place. Needless to say, it must be properly policed, implemented, reviewed, and updated appropriately.
- Once a breach does occur, a proper procedure can assist in containing and recovering from the breach, assessing the ongoing risk, notifying the breach as appropriate, and evaluating and reacting to the breach and the risk.
- All of the appropriate personnel within the organization should be aware of the procedures and consulted as appropriate, including, for example, the managing director and the legal, IT, and media/press officers.
- A part of the procedure will have a designated list of external contact points, some or all of whom may need to be notified and contacted, as appropriate.
- Obviously, the nature of organizations, and of breaches themselves, differs, and the IT security incident handling procedure policy will need to be tailored. After all, the cause of a data security breach can be any one of a number of reasons.

- Also, such a policy, while covering breaches of data protection and privacy, may well encompass wider issues, such as outsourcing, backups, disaster recovery, business continuity, and so on.
- Business in other jurisdictions may require additional measures. For example, if a business owns or has access to the personal information of Californian residents, it may have a legal duty to notify those individuals if that information (such as names and credit card details) has been accessed illegally.

Legislative Data Protection Reviews

Member states must consult the data protection supervisory authority during the preparation of a proposal for a legislative measure to be adopted by a national parliament, or of a regulatory measure based on such a legislative measure, which relates to processing.*

Specific Public Interest Prior Consultations

Notwithstanding this, member state law may require controllers to consult with, and obtain *prior authorization* from, the data protection supervisory authority in relation to processing by a controller for the performance of a task carried out by the controller in the *public interest*, including processing in relation to *social protection* and *public health*.†

Security Directive

The new Security Directive provisions, once enacted, will also need careful consideration by organizations.‡

---

* GDPR Article 36(4).
† GDPR Article 36(5).
‡ See generally, James, "The Network and Information Security Directive" ("Cybersecurity" Directive), SCL.

Security Awareness

EU Council Resolution 2002/C43/02* indicates the recognition and official concern in relation to the loss of personal data, and the fact that technology has changed significantly since the DPD95.

It refers to the dangers of information loss, attacks on organizations, and issues of network and information security for organizations and individuals. It indicates that EU member states should engage in information campaigns addressing the issues of security and personal data. There is a need to promote best practice, such as the internationally recognized standards for IT; for example, ISO 15408, ISO 27001, ISO 31000, and BS10012:2009.

There is also an increase in eGovernment and an associated need to promote secure eGovernment.

It notes the increase of attacks on the security of personal data through technology, but some of the solutions may also come from new technologies. Some of these are referred to as privacy-enhancing technologies (PETs).[†]

In addition, it refers to the increase of mobile and wireless communications technologies and the need for introducing and enhancing wireless security.

Keeping on top of the increasing threats to information security is an ongoing task. The threats are ever-changing, and so equally should be the effort to prevent breaches and to deal with them if and when they occur. Some of the most current information security threats are highlighted annually by various IT security vendors as well as police and investigative officials.

Data Protection Supervisory Authorities Guides

Data protection supervisory authorities advise that that appropriate security measures be put in place that take account of the harm that would result from unauthorized access to the information. This

---

* Of January 28, 2002.
† See, for example, Beric and Carlisle, "Investigating the Legal Protection of Data, Information and Knowledge under the EU Data Protection Regime," *International Review of Law, Computers & Technology* (2009) (23) 189.

should take account of available technology and the cost of installation. In addition to technical security measures, due regard should be given to physical security measures such as access control for central IT servers and local PCs.*

According to one data protection supervisory authority, physical security safeguards should include the following considerations:

- Perimeter security (monitoring of access, office locked and alarmed when not in use).
- Restrictions on access to sensitive areas within the building (such as server rooms).
- Computer location (so that the screen may not be viewed by members of the public).
- Storage of files (files not stored in public areas, with access restricted to staff with a need to access particular files).
- Secure disposal of records (effective "wiping" of data stored electronically; secure disposal of paper records).†

Many data protection supervisory authorities have issued guides and codes of conduct in relation to data security, breach issues, and breach reporting rules to help organizations to react appropriately when they become aware of breaches of security involving customer or employee personal information.‡

National ePrivacy rules can also place specific obligations on providers of publicly available electronic communications networks or services to safeguard the security of their services.§

---

* See, for example, DPC at https://www.dataprotection.ie.
† See DPC at https://www.dataprotection.ie. The UK data protection supervisory authority (ICO) has also issued a guide entitled *A Practical Guide to IT Security, Ideal for Small Businesses*, at https://ico.org.uk. The ICO has commented in relation to encryption issues and general security for personal data, including computers, emails, and so on.
‡ The data protection supervisory authority in Ireland (DPC), for example, has issued a Personal "Data Security Breach Code of Practice."
§ For example, the European Communities (Electronic Communications Networks and Services) (Privacy and Electronic Communications) Regulations 2011, SI 336/2011 in Ireland, and similar rules in other EU member states.

Prior to the new GDPR, the UK data protection supervisory authority (Information Commissioner's Office [ICO]), for example, has issued recommendations in relation security issues, namely

- *A Practical Guide to IT Security: Ideal for the Small Business.*
- *Guidance on Data Security Breach Management.*
- *Notification of Data Security Breaches to the Information Commissioner's Office.*
- *Notification of Privacy and Electronic Communications Security Breaches.*

These now need to be read in light of the GDPR changes, as, indeed, do similar guides elsewhere.

Security and Article 29 Data Protection Working Party (WP29)/EDPB

The influential EU WP29 (now replaced by the new EDPB) has published a document relating to personal data and information security.* This is an EU organization made up of representatives of all EU data protection authorities.† It refers to the surveillance of employees' electronic communications.

In terms of compliance, it raises a number of concerns for organizations to consider when dealing with their policies and activities regarding such personal data. It suggests that organizations ask whether the proposed processing of the employees' personal data is

- Transparent?
- Necessary?
- Fair?
- Proportionate?
- And to be used for what purpose?‡

It suggests that organizations should consider whether each proposed processing activity can be achieved through some other, less

---

* See http://ec.europa.eu/justice/data-protection/article-29/index_en.htm.
† Article 29 Working Party, Working document on the surveillance of electronic communications in the workplace (WP 55), at http://ec.europa.eu/justice/policies/privacy/docs/wpdocs/2002/wp55_en.pdf.
‡ Article 29 Working Party, Working document on the surveillance of electronic communications in the workplace (WP 55), at http://ec.europa.eu/justice/policies/privacy/docs/wpdocs/2002/wp55_en.pdf.

obtrusive means.* It refers to the organization informing those outside of the organization as appropriate in relation to the proposed processing.† It also highlights issues of proportionality in suggesting that an organization, in processing personal data, should adopt the minimum processing necessary and pursue a strategy of prevention versus detection. Detection leans more toward blanket monitoring of employees. Prevention is viewed as more appropriate and employee privacy friendly. Of course, where an issue comes to the organization's attention, it could then investigate that issue, as opposed to actively monitoring all employees continuously. An example would be using IT filtering systems, which alert the IT manager that there may be an issue to look at further, rather than the IT manager actively looking at and monitoring all employee communications.‡

Organizational Security Awareness

There is a need to ensure security awareness within the organization. Controllers and processors must take all reasonable steps to ensure that persons employed by them and other persons at the place of work are aware of and comply with the relevant security measures.

Identifying and Controlling Organizational IT Security

Who needs to be in charge of IT and data security in an organization? What organizational security measures should be in place?

The data protection rules do not require that a named individual be appointed with responsibility for security compliance. However, there are specific organizational responsibilities regarding security set out in the data protection rules, and these include a specific requirement that all staff are aware of and comply with the security standards set out in the data protection regime.

These security requirements apply where an organization collects and processes any personal data. Typically, personal data would include information that identifies living individuals, such as employees or

---

* Ibid.
† Ibid.
‡ Ibid.

customers. Accordingly, for most organizations, data protection compliance is likely to be an issue that crosses various aspects of the business, such as human resources, IT, and customer support. It is not necessarily just an IT function. An organization's decision as to who should be responsible for IT and data security should be made with this in mind.

The security standards set out in the data protection rules can be summarized as obliging the organization to take "appropriate" security measures to guard against unauthorized access, alteration, disclosure, or destruction of any personal data.

In determining what is "appropriate," the organization can take into account the state of technological development and the cost of implementing the security measures. However, the organization is obliged to ensure that the measures it decides to adopt provide a level of security appropriate to the harm that might result from a security compromise given the nature of the data concerned. For example, a hospital processing sensitive health data would be expected to adopt a particularly high security standard, while a corner shop processing personal data for a paper round might be subject to a less onerous standard.

In light of some high-profile cases of personal data theft or personal data loss, it should also be noted that the data protection supervisory authority's office may take the view that an appropriate level of security for laptop computers used in the financial services and health industries requires the use of encryption in respect of the data stored on the hard drive (over and above the use of user name and password log-in requirements).

In adopting security measures within an organization, it should be noted that the legal standard governing personal data is over and above any other legal obligations of confidentiality that could be owed to third parties at common law or under a contract that contains confidentiality provisions.

Appraising Employees

What guidance should be given to an organization's employees regarding IT and data security? An organization might consider these issues.

The overriding principle here is that, for it to be effective, an employee must have clear notice of all aspects of the organization's IT and data security policy. The following refers to some of these in greater detail. This is an illustrative list and is not meant as a comprehensive list of issues arising.

General Policy

Organizations should reserve the right to monitor use of the computer and telephone system, including email. Disclosure of sensitive or confidential information about the company or personal data about any individual without authorization should be forbidden.

Email

Employees should be made aware that email is an essential business tool but not without its risks. Business communications should be suitable and not too chatty and should not contain inappropriate material. Personal use of email must be reasonable.

Internet Access

Downloading any software without approval should be forbidden. No improper or illegal activities (hacking, etc.) should be tolerated. Access to certain types of websites (adult, criminal, hate, violent, etc.) should be expressly restricted. The origination or dissemination of inappropriate material should be forbidden.

Mobile Telephones and Devices

Downloading any software, and content, without approval should be forbidden. No improper or illegal activities (hacking, etc.) should be tolerated. Access to certain types of websites (adult, criminal, hate, violent, etc.) should be expressly restricted. The origination or dissemination of inappropriate material should be forbidden.

Vehicles

Increasingly, tracking and other data from vehicles can be related to identified employees. It is important for organizations to consider these personal data issues.

Internet Social Media

Downloading any software without approval should be forbidden. No improper or illegal activities (hacking, etc.) should be tolerated. Access to certain types of websites (adult, criminal, hate, violent, etc.) should be expressly restricted. The origination or dissemination of inappropriate material should be forbidden.

Software Installation and Management

Purchase and/or installation of software and/or content not approved by you should be forbidden. All software must be required to be tested before installation on the system to ensure that it is free from viruses, malware, and so on.

Password Security

Clear guidelines as to the use of passwords should be given, including the strength of password required, the importance of keeping one's password(s) confidential, the changing of passwords at regular intervals, and (in the light of recent events) the application of password security (at least) to laptops, mobile phones, and personal digital assistants. In some businesses, stronger encryption may be appropriate, and employees should be required to comply with procedures in this regard. Carrying organizational data on vulnerable media such as memory sticks should be discouraged.

Connecting Hardware

Employees should be required not to connect any hardware (memory sticks, hard drives, etc.) without following specified procedures and obtaining appropriate authorization.

Remote Access

For many businesses, remote access, including web-based remote access, is a vital tool. However, policies should deal with such matters as accessing remotely from insecure locations such as Internet cafés and emphasize the importance of logging off effectively.

Bring Your Own Device (BYOD)

Increasingly, organizations are faced with the dilemma of permitting employees to bring their own electronic devices into the work environment, which may interact with the organization's network systems and data. This creates inevitable risks and complications for organizations if permitted.

Organizational Security Measures

What security measures should an organization take? Some suggestions may include

- Ensure that the organization has the appropriate security equipment and software to protect the organization's systems if granting third-party access. If providing access to a third party involves opening its business systems up to a public network such as the Internet, it is essential that suitable security measures are taken.
- Obtain a complete listing of the IT provider personnel who have access to organizational systems, detail their level and status (full-time/contractor), and ensure that their employment contracts incorporate appropriate security terms.
- Grant third parties access to the organization's systems only when the relevant individuals in the organization (e.g., a business manager, in conjunction with IT staff) have agreed that there is a business need for such access to be granted. Access should be only for a temporary period and renewed at regular intervals.
- Monitor third-party computer accounts (subject to legal agreements between the organization and the third party and in accordance with legal requirements) and disable them as soon as access is no longer required.
- Ensure that sensitive files are segregated in secure areas/computer systems and available only to qualified persons.
- Ensure that the organization has inventoried the various types of data being stored and classified according to how important they are and how costly it would be for the organization if they were lost or stolen.

- Scan computers (especially servers) for unauthorized programs that transmit information to third parties such as hackers.
- Be aware of programs that have a hidden purpose, known as Trojans. Individuals may have inadvertently or deliberately downloaded free programs from the Internet that send back information such as passwords to hackers or Internet usage information to marketers to build up trends of people's tastes.
- Ensure that third parties only have access to information and computer settings on a need-to-know basis.
- Ensure that the system administrator for the organization's computer systems sets up computer accounts for third parties so that these third parties do not have access to all information on the organization's systems or have the permission to install non-standard software and change computer settings.
- When engaging an external business to destroy records or electronic media, ensure that references are checked. Draft a contract setting out the terms of the relationship. Ensure that destruction is done on-site, and require that a certificate of destruction be issued on completion.

Particular attention also needs to be given to the deletion of data and the decommissioning or transfer of devices so that all personal data are deleted. This requires expert advice. Just because certain data may be deleted does not mean that it is not retrievable or that it is deleted from all locations.

Breach Laws to Consider

What laws might affect an organization if an organization has an IT or data security breach? Suggested legal issues and laws to consider include

- GDPR.
- DPD95.
- The ePrivacy Directive and the proposed ePrivacy Regulation
- The new EU Security Directive, once enacted.
- National data protection laws.
- eCommerce laws.

- Protection of consumers in respect of contracts made by means of distance communication laws.
- Unfair terms in consumer contract laws.
- Unfair terms in consumer contracts laws.
- Child pornography laws.
- Child trafficking and pornography laws.
- Children laws.
- Consumer credit laws.
- Consumer information laws.
- Copyright laws.
- Criminal damage laws.
- Criminal evidence laws.
- Criminal justice laws.
- Employment and equality laws.
- The Human Rights Convention.
- Human rights laws.
- Evidence.
- Freedom of information laws.
- Human rights laws.
- Interception and data retention laws.
- Employment notice and terms of employment laws.
- Civil liability laws.
- Prohibition of incitement to hatred laws.
- Health and safety laws.
- ePrivacy rules.

Other issues to consider include

- Official guidance and current stated positions of regulators and guidance bodies.
- International standards for organizations; for example, technical security standards, and so on.

Third-Party Security Providers

What actions should an organization take if a third party is responsible for IT security or has access to its IT system? This is becoming increasingly popular in practice through outsourcing arrangements and vendor agreements. Some issues to consider include

- Understand the organization's security framework, and document stakeholder exposure throughout the organization.
- Evaluate what measures to take with the organization's IT provider.
- Take legal advice on drafting appropriate contracts that secure what your IT provider is securing.
- Ensure that confidentiality clauses are included to protect all of the organization's intellectual property assets.
- Have the organization's IT provider supply a complete security document outlining the hardware, topology, software, and methodologies deployed.
- Ensure that the organization's IT provider has staff participate in regular training programs to keep abreast of technical and legal issues.
- Ensure that the organization's IT provider develops a security breach response plan in the event that your company experiences a data breach.
- Develop security guidelines for laptops and other portable devices when transported off-site.
- Have the organization's IT provider ensure that all employees follow strict password and virus-protection procedures and develop a mechanism where employees are required to change passwords often, using foolproof methods, especially for terminating employees.
- Ensure that the organization's IT provider has a records retention/disposal schedule for personally identifiable information, whether stored in paper, micrographic. or magnetic/electronic (computer) media.

Disposal of Computer Hardware

Particular care is needed when considering the disposal of IT hardware, equipment and software, as they may still contain personal data files. This can continue to be the case even when it appears that files have been wiped or deleted. It is always advised to take professional legal, IT and/or forensic advice. This also applies to mobile devices.

Conclusion

Security is a legal data protection compliance requirement, as well as best business practice. This is one of the more prominent areas of compliance where time never stands still. The security risks and needs must constantly be appraised and updated. It is also essential to ensure that outsourced data processing activities are undertaken in an appropriately secure manner. Increasingly, the area of appraisals and procedures surrounding security breaches and data loss instances is regulated. If such an event arises, the data protection commissioner as well as individual data subjects may have to be informed. Liability issues should also be a constant concern for organizations as regards security and risk, notwithstanding that the penalties have increased significantly. Security is also an issue of both inward- and outward-facing concern. Employees and customers, respectively, expect their personal data to be respected. While the new Security Directive will have further provisions, it is also possible for further specifics to come from the EU Commission, national data protection supervisory authorities, and international technical standards organizations.

KEY CONCEPTS

Security is a legal data protection compliance requirement as well as best business practice. This is one of the more prominent areas of compliance for organizations.

KEYWORDS

- Security of personal data.
- Data breach.
- Notification of breach to data protection supervisory authority.
- Fines and penalties.
- Notification of breach to individual data subjects.
- Risks.
- Heightened risks.

FURTHER READING

- Calder, *A Business Guide to Information Security: How to Protect Your Company's IT Assets, Reduce Risks and Understand the Law* (Kogan, 2005).
- Dort and Criss, "Trends in Cybersecurity Law, The Privacy Shield, and Best Practices for Businesses Operating in the Global Marketplace," *Computer & Internet Lawyer* (2016) (33:7) 1.
- Gough, ed., *Data Protection for Financial Firms: A Practical Guide to Managing Privacy and Information Risk* (Risk Books, 2009).
- Harrington, "What Lawyers Need to Know about Cyber Insurance," *Computer and Internet Lawyer* (2016) (33:2) 1.
- Heim, "The Quest for Clarity on Data Protection and Security," *Network Security* (2014) (2014:2) 8.
- Hurwitz, "Data Security and the FTC's Uncommon Law," *Iowa Law Review* (2016) (101:3) 955.
- King and Raja, "Protecting the Privacy and Security of Sensitive Customer Data in the Cloud," *Computer Law & Security Review* (2012) (28) 308.
- Martecchini, "A Day in Court for Data Breach Plaintiffs: Preserving Standing Based on Increased Risk of Identity Theft after *Clapper v Amnesty International USA*," *Michigan Law Review* (2016) (114:8) 1471.
- Phan, Flo and Patel, "Recent Trends in the FTC's Data Security and Privacy Enforcement Actions," *Journal of Internet Law* (2016) (19:9) 18.
- Pierce, "Shifting Data Breach Liability: A Congressional Approach," *William and Mary Law Review* (2016) (57:3) 22.
- Tauwhare, "Improving Cybersecurity in the European Union: The Network and Information Security Directive," *Journal of Internet Law* (2016) (19:12) 3.

29
Data Breaches

Introduction

The new General Data Protection Regulation (GDPR) defines "personal data breach" as "a breach of security leading to the accidental or unlawful destruction, loss, alteration, unauthorised disclosure of, or access to, personal data transmitted, stored or otherwise processed." The importance attached to dealing with data breaches and data breach incidents is highlighted in the GDPR. Now, data breaches must be notified to the data protection supervisory authority and the individual data subjects. (Bear in mind that employees can also be individual data subjects.) Individual data subjects can suffer loss and damage if there has been a data breach, and particularly so if they are unaware of it and are not notified when the organization becomes aware so that, for example, remedial measures can be undertaken by the individual data subject. For example, they may wish to change passwords or cancel credit cards, depending on the nature of the reach. Indeed, in some instances, organizations may need to recommend remedial or safety measures to individual data subjects after a data breach.

Data Breach Incidents in Context

The issue and frequency of data breaches and data breach incidents are highlighted in Part 1. In addition, it is clear that national data protection supervisory authorities take data breaches very seriously. Significant fines are now regularly leveled at organizations, including large organizations and public organizations, in relation to data breaches. Similarly, even smaller organizations have been fined.

Data protection supervisory authorities can carry out audits and inspections of organizations, which can include security and data breach preparedness as well as resulting from a recent data breach incident. In fact, many data breaches result in media publicity for the organization, in which case the data protection supervisory authority is likely to contact the organization.

Background Guidance

Data Breach

A personal data breach may, if not addressed in an appropriate and timely manner, result in physical, material, or non-material damage to natural persons, such as loss of control over their personal data or limitation of their rights, discrimination, identity theft or fraud, financial loss, unauthorized reversal of pseudonymization, damage to reputation, loss of confidentiality of personal data protected by professional secrecy, or any other significant economic or social disadvantage to the natural person concerned. Therefore, as soon as the controller becomes aware that a personal data breach has occurred, the controller should notify the personal data breach to the data protection supervisory authority without undue delay and, where feasible, not later than 72 hours after having become aware of it, unless the controller is able to demonstrate, in accordance with the accountability principle, that the personal data breach is unlikely to result in a risk to the rights of natural persons. Where such notification cannot be achieved within 72 hours, the reasons for the delay should accompany the notification, and information may be provided in phases without undue further delay.*

Notifying Data Breach to Individual Data Subjects

The controller should communicate to the individual data subject a personal data breach, without undue delay, where that personal data breach is likely to result in a high risk to the rights of the natural person, to allow them to take the necessary precautions. The communication should describe the nature of the personal data breach as well as recommendations for the natural person concerned to mitigate potential adverse effects. Such communications to individual data subjects should be made as soon as reasonably feasible and in close cooperation with the data protection supervisory authority, respecting guidance provided by it or by other relevant authorities, such as law enforcement authorities.

---

* GDPR Recital 85.

For example, the need to mitigate an immediate risk of damage would call for prompt communication with individual data subjects. The need to implement appropriate measures against continuing or similar personal data breaches may justify more time for communication.*

Notifications and Measures re Data Breaches

It should be ascertained whether all appropriate technological protection and organizational measures have been implemented to establish immediately whether a personal data breach has taken place and to inform promptly the data protection supervisory authority and the individual data subject. The fact that the notification was made without undue delay should be established, taking into account in particular the nature and gravity of the personal data breach and its consequences and adverse effects for the individual data subject. Such notification may result in an intervention of the data protection supervisory authority in accordance with its tasks and powers laid down in the GDPR.† In setting detailed rules concerning the format and procedures applicable to the notification of personal data breaches, due consideration should be given to the circumstances of that breach, including whether or not personal data had been protected by appropriate technical protection measures, effectively limiting the likelihood of identity fraud or other forms of misuse. Moreover, such rules and procedures should take into account the legitimate interests of law enforcement authorities where early disclosure could unnecessarily hamper the investigation of the circumstances of a personal data breach.‡

Legal Rule

Notification of a Data Breach to Data Protection Supervisory Authority

In the case of a personal data breach, the new GDPR requires that the controller must without undue delay and, where feasible, not later

---

* GDPR Recital 86.
† GDPR Recital 87.
‡ GDPR Recital 88. Such rules and procedures should take into account the legitimate interests of law enforcement authorities in cases where early disclosure could unnecessarily hamper the investigation of the circumstances of a breach; ibid.

than 72 hours after having become aware of it notify the personal data breach to the competent data protection supervisory authority in accordance with Article 55, unless the personal data breach is unlikely to result in a risk to the rights of natural persons. Where the notification to the data protection supervisory authority is not made within 72 hours, it must be accompanied by reasons for the delay.*

The processor must notify the controller without undue delay after becoming aware of a personal data breach.†

This notification must at least

- Describe the nature of the personal data breach, including, where possible, the categories and approximate number of data subjects concerned and the categories and approximate number of personal data records concerned.
- Communicate the name and contact details of the data protection officer or other contact point from which more information can be obtained.
- Describe the likely consequences of the personal data breach.
- Describe the measures taken or proposed to be taken by the controller to address the personal data breach, including, where appropriate, measures to mitigate its possible adverse effects.‡

Where, and insofar as, it is not possible to provide the information at the same time, the information may be provided in phases without undue further delay.§

The controller must document any personal data breaches, comprising the facts relating to the personal data breach, its effects, and the remedial action taken. That documentation must enable the data protection supervisory authority to verify compliance with this Article.¶

---

* GDPR Article 33(1). Generally, see Breaux, Black and Newman, "A Guide to Data Protection and Breach Response," *Intellectual Property and Technology Law Journal* (2014) (26:7) 3.
† GDPR Article 33(2).
‡ GDPR Article 33(3).
§ GDPR Article 33(4).
¶ GDPR Article 33(5).

Communication of a Data Breach to the Data Subject

When the personal data breach is likely to result in a high risk to the rights of natural persons, the controller must communicate the personal data breach to the data subject without undue delay.*

The communication to the data subject referred to in paragraph 1 of this Article must describe in clear and plain language the nature of the personal data breach and contain at least the information and measures referred to in Article 33(3)(b), (c), and (d).†

The communication to the data subject referred to must not be required if any of the following conditions are met

- The controller has implemented appropriate technical and organizational protection measures, and those measures were applied to the personal data affected by the personal data breach, in particular those that render the personal data unintelligible to any person who is not authorized to access it, such as encryption.
- The controller has taken subsequent measures that ensure that the high risk to the rights of data subjects referred to is no longer likely to materialize.
- It would involve disproportionate effort. In such a case, there must instead be a public communication or similar measure whereby the data subjects are informed in an equally effective manner.‡

If the controller has not already communicated the personal data breach to the data subject, the data protection supervisory authority, having considered the likelihood of the personal data breach resulting in a high risk, may require it to do so or may decide that any of the conditions referred to in paragraph 3 are met.§

---

* GDPR Article 34(1). Note, for example, Wainman, "Data Protection Breaches: Today and Tomorrow," *Computers and Law* (June 30, 2012). Also see Dekker, Christoffer Karsberg and Daskala, *Cyber Incident Reporting in the EU* (European Network and Information Security Agency, 2012).

† GDPR Article 34(2).

‡ GDPR Article 34(3).

§ GDPR Article 32(4).

Employee Data Breaches

Employee involvement is critical in dealing with—and preparing for—data breach incidents. Various teams of employees will be involved. However, as employee personal data can also be the subject of a data breach incident, employees may need to be specifically considered in this context also. For example, they may need to be separately informed that there is a breach relating to their personal data and what actions and safeguards are being followed by the organization to deal with the issue. If the employees need to take specific actions, they may also need to be appraised of this possibility. Potentially, liability issues may also arise. For example, employees in the massive Sony data breach incidents may have considered suing Sony for breaches in relation to their data.

Notification Timelines

Organizations will need to assess the categories of personal data they have that may be involved in a data breach. They also need to assess what type of organization or sector they are involved in. These factors may dictate how the data protection regime may impose time limits for respective notification of breaches.

Notification Processes

Data protection officers and organizations need to develop, and update as appropriate, breach notification procedures. There needs to be an appropriate response plan for the different types of breach incidents, data protection supervisory authority, other regulators if appropriate or required, individual data subjects and other organizations, whether partners, processors, outsource security, and so on.

Contracts and agreements should also be reviewed to ensure appropriate breach, notification, and security provisions.

Security Standards

The requirement to comply with the new GDPR regime, to maintain security, and to prevent and to deal with data breaches increasingly directs attention to detailed standards and implementation measures; for example, ISO 15408, ISO 27001, ISO 31000, and BS10012:2009. One example is compliance with the ISO 27001 international standard for confidentiality and security. In particular, it refers to

- Security policies.
- Organizational information security.
- HR security issues (including employees, families, and contractors previously and currently).
- Asset identification and control.
- Encryption.
- Physical and environmental security factors.
- Operational security.
- Communications security.
- Acquisition, development, and maintenance of systems.
- Supplier relations.
- Security incident management.
- Security issues and business continuity.
- Compliance with internal policies and external issues such a data protection regime and other laws.

Also consider ISO 31000, on international risk management standards, and BS10012:2009, a standard for personal information management systems.

Organizations, including processors, must implement appropriate security measures, considering

- Impact assessments.
- Anonymizing data.
- Deleting after use purpose.
- Confidentiality.
- Integrity.
- Availability.
- Access controls and restrictions.
- Approved codes of conduct and certification.
- Separating, segregating, and securing different data sets.
- Encryption.

Incident Response

Some of the incident response and action points include, not in order of priority

- Incident detection and reporting.
- Incident notification to organization (e.g., notification or demand from hacker; posting online; etc.).
- Internal notification(s).
- Team notifications.
- Risk assessment.
- Impact assessments.
- Disciplinary action.
- Hacker relation action.
- Data protection supervisory authority external breach notification.
- Individual data subject breach notification.
- Customer breach notification.

Conclusion

Data breach issues should be considered in conjunction with the various risk reduction mechanisms referred to under the new GDPR regime, such as impact assessments, data protection by design, mandatory breach reporting, mandatory prior consultations with the data protection supervisory authority in the case of identified high risks, codes of conduct, and certification mechanisms.

KEY CONCEPTS

Data breaches are one of the most significant current threats to organizations. This includes the risk associated with personal data being accessed by unauthorized parties or otherwise being accessed, lost, or stolen in an unauthorized manner.

KEYWORDS

- Data breach.
- Data loss.
- Data incident.
- Security.
- Notifying data breaches.
- Responsibility and safeguards.
- Data protection officer.
- IT.

FURTHER READING

- Harrington, "What Lawyers Need to Know about Cyber Insurance," *Computer and Internet Lawyer* (2016) (33:2) 1.
- Pierce, "Shifting Data Breach Liability: A Congressional Approach," *William and Mary Law Review* (2016) (57:3) 22.

DATA PROTECTION
IMPACT ASSESSMENT AND
PRIOR CONSULTATION

Introduction

Part of the process of dealing with security threats, data breach prevention, and security breaches can involve assessment or impact assessments in advance of incidents arising. In addition, post-event or post-incident reviews and assessments are necessary. These issues are referred to in the new General Data Protection Regulation (GDPR).

Background Guidance

High Risks

To enhance compliance with the GDPR where processing operations are likely to result in a high risk to the rights of natural persons, the controller should be responsible for the carrying-out of a data protection impact assessment to evaluate, in particular, the origin, nature, particularity, and severity of that risk. The outcome of the assessment should be taken into account when determining the appropriate measures to be taken to demonstrate that the processing of personal data complies with the GDPR. Where a data protection impact assessment indicates that processing operations involve a high risk that the controller cannot mitigate by appropriate measures in terms of available technology and costs of implementation, a consultation of the data protection supervisory authority should take place prior to the processing.*

---

* GDPR Recital 84.

Data Protection Impact Assessment

A data protection impact assessment should be carried out by the controller prior to the processing to assess the particular likelihood and severity of the high risk, taking into account the nature, scope, context, and purposes of the processing and the sources of the risk. That impact assessment should include, in particular, the measures, safeguards, and mechanisms envisaged for mitigating that risk, ensuring the protection of personal data and demonstrating compliance with the GDPR.*

This should in particular apply to large-scale processing operations that aim to process a considerable amount of personal data at regional, national, or supranational level, that could affect a large number of individual data subjects, and that are likely to result in a high risk, for example, on account of their sensitivity, where in accordance with the achieved state of technological knowledge, a new technology is used on a large scale, as well as to other processing operations that result in a high risk to the rights of individual data subjects, in particular where those operations render it more difficult for individual data subjects to exercise their rights. A data protection impact assessment should also be made where personal data are processed for taking decisions regarding specific natural persons following any systematic and extensive evaluation of personal aspects relating to natural persons based on profiling those data or following the processing of special categories of personal data, biometric data, or data on criminal convictions and offenses or related security measures.

A data protection impact assessment is equally required for monitoring publicly accessible areas on a large scale, especially when using optic-electronic devices or for any other operations where the competent data protection supervisory authority considers that the processing is likely to result in a high risk to the rights of individual data subjects, in particular because they prevent individual data subjects from exercising a right or using a service or a contract, or because they are carried out systematically on a large scale. The processing of personal data should not be considered to be on a large scale if the processing concerns personal data obtained from patients or clients by

---

* GDPR Recital 90.

an individual physician, other health-care professional or lawyer. In such cases, a data protection impact assessment should not be mandatory.* It may be necessary to carry out such an assessment prior to the processing activities.†

Where a data protection impact assessment indicates that the processing would, in the absence of safeguards, security measures, and mechanisms to mitigate the risk, result in a high risk to the rights of natural persons, and the controller is of the opinion that the risk cannot be mitigated by reasonable means in terms of available technologies and costs of implementation, the data protection supervisory authority should be consulted prior to the start of processing activities. Such high risk is likely to result from certain types of processing and the extent and frequency of processing, which may result also in a realization of damage or interference with the rights of the natural person. The data protection supervisory authority should respond to the request for consultation within a specified period. However, the absence of a reaction of the data protection supervisory authority within that period should be without prejudice to any intervention of the data protection supervisory authority in accordance with its tasks and powers laid down in the GDPR, including the power to prohibit processing operations. As part of that consultation process, the outcome of a data protection impact assessment carried out with regard to the processing at issue may be submitted to the data protection supervisory authority, in particular the measures envisaged to mitigate the risk to the rights of natural persons.‡

The processor should assist the controller, where necessary and on request, in ensuring compliance with the obligations deriving from the carrying-out of data protection impact assessments and from prior consultation of the data protection supervisory authority.§

---

* GDPR Recital 91. The Recital also refers to particular caveats.
† GDPR Recital 93.
‡ GDPR Recital 94.
§ GDPR Recital 95. A consultation of the data protection supervisory authority should also take place in the course of the preparation of a legislative or regulatory measure that provides for the processing of personal data to ensure compliance of the intended processing with this Regulation and in particular to mitigate the risk involved for the data subject; GDPR Recital 96.

There is also specific reference to processing carried out by a public authority. Where the processing is carried out by a public authority, except for courts or independent judicial authorities when acting in their judicial capacity; where, in the private sector, processing is carried out by a controller whose core activities consist of processing operations that require regular and systematic monitoring of the individual data subjects on a large scale; or where the core activities of the controller or the processor consist of processing on a large scale of special categories of personal data and data relating to criminal convictions and offenses, a person with expert knowledge of data protection law and practices should assist the controller or processor to monitor internal compliance with the GDPR. In the private sector, the core activities of a controller relate to its primary activities and do not relate to the processing of personal data as an ancillary activity. The necessary level of expert knowledge should be determined, in particular according to the data processing operations carried out and the protection required for the personal data processed by the controller or the processor. Such data protection officers, whether or not they are employees of the controller, should be in a position to perform their duties and tasks in an independent manner.*

Legal Rule

Chapter IV, Section 3 of the GDPR refers to data protection impact assessment (sometimes also referred to as *privacy impact assessments*) and prior consultation.

As a result of the new GDPR regime, there is now a mandatory impact assessment regime. These assessments must be undertaken when data processing activities involve specific data protection and privacy risks. In particular when new products and services, or other changes to existing products and services, arise, the organization should ensure that these activities are the subject of a data protection impact assessment.

These impact assessments will help organizations to identify and understand current and new risks in their processing activities, or indeed to their processing activities. Considerations include

---

* GDPR Recital 97.

- Identifying when a project involves the collection of new information about individuals.
- Identifying whether information about individuals will be disclosed to organizations or people who have not previously had routine access to the information.
- Identifying whether the project involves the use of new technology that may raise privacy and data protection issues, such as overreach or privacy intrusion.
- Identifying whether the personal data raise issues or concerns or are in some way objectionable.

Article 35 is headed "Data Protection Impact Assessment." Where a type of processing in particular using new technologies, and taking into account the nature, scope, context, and purposes of the processing, is likely to result in a high risk to the rights of natural persons, the controller must, prior to the processing, carry out an assessment of the impact of the envisaged processing operations on the protection of personal data. A single assessment may address a set of similar processing operations that present similar high risks.[*]

The controller must seek the advice of the data protection officer, where designated, when carrying out a data protection impact assessment.[†]

A data protection impact assessment is required in the case of

- A systematic and extensive evaluation of personal aspects relating to natural persons that is based on automated processing, including profiling, and on which decisions are based that produce legal effects concerning the natural person or similarly significantly affect the natural person.
- Processing on a large scale of special categories of data[‡] or of personal data relating to criminal convictions and offenses;[§] or.
- A systematic monitoring of a publicly accessible area on a large scale.[¶]

---

[*] GDPR Article 35(1).
[†] GDPR Article 35(2).
[‡] Referred to in GDPR Article 9(1).
[§] Referred to in GDPR Article 10.
[¶] GDPR Article 35(3).

The data protection supervisory authority must establish and make public a list of the kinds of processing operations that are subject to the requirement for a data protection impact assessment. The data protection supervisory authority must communicate those lists to the European Data Protection Board (EDPB).*

The data protection supervisory authority may also establish and make public a list of the kinds of processing operations for which no data protection impact assessment is required. The data protection supervisory authority must communicate those lists to the EDPB.[†]

Prior to the adoption of the lists referred to, the competent data protection supervisory authority must apply the consistency mechanism[‡] where such lists involve processing activities that are related to the offering of goods or services to data subjects or to the monitoring of their behavior in several member states, or may substantially affect the free movement of personal data within the EU.[§]

The assessment must contain at least

- A systematic description of the envisaged processing operations and the purposes of the processing, including, where applicable, the legitimate interest pursued by the controller.
- An assessment of the necessity and proportionality of the processing operations in relation to the purposes.
- An assessment of the risks to the rights of data subjects referred to; and.
- The measures envisaged to address the risks, including safeguards, security measures, and mechanisms to ensure the protection of personal data and to demonstrate compliance with the GDPR, taking into account the rights and legitimate interests of data subjects and other persons concerned.[¶]

Compliance with approved codes of conduct referred to in Article 40 by the relevant controllers or processors must be taken into due account in assessing the impact of the processing operations performed

---

* GDPR Article 35(4).
[†] GDPR Article 35(5).
[‡] Referred to in Article 63.
[§] GDPR Article 35(6).
[¶] GDPR Article 35(7).

by such controllers or processors, in particular for the purposes of a data protection impact assessment.*

Where appropriate, the controller must seek the views of data subjects or their representatives on the intended processing, without prejudice to the protection of commercial or public interests or the security of processing operations.†

Where processing pursuant to Article 6(1)(c) or (e) has a legal basis in EU law or in the law of the member state to which the controller is subject, that law regulates the specific processing operation or set of operations in question, and a data protection impact assessment has already been carried out as part of a general impact assessment in the context of the adoption of that legal basis, paragraphs 1 to 7 must not apply unless member states deem it to be necessary to carry out such an assessment prior to processing activities.‡

Where necessary, the controller must carry out a review to assess whether processing is performed in accordance with the data protection impact assessment, at least when there is a change of the risk represented by the processing operations.§

Reasons for Assessments

Vodafone refers to the following reasons for assessments

- *Accountability*: To demonstrate that the assessment process was performed appropriately and in accord with the program of assessments agreed with the board sponsor for privacy.
- *Provides basis for post-implementation review*: To ensure that any privacy risks identified are allocated a business owner and a timetable for delivery mitigation actions, therefore providing the data protection officer with a mechanism for ensuring that the agreed actions are delivered with agreed timescales.
- *Provides a basis for audit*: Vodafone distinguishes between review, which is undertaken by the data protection officer, who is responsible for ensuring it is implemented and the

---

* GDPR Article 35(8).
† GDPR Article 35(9).
‡ GDPR Article 35(10).
§ GDPR Article 35(11).

controls required are delivered, and the audit, which is an objective and neutral assessment undertaken by the group or local audit function or any other suitably qualified audit function that is not part of delivering the overall privacy risk management system.

- *Provides corporate memory*: Ensures that the information gained is available to those completing new assessments especially if original staff have left.
- Enables the experience gained during the project to be shared with the future assessment teams and others outside the organization.[*]

Nokia also give reasons for undertaking assessments

- "To measure the implementation of privacy requirements, to get an understanding of the current status (risk, controls, root causes, etc.)."[†]
- The assessment is part of technical and organizational measures. It assists in finding out whether new projects follow the privacy requirements; project management; communicating the fulfillment of requirements; and generating status reports for management teams, and is an effective tool for assigning responsibility and fixing problems.
- The impact assessment serves as "a repository for information requests from authorities and consumers. Consumers might ask Nokia where and for how long their data is stored. A data protection authority might, for example, ask how consumers are informed about privacy practices or who the controller of the data is. Privacy assessment might also be used to prepare notifications for data protection authorities."[‡]
- "A means to improve general awareness. The assessment process ... builds up competencies and privacy awareness, as it

---

[*] Deadman and Chandler, "Vodafone's Approach to Privacy Impact Assessments," in Wright and de Hert, eds, *Privacy Impact Assessment* (Springer, 2012) 298.

[†] Brautigam, "PIA: Cornerstone of Privacy Compliance in Nokia," in Wright and de Hert, eds, *Privacy Impact Assessment* (Springer, 2012) 260.

[‡] ibid.

offers an extensive set of questions that might be relevant for privacy compliance."*

Assessment Reports

Some key elements of an assessment report include

- The scope of the assessment undertaken.
- A summary of the consultative process undertaken.
- The project background paper(s) provided to those consulted
- Analysis of the privacy issues and risks arising from the assessment.
- The business case justifying privacy intrusion, implications, mitigation action, together with timelines for implementation.
- References to relevant laws, codes, and guidelines, including internal Vodafone local group policies.†

Assessment Characteristics

Common characteristics of impact assessments include

- *Statement of problem*: Is government intervention both necessary and desirable?
- *Definition of alternative remedies*: These include different approaches, such as the use of economic incentives or voluntary approaches.
- *Determination of the physical effects of each alternative, including potential unintended consequences*: The net should be cast wide. Generally speaking, regulations or investments in many areas of public policy can have social, environmental, and other implications that must be kept in mind.
- *Estimation of benefits and costs of each alternative*: Benefits should be quantified and where possible monetized. Benefits should be true opportunity and costs not simply expenditures.

---

* ibid.
† Deadman and Chandler, "Vodafone's Approach to Privacy Impact Assessments," in Wright and de Hert, eds, *Privacy Impact Assessment* (Springer, 2012), 299.

- Assessment of other economic impacts, including effects on competition, effects on small firms, and international trade implications.
- Identification of winners and losers: those in the community who stand to gain and lose from each alternative and, if possible, the extent of their gains and losses.
- *Communication with the interested public, including the following activities*: Notification of intent to regulate, request for compliance costs and other data, public disclosure of regulatory proposals and supporting analysis, and consideration of and response to public comments.
- A clear choice of the preferred alternative, plus a statement defending that choice.
- *Provision of a plan for ex post analysis of regulatory outcomes*: It is important to establish a benchmark against which to measure performance. Planning is needed to ensure that procedures are in place for the collection of data to permit such benchmarking.*

Some assessment characteristics distinguishing it from other data protection–related processes include the following

- An assessment focuses on a particular initiative or project.
- An assessment is performed at depth, through the project life cycle, and involves engagement with stakeholders.
- An assessment assesses a project against the needs, expectations, and concerns of all stakeholders, including but not limited to legal requirements.
- An assessment assesses all aspects of privacy and data protection.
- An assessment adopts a multi-perspective approach, taking into account the costs and benefits as perceived by all stakeholders.

---

* OECD, Regulatory performance: Ex post evaluation of regulatory tools and institutions, Working Party on Regulatory Management and Reform, Draft Report by the Secretariat, OECD, Paris (2004) 7; referred to in Parker, "(Regulatory) Impact Assessment and Better Regulation," in Wright and de Hert, eds, *Privacy Impact Assessment* (Springer, 2012) 80.

- An assessment adopts a multi-perspective approach, taking into account the risks as perceived by all stakeholders.
- An assessment is a process used to establish what the organization needs to give.
- An assessment is a process that identifies the problems and identifies solutions to them.
- An assessment is conducted before and in parallel with a project, and ensures that harmful and expensive problems that an audit would later expose are avoided, and that unavoidable negative impacts on privacy are minimized and harms mitigated.*

Steps and Methodologies

The key steps and methodologies in an assessment can include

- Identifying all of the personal data related to a program or service and looking at how they will be used.
- Mapping where personal data are sent after collection.
- Identifying privacy and data protection risks and the level of the risks.
- Finding methods to eliminate or reduce the risks.†

Organizations might consider issues such as the following:

- Preparation.
- Undertaking of the assessment.
- Timing of the assessment.
- Cost and resourcing the assessment.
- Whom the report is for.
- Issues and problems raised.
- Independence of those undertaking the assessment.
- Any constraints.

---

* Clarke, PIAs in Australia: A Work-in-Progress Report, in Wright and de Hert, eds, *Privacy Impact Assessment* (Springer, 2012) 121.
† Office of the Privacy Commissioner of Canada, Fact Sheet on Privacy Impact Assessment. Also note OIPC of Alberta, Commissioner accepts privacy impact assessment for the Alberta Security Screening Directive, press release, January 16, 2003.

- Legal professional privilege and confidentiality
- After undertaking the assessment, draft report, comments, final report
- Whether the assessment is a one-off or an ongoing assessment in a (rolling) series

Prior Consultation and Risk

Article 36 refers to prior consultation obligations. The controller must consult the data protection supervisory authority prior to processing where a data protection impact assessment under Article 35 indicates that the processing would result in a high risk in the absence of measures taken by the controller to mitigate the risk.*

Where the data protection supervisory authority is of the opinion that the intended processing would infringe the GDPR, in particular where the controller has insufficiently identified or mitigated the risk, the data protection supervisory authority must, within a period of up to 8 weeks of receipt of the request for consultation, provide written advice to the controller and, where applicable, to the processor, and may use any of its powers. That period may be extended by 6 weeks, taking into account the complexity of the intended processing. The data protection supervisory authority must inform the controller and, where applicable, the processor of any such extension within 1 month of receipt of the request for consultation together with the reasons for the delay. Those periods may be suspended until the data protection supervisory authority has obtained information it has requested for the purposes of the consultation.†

When consulting the data protection supervisory authority, the controller must provide the data protection supervisory authority with

- Where applicable, the respective responsibilities of the controller, joint controllers, and processors involved in the processing, in particular for processing within a group of undertakings.
- The purposes and means of the intended processing.

---

* GDPR Article 36(1).
† GDPR Article 36(2).

- The measures and safeguards provided to protect the rights of data subjects pursuant to the GDPR.
- Where applicable, the contact details of the data protection officer.
- The data protection impact assessment; and.
- Any other information requested by the data protection supervisory authority.*

Member states must consult the data protection supervisory authority during the preparation of a proposal for a legislative measure to be adopted by a national parliament, or of a regulatory measure based on such a legislative measure, which relates to processing.†

Notwithstanding this, member state law may require controllers to consult with, and obtain prior authorization from, the data protection supervisory authority in relation to processing by a controller for the performance of a task carried out by the controller in the public interest, including processing in relation to social protection and public health.‡

Conclusion

Carrying out impact assessments and the like not only helps to identify privacy and data protection problems, in which case these can then be addressed, but it helps to raise these at the earliest stage possible. Therefore, the least expensive and least problematic time to make remedial changes is engaged. Carrying out such assessments is not a requirement under the new GDPR regime. This is especially so for high-risk activities and when sensitive personal data may be involved. These assessments ensure that organizations understand the data they hold and understand the likely problem issues arising. The organization, its processes, and the ultimate customer relationship will all be improved. Impact assessments are ultimately one of the mechanisms under the new GDPR for assessing, and thus minimizing, risk in the personal data environment.

---

* GDPR Article 36(3).
† GDPR Article 36(4).
‡ GDPR Article 37(5).

Organizations must now be proactive and assess when processing activities are likely to raise risks in relation to personal data and processing. The data protection officer and other relevant parties/teams must be involved. Assessments must be more systematic. Risk identification and evaluation are now key considerations. Measures to mitigate and address risks must be considered and documented, including risk assessments. In situations where there are substantial risk issues, it may be necessary to consult with the data protection supervisory authority.

KEY CONCEPTS

Organizations should be proactive in seeking to identify, assess, and implement mechanisms to prevent and reduce potential incidents regarding personal data. Certain activities and certain sets of data may require impact assessment(s)

KEY WORDS

- Data protection impact assessment.
- Where processing is likely to result in high risk to rights, the organization must, prior to processing, carry out an assessment of the impact of the envisaged processing on the protection of personal data.
- In particular, processing using new technologies.
- Nature, scope, context, and purposes of processing.
- Single assessment.
- Multiple assessments.
- Prior consultation.

FURTHER READING

- Wright, "The State of the Art in Privacy Impact Assessments," *Computer Law & Security Review* (2012) (28) 54.

31
DATA PROTECTION
BY DESIGN

Introduction

It has been suggested that "law should play a more active role in establishing best practices for emerging online trends."* Data protection by design and by default is a prime example. One of the most important and developing practical areas of data protection is the concept of data protection by design as referred to in the General Data Protection Regulation (GDPR). Originally developed as a follow-on from the data protection legal regime, it is now being recognized more widely and is also being explicitly referred to and recognized in primary legislation itself.

Data protection by design is important for organizations not only in terms of being a legal obligation but also commercially in terms of being a competitive advantage.†

Background

Previously, data protection by design has been referred to as *privacy by design* or PbD. The concept of data protection by design is complementary to data protection law and regulation. The idea is acknowledged to have started with Dr. Ann Cavoukian, the Information & Privacy Commissioner for Ontario, Canada. She states that

> the increasing complexity and interconnectedness of information technologies [require] building privacy right into system design ... the

---

* McGeveran, "Disclosure, Endorsement, and Identity in Social Marketing," *Illinois Law Review* (2009) (4) 1105.

† See, for example, Mantelero, "Competitive Value of Data Protection: The Impact of Data Protection Regulation on Online Behaviour," *International Data Privacy Law* (2013) (3:4) 229.

concept of Privacy by Design (PbD)… describe[s] the philosophy of embedding privacy proactively into technology itself – making it the default."*

Principles of Data Protection by Design

The Information and Privacy Commissioner for Ontario refers to seven principles of PbD.† These are set out here:

> *Proactive Not Reactive; Preventive Not Remedial*: The Privacy by Design (PbD) approach is characterized by proactive rather than reactive measures. It anticipates and prevents privacy-invasive events before they happen. PbD does not wait for privacy risks to materialize, nor does it offer remedies for resolving privacy infractions once they have occurred—it aims to prevent them from occurring. In short, PbD comes before the fact, not after.
>
> *Privacy as the Default Setting*: We can all be certain of one thing—the default rules. PbD seeks to deliver the maximum degree of privacy by ensuring that personal data are automatically protected in any given information technology (IT) system or business practice. If an individual does nothing, their privacy still remains intact. No action is required on the part of the individual to protect their privacy—it is built into the system, by default.
>
> *Privacy Embedded into Design*: PbD is embedded into the design and architecture of IT systems and business practices. It is not bolted on as an add-on, after the fact. The result is that privacy becomes an essential component of the core functionality being delivered. Privacy is integral to the system without diminishing functionality.
>
> *Full Functionality: Positive-Sum, Not Zero-Sum*: PbD seeks to accommodate all legitimate interests and objectives in a positive-sum "win-win" manner, not through a dated, zero-sum approach where unnecessary trade-offs are made. PbD avoids

---

* At http://privacybydesign.ca/about/.

† At www.privacybydesign.ca/content/uploads/2009/08/7foundationalprinciples.pdf.

the pretense of false dichotomies, such as privacy vs. security, demonstrating that it is possible to have both.

End-to-End Security: Full Lifecycle Protection: PbD, having been embedded into the system prior to the first element of information being collected, extends securely throughout the entire lifecycle of the data involved—strong security measures are essential to privacy, from start to finish. This ensures that all data are securely retained, and then securely destroyed at the end of the process, in a timely fashion. Thus, PbD ensures cradle-to-grave, secure lifecycle management of information, end-to-end.

Visibility and Transparency: Keep It Open: PbD seeks to assure all stakeholders that whatever the business practice or technology involved, it is, in fact, operating according to the stated promises and objectives, subject to independent verification. Its component parts and operations remain visible and transparent to users and providers alike. Remember, trust but verify.

Respect for User Privacy: Keep It User-Centric: Above all, PbD requires architects and operators to keep the interests of the individual uppermost by offering such measures as strong privacy defaults, appropriate notice, and empowering user-friendly options. Keep it user-centric.*

Legal Rule: Data Protection by Design

The EU Commission proposed an enhanced data protection regime including data protection by design.† Article 25 of the data protection by design refers to data protection by design and by default. This is an increasingly important area in data protection.

---

* At www.privacybydesign.ca/content/uploads/2009/08/7foundationalprinciples.pdf.
† See Spiekermann, "The Challenges of Privacy by Design," *Communications of the ACM* (2012) (55) 38; Spiekermann and Cranor, "Engineering Privacy," *IEEE Transactions on Software Engineering* (2009) (35) 67; Tielemans and Hildebrandt, "Data Protection by Design and Technology Neutral Law," *Computer Law and Security Review* (2013) (29:5) 509.

Individual data subjects' rights and legitimate interests are in place and must be respected, both generally and in business planning and processes. This involves compliance per se as well as pre-problem-solving to eliminate personal data problems arising.

Article 25 of the new GDPR refers to data protection by design and by default. Note also the related concept of PbD. In some ways, PbD is the impetus or precursor for the current data protection by design rules.

Taking into account the state of the art, the cost of implementation, and the nature, scope, context, and purposes of processing as well as the risks of varying likelihood and severity for rights of natural persons posed by the processing, the controller must, both at the time of the determination of the means for processing and at the time of the processing itself, implement appropriate technical and organizational measures, such as pseudonymization, which are designed to implement data protection principles, such as data minimization, in an effective manner and to integrate the necessary safeguards into the processing so as to meet the requirements of the GDPR and protect the rights of data subjects.*

The controller must implement appropriate technical and organizational measures for ensuring that, by default, only personal data that are necessary for each specific purpose of the processing are processed. That obligation applies to the amount of personal data collected, the extent of their processing, the period of their storage, and their accessibility. In particular, such measures must ensure that by default, personal data are not made accessible without the individual's intervention to an indefinite number of natural persons.†

An approved certification mechanism pursuant to Article 42 may be used as an element to demonstrate compliance with the requirements set out in paragraphs 1 and 2 of this Article.‡

Data protection by design is embraced by EU data protection supervisory authorities. Prior to the new GDPD, the UK data protection supervisory authority (Information Commissioner's Office [ICO]) has issued recommendations in relation to privacy notices, namely,

---

* GDPR Article 25(1).
† GDPR Article 25(2).
‡ GDPR art 25(3).

the Privacy Impact Assessment Code of Practice. This now needs to be read in light of the GDPR changes. The UK data protection supervisory authority refers to data protection by design by saying that it is "an approach whereby privacy and data protection compliance is designed into systems holding information right from the start, rather than being bolted on afterwards or ignored, as has too often been the case."[*] It provides various documents and guidance.[†]

Many multinationals and other organizations are embracing data protection by design. Microsoft, for example, has endorsed data protection by design for a number of years now.

Conclusion

Organizations must be proactive and not reactive. Data protection considerations need to be considered and built in from the earliest stage in processes that potentially impact data protection. They must be transparent and visible. Problem issues are addressed and solutions incorporated into the process design and process cycle so that pre-problem-solving is achieved for personal data. Data protection by design needs to be built in, not merely added or considered once a problem arises at the end or after go-live. However, data protection by design means incorporating these considerations into the whole life cycle and not just at the beginning and/or the end. It is also incorporated into engineering processes and not just system consideration and data categories. Data protection regime is now a key concept and requirement under the new data protection by design. There is increasing emphasis on data protection engineering as a part of the mechanisms needed to achieve data protection by design.

---

[*] UK data protection supervisory authority (ICO), *Privacy by Design*.

[†] ibid. Privacy by Design report; Privacy by Design implementation plan; privacy impact assessment (PIA) handbook, PbD ICO Implementation Plan; privacy impact assessment; ICO technical guidance note on Privacy-Enhancing Technologies (PETs), Privacy by Design, An Overview of Privacy Enhancing Technologies; Enterprise Privacy Group paper on PETs; Homeland security, biometric Identification and personal Detection Ethics (HIDE); Glossary of privacy and data protection terms; Privacy Impact Assessments—international study (Loughborough University).

Data protection by design is one of the more important innovations in data protection generally. This is reflected in the data protection by design. All organizations will need to apprise themselves of the concept and the regulatory compliance issues. The Google requirement to implement data protection by design is also timely and reflects the importance of enterprise, both large and small, needing to engage the benefits, as well as the requirements, of data protection by design.

Data protection impact assessments* are also referred to in the GDPR and may also be relevant in the context of data protection by design. Data protection impact assessments are also relevant in the context of developing cloud services.† Cloud services also raise important data protection and security considerations, and these should be carefully considered by customers as well as providers.‡ The Article 29 Data Protection Working Party (WP29) has also commented in relation to cloud issues,§ Big Data issues,¶ Internet of Things (IoT),**

---

* Wright, "The State of the Art in Privacy Impact Assessments," *Computer Law & Security Review* (2012) (28) 54.

† Cloud and data protection reliability and compliance issues are referred to in Clarke, "How Reliable Is Cloudsourcing? A Review of Articles in the Technical Media 2005–11," *Computer Law & Security Review* (2012) (28) 90. King and Raja also research the area of the protections of sensitive personal data and cloud computing; see King and Raja, "Protecting the Privacy and Security of Sensitive Customer Data in the Cloud," *Computer Law & Security Review* (2012) (28) 308; Peng, "A New Model of Data Protection on Cloud Storage," *Journal of Networks* (03/2014) (9:3) 666.

‡ See, for example, UK data protection supervisory authority (ICO), *Guidance on the Use of Cloud Computing*; WP29, *Opinion 05/2012 on Cloud Computing*, WP 196; Lanois, "Caught in the Clouds: The Web 2.0, Cloud Computing, and Privacy?" *Northwestern Journal of Technology and Intellectual Property* (2010) (9) 29; Pinguelo and Muller, "Avoid the Rainy Day: Survey of US Cloud Computing Caselaw," *Boston College Intellectual Property & Technology Forum* (2011) 1; Kattan, "Cloudy Privacy Protections: Why the Stored Communications Act Fails to Protect the Privacy of Communications Stored in the Cloud," *Vandenburg Journal of Entertainment and Technology Law* (2010–2011) (13) 617.

§ WP29, Opinion 02/2015 on C-SIG Code of Conduct on Cloud Computing; and Opinion 05/2012 on cloud computing.

¶ WP29, Statement of the WP29 on the impact of the development of Big Data on the protection of individuals with regard to the processing of their personal data in the EU, 2014. The ICO also issued guidance on Big Data and data protection issues prior to the new GDPR.

**WP29, Opinion 8/2014 on the recent developments on the Internet of Things. Weber, "Internet of Things: Privacy Issues Revisited," *Computer Law and Security Report* (2015) (31:5) 618.

drones,* apps on smart devices,† cookies,‡ device fingerprinting,§ anonymization techniques,¶ purpose limitation,** smart devices,†† and so on.

KEY CONCEPTS

There are various problems that can arise after the event if data
protection compliance and security issues have not been considered in advance of the roll out of new processes, services, and
activities. However, if data protection, risk minimization, security, and so on are introduced at the very initial conception stage
and included throughout the development process, the data protection risks, problems, and so on that can arise will be minimized
in number and scale. This policy of incorporating data protection
throughout the life cycle is known as *data protection by design*.
This is expressly included as part of the GDPR obligations.

KEY WORDS

- Data protection by design.
- Privacy by design.
- The state of the art.
- Cost of implementation.
- Nature, scope, context, and purposes of processing.
- Risks of varying likelihood and severity for rights of processing.
- Organizations must both at determination of means for pro-
  cessing, and at the time of the processing.

---

* WP29, Opinion 01/2015 on privacy and data protection issues relating to the utili-
zation of drones.
† WP29, Opinion 02/2013 on apps on smart devices.
‡ WP29, Cookie sweep combined analysis 2015; Opinion 04/2012 on cookie consent
exemption.
§ WP29, Opinion 9/2014 on the application of Directive 2002/58/EC to device
fingerprinting.
¶ WP29, Opinion 05/2014 on anonymisation techniques. The ICO has previously
issued guidance on anonymization techniques prior to the GDPR in an anonymiza-
tion code of practice (2012).
**WP29, Opinion 03/2013 on purpose limitation.
††WP29, Opinion 02/2013 on apps on smart devices.

- At determination of means for processing.
- at the time of the processing.
- Implement appropriate technical and organizational measures.
- Such as pseudonymization.
- Designed to implement data protection principles, such as data minimization, in an effective manner and to integrate necessary safeguards into the processing.
- To meet the requirements of GDPR and protect individual data subjects' rights.

FURTHER READING

- Finneran Dennedy, Fox, Finneran, *The Privacy Engineer's Manifesto, Getting from Policy to Code to QA* (Aspen Open, 2014).
- Schartum, "Making Privacy by Design Operative," *International Journal of Law and Information Technology* (2016) (24:2) 151.

32

DATA PROTECTION AS DEFAULT

Introduction

Following on from data protection by design, the General Data Protection Regulation (GDPR) introduces a complimentary concept of data protection by default. Consider the example of Google outdoor mapping and imaging in Streetview in the United Kingdom (and possibly elsewhere). In addition to the main imaging, the equipment is also said to have collected individuals' Wi-Fi data and Wi-Fi passwords. The company later claimed that this secondary activity was unintended. Without getting into the specific details, this serves as an example of how default policies and procedures can help to prevent unintended consequences.

Legal Rule

The controller must implement appropriate technical and organizational measures for ensuring that, by default, only personal data that are necessary for each specific purpose of the processing are processed. That obligation applies to the amount of personal data collected, the extent of their processing, the period of their storage, and their accessibility. In particular, such measures must ensure that by default, personal data are not made accessible without the individual's intervention to an indefinite number of natural persons. This is contained in GDPR Article 25(2).

Assessments

Data protection impact assessments* are also referred to in the GDPR and may also be relevant in the context of data protection by default. Data protection impact assessments are also relevant in the context of

---

* Wright, "The State of the Art in Privacy Impact Assessments," *Computer Law & Security Review* (2012) (28) 54.

developing cloud services.* Cloud services also raise important data protection and security considerations, and these should be carefully considered by customers as well as providers.† The Article 29 Data Protection Working Party (WP29) has also commented in relation to cloud issues,‡ Big Data issues,§ Internet of Things (IoT),¶ drones,** apps on smart devices,†† cookies,‡‡ device fingerprinting,§§ anonymization techniques,¶¶ purpose limitation,*** smart devices,††† and so on.

---

* Cloud and data protection reliability and compliance issues are referred to in Clarke, "How Reliable Is Cloudsourcing? A Review of Articles in the Technical Media 2005–11," *Computer Law & Security Review* (2012) (28) 90. King and Raja also research the area of the protections of sensitive personal data and cloud computing; see King and Raja, "Protecting the Privacy and Security of Sensitive Customer Data in the Cloud," *Computer Law & Security Review* (2012) (28) 308; Peng, "A New Model of Data Protection on Cloud Storage," *Journal of Networks* (03/2014) (9:3) 666.

† See, for example, UK data protection supervisory authority (Information Commissioner's Office [ICO]), Guidance on the use of cloud computing; WP29, Opinion 05/2012 on cloud computing, WP 196; Lanois, "Caught in the Clouds: The Web 2.0, Cloud Computing, and Privacy?" *Northwestern Journal of Technology and Intellectual Property* (2010) (9) 29; Pinguelo and Muller, "Avoid the Rainy Day: Survey of US Cloud Computing Caselaw," *Boston College Intellectual Property & Technology Forum* (2011) 1; Kattan, "Cloudy Privacy Protections: Why the Stored Communications Act Fails to Protect the Privacy of Communications Stored in the Cloud," *Vandenburg Journal of Entertainment and Technology Law* (2010–2011) (13) 617.

‡ WP29, Opinion 02/2015 on C-SIG code of conduct on cloud computing; and Opinion 05/2012 on cloud computing.

§ WP29, Statement of the WP29 on the impact of the development of Big Data on the protection of individuals with regard to the processing of their personal data in the EU, 2014. The ICO also issued guidance on Big Data and data protection issues prior to the new GDPR.

¶ WP29, Opinion 8/2014 on the recent developments on the Internet of Things. Weber, "Internet of Things: Privacy Issues Revisited," *Computer Law and Security Report* (2015) (31:5) 618.

** WP29, Opinion 01/2015 on privacy and data protection issues relating to the utilization of drones.

†† WP29, Opinion 02/2013 on apps on smart devices.

‡‡ WP29, Cookie sweep combined analysis 2015; Opinion 04/2012 on cookie consent exemption.

§§ WP29, Opinion 9/2014 on the application of Directive 2002/58/EC to device fingerprinting.

¶¶ WP29, Opinion 05/2014 on anonymisation techniques. The ICO has previously issued guidance on anonymization techniques prior to the GDPD in an anonymization code of practice (2012).

*** WP29, Opinion 03/2013 on purpose limitation.

††† WP29, Opinion 02/2013 on apps on smart devices.

Certification

An approved certification mechanism pursuant to Article 42 may be used as an element to demonstrate compliance with the requirements set out. This is contained in GDPR Article 25(3).

Conclusion

Organizations must be proactive and not reactive. Data protection considerations need to be considered and built in from the earliest stage in processes that potentially impact data protection. They must be transparent and visible. Problem issues are addressed and solutions incorporated into the process design and process cycle so that pre-problem-solving is achieved for personal data. Data protection by default needs to be built in, not merely added or considered once a problem arises at the end or after go-live. However, data protection by default means incorporating these considerations into the whole life cycle and not just at the beginning and/ or the end. It is also incorporated into engineering processes and not just system consideration and data categories. Data protection by default is now a key concept and requirement under the new GDPD. There is increasing emphasis on privacy engineering as a part of the mechanisms needed to achieve data protection by design.

Data protection by default is one of the more important innovations in data protection generally. This is reflected in the GDPR. All organizations will need to apprise themselves of the concept and the regulatory compliance issues.

KEY CONCEPTS

Data protection by default can assist organizations in reducing adverse data protection incidents. As stated previously, incorporating data protection by default can assist in avoiding problems that might otherwise arise, whether predictable or unanticipated.

KEYWORDS

- Data protection as default.
- Organizations must implement measures to ensure by default that only personal data necessary for each specific purpose of the processing are processed.
- Amount of personal data collected.
- Extent of processing.
- Period of storage.
- Accessibility.
- Must ensure that by default, personal data are not made accessible without the individual's intervention to an indefinite number of natural persons.

FURTHER READING

- UK supervisory authority (ICO), Guidance on the use of cloud computing; WP29, Opinion 05/2012 on cloud computing, WP 196.

33

CROSS-BORDER TRANSFERS OF DATA

Introduction

Organizations are under ever-increasing pressure to reduce costs. This can sometimes involve consideration of outsourcing to countries outside of the EU. Any transfers, unless specifically excepted, are restricted.

In addition, the global nature of commercial activities means that organizations as part of normal business processes may seek to transfer particular sets of personal data to group entities that may be located outside of the EU. There can be similar situations where an organization wishes to make trans-border data flows to agents, partners, or outsourced processors.

The data protection regime controls and regulates transfers of personal data* from the United Kingdom to jurisdictions outside of the EU. Transfers of personal data outside of the EU are known as *cross-border transfers*.† Frequently, organizations would have transferred personal data to other sections within their international organizations, such as banks. This could be personal data in relation to customers as well as employees (e.g., where the personnel or payroll section may be in a different country).

---

* See Nugter, *Transborder Flow of Personal Data within the EC* (Kluwer Law and Taxation Publishers, 1990).
† Previously referred to as *trans-border data flows*. Beling, "Transborder Data Flows: International Privacy Protection and the Free Flow of Information," *Boston College International and Comparative Law Review* (1983) (6) 591; "Declaration on Transborder Data Flows," *International Legal Materials* (1985) (24) 912; "Council Recommendation Concerning Guidelines Governing the Protection of Privacy and Transborder Flows of Personal Data," *International Legal Materials* (1981) (20) 422; "Draft Recommendation of the Council Concerning Guidelines Governing the Protection of Privacy and Transborder Flows of Personal Data," *International Legal Materials* (1980) (19) 318.

This trend of cross-border transfers has increased, however, as more and more activity is carried out online, such as eCommerce and social media. Personal data are frequently transferred or mirrored on computer servers in more than one country as a matter of technical routine.

However, organizations need to be aware that any transfer of personal data of EU citizens needs to be in compliance with the EU data protection regime. One of the obligations is that cross-border transfers of personal data may not occur.* This default position can be derogated from if one of a limited number of criteria is satisfied.

Background Guidance

Cross-Border Flows

Economic and social integration increases cross-border flows. The exchange of data has increased.† Rapid technological developments and globalization have brought new challenges for the protection of personal data. The scale of the collection and sharing of personal data has increased significantly. Technology allows both private companies and public authorities to make use of personal data on an unprecedented scale to pursue their activities. Natural persons increasingly make personal information available publicly and globally. Technology has transformed both the economy and social life and should, further, facilitate the free flow of personal data within the EU and the transfer to third countries and international organizations, while ensuring a high level of protection of personal data.‡ Those developments require a strong and more coherent data protection framework in the EU, backed by strong enforcement, given the importance of creating the trust that will allow the digital economy to develop across the internal market. Natural persons should have control of their own personal data. Legal and practical certainty for natural persons, economic operators, and public authorities should be

---

* For one article noting the difficulties that the data protection regime creates in terms of trans-border data flows, see Kong, "Data Protection and Trans Border Data Flow in the European and Global Context," *European Journal of International Law* (2010) (21) 441.
† GDPR Recital 5.
‡ GDPR Recital 6.

enhanced.* Flows of personal data to and from countries outside the EU and international organizations are necessary for the expansion of international trade and international cooperation. The increase in such flows has raised new challenges and concerns with regard to the protection of personal data. However, when personal data are transferred from the EU to controllers, processors, or other recipients in third countries or to international organizations, the level of protection of natural persons ensured in the EU by the General Data Protection Regulation (GDPR) should not be undermined, including in cases of onward transfers of personal data from the third country or international organization to controllers and processors in the same or another third country or international organization. In any event, transfers to third countries and international organizations may only be carried out in full compliance with the GDPR. A transfer can take place only if, subject to the other provisions of the GDPR, the conditions laid down in the provisions of the GDPR relating to the transfer of personal data to third countries or international organizations are complied with by the controller or processor.[†]

Transfer Agreements and Mechanisms

The GDPR is without prejudice to international agreements concluded between the EU and third countries regulating the transfer of personal data including appropriate safeguards for the individual data subjects. Member states may conclude international agreements that involve the transfer of personal data to third countries or international organizations, as far as such agreements do not affect the GDPR or any other provisions of EU law and include an appropriate level of protection for the fundamental rights of the individual data subjects.[‡] The EU Commission may decide with effect for the entire EU that a third country, a territory or specified sector within a third country, or an international organization offers an adequate level of data protection, thus providing legal certainty and uniformity throughout the EU as regards the third country or international organization that is

---

* GDPR Recital 7.
[†] GDPR Recital 101.
[‡] GDPR Recital 102.

considered to provide such level of protection. In such cases, transfers of personal data to that third country or international organization may take place without the need to obtain any further authorization. The EU Commission may also decide, having given notice and a full statement setting out the reasons to the third country or international organization, to revoke such a decision.*

In line with the fundamental values on which the EU is founded, in particular the protection of human rights, the EU Commission should, in its assessment of the third country or of a territory or specified sector within a third country, take into account how a particular third country respects the rule of law and access to justice as well as international human rights norms and standards and its general and sectoral law, including legislation concerning public security, defense, and national security as well as public order and criminal law. The adoption of an adequacy decision with regard to a territory or a specified sector in a third country should take into account clear and objective criteria, such as specific processing activities and the scope of applicable legal standards and legislation in force in the third country. The third country should offer guarantees ensuring an adequate level of protection essentially equivalent to that ensured within the EU, in particular where personal data are processed in one or several specific sectors. In particular, the third country should ensure effective independent data protection supervision and should provide for cooperation mechanisms with the member states' data protection authorities, and the individual data subjects should be provided with effective and enforceable rights and effective administrative and judicial redress.†

Apart from the international commitments the third country or international organization has entered into, the EU Commission should take account of obligations arising from the third country's or international organization's participation in multilateral or regional systems, in particular in relation to the protection of personal data, as well as the implementation of such obligations. In particular, the third country's accession to the Council of Data Protection Convention should be taken into account. The EU Commission should consult the

---

* GDPR Recital 103.
† GDPR Recital 104.

European Data Protection Board (EDPB) when assessing the level of protection in third countries or international organizations.*

The EU Commission should monitor the functioning of decisions on the level of protection in a third country, a territory or specified sector within a third country, or an international organization and monitor the functioning of decisions adopted on the basis of Article 25(6) or Article 26(4) of the 1995 data protection directive (DPD95). In its adequacy decisions, the EU Commission should provide for a periodic review mechanism of their functioning. That periodic review should be conducted in consultation with the third country or international organization in question and take into account all relevant developments in the third country or international organization. For the purposes of monitoring and of carrying out the periodic reviews, the EU Commission should take into consideration the views and findings of the European Parliament and of the Council as well as of other relevant bodies and sources. The EU Commission should evaluate, within a reasonable time, the functioning of the latter decisions and report any relevant findings to the Committee within the meaning of Regulation 182/2011 as established under the GDPR, to the European Parliament and to the EU Council.†

The EU Commission may recognize that a third country, a territory or a specified sector within a third country, or an international organization no longer ensures an adequate level of data protection. Consequently, the transfer of personal data to that third country or international organization should be prohibited, unless the requirements in the GDPR relating to transfers subject to appropriate safeguards, including binding corporate rules, and derogations for specific situations are fulfilled. In that case, provision should be made for consultations between the EU Commission and such third countries or international organizations. The EU Commission should, in a timely manner, inform the third country or international organization of the reasons and enter into consultations with it to remedy the situation.‡

In the absence of an adequacy decision, the controller or processor should take measures to compensate for the lack of data protection in

---

* GDPR Recital 105. Data Protection Convention.
† GDPR Recital 106.
‡ GDPR Recital 107.

a third country by way of appropriate safeguards for the individual data subject. Such appropriate safeguards may consist of making use of binding corporate rules, standard data protection clauses adopted by the EU Commission, standard data protection clauses adopted by a data protection supervisory authority, or contractual clauses authorized by a data protection supervisory authority. Those safeguards should ensure compliance with data protection requirements and the rights of the individual data subjects appropriate to processing within the EU, including the availability of enforceable individual data subject rights and of effective legal remedies, including to obtain effective administrative or judicial redress and to claim compensation, in the EU or in a third country. They should relate in particular to compliance with the general principles relating to personal data processing, the principles of data protection by design and by default. Transfers may also be carried out between public authorities or bodies and public authorities or bodies in third countries or international organizations with corresponding duties or functions, including on the basis of provisions to be inserted into administrative arrangements, such as a memorandum of understanding, providing enforceable and effective rights for individual data subjects. Authorization by the competent data protection supervisory authority should be obtained when the safeguards are provided for in administrative arrangements that are not legally binding.*

The possibility for the controller or processor to use standard data protection clauses adopted by the EU Commission or by a data protection supervisory authority should not prevent controllers or processors either from including the standard data-protection clauses in a wider contract, such as a contract between the processor and another processor, or from adding other clauses or additional safeguards provided that they do not contradict, directly or indirectly, the standard contractual clauses adopted by the EU Commission or by a data protection supervisory authority or prejudice the fundamental rights or freedoms of the individual data subjects. Controllers and processors should be encouraged to provide additional safeguards via contractual commitments that supplement standard protection clauses.†

---

* GDPR Recital 108.
† GDPR Recital 109.

A group of undertakings, or a group of enterprises engaged in a joint economic activity, should be able to make use of approved binding corporate rules for its international transfers from the EU to organizations within the same group of undertakings, or groups of enterprises engaged in a joint economic activity, provided that such corporate rules include all the essential principles and enforceable rights to ensure appropriate safeguards for transfers or categories of transfers of personal data.*

Provisions should be made for the possibility for transfers in certain circumstances where the individual data subject has given their explicit consent, where the transfer is occasional and necessary in relation to a contract or a legal claim, regardless of whether this is in a judicial procedure or in an administrative or any out-of-court procedure, including procedures before regulatory bodies. Provision should also be made for the possibility for transfers where important grounds of public interest laid down by EU or member state law so require or where the transfer is made from a register established by law and intended for consultation by the public or persons having a legitimate interest. In the latter case, such a transfer should not involve the entirety of the personal data or entire categories of the data contained in the register, and when the register is intended for consultation by persons having a legitimate interest, the transfer should be made only at the request of those persons or, if they are to be the recipients, taking into full account the interests and fundamental rights of the individual data subject.†

Those derogations should in particular apply to data transfers required and necessary for important reasons of public interest, for example in cases of international data exchange between competition authorities or tax or customs administrations, between financial supervisory authorities, or between services competent for social security matters or for public health, for example in the case of contact tracing for contagious diseases or to reduce and/or eliminate doping in sport. A transfer of personal data should also be regarded as lawful where it is necessary to protect an interest that is essential for the individual data subject's or another person's vital interests, including

---

* GDPR Recital 110.
† GDPR Recital 111.

physical integrity or life, if the individual data subject is incapable of giving consent. In the absence of an adequacy decision, EU or member state law may, for important reasons of public interest, expressly set limits to the transfer of specific categories of data to a third country or an international organization. Member states should notify such provisions to the EU Commission. Any transfer to an international humanitarian organization of personal data of an individual data subject who is physically or legally incapable of giving consent, with a view to accomplishing a task incumbent under the Geneva Conventions or to complying with international humanitarian law applicable in armed conflicts, could be considered to be necessary for an important reason of public interest or because it is in the vital interest of the individual data subject.*

Transfers that can be qualified as not repetitive, and that only concern a limited number of individual data subjects, could also be possible for the purposes of the compelling legitimate interests pursued by the controller when those interests are not overridden by the interests or rights of the individual data subject and when the controller has assessed all the circumstances surrounding the data transfer. The controller should give particular consideration to the nature of the personal data and the purpose and duration of the proposed processing operation or operations, as well as the situation in the country of origin, the third country, and the country of final destination, and should provide suitable safeguards to protect the fundamental rights of natural persons with regard to the processing of their personal data. Such transfers should be possible only in residual cases where none of the other grounds for transfer are applicable. For scientific or historical research purposes or statistical purposes, the legitimate expectations of society for an increase of knowledge should be taken into consideration. The controller should inform the data protection supervisory authority and the individual data subject about the transfer.†

In any case, where the EU Commission has taken no decision on the adequate level of data protection in a third country, the controller or processor should make use of solutions that provide individual data subjects with enforceable and effective rights as regards the processing

---

* GDPR Recital 112.
† GDPR Recital 113.

of their data in the EU once those data have been transferred so that that they will continue to benefit from fundamental rights and safeguards.[*]

Legal Rule

Background Recitals 5, 6, 48, 53, 101, 102, 103, 107, 108, 110–116, 138, and 153 and Articles 44, 45, 47, 48, 49, 4, 13, 14, 15, 23, 28, 30, 40, and 42 refer to cross-border data transfers. The WP29 also refers to transfers.[†] Chapter V of the GDPR refers to data transfers and transfer of personal data to third countries or international organizations. Various data protection supervisory authorities have also issued recommendations in relation to personal data transfer issues.

Any transfer of personal data that are undergoing processing or are intended for processing after transfer to a third country or to an international organization must take place only if, subject to the other provisions of the GDPR, the conditions laid down in this Chapter are complied with by the controller and processor, including for onward transfers of personal data from the third country or an international organization to another third country or to another international organization. All provisions in this Chapter must be applied to ensure that the level of protection of natural persons guaranteed by the GDPR is not undermined.[‡]

---

[*] GDPR Recital 114.

[†] WP29, Statement on the implementation of the judgement of the Court of Justice of the European Union of 6 October 2015 in the *Maximilian Schrems v Data Protection Commissioner* case (C-362-14); Recommendation 1/2012 on the Standard Application form for Approval of Binding Corporate Rules for the Transfer of Personal Data for Processing Activities; Opinion 3/2009 on the Draft Commission Decision on standard contractual clauses for the transfer of personal data to processors established in third countries, under Directive 95/46/EC (data controller to data processor); FAQs in order to address some issues raised by the entry into force of the EU Commission Decision 2010/87/EU of 5 February 2010 on standard contractual clauses for the transfer of personal data to processors established in third countries under Directive 95/46/EC 2010; Recommendation 1/2007 on the Standard Application for Approval of Binding Corporate Rules for the Transfer of Personal Data.

[‡] GDPR Article 44. The DPD95 referred to transfer issues, and the default transfer ban on transfers to outside of the EU in Article 25.

Permitting Transfers via Adequacy Decision

A transfer of personal data to a third country or an international organization may take place where the EU Commission has decided that the third country, a territory or one or more specified sectors within that third country, or the international organization in question ensures an adequate level of protection. Such a transfer must not require any specific authorization.*

When assessing the adequacy of the level of protection, the EU Commission must, in particular, take account of the following elements

- The rule of law, respect for human rights and fundamental freedoms, relevant legislation, both general and sectoral, including concerning public security, defense, national security and criminal law and the access of public authorities to personal data, as well as the implementation of such legislation, data protection rules, professional rules and security measures, including rules for the onward transfer of personal data to another third country or international organization that are complied with in that country or international organization, case law, as well as effective and enforceable data subject rights and effective administrative and judicial redress for the data subjects whose personal data are being transferred.
- The existence and effective functioning of one or more independent data protection supervisory authorities in the third country or to which an international organization is subject, with responsibility for ensuring and enforcing compliance with the data protection rules, including adequate enforcement powers, for assisting and advising the data subjects in exercising their rights and for cooperation with the data protection supervisory authorities of the member states; and
- The international commitments the third country or international organization concerned has entered into, or other obligations arising from legally binding conventions or

---

* GDPR Article 45(1).

instruments as well as from its participation in multilateral or regional systems, in particular in relation to the protection of personal data.*

The EU Commission, after assessing the adequacy of the level of protection, may decide, by means of implementing act, that a third country, a territory or one or more specified sectors within a third country, or an international organization ensures an adequate level of protection. The implementing act must provide for a mechanism for a periodic review, at least every 4 years, which must take into account all relevant developments in the third country or international organization. The implementing act must specify its territorial and sectoral application and, where applicable, identify the data protection supervisory authority or authorities referred to in point (b) of paragraph 2 of this Article.†

The EU Commission must, on an ongoing basis, monitor developments in third countries and international organizations that could affect the functioning of decisions adopted pursuant to paragraph 3 of this Article and decisions previously adopted on the basis of the DPD95.‡

The EU Commission must, where available information reveals, in particular following the review referred to in paragraph 3 of this Article, that a third country, a territory or one or more specified sectors within a third country, or an international organization no longer ensures an adequate level of protection within the meaning of paragraph 2 of this Article, to the extent necessary, repeal, amend, or suspend the decision referred to in paragraph 3 of this Article by means of implementing acts without retro-active effect.§

The EU Commission must enter into consultations with the third country or international organization with a view to remedying the situation giving rise to the decision made.¶

---

* GDPR Article 45(2).
† GDPR Article 45(3). The implementing act must be adopted in accordance with the examination procedure referred to in Article 93(2).
‡ GDPR Article 45(4).
§ GDPR Article 45(5).
¶ GDPR Article 45(6).

A decision pursuant to paragraph 5 of this Article is without prejudice to transfers of personal data to the third country, a territory or one or more specified sectors within that third country, or the international organization in question.*

The EU Commission must publish in the *Official Journal of the EU* and on its website a list of the third countries, territories and specified sectors within a third country, and international organizations for which it has decided that an adequate level of protection is or is no longer ensured.[†]

Decisions adopted by the EU Commission on the basis of Article 25(6) of DPD95 must remain in force until amended, replaced, or repealed by an EU Commission Decision.[‡]

Note that the EU–US Safe Harbor data transfer regime was struck down by the EU Court of Justice in the *Schrems* case.[§] The Safe Harbor regime was held to be invalid. Notwithstanding the GDPR, the previous Safe Harbor regime will have to be replaced. Negotiations between the EU Commission and the US authorities seem to have reached a new agreement entitled the EU–US Privacy Shield.

It should be noted also that there have been some concerns that the same or similar reasons for the striking down of the Safe Harbor regime may cause concerns for some of the other transfer-legitimizing mechanisms. It remains to be seen whether further challenges or concerns will arise.

Adequate Protection Exception

If the recipient country has been deemed by the EU to already have an adequate level of protection for personal data, then the transfer is permitted. It is provided that a transfer can occur where there

---

* GDPR Article 45(7). Pursuant to Articles 46 to 49.
† GDPR Article 45(8).
‡ GDPR Article 45(9). Adopted in accordance with paragraph 3 or 5 of this Article.
§ *Schrems v Commissioner*, Court of Justice, Case C-362/14, October 6, 2015. The case technically related to Prism and Facebook Europe and transfers to the United States. However, the wider import turned out to be the entire EU-US Safe Harbor Agreement and data transfers to the United States. Note WP29 statement on the case, Statement on the implementation of the judgement of the Court of Justice of the European Union of 6 October 2015 in the *Maximilian Schrems v Data Protection Commissioner* case (C-362-14).

has been a positive Community finding in relation to the type of transfer proposed. A Community finding means a finding of the EU Commission, under the procedure provided for in Article 31(2) of the DPD95, that a country or territory outside the European Economic Area does, or does not, ensure an adequate level of protection within the meaning of Article 25(2) of the Directive.

The EU Commission provides a list of EU Commission decisions on the adequacy of the protection of personal data in third countries.* The EU Commission has thus far recognized Switzerland, Canada, Argentina, Guernsey, the Isle of Man, the US Department of Commerce's Safe Harbor Privacy Principles, and the transfer of air passenger name records to the United States Bureau of Customs and Border Protection as providing adequate protection.

Transfers via Appropriate Safeguards

In the absence of a decision pursuant to Article 45(3), a controller or processor may transfer personal data to a third country or an international organization only if the controller or processor has adduced appropriate safeguards and on condition that enforceable individual data subject rights and effective legal remedies for individual data subjects are available.[†]

The appropriate safeguards referred to in Article 46(1) may be provided for, without requiring any specific authorization from a data protection supervisory authority, by

- A legally binding and enforceable instrument between public authorities or bodies.
- Binding corporate rules.[‡]
- Standard data protection clauses adopted by the EU Commission.[§]
- Standard data protection clauses adopted by a data protection supervisory authority and approved by the EU Commission

---

* At http://ec.europa.eu/justice/policies/privacy/thridcountries/index_en.htm.
† GDPR Article 44(1).
‡ In accordance with Article 47.
§ In accordance with the examination procedure referred to in Article 93(2).

pursuant to the examination procedure referred to in Article 93(2).

- An approved code of conduct pursuant to Article 40 together with binding and enforceable commitments of the controller or processor in the third country to apply the appropriate safeguards, including as regards data subjects' rights; or.
- An approved certification mechanism pursuant to Article 42 together with binding and enforceable commitments of the controller or processor in the third country to apply the appropriate safeguards, including as regards data subjects' rights.*

Subject to the authorization from the competent data protection supervisory authority, the appropriate safeguards† may also be provided for, in particular, by

- Contractual clauses between the controller or processor and the controller, the processor or the recipient of the personal data in the third country or international organization; or
- Provisions to be inserted into administrative arrangements between public authorities or bodies that include enforceable and effective data subject rights.‡

Authorizations by a member state or data protection supervisory authority on the basis of Article 26(2) of DPD95 must remain valid until amended, replaced, or repealed, if necessary, by that data protection supervisory authority. Decisions adopted by the EU Commission on the basis of Article 26(4) of DPD95 must remain in force until amended, replaced, or repealed, if necessary, by a Commission Decision adopted in accordance with paragraph 2 of this Article.§

Creating Adequacy through Consent, Contract

One solution involves "creating adequacy" through consent. Under Article 26 of the DPD95, transfers can be made to a non-EU country where the unambiguous consent of the individual data subject to

---

* GDPR Article 46(2).
† Referred to in Article 46(1).
‡ GDPR Article 46(3).
§ GDPR Article 46(5).

that transfer is obtained. Transfers of data to a third country may be made even though there is not adequate protection in place if the controller secures the necessary level of protection through contractual obligations. This refers to the model contract clauses from the EU Commission. The EU Commission has issued what it considers to be adequate clauses that, incorporated into the contract relationship of the data exporter and the data importer, should then provide an adequate level of consent.

Transfers via Binding Corporate Rules (BCRs)

The EU Commission and the WP29* also developed a policy of recognizing adequate protection of the policies of multinational organizations transferring personal data that satisfy the determined BCRs, pursuant to the DPD95 Article 26(2).[†] Organizations that have contracts, policies, and procedures that satisfy the binding corporate rules and are accepted as doing so after a review process with the EU Commission or one of the member states' data protection authorities can transfer personal data outside of the EU within the organization. Recently, Intel and its BCRs have been examined and approved by one of the data protection supervisory authorities.[‡] This now provides a passporting recognition in the EU member states.

The competent data protection supervisory authority must approve BCRs in accordance with the consistency mechanism set out in Article 63, provided that they

---

* WP29, Recommendation 1/2007 on the Standard Application for Approval of Binding Corporate Rules for the Transfer of Personal Data; Working document setting up a table with the elements and principles to be found in binding corporate rules (WP 153); Working document setting up a framework for the structure of binding corporate rules (WP154); Working document on frequently asked questions (FAQs) related to binding corporate rules (WP155).

† See http://ec.europa.eu/justice/policies/privacy/binding_rules/index_en.htm; Moerel, *Binding Corporate Rules, Corporate Self-Regulation of Global Data Transfers* (OUP, 2012).

‡ See DPC, *Commissioner Approves Intel Corporation Binding Corporate Rules.*

- Are legally binding and apply to and are enforced by every member concerned of the group of undertakings or group of enterprises engaged in a joint economic activity, including their employees.
- Expressly confer enforceable rights on data subjects with regard to the processing of their personal data.
- Fulfill the requirements laid down in paragraph 2.*

The BCRs must specify at least

- The structure and contact details of the group of undertakings or group of enterprises engaged in a joint economic activity and of each of its members.
- The data transfers or set of transfers, including the categories of personal data, the type of processing and its purposes, the type of data subjects affected, and the identification of the third country or countries in question.
- Their legally binding nature, both internally and externally.
- The application of the general data protection principles, in particular purpose limitation, data minimization, limited storage periods, data quality, data protection by design and by default, legal basis for processing, processing of special categories of personal data, measures to ensure data security, and the requirements in respect of onward transfers to bodies not bound by the BCRs [d].
- The rights of data subjects in regard to processing and the means to exercise those rights, including the right not to be subject to decisions based solely on automated processing, including profiling in accordance with Article 22, the right to lodge a complaint with the competent data protection supervisory authority and before the competent courts of the member states in accordance with Article 79, and to obtain redress and, where appropriate, compensation for a breach of the BCRs [e].
- The acceptance by the controller or processor established on the territory of a member state of liability for any breaches of the BCRs by any member concerned not established in the

---

* GDPR Article 47(1).

EU; the controller or the processor must be exempt from that liability, in whole or in part, only if it proves that that member is not responsible for the event giving rise to the damage [f].

- How the information on the BCRs, in particular on the provisions referred to in points (d), (e), and (f) of this paragraph, is provided to the data subjects in addition to Articles 13 and 14.

- The tasks of any data protection officer designated in accordance with Article 37 or any other person or entity in charge of monitoring compliance with the BCRs within the group of undertakings or group of enterprises engaged in a joint economic activity, as well as monitoring training and complaint-handling [h].

- The complaint procedures.

- The mechanisms within the group of undertakings or group of enterprises engaged in a joint economic activity for ensuring the verification of compliance with the BCRs. Such mechanisms must include data protection audits and methods for ensuring corrective actions to protect the rights of the data subject. The results of such verification should be communicated to the person or entity referred to in Point (h) and to the board of the controlling undertaking of a group of undertakings, or of the group of enterprises engaged in a joint economic activity, and should be available on request to the competent data protection supervisory authority [i].

- The mechanisms for reporting and recording changes to the rules and reporting those changes to the data protection supervisory authority [j].

- The cooperation mechanism with the data protection supervisory authority to ensure compliance by any member of the group of undertakings or group of enterprises engaged in a joint economic activity, in particular by making available to the data protection supervisory authority the results of verifications of the measures referred to in Point (j).

- The mechanisms for reporting to the competent data protection supervisory authority any legal requirements to which a member of the group of undertakings or group of enterprises engaged in a joint economic activity is subject in a third country that are likely to have a substantial adverse effect on the guarantees provided by the binding corporate rules

- The appropriate data protection training to personnel having permanent or regular access to personal data.[*]

The EU Commission may specify the format and procedures for the exchange of information between controllers, processors, and data protection supervisory authorities for BCRs within the meaning of this Article. Those implementing acts must be adopted in accordance with the examination procedure set out in Article 93(2).[†]

Given that the EU–US Safe Harbor data transfer regime was struck down by the EU Court of Justice in the *Schrems* case,[‡] there have been some concerns that a similar strike-down problem could arise for other transfer-legitimizing mechanisms, including BCRs. The WP29 also refers to BCR issues, including the *Schrems* case.[§]

---

[*] GDPR Article 47(2).

[†] GDPR Article 47(3).

[‡] *Schrems v Commissioner*, Court of Justice, Case C-362/14, October 6, 2015. The case technically related to Prism and Facebook Europe and transfers to the United States. However, the wider import turned out to be the entire EU-US Safe Harbor Agreement and data transfers to the United States. Note WP29 statement on the case, Statement on the implementation of the judgement of the Court of Justice of the European Union of 6 October 2015 in the Maximilian Schrems v Data Protection Commissioner case (C-362-14).

[§] WP29, Statement on the implementation of the judgement of the Court of Justice of the European Union of 6 October 2015 in the *Maximilian Schrems v Data Protection Commissioner* case (C-362-14); Explanatory document on the processor binding corporate rules, revised version May 2015 - WP 204; Opinion 02/2014 on a referential for requirements for binding corporate rules submitted to national data protection authorities in the EU and cross border privacy rules submitted to APEC CBPR accountability agents; Opinion 07/2013 on the Data Protection Impact Assessment Template for Smart Grid and Smart Metering Systems ("DPIA Template") prepared by Expert Group 2 of the Commission's Smart Grid Task Force; Opinion 04/2013 on the Data Protection Impact Assessment Template for Smart Grid and Smart Metering Systems ("DPIA Template") prepared by Expert Group 2 of the Commission's Smart Grid Task Force; Working document 02/2012 setting up a table with the elements and principles to be found in processor binding corporate rules; Recommendation 1/2012 on the Standard Application form for Approval of Binding Corporate Rules for the Transfer of Personal Data for Processing Activities; Opinion 5/2010 on the industry proposal for a privacy and data protection impact assessment framework for RFID applications.

Transfers or Disclosures Not Authorized by EU Law

Any judgment of a court or tribunal and any decision of an administrative authority of a third country requiring a controller or processor to transfer or disclose personal data may only be recognized or enforceable in any manner if based on an international agreement, such as a mutual legal assistance treaty, in force between the requesting third country and the EU or a member state, without prejudice to other grounds for transfer.*

Transfers via Derogations for Specific Situations

In the absence of an adequacy decision pursuant to Article 45(3) or of appropriate safeguards pursuant to Article 46, including BCRs, a transfer or a set of transfers of personal data to a third country or an international organization must take place only on one of the following conditions

- The data subject has explicitly consented to the proposed transfer after having been informed of the possible risks of such transfers for the data subject due to the absence of an adequacy decision and appropriate safeguards. [a]
- The transfer is necessary for the performance of a contract between the data subject and the controller or the implementation of pre-contractual measures taken at the data subject's request. [b]
- The transfer is necessary for the conclusion or performance of a contract concluded in the interest of the data subject between the controller and another natural or legal person. [c]
- The transfer is necessary for important reasons of public interest.
- The transfer is necessary for the establishment, exercise, or defense of legal claims.
- The transfer is necessary to protect the vital interests of the data subject or of other persons where the data subject is physically or legally incapable of giving consent.

---

* GDPR Article 48.

- The transfer is made from a register that, according to EU or member state law, is intended to provide information to the public and that is open to consultation either by the public in general or by any person who can demonstrate a legitimate interest, but only to the extent that the conditions laid down by EU or member state law for consultation are fulfilled in the particular case.* [g]

Where a transfer could not be based on a provision in Article 45 or 46, including the provisions on BCRs, and none of the derogations for a specific situation referred to in the first subparagraph of this paragraph is applicable, a transfer to a third country or an international organization may take place only if the transfer is not repetitive, concerns only a limited number of data subjects, and is necessary for the purposes of compelling legitimate interests pursued by the controller that are not overridden by the interests or rights of the data subject, and the controller has assessed all the circumstances surrounding the data transfer and has on the basis of that assessment provided suitable safeguards with regard to the protection of personal data. The controller must inform the data protection supervisory authority of the transfer. The controller must, in addition to providing the information referred to in Articles 13 and 14, inform the data subject of the transfer and of the compelling legitimate interests pursued.†

A transfer pursuant to point (g) of the first subparagraph of paragraph 1 must not involve the entirety of the personal data or entire categories of the personal data contained in the register. Where the register is intended for consultation by persons having a legitimate interest, the transfer must be made only at the request of those persons or if they are to be the recipients.‡

Points (a), (b), and (c) of the first subparagraph of paragraph 1 and the second subparagraph thereof must not apply to activities carried out by public authorities in the exercise of their public powers.§

---

* GDPR Article 49(1).
† ibid.
‡ GDPR Article 49(2).
§ GDPR Article 49(3).

The public interest referred to in point (d) of the first subparagraph of paragraph 1 must be recognized in EU law or in the law of the member state to which the controller is subject.*

In the absence of an adequacy decision, EU or member state law may, for important reasons of public interest, expressly set limits to the transfer of specific categories of personal data to a third country or an international organization. Member states must notify such provisions to the EU Commission.†

The controller or processor must document the assessment as well as the suitable safeguards referred to in the second subparagraph of paragraph 1 of this Article in the records referred to in Article 30.‡

Exceptions

If the recipient country's protection is not adequate or perhaps not ascertainable, but it is intended that cross-border transfers are required, the organization should then ascertain whether the transfer comes within one of the excepted categories.

Transfers of personal data from the EU to outside the EU cannot occur unless exempted, such as

- The individual data subject has given consent.
- The transfer is necessary for the performance of a contract between an individual data subject and a controller.
- The transfer is necessary for taking steps at the request of an individual data subject with a view to entering into a contract with the controller.
- The transfer is necessary for the conclusion of a contract between the controller and a person other than the individual data subject, which is entered into at the request of the individual data subject and is in the interests of the individual data subject.
- The transfer is necessary for the performance of such a contract.

---

* GDPR Article 49(4).
† GDPR Article 49(5).
‡ GDPR Article 49(6).

- The transfer is required or authorized under any enactment or instrument imposing international obligation.
- The transfer is necessary for reasons of substantial public interest.
- The transfer is necessary for purposes of or in connection with legal proceedings or prospective legal proceedings.
- The transfer is necessary to prevent injury or damage to the health of the individual data subject or serious loss of or damage to the property of the individual data subject or otherwise to protect vital interests.
- Subject to certain conditions, the transfer is only part of the personal data on a register established by or under an enactment.
- The transfer has been authorized by data protection supervisory authorities where the controller adduces adequate safeguards.
- The transfer is made to a country that has been determined by the EU Commission as having "adequate levels of protection."
- The transfer is made to a US entity that has signed up to the EU–US Safe Harbor arrangements; or
- The EU Commission contract provisions (i.e., the model contract clauses issues by the EU Commission) apply.

Therefore, for example, where a customer books a hotel in New York through an agent in London, it is necessary for the ultimate performance of the contract for the personal data to be transferred to the hotel in New York from the United Kingdom. The transfer of the personal data is permitted.

However, when an EU company processes its employee payroll personal data to a US parent company, such a transfer is for the convenience of the company and is not strictly necessary for the performance of a contract.

Issues

Certain issues may arise in relation to the following:

- What is a "transfer"? Is there a difference between transfer and transit?

- "Data" and anonymized data: Is there a restriction on cross-border transfers of anonymized data? For example, can certain anonymized data fall outside the definition of personal data?
- "Third country" currently includes the EU countries and the European Economic Area (EEA) countries of Iceland, Norway, and Liechtenstein. The EU countries are expanding over time. In addition, the list of permitted additional third countries is expanding over time; for example, Safe Harbor.
- How the EU–US Safe Harbor transfer problem will be resolved after the EU Court of Justice struck down the original EU–US Safe Harbor data transfer agreement.* Many organizations used this as the legitimizing basis for the lawful transfer of personal data from the EU to the United States.

Establishing Whether the Ban Applies

Criteria for assessing whether the ban applies include the following issues

- Identifying whether the organization transfers personal data.
- Identifying whether there is a transfer.
- Identifying whether there is a transfer to a "third country."
- Identifying whether that third country has an adequate level of protection.
- Identifying, in relation to transfers to the United States, whether the Safe Harbor (or now the Privacy Shield) rules apply.
- Identifying whether any of the white list countries are recipients; considering what constitutes adequacy.
- Identifying the nature of the data; identifying how it is to be used.
- Considering the laws and practices in place in the third country; identifying whether there is a transfer by a controller to a processor. Under Article 7 [of the DPD95], such a transfer requires a contract to be put in place relating to security measures to date. The controller retains control of the personal

---

* *Digital Rights Ireland and Seitlinger and Others,* Joined Cases C-293/12 and C-594/12, Court of Justice, April 8, 2014.

data, so that the risk to the individual data subject is minimal; identify whether there is a transfer within an international or multinational company or group of companies where an internal privacy code or agreement is in place; identify whether there is a transfer within a consortium established to process international transactions; for example, banking; identify whether there is a transfer between professionals such as lawyers or accountants where a client's business has an international dimension. The EU Commission has identified core principles that must be present in the foreign laws or codes of practice or regulations to achieve the requisite standard of "adequacy" in third-party countries; identify whether these are applicable in the particular instance. Personal data must be processed for a specific purpose; identify what this purpose is.

- Personal data must be accurate and kept up to date; ensuring that this applies. The individual data subject must be provided with adequate information in relation to the transfer; ensuring that this principle is complied with. Technical and organizational security measures should be taken by the controller.
- Ensuring that there is a right of access to the data by the individual data subject; there should be a prohibition on onward transfer of data along the lines of Article 25 of the DPD95; and
- Ensuring that there is an effective procedure or mode of enforcement.

Organizations should be aware that if they wish to transfer personal data outside of the EU, additional considerations arise, and that unless there is a specific exemption, the transfer may not be permitted. Once a transfer possibility arises, the organization should undertake a compliance exercise to assess whether the transfer can be permitted, and if so, how. Additional compliance documentation and contracts may be required.

The increasing number of locations and methods by which personal data may be collected by organizations, in particular Internet, communications, and social media, will increasingly be scrutinized in terms of transparency, consent, and compliance. Equally, cloud computing is receiving particular data protection attention. Apps are also being considered, as is the developing area of the Internet of Things (IoT) and related data protection compliance issues.

Schrems, EU–US Safe Harbor, and EU–US Privacy Shield

One of the transfer mechanisms enabling the transfer of data from the EU to the United States was the EU Commission arrangement with the United States entitled the Safe Harbor arrangement. US companies would self-certify that they would adhere to the Safe Harbor principles and register in the United States as being Safe Harbor compliant. However, in one of the ripples from the Snowden disclosures, Austrian law student Max Schrems asked the Data Protection Commissioner to investigate Facebook as being in breach of the EU law in relation to transfers of data from Facebook to US authorities. The Commissioner felt constrained by the Commission Safe Harbor arrangement. Schrems took a Judicial Review case in the Irish High Court, which was ultimately referred to the EU Court of Justice.

The EU Court of Justice in the *Schrems* case referral* struck down the Safe Harbor regime as invalid under the EU data protection regime. That is, it was struck down under the DPD95 and the current data protection regime, and not the later GDPR and the updated data protection regime.

The questions referred to the EU Court of Justice by the High Court were

> Whether in the course of determining a complaint which has been made to an independent office holder who has been vested by statute with the functions of administering and enforcing data protection legislation that personal data is being transferred to another third country

---

* *Schrems v Commissioner*, Court of Justice, Case C-362/14, October 6, 2015. The case technically related to Prism and Facebook Europe and transfers to the United States. However, the wider import turned out to be the entire EU-US Safe Harbor Agreement and data transfers to the United States. Note WP29 statement on the case, Statement on the implementation of the judgement of the Court of Justice of the European Union of 6 October 2015 in the *Maximilian Schrems v Data Protection Commissioner* case (C-362-14).

(in this case, the US) the laws and practices of which, it is claimed, do not contain adequate protections for the individual data subject, that office holder is absolutely bound by the Community finding to the contrary contained in Commission Decision of 26 July 2000 (2000/520/EC) having regard to Article 7, Article 8 and Article 47 of the EU Charter, the provisions of Article 25(6) of DPD95 notwithstanding?

Or, alternatively, may and/or must the office holder conduct their own investigation of the matter in the light of factual developments in the meantime since that Commission Decision was first published?

The EU Court of Justice (Grand Chamber) held that

Article 25(6) of [DPD95]* ... read in the light of Articles 7, 8 and 47 of the Charter of Fundamental Rights of the European Union, must be interpreted as meaning that a decision adopted pursuant to that provision, such as Commission Decision 2000/520/EC of 26 July 2000 pursuant to [DPD95] on the adequacy of the protection provided by the safe harbor privacy principles and related frequently asked questions issued by the US Department of Commerce, by which the EU Commission finds that a third country ensures an adequate level of protection, does not prevent a [data protection] supervisory authority of a member state, within the meaning of Article 28 of that directive as amended, from examining the claim of a person concerning the protection of their rights and freedoms in regard to the processing of personal data relating to them which has been transferred from a member state to that third country when that person contends that *the law and practices in force in the third country do not ensure an adequate level of protection*.

Decision 2000/520 is invalid [i.e., the decision on which the US–EU Safe Harbor transfer exemption was based]

Notwithstanding the case itself, there were already longstanding negotiations going on between the EU and the United States to amend, update, and/or replace the Safe Harbor regime. This has recently resulted in the EU–US Privacy Shield arrangement being

---

* As amended by Regulation (EC) No 1882/2003 of the European Parliament and of the Council of September 29, 2003.

agreed to facilitate such data transfers.* The full details remain to be examined, and the WP29 has sought further details. It will ultimately also need to be assessed whether further legal challenges will transpire.

One issue that does arise, however, is the issue of EU citizens being able to make challenges in the United States in relation to what is happening with their data. One of the concerns addressed before the EU Court of Justice was that EU citizens did not have such a mechanism. The new Privacy Shield seeks to address this with a new law in the United States expressly permitting EU citizens to take action in US courts: the Judicial Redress Act, which has passed the legislative approval stage in the United States.

The new arrangement will, according to the EU Commission, include the following elements

* *Strong obligations on companies handling Europeans' personal data and robust enforcement*: US companies wishing to import personal data from Europe will need to commit to robust obligations on how personal data is processed and individual rights are guaranteed. The Department of Commerce will monitor that companies publish their commitments, which makes them enforceable under US law by the US Federal Trade Commission (FTC). In addition, any company handling human resources data from Europe has to commit to comply with decisions by EU data protection supervisory authorities.

* *Clear safeguards and transparency obligations on US government access*: For the first time, the United States has given the EU written assurances that the access of public authorities for law enforcement and national security will be subject to clear limitations, safeguards, and oversight mechanisms. These exceptions must be used only to the extent necessary and proportionate. The United States has ruled out indiscriminate mass surveillance on the personal data transferred to the United States under the new arrangement. To regularly

---

* See EU Commission press release, at http://europa.eu/rapid/press-release_IP-16-216_en.htm.

monitor the functioning of the arrangement, there will be an annual joint review, which will also include the issue of national security access. The EU Commission and the US Department of Commerce will conduct the review and invite national intelligence experts from the US and European data protection supervisory authorities to it.

- *Effective protection of EU citizens' rights with several redress possibilities*: Any citizen who considers that their data has been misused under the new arrangement will have several redress possibilities. Companies have deadlines to reply to complaints. European data protection supervisory authorities can refer complaints to the Department of Commerce and the Federal Trade Commission. In addition, alternative dispute resolution will be free of charge. For complaints on possible access by national intelligence authorities, a new ombudsperson will be created.

The WP29 also comments on the *Schrems* case

- The consequences of the *Schrems* EU Court of Justice judgement:* The full details of the proposed details and formal decision in relation to the new EU–US Privacy Shield have just been issued.† It remains to be seen how this will work in practice, and indeed whether further challenge will arise.

Conclusion

Data protection compliance practice for organizations means that they will have to include a compliance assessment as well as an assessment of the risks associated with transfers of personal data outside of the EU. This applies to transfers from parent to subsidiary or to a branch office in the same way as a transfer to an unrelated company or entity.

---

* WP29, press release, *Statement Consequences Schrems Judgement*, February 3, 2016.
† At   http://ec.europa.eu/justice/newsroom/data-protection/news/160229_en.htm; and the draft adequacy decision at http://ec.europa.eu/justice/data-protection/files/privacy-shield-adequacy-decision_en.pdf.

Organizations should at least be aware that if they wish to transfer personal data outside of the EU, additional considerations arise, and that unless there is a specific exemption process, the transfer may not be permitted. Once a transfer possibility arises, the organization should undertake a compliance exercise to assess whether the transfer can be permitted, and if so, how. Additional compliance documentation may be required.

KEY CONCEPTS

Organizations in the United States need to be aware that they cannot receive EU personal data from third-party organizations or sister or group organizations. There is a default position banning such transfers from the EU to third countries, as such recipient countries may not have the same data protection standards and rules as exist in the EU. The United States is deemed not to have such equivalent standards, and as such, there is a default transfer ban applicable.

To deal with this transfer ban, organizations must fall within a limited number of exemptions.

KEY WORDS

- Transfers of personal data.
- Default transfer ban on cross-border transfer to countries outside of the EU.
- *White list third countries*.
- US–EU Safe Harbor transfer arrangement.
- Safe Harbor deemed invalid.
- Now replaced by US–EU Privacy Shield.
- Contract clauses.
- Binding corporate rules.

FURTHER READING

- Dort and Criss, "Trends in Cybersecurity Law, the Privacy Shield, and Best Practices for Businesses Operating in the Global Marketplace," *Computer & Internet Lawyer* (2016) (33: 7) 1.
- Johnson, "Foreign Nationals' Privacy Interests under US Foreign Intelligence Law," *Texas International Law Journal* (2016) (51:2–3) 229.
- Kuschewsky, *Data Protection & Privacy: Jurisdictional Comparisons* (Thomson Reuters, 2012).
- Myers, "Cross-Border Commerce without Constraint: Shifting from Territorial-Based Regulation to an Industry-Based Code of Conduct for the Online Payment Processing Industry," *Computer & Internet Lawyer* (2016) (33:7) 11.
- Voss, "The Future of Transatlantic Data Flows: Privacy Shield or Bust?" *Journal of Internet Law* (2016) (19:11) 9.
- WP29 Recommendation 1/2012 on the Standard Application form for Approval of Binding Corporate Rules for the Transfer of Personal Data for Processing Activities.

34

RIGHT TO BE INFORMED OF THIRD-COUNTRY SAFEGUARDS

Introduction

The right to be informed of third-country safeguards is an important new right that individual data subjects will be aware of. Given that there is increasing frequency, and sometimes contention, regarding cross-border transfers of personal data, individuals will often like to be made aware of the existence of such proposed transfers and also additional information on the nature of the safeguards that the third countries or third-country organizations may have in relation to their personal data.

Background Guidance

Background Recital 39 states that any processing of personal data should be lawful and fair. It should be transparent to natural persons that personal data concerning them are collected, used, consulted, or otherwise processed and to what extent the personal data are or will be processed. The principle of transparency requires that any information and communication relating to the processing of those personal data be easily accessible and easy to understand, and that clear and plain language be used. That principle concerns, in particular, information to the data subjects on the identity of the controller and the purposes of the processing and further information to ensure fair and transparent processing in respect of the natural persons concerned and their right to obtain confirmation and communication of personal data concerning them that are being processed. Natural persons should be made aware of risks, rules, safeguards, and rights in relation to the processing of personal data and how to exercise their rights in relation to such processing. In particular, the specific purposes for which personal data are processed should be explicit and legitimate and determined at the time of the collection of the personal data. The personal data should be adequate, relevant, and limited to what is necessary for the purposes for which they are processed. This requires, in particular, ensuring that the period for which the personal data are stored is limited to a strict minimum. Personal data should be processed only if the purpose of the processing could not reasonably be fulfilled by other means. To ensure that the personal data are not kept longer than necessary, time limits should be established by the controller for erasure or for a periodic review. Every reasonable step should be taken to ensure that personal data that are inaccurate are rectified or deleted. Personal data should be processed in a manner that ensures appropriate security and confidentiality of the personal data, including for preventing unauthorized access to or use of personal data and the equipment used for the processing.

Background Recital 108 states that in the absence of an adequacy decision, the controller or processor should take measures to compensate for the lack of data protection in a third country by way of appropriate safeguards for the data subject. Such appropriate safeguards may consist of making use of binding corporate rules, standard data protection clauses adopted by the Commission, standard data protection clauses adopted by a data protection supervisory authority, or contractual clauses authorized by a data protection supervisory authority. Those safeguards should ensure compliance with data protection requirements and the rights of the data subjects appropriate to processing within the EU, including the availability of enforceable data subject rights and of effective legal remedies, including to obtain effective administrative or judicial redress and to claim compensation, in the EU or in a third country. They should relate in particular to compliance with the general principles relating to personal data processing, the principles of data protection by design and by default. Transfers may also be carried out between public authorities or bodies and public authorities or bodies in third countries or international organizations with corresponding duties or functions, including on the basis of provisions to be inserted into administrative arrangements, such as a memorandum of understanding, providing for enforceable and effective rights for data subjects. Authorization by the competent data protection supervisory authority should be obtained when the safeguards are provided for in administrative arrangements that are not legally binding.

Background Recital 113 states that transfers that can be qualified as not repetitive and that only concern a limited number of data subjects could also be possible for the purposes of the compelling legitimate interests pursued by the controller when those interests are not overridden by the interests or rights of the data subject and when the controller has assessed all the circumstances surrounding the data transfer. The controller should give particular consideration to the nature of the personal data and the purpose and duration of the proposed processing operation or operations, as well as the situation in the country of origin, the third country, and the country of final destination, and should provide suitable safeguards to protect the fundamental rights of natural persons with regard to the processing of their personal data. Such transfers should be possible only in residual cases where none of the other grounds for transfer are applicable. For scientific or historical research purposes or statistical purposes, the legitimate expectations of society for an increase of knowledge should be taken into consideration. The controller should inform the data protection supervisory authority and the data subject about the transfer.

Background Recital 114 states that in any case where the EU Commission has taken no decision on the adequate level of data protection in a third country, the controller or processor should make use of solutions that provide data subjects with enforceable and effective rights as regards the processing of their data in the EU once those data have been transferred so that that they will continue to benefit from fundamental rights and safeguards.

Legal Rule

Where personal data are transferred to a third country or to an international organization, the data subject must have the right to be informed of the appropriate safeguards pursuant to Article 46 relating to the transfer of data (Article 15(2)). This has added relevance as part of the potential ripples from the *Schrems* EU Court of Justice decision.

Where personal data are transferred to a third country or to an international organization, the data subject must have the right to be informed of the appropriate safeguards pursuant to Article 46 relating to the transfer.*

This has added relevance as part of the potential ripples from the *Schrems* EU Court of Justice decision.

Conclusion

Frequently, organizations may consider the direct issues within organizations in relation to inward-facing (e.g., employees) and outward-facing (e.g., customers) data protection issues. There is a danger that a narrow focus on these issues can lead to transparency issues as regards data subjects, and third parties may fall through the gaps. For example, many organizations may have third parties carrying out certain data processing activities for them, or in other scenarios, may seek to pass on personal data to third parties. When fulfilling transparency and information on such activities to third parties, data subjects must also be informed of appropriate safeguards being taken.

KEY CONCEPTS

Organizations need to consider how they inform individuals as regards potential third-country destinations and organization recipients of their personal data and the associated security precautions. Consent issues may also arise.

KEYWORDS

- Data transfers.
- Cross-border data transfers.
- Transfers to third-party organizations.
- Safeguards.
- Right to be informed of the safeguards.

---

* GDPR Article 15(2).

35
TRANSPARENCY

Introduction

One of the routes by which individuals can consent to data collection, specific uses, and on occasion onward transfers of their personal data, and enforce their various rights, is to have transparency from the organizational data controller in relation to data collection and use. When organizations propose to collect, use, and process personal data, they must do so in a transparent manner. In effect, transparency is needed as a trigger for individual data subjects to understand that there is a proposal to collect and process their personal data, by whom, for what purposes, and whether any third parties may also receive their personal data. Transparency effectively acts as a trigger for individuals to be able to enforce their respective data protection rights.

Background Guidance

Background Recital 13 refers to the need to ensure a consistent level of protection for natural persons throughout the EU, and to prevent divergences hampering the free movement of personal data within the internal market, a regulation (not a directive) is necessary to provide legal certainty and transparency for economic operators, including micro, small, and medium-sized enterprises.

It adds that a regulation is also needed to provide natural persons in all member states with the same level of legally enforceable rights and obligations and responsibilities for controllers and processors, and to ensure consistent monitoring of the processing of personal data and equivalent sanctions in all member states as well as effective cooperation between the data protection supervisory authorities of different member states. The proper functioning of the internal market requires that the free movement of personal data within the EU is not restricted or prohibited for reasons connected with the protection of natural persons with regard to the processing of personal data.

To take account of the specific situation of micro, small, and medium-sized enterprises, the General Data Protection Regulation (GDPR) includes a derogation for organizations with fewer than 250 employees with regard to record-keeping. In addition, EU institutions and bodies, and member states and their data protection supervisory authorities, are encouraged to take account of the specific needs of micro, small, and medium-sized enterprises in the application of the GDPR.*

Background Recital 39 also refers to transparency requirements. Any processing of personal data should be lawful and fair. It should be transparent to natural persons that personal data concerning them are collected, used, consulted, or otherwise processed and to what extent the personal data are or will be processed. The principle of transparency requires that

- Any information and communication relating to the processing of those personal data be easily accessible and easy to understand, and that clear and plain language be used.
- The principle concerns, in particular, information to the data subjects on the identity of the controller and the purposes of the processing and further information to ensure fair and transparent processing in respect of the natural persons concerned and their right to obtain confirmation and communication of personal data concerning them that are being processed.
- Natural persons should be made aware of risks, rules, safeguards, and rights in relation to the processing of personal data and how to exercise their rights in relation to such processing.
- In particular, the specific purposes for which personal data are processed should be explicit and legitimate and determined at the time of the collection of the personal data.
- The personal data should be adequate, relevant, and limited to what is necessary for the purposes for which they are processed.

---

* The notion of micro, small, and medium-sized enterprises should draw from Article 2 of the Annex to Commission Recommendation 2003/361/EC.

- This requires, in particular, ensuring that the period for which the personal data are stored is limited to a strict minimum,
- Personal data should be processed only if the purpose of the processing could not reasonably be fulfilled by other means.
- To ensure that the personal data are not kept longer than necessary, time limits should be established by the controller for erasure or for a periodic review.
- Every reasonable step should be taken to ensure that personal data that are inaccurate are rectified or deleted. Personal data should be processed in a manner that ensures appropriate security and confidentiality of the personal data, including for preventing unauthorized access to or use of personal data and the equipment used for the processing.

Background Recital 58 also refers to transparency. The principle of transparency requires that

- Any information addressed to the public or to the data subject must be concise, easily accessible, and easy to understand.
- Clear and plain language and additionally, where appropriate, visualization should be used.
- Such information could be provided in electronic form; for example, when addressed to the public, through a website.
- This is of particular relevance in situations where the proliferation of actors and the technological complexity of practice make it difficult for the data subject to know and understand whether, by whom. and for what purpose personal data relating to them are being collected, such as in the case of online advertising.
- Given that children merit specific protection, any information and communication, where processing is addressed to a child, should be in such clear and plain language that the child can easily understand it.

Background Recital 60 refers to transparency as follows. The principles of fair and transparent processing require that

- The data subject be informed of the existence of the processing operation and its purposes.

- The controller should provide the data subject with any further information necessary to ensure fair and transparent processing, taking into account the specific circumstances and context in which the personal data are processed.
- The data subject should be informed of the existence of profiling and the consequences of such profiling.
- Where the personal data are collected from the data subject, the data subject should also be informed whether they are obliged to provide the personal data and of the consequences where they do not provide such data.
- Information may be provided in combination with standardized icons to give in an easily visible, intelligible, and clearly legible manner a meaningful overview of the intended processing.
- Where the icons are presented electronically, they should be machine-readable.

Background Recital 71 also refers to transparency and that the data subject should have the right not to be subject to a decision that may include a measure, evaluating personal aspects relating to them, that is based solely on automated processing and that produces legal effects concerning them or similarly significantly affects them, such as automatic refusal of an online credit application or e-recruiting practices without any human intervention. Such processing includes "profiling" that consists of any form of automated processing of personal data evaluating the personal aspects relating to a natural person, in particular to analyze or predict aspects concerning the data subject's

- Performance at work.
- Economic situation.
- Health.
- Personal preferences or interests.
- Reliability or behavior.
- Location or movements.
- Or where it produces legal effects concerning them or similarly significantly affects them.

However, decision-making based on such processing, including profiling, should be allowed where expressly authorized by EU or member state law to which the controller is subject, including for fraud and tax-evasion monitoring and prevention purposes conducted in accordance with the regulations, standards, and recommendations of EU institutions or national oversight bodies and to ensure the security and reliability of a service provided by the controller, or necessary for the entering or performance of a contract between the data subject and a controller, or when the data subject has given their explicit consent.

In any case, such processing should be subject to suitable safeguards, which should include specific information to the data subject and the right to obtain human intervention, to express their point of view, to obtain an explanation of the decision reached after such assessment, and to challenge the decision. Such measures should not concern a child.

Background Recital 71 also states that to ensure fair and transparent processing in respect of the data subject, taking into account the specific circumstances and context in which the personal data are processed, the controller should

- Use appropriate mathematical or statistical procedures for the profiling.
- Implement technical and organizational measures appropriate to ensure, in particular, that factors which result in inaccuracies in personal data are corrected and the risk of errors is minimized.
- Secure personal data in a manner that takes account of the potential risks involved to the interests and rights of the data subject and that prevents, *inter alia*, discriminatory effects on natural persons on the basis of
  - Racial or ethnic origin
  - Political opinion
  - Religion or beliefs
  - Trade union membership
  - Genetic or health status or sexual orientation
  - Or that result in measures having such an effect.

Automated decision-making and profiling based on special categories of personal data should be allowed only under specific conditions.

Background Recital 78 states that the protection of the rights of natural persons with regard to the processing of personal data requires that appropriate technical and organizational measures be taken to ensure that the requirements of the GDPR are met. To be able to demonstrate compliance with the GDPR, the controller should adopt internal policies and implement measures that meet in particular the principles of data protection by design and data protection by default. Such measures could consist, *inter alia*, of

- Minimizing the processing of personal data.
- Pseudonymizing personal data as soon as possible.
- Transparency with regard to the functions and processing of personal data.
- Enabling the data subject to monitor the data processing.
- Enabling the controller to create and improve security features.

When developing, designing, selecting, and using applications, services, and products that are based on the processing of personal data or process personal data to fulfill their task, producers of the products, services, and applications should be encouraged to take into account the right to data protection when developing and designing such products, services, and applications and, with due regard to the state of the art, to make sure that controllers and processors are able to fulfill their data protection obligations. The principles of data protection by design and by default should also be taken into consideration in the context of public tenders.

Background Recital 100 states that to enhance transparency and compliance with the GDPR, the establishment of certification mechanisms and data protection seals and marks should be encouraged, allowing data subjects to quickly assess the level of data protection of relevant products and services.

Legal Rule

Article 5 of the earlier original draft proposal for the GDPR provided that personal data shall be "processed lawfully, fairly and in a transparent manner in relation to the data subject." Transparency breaches "[require] greater awareness among citizens about the processing going on: its existence, its content and the flows generated in and out by using terminals."

Organizations should ensure transparency in relation to security of data and risk management.* It is noted that "the greater the flow of information systems the more opaque it becomes in modern information systems and with new ICT applications. In that case the right to transparency must increase alongside these new processes."†

Article 5 of the final version of the new GDPR now refers to the data protection principles. The first principle now reads

> "processed lawfully, fairly and in a transparent manner in relation to the data subject ('lawfulness, fairness and transparency')."

This is the Transparency Principle.

The GDPR also refers to transparent information, communication, and modalities for the exercise of the rights of the data subject. Chapter III (rights of the data subject), Section 1 of the GDPR refers to transparency and modalities. Article 12 of the GDPR is headed "Transparent information, communication and modalities for exercising the rights of the data subject." Under Article 12(1), the controller must take appropriate measures to provide any information referred to in Articles 13 and 14 and any communication under Articles 15 to 22 and 34 relating to processing to the individual data subject in a concise, transparent, intelligible, and easily accessible form, using clear and plain language, in particular for any information addressed specifically to a child. The information must be provided in writing or by other means, including, where appropriate, by electronic means. When requested by the individual data subject, the information may be provided orally, provided that the identity of the individual data subject is proven by other means.

The controller must facilitate the exercise of individual data subject rights under Articles 15 to 22.‡ In the cases referred to in Article 11(2), the controller must not refuse to act on the request of the individual

---

* Costa and Poullet, "Privacy and the Regulation of 2012," *Computer Law & Security Review* (2012) (28) 254, at 256.
† ibid.
‡ GDPR Article 12(2).

data subject for exercising their rights under Articles 15 to 22, unless the controller demonstrates that it is not in a position to identify the individual data subject.

The controller must provide information on action taken on a request under Articles 15 to 22 to the individual data subject without undue delay and in any event within 1 month of receipt of the request.* That period may be extended by two further months where necessary, taking into account the complexity and number of the requests. The controller must inform the individual data subject of any such extension within 1 month of receipt of the request, together with the reasons for the delay. Where the individual data subject makes the request by means of an electronic form, the information must be provided by electronic means where possible, unless otherwise requested by the individual data subject.

If the controller does not take action on the request of the individual data subject, the controller must inform the individual data subject without delay and at the latest within 1 month of receipt of the request of the reasons for not taking action and on the possibility of lodging a complaint with a data protection supervisory authority and seeking a judicial remedy.†

Information provided under Articles 13 and 14 and any communication and any actions taken under Articles 15 to 22 and 34 must be provided free of charge.‡ Where requests from an individual data subject are manifestly unfounded or excessive, in particular because of their repetitive character, the controller may either

- Charge a reasonable fee taking into account the administrative costs of providing the information or communication or taking the action requested; or
- Refuse to act on the request.

The controller must bear the burden of demonstrating the manifestly unfounded or excessive character of the request.

Without prejudice to Article 11, where the controller has reasonable doubts concerning the identity of the natural person making the

---

* GDPR Article 12(3).
† GDPR Article 12(4).
‡ GDPR Article 12(5).

request referred to in Articles 15 to 21, the controller may request the provision of additional information necessary to confirm the identity of the individual data subject.*

The information to be provided to individual data subjects pursuant to Articles 13 and 14 may be provided in combination with standardized icons to give in an easily visible, intelligible, and clearly legible manner a meaningful overview of the intended processing. Where the icons are presented electronically, they must be machine-readable.[†]

Conclusion

Organizations should continue to see what further developments arise, such as codes of conduct, security standards, and standardized icons for particular data protection matters. Icons may serve to assist the transparency and awareness of specific issues to the public and to individual data subjects. For example, the EU Commission must be empowered to adopt delegated acts in accordance with Article 92 for the purpose of determining the information to be presented by the icons and the procedures for providing standardized icons.[‡] Prior to the new GDPR, the UK data protection supervisory authority (Information commissioner's office [ICO]) has issued recommendations in relation to privacy notices, namely

- Getting it right: Collecting information about your customers.
- Privacy notices code of practice.

These now need to be read in light of the GDPR changes but may be useful to consider. The same applies to particular previous guidance from other data protection supervisory authorities.

KEY CONCEPTS

Transparency assists organizations to conceptualize lawful data processing, processes, and procedures and assists individuals

---

* GDPR Article 12(6).
[†] GDPR Article 12(7).
[‡] GDPR Article 12(8).

in enforcing their rights and being assured in relation to data processing activities.

KEYWORDS

- Transparency.
- Fairness.
- Lawfulness, fairness, and transparency principle.
- Transparent information, communication, and modalities for exercising rights of the individual data subject.
- Adults.
- Children.
- General personal data.
- Sensitive personal data.
- Transfers.
- Third parties.
- Third-party safeguards.
- Purposes of processing.
- Security.
- Transparency of rights.

36
HEALTH DATA

Introduction

There is an explosion in the use of personal health data and potential treatment and lifestyle advances. This type of data counts as additionally confidential and important. It is classed and protected as sensitive personal data, which requires additional compliance safeguards.

Health-Related Definitions

Article 4 of the General Data Protection Regulation (GDPR) contains a number of definitions relevant to the collection and processing of health-related personal data.

Data Concerning Health

"Data concerning health" means "personal data related to the physical or mental health of a natural person, including the provision of health care services, which reveal information about his or her health status."

The background Recitals refer to the increasingly important issue of health-related personal data. Personal data concerning health should include all data pertaining to the health status of an individual data subject that reveal information relating to the past, current, or future physical or mental health status of the individual data subject. This includes information about the natural person collected in the course of the registration for, or the provision of, health-care services as referred to in Directive 2011/24 to that natural person; a number, symbol, or particular assigned to a natural person to uniquely identify the natural person for health purposes; information derived from the testing or examination of a body part or bodily substance, including from genetic data and biological samples; and any information on, for example, a disease, disability, disease risk, medical history, clinical treatment, or the physiological or biomedical state of the individual data subject independent of its source; for example, from a physician or other health professional, a hospital, a medical device, or an in vitro diagnostic test.*

Genetic Data

"Genetic data" means "personal data relating to the inherited or acquired genetic characteristics of a natural person which give unique information about the physiology or the health of that natural person and which result, in particular, from an analysis of a biological sample from the natural person in question."

Background Recital 34 states that genetic data should be defined as personal data relating to the inherited or acquired genetic characteristics of a natural person that result from the analysis of a biological sample from the natural person in question, in particular chromosomal, deoxyribonucleic acid (DNA), or ribonucleic acid (RNA) analysis, or from the analysis of another element enabling equivalent information to be obtained.†

Biometric Data

"Biometric data" means "personal data resulting from specific technical processing relating to the physical, physiological or behavioural characteristics of a natural person, which allow or confirm the unique identification of that natural person, such as facial images or dactyloscopic data."

Pseudonymization

"Pseudonymization" means the "processing of personal data in such a manner that the personal data can no longer be attributed to a specific data subject without the use of additional information, provided that such additional information is kept separately and is subject to

---

* GDPR Recital 35.
† GDPR Recital 34.

technical and organisational measures to ensure that the personal data are not attributed to an identified or identifiable natural person."

Profiling

"Profiling" means any form of automated processing of personal data consisting of the use of personal data to evaluate certain personal aspects relating to a natural person, in particular to analyze or predict aspects concerning that natural person's performance at work, economic situation, health, personal preferences, interests, reliability, behavior, location, or movements.

Legal Rule: Special Data

Article 9 of the GDPR also refers to health processing as regards health data comprising or being encompassed in sensitive data. The Article expressly refers to "[p]rocessing of special categories of personal data." The rule states:

> "Processing of personal data revealing racial or ethnic origin, political opinions, religious or philosophical beliefs, or trade union membership, and the processing of genetic data, biometric data for the purpose of uniquely identifying a natural person, data concerning health or data concerning a natural person's sex life or sexual orientation shall be prohibited."

There are carveouts, such as express consent.* In the carveouts the following clause is contained:

> "processing is necessary for the purposes of preventive or occupational medicine, for the assessment of the working capacity of the employee, medical diagnosis, the provision of health or social care or treatment or the management of health or social care systems and services on the basis of EU or member state law or pursuant to contract with a health

---

* See GDPR Article 9(2).

professional and subject to the conditions and safeguards referred to in paragraph 3."*

Another states:

"processing is necessary for reasons of public interest in the area of public health, such as protecting against serious cross-border threats to health or ensuring high standards of quality and safety of health care and of medicinal products or medical devices, on the basis of EU or member state law which provides for suitable and specific measures to safeguard the rights and freedoms of the data subject, in particular professional secrecy."†

Member states may maintain or introduce further conditions, including limitations, with regard to the processing of genetic data, biometric data, or data concerning health.‡

Health Research

The issue of health research was just one of the matters that proved to be of some controversy during the discussions for the GDPR. The final provisions include the following. The sensitive data processing prohibition must not apply in the following health research instances

- Processing is necessary for the purposes of preventive or occupational medicine, for the assessment of the working capacity of the employee, medical diagnosis, the provision of health or social care or treatment or the management of health or social care systems and services on the basis of EU or member state law or pursuant to contract with a health professional and subject to the conditions and safeguards referred to in paragraph 3 (personal data referred to in paragraph 1 may be processed for the purposes referred to in point (h) of paragraph 2 when those data are processed by or under the responsibility of a professional subject to the obligation of professional

---

* See GDPR Article 9(2)(h).
† See GDPR Article 9(2)(i).
‡ See GDPR Article 9(4).

secrecy under EU or member state law or rules established by national competent bodies or by another person also subject to an obligation of secrecy under EU or member state law or rules established by national competent bodies*).

- Processing is necessary for reasons of public interest in the area of public health, such as protecting against serious cross-border threats to health or ensuring high standards of quality and safety of health care and of medicinal products or medical devices, on the basis of EU or member state law that provides for suitable and specific measures to safeguard the rights and freedoms of the individual data subject, in particular professional secrecy.
- Processing is necessary for ... scientific ... or statistical purposes in accordance with Article 89(1) based on EU or member state law, which shall be proportionate to the aim pursued, respect the essence of the right to data protection, and provide for suitable and specific measures to safeguard the fundamental rights and the interests of the individual data subject.†

Right to Be Forgotten Exception

The right to erasure (right to be forgotten) does not apply to the extent that processing is necessary, *inter alia*, for reasons of public interest in the area of public health in accordance with Article 9(2)(h) and (i) as well as Article 9(3).‡

There is also a form of exclusion in relation to "other important objectives of general public interest of the EU or of a member state, in particular an important economic or financial interest of the EU or of a member state, including monetary, budgetary and taxation matters, public health and social security."§

---

* GDPR Article 9(3).
† GDPR Article 9(2).
‡ See GDPR Article 17(3)(c).
§ See GDPR Article 23(1)(e).

Conclusion

Health data and health issues are very important in the context of the data protection rules. First, health data are recognized as being particularly important and fall within the concept of sensitive personal data. They are also important because the new GDPR expressly includes a number of new concepts and definitions recognizing some of the nuances and types of health personal data. Issues of archiving and archiving of health or medical data (whether for research or practice) also need careful consideration by organizations.

KEY CONCEPTS

The processing of personal data revealing racial or ethnic origin and the processing of genetic data, biometric data for the purpose of uniquely identifying a natural person, data concerning health, or data concerning a natural person's sex life or sexual orientation shall be prohibited.

Therefore, organizations need to consider how otherwise, if at all, they may legitimately propose the processing of health-related personal data. Given the complexity of the rule, this may not always be easy.

KEY WORDS

- Health data.
- Right to erasure.
- Right to be forgotten.
- Research.
- Data concerning health.
- Genetic data.
- Biometric data.
- Pseudonymization.
- Profiling.

FURTHER READING

- Beyleveld, Townend, Rouillé-Mirza and Wright, *Implementation of the Data Protection Directive in Relation to Medical Research in Europe* (Ashgate, 2005).
- Beyleveld, Townend and Wright, *Research Ethics Committees, Data Protection and Medical Research in European Countries* (Ashgate, 2005).
- Earle, *Data Protection in the NHS* (Informa, 2003).
- Forgo, "My Health Data: Your Research—Some Preliminary Thoughts on Different Values in the General Data Protection Regulation," *International Data Privacy Law* (2015) (5:1) 54.
- Harrell and Rothstein, "Biobanking Research and Privacy Laws in the United States," *Journal of Law, Medicine & Ethics* (2016) (44:1) 106.
- Herveg, "Data Protection and the Patient's Right to Safety," *European Journal of Health Law* (2014) (21:3) 260.
- Jasserand, "Avoiding Terminological Confusion between the Notions of 'Biometrics' and 'Biometric Data': An Investigation into the Meanings of the Terms from a European Data Protection and a Scientific Perspective," *International Data Privacy Law* (2015) (6:1) 63.
- Schropp, "Biometric Data Collection and RFID Tracking in Schools: A Reasoned Approach to Reasonable Expectations of Privacy," *North Carolina Law Review* (2016) (94:3) 1068.
- Townend, "EU Laws on Privacy in Genomic Databases and Biobanking," *Journal of Law, Medicine & Ethics* (2016) (44:1) 128.

37
ePrivacy

Introduction

There is increasing use of electronically transmitted personal data. This is protected and regulated in certain respects separately from the general data protection regime under the 1995 data protection directive (DPD95) (and the General Data Protection Regulation [GDPR]). While originally the regulation of telecommunications-related personal data centered on telecoms companies, it is now recognized as encompassing telecoms companies and almost any company engaged in activities involving the collection or transmission of particular personal data over electronic communications networks, including the Internet.

Organizations undertaking marketing, email marketing, text marketing, telephone marketing, or fax marketing and using location-based data, cookies, and identification regarding telephone calls need to comply with the rules in relation to ePrivacy and electronic communications.

The GDPR indicates that it must not impose additional obligations on natural or legal persons in relation to the processing of personal data in connection with the provision of publicly available electronic communications services in public communication networks in the EU in relation to matters for which they are subject to specific obligations with the same objective as set out in Directive 2002/58.* This is because certain issues are referred to or catered for separately than in the prior DPD95 and the new GDPR, in the ePrivacy Directive (ePD). However, other Directives (apart from ePrivacy) may be

---

* Article 89. Directive 2002/58/EC of the European Parliament and of the Council of 12 July 2002 concerning the processing of personal data and the protection of privacy in the electronic communications sector (Directive on privacy and electronic communications).

reviewed in terms of amendments required to smoothly comply with the GDPR.

Organizations must also note that it is proposed to amend the rules in relation to ePrivacy issues, again by way of an EU regulation similar to the GDPR. The contents of the proposal are referred to in this chapter, although the timeframe—and any potential amendments—are as yet unclear. The draft proposed ePrivacy Regulation also arises, as technology and events have changed significantly since it was originally enacted.

Background

There has been a separation between the data protection of general personal data, in the DPD95, and the regulation of personal data in (tele)communications networks. The latter were legislated for in the Data Protection Directive of 1997.* This was later replaced with the ePD.† The ePD concerns the processing of personal data and the protection of privacy in the electronic communications sector. It is also known as the Directive on privacy and electronic communications, hence the ePrivacy Directive. One of the concerns has been how electronic communications and electronic information are increasingly used for profiling for marketing purposes, including by electronic means.‡

Costa and Poullet indicate that once the GDPR "comes into force, the document will be the new general legal framework of data protection, repealing [the DPD95] more than 27 years after its adoption."§ The GDPR, as well as Article 8(1) of the EU Charter and Article 16(1), reasserts the importance of privacy and data protection "as a

---

* Directive 97/66/EC.

† Directive 2002/58/EC of the European Parliament and of the Council of 12 July 2002 concerning the processing of personal data and the protection of privacy in the electronic communications sector (Directive on privacy and electronic communications) (as amended by Directives 2006/24/EC and 2009/136/EC) (ePD). The ePD was also later amended. The ePrivacy Directive was amended by Directives 2006/24/EC and 2009/136/EC.

‡ See, for example, McGeveran, "Disclosure, Endorsement, and Identity in Social Marketing," *University of Illinois Law Review* (2009) (4) 1105.

§ Costa and Poullet, "Privacy and the Regulation of 2012," *Computer Law & Security Review* (2012) (28) 254.

fundamental right."* "[E]ffective and more coherent protection" is required.†

In terms of policy, as between modernizing via a directive or via a regulation, "in order to ensure a full consistent and high level of protection equivalent in all the EU member states, a Regulation was judged as the adequate solution to ensure full harmonisation"‡ throughout the EU. The EU Commission may also oversee and monitor the national data protection authorities.§

"Individuals are rarely aware of how their data are collected and processed while they are surfing on the internet at home, using their cellphones, walking down a video-surveyed street or with a TFID tag embedded in their clothes and so on."¶ There is a need for greater transparency. As regards data processing, "transparency translates the widening of the knowledge about information systems … coupled with fairness."**

The GDPR provides that personal data must be "processed lawfully, fairly and in a transparent manner in relation to the individual data subject ('lawfulness, fairness and transparency')."†† Transparency "requires greater awareness among citizens about the processing going on: its existence, its content and the flows generated in and out by using terminals."‡‡ Transparency also relates to security of data and risk management.§§

Some commentators have suggested that the GDPR could go further. It is suggested that "the greater the flow of information systems, the more opaque it becomes in modern information systems and with new ICT applications. In that case the right to transparency must increase alongside these new processes."¶¶

---

* Costa and Poullet, "Privacy and the Regulation of 2012," *Computer Law & Security Review* (2012) (28) at 254.
† ibid.
‡ ibid. at 255.
§ ibid.
¶ ibid. at 256.
** ibid.
†† GDPR Article 5(1)(a), Data Protection Principle 1.
‡‡ Costa and Poullet, "Privacy and the Regulation of 2012," *Computer Law & Security Review* (2012) (28), 254.
§§ ibid. at 256.
¶¶ ibid. at 256.

DPD95 and ePD

Article 94 of the GDPR repeals the DPD95. It is repealed with effect from May 25, 2018. Under Article 94(2), it provides that references to the repealed Directive will be construed as references to the GDPR. References to Article 29 Data Protection Working Party (WP29) of DPD95 must be construed as references to the European Data Protection Board (EDPB) established by the GDPR.

The GDPR also refers to the ePD.* Article 95 refers to the relationship to and amendment of the ePD. It states that the GDPR must not impose additional obligations on natural or legal persons in relation to processing in connection with the provision of publicly available electronic communications services in public communication networks in the EU in relation to matters for which they are subject to specific obligations with the same objective as set out in the ePrivacy Directive.

GDPR Article 96 provides that international agreements involving the transfer of personal data to third countries or international organizations that were concluded by member states prior to May 24, 2016, and that comply with EU law as applicable prior to that date, must remain in force until amended, replaced, or revoked.

Scope of ePD

The ePD† broadly relates to

- Security.
- Confidentiality.

---

* Directive 2002/58/EC of the European Parliament and of the Council of 12 July 2002 concerning the processing of personal data and the protection of privacy in the electronic communications sector (Directive on privacy and electronic communications) (as amended by Directives 2006/24/EC and 2009/136/EC).
† As amended, Directive 2002/58/EC of the European Parliament and of the Council of 12 July 2002 concerning the processing of personal data and the protection of privacy in the electronic communications sector (Directive on privacy and electronic communications) (as amended by Directives 2006/24/EC and 2009/136/EC). The ePrivacy Directive was amended by Directive 2006/24. This includes, *inter alia*, obligation to retain data; access; data categories; periods of retention; security; storage requirements for retained data; supervisory authorities; statistics on retention; and ePD remedies, liability and penalties.

- Traffic data.
- Non-itemized bills.
- Call and connected line identification.
- Location data.
- Exceptions.
- Directories.
- Unsolicited communications.
- Technical features.

It also provides various rules in particular in relation to

- Email marketing.
- Text marketing.
- Telephone marketing.
- Fax marketing.
- Cookies.

The ePD harmonizes member states' rules on the protection of fundamental rights, in particular privacy, with respect to the processing of personal data in the electronic communications sector. It complements the DPD95* and applies to the processing of personal data in connection with the provision of publicly available electronic communications services in public communications networks in the EU.†

Security

Article 4 of the ePD relates to security. The provider of a publicly available electronic communications service must take appropriate technical and organizational measures to safeguard the security of its services, if necessary in conjunction with the provider of the public communications network with respect to network security. Having regard to the state of the technology and the cost of their implementation, these measures must ensure a level of security appropriate to the risk presented. In the case of a particular risk of a breach of the

---

* ePD Article 1 refers to the scope and aim. Article 2 of the ePD refers to definitions. The definitions in the DPD95 and in the ePD apply. The following terms are also defined: "User"; "Traffic data"; "Location data"; "Communication"; "Call"; "Consent"; "Value added service"; "Electronic mail."
† ePD Article 3.

security of the network, the provider of a publicly available electronic communications service must inform the subscribers concerning such risk and, where the risk lies outside the scope of the measures to be taken by the service provider, of any possible remedies, including an indication of the likely costs involved.*

Confidentiality

Article 5 refers to the confidentiality of the communications. Member states must ensure the confidentiality of communications and the related traffic data by means of a public communications network and publicly available electronic communications services, through member state legislation. In particular, they must prohibit listening, tapping, storage, or other kinds of interception or surveillance of communications and the related traffic data by persons other than users without user consent, unless legally authorized to do so. (There is a technical storage exception† and an exception for proving a transaction or business communication.‡ There is also a user right to refuse processing of data stored in terminal equipment.§)

---

* ePD Article 4(2).

† The exception is that this shall not prevent technical storage that is necessary for the conveyance of a communication without prejudice to the principle of confidentiality. ePD Article 5.

‡ The restriction does not affect any legally authorized recording of communications and the related traffic data when carried out in the course of lawful business practice for the purpose of providing evidence of a commercial transaction or of any other business communication. ePD Article 5(2).

§ Member states shall ensure that the use of electronic communications networks to store information or to gain access to information stored in the terminal equipment of a subscriber or user is only allowed on condition that the subscriber or user concerned is provided with clear and comprehensive information in accordance with the DPD95, *inter alia* about the purposes of the processing, and is offered the right to refuse such processing by the controller. This shall not prevent any technical storage or access for the sole purpose of carrying out or facilitating the transmission of a communication over an electronic communications network, or as strictly necessary to provide an information society service explicitly requested by the subscriber or user. ePD Article 5(3).

Traffic Data

Subscriber and user traffic data must be erased or made anonymous by communications providers when no longer needed for communication transmission purposes.* Communications providers may process the data to the extent and for the duration necessary for value-added services or marketing if the subscriber/user has given consent. Users or subscribers must be given the possibility to withdraw their consent for the processing of traffic data at any time. The service provider must inform the subscriber or user of the types of traffic data that are processed and of the duration of such processing and prior to obtaining consent.† There are also restrictions on the types of personnel who may process traffic data.‡

Non-Itemized Billing

Subscribers have the right to receive non-itemized bills.§

Call Line Identification

Article 8 relates to the presentation and restriction of calling and connected line identification. Service providers must offer users simple, free of charge means to prevent call line identification.¶

---

* Traffic data relating to subscribers and users processed and stored by the provider of a public communications network or publicly available electronic communications service. ePD Article 6. Traffic data necessary for subscriber billing and interconnection payments may be processed, but only up to the end of the period during which the bill may lawfully be challenged or payment pursued. ePD Article 6(2).

† Processing of traffic data must be restricted to persons handling billing or traffic management, customer enquiries, fraud detection, marketing electronic communications services, or providing a value-added service and must be restricted to what is necessary for the purposes of such activities. ePD Article 6(3).

‡ ePD Article 6(3).

§ Member states must apply national provisions to reconcile the rights of subscribers receiving itemized bills with the right to privacy of calling users and called subscribers; for example, by ensuring that sufficient alternative privacy-enhancing methods of communications or payments are available to such users and subscribers. ePD Article 7.

¶ ePD Article 8(1).

Location Data

This is increasingly important as more and more smartphones and electronic devices permit the capture of location-based data relating to individuals and/or their personal equipment. User or subscriber location data may only be processed if made anonymous, or with *consent* and for the duration necessary for the provision of a value-added service. The users or subscribers, prior to consent, must be informed of the type of location data, the purposes, the duration of processing, and any third-party recipients. Users or subscribers must be given the possibility to withdraw their consent at any time.* There are also personnel restrictions on who can process the data.† There are also certain exceptions relating to the tracing of malicious or nuisance calls and emergency calls. There are also rights in relation to stopping automatic call forwarding by a third party.‡

Directories

Article 12 refers to directories of subscribers (in this instance, both persons and organizations), who have certain rights in relation to directories,§ including prior information, consent, and to verify, correct, or withdraw personal data from a directory.¶

Unsolicited Communications, Direct Marketing, and Spam

How should organizations go about data protection compliance direct marketing? When is direct marketing permitted? All organizations should carefully assess compliance issues when considering any direct marketing activities. Getting it wrong can be costly and can have enforcement and investigation consequences.

Direct marketing tends to be one of the most contentious areas of data protection practice, with the possible exceptions of data breach/data loss and Internet/social media data protection issues. Most

---

* Article 9 of the ePD relates to location data other than traffic data.
† ePD Article 9(1).
‡ ePD Article 11.
§ ePD Article 12.
¶ ePD Article 12(2) and (4).

organizations need to engage in direct marketing at some stage, some more heavily than others. Many organizations may even go so far as to say that direct marketing is an essential ingredient of continued commercial success.

However, direct marketing is sometimes viewed as spam and unsolicited commercial communications, which are unwanted and also unlawful. The data protection regime (and the eCommerce legal regime) refers to permissible direct marketing and sets out various obligatory requirements while at the same time setting a default position of prohibiting non-exempted or non-permitted electronic direct marketing.

The GDPR provides that it must not impose additional obligations on natural or legal persons in relation to the processing of personal data in connection with the provision of publicly available electronic communications services in public communication networks in the EU in relation to matters for which they are subject to specific obligations with the same objective as set out in Directive 2002/58.* There may be a review to ensure that the ePD fully complements and does not conflict with the GDPR, and if so, amendments may be required.

If the organization anticipates that personal data kept by it will be processed for the purposes of direct marketing, it must inform the persons to whom the data relate that they may object by means of a request in writing to the controller and free of charge.†

Article 13 of the ePD refers to unsolicited communications. The use of automated calling systems without human intervention (automatic calling machines), facsimile machines (fax), or electronic mail, for the purposes of direct marketing, may *only* be allowed in respect of subscribers who have given their *prior consent*. This means that there is a default rule prohibiting direct marketing without prior consent.

---

* GDPR Article 95. Directive 2002/58/EC of the European Parliament and of the Council of 12 July 2002 concerning the processing of personal data and the protection of privacy in the electronic communications sector (Directive on privacy and electronic communications).
† See, for example, Edwards, "Consumer Privacy Law 1: Online Direct Marketing" and Edwards and Hatcher, "Consumer Privacy Law: Data Collection, Profiling and Targeting," each in Edwards and Waelde (eds), *Law and the Internet* (Hart, 2009) 489 and following and 511 and following, respectively.

Many marketing-orientated organizations may be surprised, if not dismayed, by this.

The Spam Problem

Spam is just one of a number of names taken to describe the problem of unsolicited electronic commercial marketing materials. The spam name comes originally from a Monty Python comic sketch. However, electronic spam is far from comic and costs industry hundreds of millions of pounds each year in employees' lost time and resources, in lost bandwidth, and in reduced capacity and network speed, as well as other problems.

Spam Internationally

The growing recognition of the problems caused by spam has meant an increasing number of local and member state laws specifically dedicated to preventing spam. In the United States, for example, there are a large number of local state laws* and national federal laws dedicated to tackling spam. These include both new specific laws and spam-specific amendments to pre-existing laws. The US federal spam act, known as the CANSPAM Act, has been introduced.[†]

Unsolicited Communications

Article 13 of the ePD refers to unsolicited communications. Article 13(1) provides that the use of automated calling systems without human intervention (automatic calling machines), facsimile machines (fax) or electronic mail for the purposes of direct marketing may only be allowed in respect of subscribers who have given their prior consent.

Article 13(2) provides that, notwithstanding Article 13(1), where a natural or legal person obtains from its customers their electronic contact details for electronic mail in the context of the sale of a product or a service, in accordance with the DPD95, the same natural or legal

---

* See www.spamlaws.com.
[†] See Reid, "Recent Developments in Private Enforcement of the Can-Spam Act," *Akron Intellectual Property Journal* (2010) (4) 281.

person may use these electronic contact details for direct marketing of its own similar products or services provided that customers clearly and distinctly are given the opportunity to object, free of charge and in an easy manner, to such use of electronic contact details when they are collected and on the occasion of each message in case the customer has not initially refused such use.

Member states must take appropriate measures to ensure that, free of charge, unsolicited communications for purposes of direct marketing, in cases other than those referred to in Article 13(1) and (2), are not allowed either without the consent of the subscribers concerned or in respect of subscribers who do not wish to receive these communications, the choice between these options to be determined by member state legislation.*

In any event, the practice of sending electronic mail for purposes of direct marketing while disguising or concealing the identity of the sender on whose behalf the communication is made, or without a valid address to which the recipient may send a request that such communications cease, must be prohibited.†

Article 13(5) provides that Article 13(1) and (3) must apply to subscribers who are natural persons. Member states must also ensure, in the framework of EU law and applicable member state legislation, that the legitimate interests of subscribers other than natural persons with regard to unsolicited communications are sufficiently protected.

Marketing Default Position

How should organizations go about data protection–compliant direct marketing? When is direct marketing permitted? All organizations should carefully assess compliance issues when considering any direct marketing activities. Getting it wrong can be costly and can have data protection supervisory authority enforcement and investigation consequences.

---

* Article 13(3) Directive 2002/58/EC of the European Parliament and of the Council of 12 July 2002 concerning the processing of personal data and the protection of privacy in the electronic communications sector.
† ibid.; Article 13(4).

Article 13 of the ePD provides a number of rules in relation to unsolicited communications. Article 13(1) provides that

- Automated calling systems without human intervention (automatic calling machines).
- Facsimile machines (fax) or
- Electronic mail.

for the purposes of direct marketing may *only* be allowed in respect of subscribers who have given their *prior consent*.

Therefore, there is a default rule prohibiting the forms of direct marketing referred to thus far *without* prior consent. Many marketing-orientated organizations may consider this a hindrance to what may have been considered legitimate marketing and business activities.

Limited Direct Marketing Permitted

Limited direct marketing is permitted; namely, of subscribers or customers who have given their prior consent. This implies consent in advance or simultaneously with the direct marketing. However, in terms of direct marketing by email, this is further restricted.

Direct Marketing to Existing Customers' Email

In the context of existing customers, there is a possibility of direct marketing using emails. Article 13(2) of the ePD provides that where an organization obtains from its customers their electronic contact details for electronic mail, in the context of the sale of a product or a service, in accordance with the DPD95, the organization may use these electronic contact details for direct marketing of its own similar products or services, provided that customers clearly and distinctly are given the opportunity to object, free of charge and in an easy manner, to such use of electronic contact details when they are collected and on the occasion of each message in case the customer has not initially refused such use.

Therefore, once the email details are obtained at the time of a product or service transaction, it will be possible to use that email for direct marketing purposes. Conditions or limitations apply, however. First, the organization is only permitted to market and promote similar products or services. This, therefore, rules out unrelated, non-identical, and non-similar products and services. Second, at the time of each subsequent act of direct marketing, the customer must be given the opportunity in an easy and accessible manner to opt out or cancel the direct marketing. Effectively, they must be taken off the organization's direct marketing list.

National Marketing Opt-Out Registers

Article 13(3) of the ePD provides that member states must take appropriate measures to ensure that, free of charge, unsolicited communications for purposes of direct marketing, in cases other than those referred to in paragraphs 1 and 2, are not allowed either without the consent of the subscribers concerned or in respect of subscribers who do not wish to receive these communications, the choice between these options to be determined by member state legislation. This means that each member state must determine and provide a means for individuals to opt out of receiving direct marketing in advance.

Deceptive Emails: Marketing Emails Must Not Conceal Identity

Article 13(4) of the ePD provides that the practice of sending electronic mail for purposes of direct marketing while disguising or concealing the identity of the sender on whose behalf the communication is made must be prohibited. This means that organizations cannot conceal their identity if permitted to engage in direct marketing. If this is not complied with, what might otherwise be permissible direct marketing can be deemed to be impermissible. Complaints, investigations, or enforcement proceedings can thus arise.

Marketing Emails Must Provide Opt-Out

In addition, Article 13(4) of the ePD provides that the practice of sending electronic mail for purposes of direct marketing without a valid address to which the recipient may send a request that such communications cease must be prohibited. This means that organizations must also include an easy contact address or other details at which the recipient can contact them if they wish to object to receiving any further direct marketing. If this is not complied with, what might otherwise be permissible direct marketing can be deemed to be impermissible. Complaints, investigations, or enforcement proceedings can thus also arise.

Marketing Protection for Organizations

Article 13(5) of the ePD provides that Article 13(1) and (3) must apply to subscribers who are natural persons. Member states must also ensure, in the framework of Community law and applicable member state legislation, that the legitimate interests of subscribers other than natural persons with regard to unsolicited communications are sufficiently protected. This means that protection from unsolicited direct marketing can also be extended to organizations.

ePrivacy Regulation Proposal

As indicated earlier, there is currently a proposal to replace the ePD with a new ePrivacy Regulation. The current proposal refers to

Article 1: Subject matter
Article 2: Material Scope
Article 3: Territorial scope and representative
Article 4: Definitions
Article 5: Confidentiality of electronic communications data
Article 6: Permitted processing of electronic communications data
Article 7: Storage and erasure of electronic communications data
Article 8: Protection of information stored in and related to end-users' terminal equipment
Article 9: Consent
Article 10: Information and options for privacy settings to be provided
Article 11: Restrictions
Article 12: Presentation and restriction of calling and connected line identification
Article 13: Exceptions to presentation and restriction of calling and connected line identification

Article 14: Incoming call blocking
Article 15: Publicly available directories
Article 16: Unsolicited communications
Article 17: Information about detected security risks
Article 18: Independent supervisory authorities
Article 19: European Data Protection Board
Article 20: Cooperation and consistency procedures
Article 21: Remedies
Article 22: Right to compensation and liability
Article 23: General conditions for imposing administrative fines
Article 24: Penalties
Article 25: Exercise of the delegation
Article 26: Committee
Article 27: Repeal
Article 28: Monitoring and evaluation clause
Article 29: Entry into force and application

Conclusion

Few organizations will not be interested in direct marketing and advertising. The key is to get it right. The consequences of sending unlawful electronic communications can include offenses, prosecutions, official enforcement, and investigations as well as being sued. This is one of the areas that are consistently areas of focus for data protection supervisory authority investigation.

These issues become more important as (a) increased competition puts pressure on organizations to engage, or increase, marketing and profiling efforts and (b) the software, devices, and technologies available to facilitate such efforts are increasing in significance. Over time, cost efforts also decrease in terms of adopting these new tools. As always, however, organizations are cautioned to ensure data protection compliance. They might also on occasion pause to question general ethical considerations in certain instances. Depending on the sector, certain third-party organizational rules may also be obligatory to consider and comply with, particularly as regards direct marketing issues. Indeed, the new GDPR also provides the impetus for representative organizations to increasingly consider industry-wide data protection Codes of Conduct. These are encouraged by data protection supervisory authorities and the new GDPR.

Originally envisaged as relating to telecoms-type data only, this secondary aspect of the data protection regime has expanded in substance, scope, and detail. While much of it is still specific to telecoms companies and entities involved in the transfer of electronic communications, certain issues are more generally applicable. The ePD as amended applies to all organizations that wish to engage in direct marketing through a variety of means. Compliance is necessary and needs to be planned in advance. If not specifically exempted from the default rule, it is difficult to envisage permissible direct marketing.

One example is the increasingly controversial area of profiling, advertising, and direct marketing in relation to children.[*]

Online behavioral advertising (OBA) and the behavioral targeting of Internet advertising are increasingly debated.[†]

Commentators and media often focus on the issue of threats to privacy, data protection, and reputation rights caused by Web 2.0 activities such as social media, search engine services, and so on. The query arises as to whether revenue versus privacy is better respected by certain online services providers than others.[‡]

KEY CONCEPTS

ePrivacy issues are one of the most frequent interfaces of compliance considerations by organizations, particularly the sales and marketing units. It is important to get data protection compliance right, whether in terms of collecting personal data, storing it, or using it for marketing, and so on.

Also note the ePD.

---

[*] Munukutla-Parker, "Unsolicited Commercial Email, Privacy Concerns related to Social Network Services, Online Protection of Children, and Cyberbullying," *I/S: A Journal of Law and Policy* (2006) (2) 628.

[†] Deane-Johns, "Behavioural Targeting of Internet Advertising," *Computers and Law* (2009) (20) 22.

[‡] Edwards and Waelde (eds), *Law and the Internet* (Hart, 2009) 539.

Note: it is proposed to replace ePrivacy with a new regulation. The draft proposal is entitled *Proposal for a Regulation on Privacy and Electronic Communications* (2017).

KEYWORDS

- ePrivacy.
- Electronic communications.
- Covered separately from new GDPR.
- Currently in ePrivacy Directive.
- New draft proposed ePrivacy Regulation.
- Electronic direct marketing.
- Spam.
- Directory databases.
- Opt-outs.
- Opt-out registries.

FURTHER READING

- Asscher and Hoogcarspel, *Regulating Spam: A European Perspective after the Adoption of the E-Privacy Directive* (TMC Asser; Cambridge University Press, 2006).
- Bainbridge, *Introduction to Information Technology Law* (Pearson Longman, 2008, updates in 2010).
- Beckstrom, "Who's Looking at Your Facebook Profile? The Use of Student Conduct Codes to Censor College Students' Online Speech," *Willamette Law Review* (2008) 261.
- Büllesbach, Poullet, Prins and Gijrath, *Concise European IT Law* (Wolters Kluwer, 2010).
- Butler, ed., *E-Commerce and Convergence: A Guide to the Law of Digital Media* (Tottel, 2012).
- Conradi, ed., *Communications Law Handbook* (Bloomsbury, 2009).

- Edwards, ed., *The New Legal Framework for E-Commerce in Europe* (Hart, 2005).
- Edwards and Waelde, eds, *Law and the Internet* (Hart, 2009) (chs 14–21).
- Edwards, "Consumer Privacy Law 1: Online Direct Marketing" and Edwards and Hatcher, "Consumer Privacy Law: Data Collection, Profiling and Targeting," each in Edwards and Waelde (eds), *Law and the Internet* (Hart, 2009) 489 and 511, respectively.
- Groppe, "A Child's Playground or a Predator's Hunting Ground?: How to Protect Children on Internet Social Networking Sites," *CommLaw Conspectus* (2007) (16) 215.
- Gourlay and Gallagher, "Collecting and Using Children's Information Online: The UK/US Dichotomy," *Computers and Law* (December 12, 2011).
- Lambert, *Social Networking: Law, Rights and Policy* (Clarus, 2014).
- Lloyd, *Information Technology Law* (Oxford University Press, 2014).
- Lambert, *International Handbook of Social Media Laws* (Bloomsbury, 2015).
- Mantelero, "Competitive Value of Data Protection: The Impact of Data Protection Regulation on Online Behaviour," *International Data Privacy Law* (2013) (3:4) 229.
- Murray, *Information Technology Law: The Law and Society* (Oxford University Press, 2013) (chs 18, 19).
- Steadman, "MySpace, But Whose Responsibility? Liability of Social Networking Websites When Offline Sexual Assault of Minors Follows Online Interaction," *Villanova Sports and Entertainment Law Journal* (2007) (14) 363.
- Reed, *Computer Law* (Oxford University Press, 2011) (chs 10, 11).
- Rowland and Kohl, *Information Technology Law* (Routledge, 2016).
- Ryan, *The EU Regulatory Framework for Electronic Communications Handbook* (Bloomsbury, 2010).

- Smith and Moseley, *The New Data Protection Liabilities & Risks for Direct Marketers: Handbook* (Forum Business Media, 2005).
- Smith, *Internet Law and Regulation* (Sweet & Maxwell, 2016) (ch. 7).
- Tauwhare, "Improving Cybersecurity in the European Union: The Network and Information Security Directive," *Journal of Internet Law* (2016) (19:12) 3.

38

Courts

Introduction

Increasingly, data protection breaches and other non-compliance will result in civil remedies and monetary awards and compensation to individual data subjects. If a request for information or other notice is received from the data protection supervisory authority, it may be appropriate to seek immediate legal advice. The data protection supervisory authority can also issue enforcement notices. In addition, the data protection supervisory authority may pursue monetary penalties. Organizations should ensure proper policies, awareness of data protection issues, and ongoing training across all personnel who have an impact on and responsibility regarding data protection operations. Organizations need to apprise themselves of the new data protection regime, not only in terms of the regime obligations being enhanced and extended but also in terms of ensuring adequate compliance procedures to avoid costly investigations, fines, penalties, and damages and compensation, as well as other consequences of non-compliance and breach.

Data protection is important. Personal data are considered important and sensitive to customers. This should be respected by organizations. Organizations are not permitted to collect or process customers' personal data without being data protection compliance. It is in this context that there can be severe consequences for an organization for non-compliance, whether in collecting personal data initially or in the subsequent processing of the personal data. The data protection supervisory authority can prosecute for non-compliance. Alternatively, enforcement notices can be imposed that specify certain actions that must be implemented by the organization. Certain types of organizations can be the recipients of a separate type of notices, namely, assessment notices. In any of these events, customers will be particularly concerned that their personal data have been collected, are being processed in a certain manner, and/or may have been subject to a breach event. This can have its own consequences. Overall, it should also be noted that the consequences of breach or non-compliance are becoming increasingly important as enforcement actions and penalties are increasing in number and financial scale. The new General Data Protection Regulation (GDPR) regime also further changes the enforcement rules.

Civil Sanctions

Certain types of data will convey inherent additional risks over others, such as loss of financial personal data. It can be argued that this requires higher obligations for the organization. Indeed, the new GDPR expressly refers to the sensitivity of certain types of personal data as well as the enhanced importance of security, risk assessment, risk minimization, consultations, and data protection by design and by default.

One interesting area to consider is online abuse and damage, such as viral publication, defamation, bulletin boards, discussion forums and websites (or sections of websites), and social media and related websites. Where damage occurs as a result of the, misuse, or loss of personal data or results in abuse, threats, defamation, or liability could, depending on the circumstances, arise for the individual tortfeasors as well as the website.

Another interesting area to consider is that of data breaches and the changing landscape in terms of responsibility and liability. Obviously, there can be a number of sources for data breaches, and the scale, complexity, length, effect, and cost can vary greatly. The new GDPR is significant (in imposing rights, obligations, security compliance, risk assessment and minimization, data protection by design and data protection by default, etc.), but it is by no means the only development for organizations to be aware of. Separately from the GDPR, there is a new Security Directive being finalized. The security landscape (in law, practice, and technology) is constantly changing internationally. Organizations cannot ignore these developments. Organizations are being sued, prosecuted, and fined internationally; executives are being prosecuted and have lost their jobs or at least have black marks on their file; services have to be stopped at significant disruption and cost; significant numbers of customers or users can be lost forever; the IT fix or replacement costs can run into millions; the brand and reputation damage can take years to recover. Just recently, the VTech (the children's electronic toy manufacturer) data breach demonstrates that the fallout can extend also to an organization reacting in an overly legalistic manner. The company drew adverse attention when it changed its terms and conditions after the breach to purport that it was not liable to customers and users when their data was hacked. The UK data protection supervisory authority (Information Commissioner's Office [ICO]) was just one avenue of the criticism that VTech received. Obviously, and as the ICO also confirms, the company is responsible for security and compliance in relation to customer and user personal data.

While there are certain limited defenses in the eCommerce Directive,* one should recall that the data protection regime (and its duty of care and liability provisions) is separate and stands alone from the eCommerce Directive legal regime. Indeed, even in terms of the eCommerce defenses, one should also recall that (a) an organization must first fall within an eCommerce defense, and not lose that defense, so as to avail itself of it and (b) there is no automatic entitlement to an Internet service provider (ISP) or website to a global eCommerce defense. In fact, there is not one eCommerce defense but three very specific defenses relating to specific and technical activities. Not every ISP activity will fall into one of these defenses. Nor will one activity fall into all three defenses. The GDPR refers to the "the liability rules of intermediary service providers in Articles 12–15 of" the eCommerce Directive, as opposed to liability defenses.[†]

It is also possible to conceive of a website that has no take-down procedures, inadequate take-down procedures (assuming there are such procedures), or non-expeditious procedures and will face potential liability under privacy and data protection as well as eCommerce liability. For example, an imposter social media profile that contains personal data and defamatory material could attract liability for the

---

* Directive 2000/31/EC of the European Parliament and of the Council of 8 June 2000 on certain legal aspects of information society services, in particular electronic commerce, in the Internal Market (Directive on electronic commerce). At http://eur-lex.europa.eu/LexUriServ/LexUriServ.do?uri=CELEX:32000L0031:en:NOT.
[†] GDPR Article 2(3).

website operator under data protection and under normal liability if none of the eCommerce defenses were unavailable or were lost. The latter could occur if, for example, the false impersonating profile was notified to the website (or it was otherwise aware) but it did not do anything.* Damages can be and have been awarded.†

Background Guidance

There are various court remedies, duty of care, and so on in relation to individual data subjects for organizations to be aware of, and which can also result in court actions. These can arise as a result of data protection supervisory authorities or from individuals.

Background Recital 22 of the GDPR states that any processing of personal data in the context of the activities of an establishment of a controller or a processor in the EU should be carried out in accordance with the GDPR, regardless of whether the processing itself takes place within the EU.‡ Therefore, the rules apply even if the processing is outsourced in-group or out-of-group.

Background Recital 23 of the GDPR states that to ensure that natural persons are not deprived of the protection to which they are entitled under the GDPR, the processing of personal data of individual data subjects who are in the EU by a controller or a processor not established in the EU should be subject to the GDPR where the processing activities are related to offering goods or services to such individual data subjects, irrespective of whether they are connected

---

* This is a complex and developing area of law, common law, civil law, Directive, new GDPR, and case law, both in the United Kingdom and internationally. A full and detailed analysis is beyond the scope of this work.

† For example, the Australian case of *Milorad Trkulja v Google* held that Google was guilty of defamation and, *inter alia*, did not operate adequate takedowns. *Milorad Trkulja v Google*, Supreme Court of Victoria, Melbourne, [2012] VSC 533, November 12, 2012. Damages of AU$200,000 were awarded. Yahoo! was also held to be a liable publisher in the amount of AU$225,000. *Trkulja v Yahoo! Inc & Anor* [2012] VSC 88. In New Zealand, a court has also indicated that online website service providers can be publishers. *A v Google*, HC AK CIV: 2011-404-002780, March 5, 2012.

‡ Establishment implies the effective and real exercise of activity through stable arrangements. The legal form of such arrangements, whether through a branch or a subsidiary with a legal personality, is not the determining factor in that respect. GDPR Recital 22.

to a payment. To determine whether such a controller or processor is offering goods or services to individual data subjects who are in the EU, it should be ascertained whether it is apparent that the controller or processor envisages offering services to individual data subjects in one or more member states in the EU.* Factors such as the use of a language or a currency generally used in one or more member states with the possibility of ordering goods and services in that other language, or the mentioning of customers or users who are in the EU, may make it apparent that the controller envisages offering goods or services to individual data subjects in the EU.

Background Recital 24 of the GDPR states that the processing of personal data of individual data subjects who are in the EU by a controller or processor not established in the EU should also be subject to the GDPR when it is related to the monitoring of the behavior of such individual data subjects insofar as their behavior takes place within the EU. To determine whether a processing activity can be considered to monitor the behavior of individual data subjects, it should be ascertained whether natural persons are tracked on the Internet, including the potential subsequent use of personal data processing techniques that consist of profiling a natural person, particularly to take decisions concerning them or for analyzing or predicting their personal preferences, behaviors, and attitudes.

Individuals are also entitled in enforcing their data protection rights, and in seeking remedies in relation to damage and loss suffered as a result of the misuse of their personal data, to seek court remedies. They are not confined to simply making complaints to the data protection supervisory authority. It is important to note that certain remedies that an individual may wish to seek are not available from or via the data protection supervisory authority.

This recognition of judicial, as well as official, routes to remedies is also contained in the recent GDPR Recitals. Every data subject should have the right to lodge a complaint with a single data protection supervisory authority, in particular in the member state of their

---

* The mere accessibility of the controller's, the processor's, or an intermediary's website in the EU, of an email address or of other contact details, or the use of a language generally used in the third country where the controller is established, is insufficient to ascertain such intention. GDPR Recital 23.

habitual residence, and have the right to an effective judicial remedy.* Where an individual data subject considers that their rights under the GDPR are infringed, they should have the right to mandate a body, organization, or association that is of non-profit-making character.† For proceedings against a controller or processor, the plaintiff should have the choice to bring the action before the courts of the member states where the controller or processor has an establishment or where the individual data subject resides, unless the controller is a public authority of a member state acting in the exercise of its public powers.‡

Any damage that a person may suffer as a result of processing that is not in compliance with the GDPR should be compensated by the controller or processor, which should be exempted from liability if they prove that they are not in any way responsible for the damage. The concept of damage should be broadly interpreted in the light of the case law of the EU Court of Justice in a manner that fully reflects the objectives of the GDPR. Individual data subjects should receive full and effective compensation for the damage they have suffered.§ Controllers and processors owe a duty of care to individual data subjects. ¶

The background Recitals refer to proceedings against controllers, processors, and jurisdiction (Recital 145); damages and compensation (Recital 146); the prevention, investigation, detection, or prosecution of criminal offenses or the execution of criminal penalties, including public security (Recital 19); and processing and courts (Recital 20).

---

* GDPR Recital 141.
† GDPR Recital 142.
‡ GDPR Recital 145.
§ GDPR Recital 118.
¶ DPD95 Chapter III. The DPD95 also refers to judicial remedies, liability, and sanctions. Article 22, referring to remedies, states that without prejudice to any administrative remedy for which provision may be made, *inter alia*, before the data protection supervisory authority, prior to referral to the judicial authority, member states must provide for the right of every person to a *judicial remedy* for any breach of the rights guaranteed them by the member state law applicable to the processing in question. Article 23 of the DPD95 refers to liability and provides that member states must provide that any person who has suffered damage as a result of an unlawful processing operation or of any act incompatible with the national provisions adopted pursuant to the Directive is entitled to receive compensation from the controller for the damage suffered.

The controller or processor should compensate any damage that a person may suffer as a result of processing that infringes the GDPR. The controller or processor should be exempt from liability if it proves that it is not in any way responsible for the damage. The concept of damage should be broadly interpreted in the light of the case law of the EU Court of Justice in a manner that fully reflects the objectives of the GDPR. This is without prejudice to any claims for damage deriving from the violation of other rules in EU or member state law. Processing that infringes the GDPR also includes processing that infringes delegated and implementing acts adopted in accordance with the GDPR and member state law specifying rules of the GDPR. Individual data subjects should receive full and effective compensation for the damage they have suffered. Where controllers or processors are involved in the same processing, each controller or processor should be held liable for the entire damage. However, where they are joined to the same judicial proceedings, in accordance with member state law, compensation may be apportioned according to the responsibility of each controller or processor for the damage caused by the processing, provided that full and effective compensation of the individual data subject who suffered the damage is ensured. Any controller or processor that has paid full compensation may subsequently institute recourse proceedings against other controllers or processors involved in the same processing.[*]

New GDPR Remedies, Legal Rules, Damage, and Compensation

The DPD95 refers to these various issues, such as courts,[†] damages and compensation,[‡] and sanctions.[§] The new GDPR changes and expands on these matters. Chapter VIII of the GDPR refers to remedies, liability, and penalties regarding data protection. Article 77 refers to the right to lodge a complaint with a data protection supervisory authority. Without prejudice to any other administrative or judicial remedy, every individual data subject must have the right to lodge

---

[*] GDPR Recital 146.
[†] DPD95 Article 22.
[‡] DPD95 Article 23.
[§] DPD95 Article 24.

a complaint with a data protection supervisory authority, in particular in the member state of their habitual residence, place of work or place of the alleged infringement if the individual data subject considers that the processing of personal data relating to them infringes the GDPR.* In addition, the data protection supervisory authority with which the complaint has been lodged must inform the complainant on the progress and the outcome of the complaint, including the possibility of a judicial remedy pursuant to Article 78.†

Right to Effective Judicial Remedy against Controller or Processor

Article 79 refers to the right to an effective judicial remedy against a controller or processor. Without prejudice to any available administrative or non-judicial remedy, including the right to lodge a complaint with a data protection supervisory authority pursuant to Article 77, each individual data subject must have the right to an effective judicial remedy where he or she considers that their rights under the GDPR have been infringed as a result of the processing of their personal data in non-compliance with the GDPR.‡

Proceedings against a controller or a processor must be brought before the courts of the member state where the controller or processor has an establishment. Alternatively, such proceedings may be brought before the courts of the member state where the individual data subject has their habitual residence, unless the controller or processor is a public authority of a member state acting in the exercise of its public powers.§

Right to Compensation and Liability

The GDPR introduces important new provisions. Article 82 of the GDPR refers to the right to compensation and liability. Any person who has suffered material or non-material damage as a result of an

---

* GDPR Article 77(1).
† GDPR Article 77(2).
‡ GDPR Article 79(1).
§ GDPR Article 79(2).

infringement of the GDPR must have the right to receive compensation from the controller or processor for the damage suffered.*

Any *controller* involved in processing must be liable for the damage caused by processing that *infringes* the GDPR. A *processor* must be liable for the damage caused by processing only where it has *not complied* with obligations of the GDPR specifically directed to processors or where it has acted *outside or contrary* to lawful *instructions of the controller.*†

A controller or processor must be exempt from liability under paragraph 2 if it proves that it is not in any way responsible for the event giving rise to the damage.‡ It is noted that the reference to "any" ensures that there is apparently a high onus on organizations to satisfy this criterion. It may point to certain factors indicating non-liability, but if there is one other factor pointing to liability, or where certain actions were not taken or risks known, this could mean that the exemption cannot or does not apply.

There is also a form of potential set off or indemnity between various parties that may be potentially liable. Where more than one controller or processor, or both a controller and a processor, are involved in the same processing, and where they are, under paragraphs 2 and 3, responsible for *any* damage caused by processing, each controller or processor must be held liable for the entire damage so as to ensure *effective compensation* of the data subject.§ It is also noted that this refers to "effective compensation" as opposed to the potentially narrower phrase "compensation" or mere "compensation."

Where a controller or processor has, in accordance with paragraph 4, paid full compensation for the damage suffered, that controller or processor must be entitled to claim back from the other controllers or processors involved in the same processing that part of the compensation corresponding to their part of responsibility for the damage, in accordance with the conditions set out in paragraph 2.¶

---

* GDPR Article 82(1).
† GDPR Article 82(2).
‡ GDPR Article 82(3).
§ GDPR Article 82(4).
¶ GDPR Article 82(5).

Court proceedings for exercising the right to receive compensation must be brought before the courts competent under the law of the member state referred to in Article 79(2).*

Right to Lodge Complaint with Data Protection Supervisory Authority

Without prejudice to any other administrative or judicial remedy, every data subject must have the right to lodge a complaint with a data protection supervisory authority, in particular in the member state of their habitual residence, place of work, or place of the alleged infringement if the data subject considers that the processing of personal data relating to them infringes the GDPR.†

The data protection supervisory authority with which the complaint has been lodged must inform the complainant on the progress and the outcome of the complaint, including the possibility of a judicial remedy pursuant to Article 78.‡

Right to an Effective Judicial Remedy against a Data Protection Supervisory Authority

Article 78 of the new GDPR refers to the right to an effective judicial remedy against a data protection supervisory authority. Article 78(1) provides that without prejudice to any other administrative or non-judicial remedy, each natural or legal person must have the right to an effective judicial remedy against a legally binding decision of a data protection supervisory authority concerning them.

Without prejudice to any other administrative or non-judicial remedy, each individual data subject must have the right to a an effective judicial remedy where the data protection supervisory authority that is competent pursuant to Articles 55 and 56 does not handle a complaint or does not inform the individual data subject within 3 months on the progress or outcome of the complaint lodged pursuant to Article 77.§

---

* GDPR Article 82(6).
† GDPR Article 77(1).
‡ GDPR Article 77(2).
§ GDPR Article 78(2).

Proceedings against a data protection supervisory authority must be brought before the courts of the member state where the data protection supervisory authority is established.*

Where proceedings are brought against a decision of a data protection supervisory authority that was preceded by an opinion or a decision of the European Data Protection Board in the consistency mechanism, the data protection supervisory authority must forward that opinion or decision to the court.†

Representation of Data Subjects

The data subject must have the right to mandate a not-for-profit body, organization, or association that has been properly constituted in accordance with the law of a member state, has statutory objectives that are in the public interest, and is active in the field of the protection of data subjects' rights with regard to the protection of their personal data to lodge the complaint on their behalf, to exercise the rights referred to in Articles 77, 78, and 79 on their behalf, and to exercise the right to receive compensation referred to in Article 82 on their behalf where provided for by member state law.‡

Member states may provide that any such body, organization, or association, independently of a data subject's mandate, has the right to lodge, in that member state, a complaint with the data protection supervisory authority that is competent pursuant to Article 77 and to exercise the rights referred to in Articles 78 and 79 if it considers that the rights of a data subject under the GDPR have been infringed as a result of the processing.§

Article 80 of the GDPR refers to representation of individual data subjects. The data subject must have the right to mandate a not-for-profit body, organization, or association that has been properly constituted in accordance with the law of a member state, has statutory objectives that are in the public interest, and is active in the field of the protection of data subjects' rights with regard to the protection of

---

* GDPR Article 78(3).
† GDPR Article 78(4).
‡ GDPR Article 80(1).
§ GDPR Article 80(2).

their personal data to lodge the complaint on their behalf, to exercise the rights referred to in Articles 77, 78, and 79 on their behalf, and to exercise the right to receive compensation referred to in Article 82 on their behalf where provided for by member state law. *

Member states may provide that any such body, organization, or association, independently of a data subject's mandate, has the right to lodge, in that member state, a complaint with the data protection supervisory authority that is competent pursuant to Article 77 and to exercise the rights referred to in Articles 78 and 79 if it considers that the rights of a data subject under the GDPR have been infringed as a result of the processing.†

Organizational Privacy Groups

Background Guidance on Representative Data Subject Organizations

Background Recital 142 of the GDPR states that where an individual data subject considers that their rights under the GDPR are infringed, he or she should have the right to mandate a not-for-profit body, organization, or association that is constituted in accordance with the law of a member state, has statutory objectives that are in the public interest, and is active in the field of the protection of personal data to lodge a complaint on their behalf with a data protection supervisory authority, exercise the right to a judicial remedy on behalf of individual data subjects, or, if provided for in member state law, exercise the right to receive compensation on behalf of individual data subjects. A member state may provide for such a body, organization, or association to have the right to lodge a complaint in that member state, independently of an individual data subject's mandate, and the right to an effective judicial remedy where it has reasons to consider that the rights of an individual data subject have been infringed as a result of the processing of personal data that infringes the GDPR. That body, organization, or association may not be allowed to claim compensation on a data subject's behalf independently of the data subject's mandate. There are an increasing number of data protection and privacy groups, both nationally and supra-nationally. Indeed, the EU Court of Justice

---

* GDPR Article 80(1).
† GDPR Article 80(2).

case striking down the Data Retention Directive was taken by one such group.*

For proceedings against a controller or processor, the plaintiff should have the choice to bring the action before the courts of the member states where the controller or processor has an establishment or where the individual data subject resides, unless the controller is a public authority of a member state acting in the exercise of its public powers.†

Jurisdiction Issues

The issues of jurisdiction are often complex. However, the GDPR provides some background and guidance.

Controller or Processor in EU

Background Recital 22 of the new GDPR states that any processing of personal data in the context of the activities of an establishment of a controller or a processor in the EU should be carried out in accordance with the GDPR, regardless of whether or not the processing itself takes place within the EU. Establishment implies the effective and real exercise of activity through stable arrangements. The legal form of such arrangements, whether through a branch or a subsidiary with a legal personality, is not the determining factor in this respect.

Controller or Processor Not in EU

Background Recital 23 of the new GDPR states that in order to ensure that individuals are not deprived of the protection to which they are entitled under the GDPR, the processing of personal data of individual data subjects who are in the EU by a controller or a processor not established in the EU should be subject to the GDPR where the processing activities are related to the offering of goods or services

---

* Cases C-293/12 and C-594/12, *Digital Rights Ireland* and *Seitlinger and Others*, Court of Justice, April 8, 2014. Directive 2006/24/EC and amending Directive 2002/58/EC.
† GDPR Recital 145.

to such individual data subjects, irrespective of whether they are connected to a payment or not. To determine whether such a controller or processor is offering goods or services to individual data subjects who are in the EU, it should be ascertained whether it is apparent that the controller envisages offering services to individual data subjects in one or more member states in the EU. While the mere accessibility of the controller's, processor's, or an intermediary's website in the EU, of an email address, or of other contact details, or the use of a language generally used in the third country where the controller is established, is insufficient to ascertain such intention, factors such as the use of a language or a currency generally used in one or more member states with the possibility of ordering goods and services in that other language, or the mentioning of customers or users who are in the EU, may make it apparent that the controller envisages offering goods or services to such individual data subjects in the EU.

Monitoring

The processing of personal data of individual data subjects who are in the EU by a controller or processor not established in the EU should also be subject to the GDPR when it is related to the monitoring of the behavior of such individual data subjects insofar as their behavior takes place within the EU. To determine whether a processing activity can be considered to monitor the behavior of individual data subjects, it should be ascertained whether natural persons are tracked on the Internet, including the potential subsequent use of personal data processing techniques that consist of profiling a natural person, particularly to take decisions concerning them or for analyzing or predicting their personal preferences, behaviors, and attitudes.[*]

Jurisdiction, Main Establishment, Groups

The main establishment of a controller in the EU should be the place of its central administration in the EU, unless the decisions on the purposes and means of the processing of personal data are taken in another establishment of the controller in the EU, in which case that

---

[*] GDPR Recital 24.

other establishment should be considered to be the main establishment. The main establishment of a controller in the EU should be determined according to objective criteria and should imply the effective and real exercise of management activities determining the main decisions as to the purposes and means of processing through stable arrangements. That criterion should not depend on whether the processing of personal data is carried out at that location. The presence and use of technical means and technologies for processing personal data or processing activities do not, in themselves, constitute a main establishment and are therefore not determining criteria for a main establishment.*

The main establishment of the processor should be the place of its central administration in the EU or, if it has no central administration in the EU, the place where the main processing activities take place in the EU. In cases involving both the controller and the processor, the competent lead data protection supervisory authority should remain the data protection supervisory authority of the member state where the controller has its main establishment, but the data protection supervisory authority of the processor should be considered to be a data protection supervisory authority concerned, and that data protection supervisory authority should participate in the cooperation procedure provided for by the GDPR. In any case, the data protection supervisory authorities of the member state or member states where the processor has one or more establishments should not be considered to be data protection supervisory authorities concerned where the draft decision concerns only the controller. Where the processing is carried out by a group of undertakings, the main establishment of the controlling undertaking should be considered to be the main establishment of the group of undertakings, except where the purposes and means of processing are determined by another undertaking.†

A group of undertakings should cover a controlling undertaking and its controlled undertakings, whereby the controlling undertaking should be the undertaking that can exert a dominant influence over the other undertakings by virtue, for example, of ownership, financial participation, or the rules that govern it or the power to have

---

* GDPR Recital 36.
† GDPR Recital 36.

personal data protection rules implemented. An undertaking that controls the processing of personal data in undertakings affiliated to it should be regarded, together with those undertakings, as a group of undertakings.*

Investigation and Evidence

The issue of electronic evidence is also critical, whether for the organization or the individual data subject wishing to use such evidence. It is recommended that organizations consider these issues proactively in advance rather than hoping to be able to deal with them adequately in a reactive manner.

Conclusion

Organizations must not only contemplate the various issues and requirements from a compliance perspective, but must also contemplate what happens when things may go wrong or a contentious issue arises. In some of these instances, there is potential for court actions to arise. These potential scenarios must also be prepared for.

KEY CONCEPTS

Organizations need to carefully consider compliance as well as contentious scenarios. There is an increase in the potential for data protection issues to end up in courts.

KEYWORDS

- Contentious data protection issues in courts
- Data protection supervisory authorities
- Individuals
- Organizational privacy groups

---

* GDPR Recital 37.

39

SOME SPECIFIC ISSUES IN GDPR

Introduction

The General Data Protection Regulation (GDPR) sets out various generally applicable rules that are applicable across all personal data (whether general personal data or sensitive personal data). In addition, the GDPR refers to a number of specific issues and how data protection will apply in those instances.

Specific Data Processing Situations

Chapter IX of the GDPR refers to provisions regarding specific data processing situations. The specified issues are

- Processing in the context of employment.[*]
- Processing of the national identification number.[†]
- Processing and public access to official documents.[‡]
- Processing and freedom of expression and information.[§]
- Safeguards and derogations relating to processing for archiving purposes in the public interest, scientific or historical research purposes, or statistical purposes.[¶]
- Obligations of secrecy.[**]
- Existing data protection rules of churches and religious associations.[††]

---

[*] GDPR Article 88.
[†] GDPR Article 87.
[‡] GDPR Article 86.
[§] GDPR Article 85(1).
[¶] GDPR Article 89.
[**] GDPR Article 90.
[††] GDPR Article 91.

Some of these issues that are potentially more pertinent to organizations are referred to in the following sections.

Employment Data

Employees, employment issues, and employee rights are all important to organizations, both large and small, and across all sectors of activity. Employment-related issues related to employee personal data are continuing to grow. The new GDPR provides that employee protections can become much more specific.* The GDPR refers to provisions relating to specific data processing situations. Article 88 refers to processing in the employment context. Article 88(1) provides that member states may, by law or by collective agreements, provide more specific rules to ensure the protection of the rights in respect of the processing of employees' personal data in the employment context, in particular for the purposes of recruitment: the performance of the contract of employment, including the discharge of obligations laid down by law or by collective agreements; the management, planning, and organization of work; equality and diversity in the workplace; health and safety at work; the protection of employer's or customers' property; and for the purposes of the exercise and enjoyment, on an individual or collective basis, of rights and benefits related to employment; and for the purpose of the termination of the employment relationship.

Article 82(2) states that those rules must include suitable and specific measures to safeguard the individual data subject's human dignity, legitimate interests, and fundamental rights, with particular regard to the transparency of processing, the transfer of personal data within a group of undertakings, or a group of enterprises engaged in a joint economic activity and monitoring systems at the workplace.

---

* GDPR Article 88. Prior to the new GDPR, the UK data protection supervisory authority (Information Commissioner's Office [ICO]) had issued recommendations in relation to personal data employment issues, namely, Employment practices code; Employment practices code—a quick guide; Employment practices code—supplementary guidance; Disclosure of employee information under TUPE; Getting it right: a brief guide to data protection for small businesses; and Monitoring under Section 75 of the Northern Ireland Act 1998. These now need to be read in light of the GDPR changes.

Processing National Identification Numbers

Member states may further determine the specific conditions for the processing of a national identification number or any other identifier of general application. In that case, the national identification number or any other identifier of general application must be used only under appropriate safeguards for the rights of the data subject pursuant to the GDPR.*

Public Authorities

There is particular reference to public authorities to whom data are disclosed, requests, limits, and compliance.†

Processing and Freedom of Expression and Information

Chapter IX of the GDPR also makes provisions relating to specific data processing situations. Article 85 refers to the processing of personal data and freedom of expression and information.

Member states must by law reconcile the right to the protection of personal data pursuant to the GDPR with the right to freedom of expression and information, including processing for journalistic purposes and the purposes of academic, artistic, or literary expression.‡

For processing carried out for journalistic purposes or the purpose of academic artistic or literary expression, member states must provide for exemptions or derogations from GDPR Chapter II (principles), Chapter III (rights of the data subject), Chapter IV (controller and processor), Chapter V (transfer of personal data to third countries or international organizations), Chapter VI (independent data protection supervisory authorities), Chapter VII (cooperation and consistency), and Chapter IX (specific data processing situations) if they are

---

* GDPR Article 87. This is an issue that is the subject of recent official Irish Oireachtas Committee consideration in relation to a new Electoral Commission and the use of identification numbers for electoral related purposes.
† GDPR Recital 31.
‡ GDPR Article 85(1).

necessary to reconcile the right to the protection of personal data with the freedom of expression and information.*

Safeguards and Derogations: Public Interest Archiving/ Scientific or Historical Research/Statistical Processing

There are also provisions in relation to safeguards and derogations relating to processing for archiving purposes in the public interest, scientific or historical research purposes, or statistical purposes.

Background Guidance

The background guidance indicates that the processing of personal data for archiving purposes in the public interest, scientific or historical research purposes, or statistical purposes should be subject to appropriate safeguards for the rights of the individual data subject pursuant to the GDPR. Those safeguards should ensure that technical and organizational measures are in place to ensure, in particular, the principle of data minimization. The further processing of personal data for archiving purposes in the public interest, scientific or historical research purposes, or statistical purposes is to be carried out when the controller has assessed the feasibility of fulfilling those purposes by processing data that do not permit or no longer permit the identification of individual data subjects, provided that appropriate safeguards exist (such as, e.g., pseudonymization of the data). Member states should provide for appropriate safeguards for the processing of personal data for archiving purposes in the public interest, scientific or historical research purposes, or statistical purposes. Member states should be authorized to provide, under specific conditions and subject to appropriate safeguards for individual data subjects, specifications and derogations with regard to the information requirements and rights to rectification, to erasure, to be forgotten, to restriction of processing, to data portability, and to object when processing personal data for archiving purposes in the public interest,

---

* GDPR Article 85(2). Each member state must notify to the EU Commission the provisions of its law that it has adopted and, without delay, any subsequent amendment law or amendment affecting them. GDPR Article 85(3).

scientific or historical research purposes, or statistical purposes. The conditions and safeguards in question may entail specific procedures for individual data subjects to exercise those rights if this is appropriate in the light of the purposes sought by the specific processing along with technical and organizational measures aimed at minimizing the processing of personal data in pursuance of the proportionality and necessity principles. The processing of personal data for scientific purposes should also comply with other relevant legislation, such as on clinical trials.[*]

Where personal data are processed for archiving purposes, the GDPR should also apply to that processing, bearing in mind that the GDPR should not apply to deceased persons. Public authorities or public or private bodies that hold records of public interest should be services that, pursuant to EU or member state law, have a legal obligation to acquire, preserve, appraise, arrange, describe, communicate, promote, disseminate, and provide access to records of enduring value for general public interest. Member states should also be authorized to provide for the further processing of personal data for archiving purposes; for example, with a view to providing specific information related to the political behavior under former totalitarian state regimes, genocide, crimes against humanity, in particular the Holocaust, or war crimes.[†]

Where personal data are processed for scientific research purposes, the GDPR should also apply to that processing. For the purposes of the GDPR, the processing of personal data for scientific research purposes should be interpreted in a broad manner, including, for example

- Technological development and demonstration.
- Fundamental research.
- Applied research.
- Privately funded research.[‡]

In addition, it should take into account the EU's objective under Article 179(1) of the Treaty on the Functioning of the European Union of achieving a European Research Area. Scientific research

---

[*] GDPR Recital 156.
[†] GDPR Recital 158.
[‡] GDPR Recital 159.

purposes should also include studies conducted in the public interest in the area of public health. To meet the specificities of processing personal data for scientific research purposes, specific conditions should apply in particular as regards the publication or otherwise disclosure of personal data in the context of scientific research purposes. If the result of scientific research, in particular in the health context, gives reason for further measures in the interest of the individual data subject, the general rules of the GDPR should apply in view of those measures.*

Where personal data are processed for historical research purposes, the GDPR should also apply to that processing. This should also include historical research and research for genealogical purposes, bearing in mind that the GDPR should not apply to deceased persons.† For the purpose of consenting to the participation in scientific research activities in clinical trials, the relevant provisions of Regulation 536/2014 should apply.‡ Where personal data are processed for statistical purposes, the GDPR should apply to that processing. EU or member state law should, within the limits of the GDPR, determine statistical content, control of access, specifications for the processing of personal data for statistical purposes, and appropriate measures to safeguard the rights of the individual data subject and for ensuring statistical confidentiality. "Statistical purposes" means any operation of collection and the processing of personal data necessary for statistical surveys or for the production of statistical results. Those statistical results may further be used for different purposes, including a scientific research purpose. The statistical purpose implies that the result of processing for statistical purposes is not personal data, but aggregate data, and that this result or the personal data are not used in support of measures or decisions regarding any particular natural person.§

Delegated acts should be adopted in respect of criteria and requirements for certification mechanisms, information to be presented by

---

* GDPR Recital 159.
† GDPR Recital 160.
‡ GDPR Recital 161.
§ GDPR Recital 162.

standardized icons, and procedures for providing such icons.* The examination procedure should be used for

- The adoption of implementing acts on standard contractual clauses between controllers and processors and between processors.
- Codes of conduct.
- Technical standards and mechanisms for certification.
- The adequate level of protection afforded by a third country, a territory or a specified sector within that third country, or an international organization.
- Standard protection clauses.
- Formats and procedures for the exchange of information by electronic means between controllers, processors, and data protection supervisory authorities for binding corporate rules.
- Mutual assistance.
- Arrangements for the exchange of information by electronic means between data protection supervisory authorities, and between data protection supervisory authorities and the European Data Protection Board.†

The EU Commission should adopt immediately applicable implementing acts where available evidence reveals that a third country, a territory or a specified sector within that third country, or an international organization does not ensure an adequate level of protection, and imperative grounds of urgency so require.‡

Legal Rule

Processing for archiving purposes in the public interest, scientific or historical research purposes, or statistical purposes must be subject to appropriate safeguards, in accordance with the GDPR, for the rights of the data subject. Those safeguards must ensure that technical and organizational measures are in place in particular to ensure respect for the principle of data minimization. Those measures may include

---

* GDPR Recital 166.
† GDPR Recital 168.
‡ GDPR Recital 169.

pseudonymization, provided that those purposes can be fulfilled in that manner. Where those purposes can be fulfilled by further processing that does not permit or no longer permits the identification of data subjects, those purposes must be fulfilled in that manner.*

Where personal data are processed for scientific or historical research purposes or statistical purposes, EU or member state law may provide for derogations from the rights referred to in Articles 15 (access right), 16 (rectification right), 18 (restriction of processing right), and 21 (right to object), subject to the conditions and safeguards referred to in previous sections, insofar as such rights are likely to render impossible or seriously impair the achievement of the specific purposes, and such derogations are necessary for the fulfillment of those purposes.†

Where personal data are processed for archiving purposes in the public interest, EU or member state law may provide for derogations from the rights referred to in Articles 15 (access right), 16 (rectification right), 18 (restriction of processing right), 19 (notification obligation regarding rectification or erasure of personal data or restriction of processing), 20 (portability right), and 21 (right to object), subject to the conditions and safeguards referred to in paragraph 1 of this Article insofar as such rights are likely to render impossible or seriously impair the achievement of the specific purposes, and such derogations are necessary for the fulfillment of those purposes.‡

Where the processing referred to serves at the same time another purpose, the derogations must apply only to processing for the purposes referred to in those paragraphs.§

Obligations of Secrecy

Article 84 is headed "Obligations of Secrecy." Member states may adopt specific rules to set out the powers of the data protection supervisory authorities laid down in Article 58(1)(e) and (f) in relation to controllers or processors that are subject, under EU or member state

---

* GDPR Article 89(1).
† GDPR Article 89(2).
‡ GDPR Article 89(3).
§ GDPR Article 89(4).

law or rules established by national competent bodies, to an obligation of professional secrecy or other equivalent obligations of secrecy, where this is necessary and proportionate to reconcile the right of the protection of personal data with the obligation of secrecy. Those rules must apply only with regard to personal data that the controller or processor has received as a result of or has obtained in an activity covered by that obligation of secrecy.*

Churches and Religious Associations

Where, in a member state, churches and religious associations or communities apply, at the time of entry into force of the GDPR, comprehensive rules relating to the protection of natural persons with regard to processing, such rules may continue to apply, provided that they are brought into line with the GDPR.†

Churches and religious associations that apply comprehensive rules in accordance with paragraph 1 of this Article must be subject to the supervision of an independent data protection supervisory authority, which may be specific, provided that it fulfills the conditions laid down in Chapter VI of the GDPR.‡

eCommerce Directive

The GDPR is without prejudice to the eCommerce Directive, particularly the limited intermediary service providers liability rules (Articles 12 to 15 therein).§

General Registration/Notification Requirement Removed

The DPD95 provided for a general obligation on organizations to notify or register the processing of personal data to the data protection

---

* GDPR Article 90(1). Each member state must notify to the EU Commission the rules adopted pursuant to paragraph 1 by May 25, 2018 and, without delay, any subsequent amendment affecting them. GDPR Article 90(2).
† GDPR Article 91(1).
‡ GDPR Article 91(2).
§ GDPR Recital 21. Directive 2000/31/EC. Directive 2000/31/EC.

supervisory authorities. The GDPR eliminated the general need for such notification or registration.

While that obligation produces administrative and financial burdens, it did not in all cases contribute to improving the protection of personal data. Such indiscriminate general notification obligations should therefore be abolished, and replaced by effective procedures and mechanisms that focus instead on those types of processing operations that are likely to result in a high risk to the rights of natural persons by virtue of their nature, scope, context, and purposes. Such types of processing operations may be those that, in particular, involve using new technologies, or are of a new kind and where no data protection impact assessment has been carried out before by the controller, or where they become necessary in the light of the time that has elapsed since the initial processing.*

Conclusion

The GDPR, following on from the DPD95, sets standards and parameters in relation to the collection, use, and processing as regards general personal data and sensitive personal data. Chapter IX of the GDPR also sets out rules in relation to a number of specific data processing situations.

KEY CONCEPTS

Organizations must comply with the prior information requirements, the principles, the legitimate processing conditions, and security, and also be aware of and comply with additional provisions, such as employment personal data processing, and other additional rules when the specific situations listed apply.

---

* GDPR Recital 89.

KEYWORDS

- Employment processing.
- National identification numbers.
- Public access to official documents.
- Processing and freedom of expression and information.
- Archiving in public interest, for scientific or historical research, or for statistical purposes.
- Secrecy obligations.
- Churches and religious associations.

40

DATA PROTECTION SUPERVISORY AUTHORITIES

Introduction

Organizations need to be familiar with the official data protection supervisory authorities in the territories that they deal with. The EU member state data protection supervisory authorities enforce, and advise on, the data protection rules. In addition, the data protection officer of the organization should liaise with and provide their contact details to the data protection supervisory authority. Individual data subjects can also complain.

Data Protection Supervisory Authorities

What happens if an organization does not comply with the data protection regime when dealing with the personal data of customers, and so on (referred to collectively as "customers")? A series of offenses are set out in the data protection rules. These are designed to ensure compliance with the data protection regime, from registration to fair use of personal data. Organizations must fully comply with their obligations. Questions arise in relation to their continued use of personal data if they have not been collected fairly. Investigations, prosecutions, and financial penalties can arise.

The GDPR sets out significant amendments to the prosecution and fines regime for non-compliance. As indicated previously, there can be consequences in terms of due diligence, value, and the ability to maintain a customer database.

When things go wrong, there can be legal and publicity consequences for the organization. The impact of a data protection breach can mean an immediate cross-team effort to deal with the data protection breach.

In dealing with an incident, and in planning for compliance with customers' personal data, organizations should be aware of the various data protection supervisory authority enforcement powers. These emphasize the importance of consequences for non-compliance. Enforcement proceedings can be issued by the data protection supervisory authority. Significant fines and penalties can result. Also, potentially, individual customers may decide to sue for damage, loss, and breach of their personal data rights.

Tasks

The General Data Protection Regulation (GDPR) provides that each data protection supervisory authority has the following tasks

- Monitor and enforce the application of the GDPR.
- Promote public awareness and understanding of the risks, rules, safeguards, and rights in relation to processing. Activities addressed specifically to children must receive specific attention.
- Advise, in accordance with member state law, the national parliament, the government, and other institutions and bodies on legislative and administrative measures relating to the protection of natural persons' rights with regard to processing.
- Promote the awareness of controllers and processors of their obligations under the GDPR.
- On request, provide information to any individual data subject concerning the exercise of their rights under the GDPR and, if appropriate, cooperate with the data protection supervisory authorities in other member states to that end.
- Handle complaints lodged by an individual data subject or by a body, organization, or association in accordance with Article 80, investigate, to the extent appropriate, the subject matter of the complaint, and inform the complainant of the progress and the outcome of the investigation within a reasonable period, in particular if further investigation or coordination with another data protection supervisory authority is necessary. [f]

- Cooperate with, including sharing information with and providing mutual assistance to, other data protection supervisory authorities with a view to ensuring the consistency of application and enforcement of the GDPR.
- Conduct investigations on the application of the GDPR, including on the basis of information received from another data protection supervisory authority or other public authority.
- Monitor relevant developments insofar as they have an impact on the protection of personal data, in particular the development of information and communication technologies and commercial practices.
- Adopt standard contractual clauses referred to in Article 28(8) and Article 46(2)(d).
- Establish and maintain a list in relation to the requirement for data protection impact assessment pursuant to Article 35(4).
- Give advice on the processing operations referred to in Article 36(2).
- Encourage the drawing up of codes of conduct, provide an opinion, and approve such codes of conduct that provide sufficient safeguards.
- Encourage the establishment of data protection certification mechanisms and of data protection seals and marks, and approve the criteria of certification.
- Where applicable, carry out a periodic review of certifications.
- Draft and publish the criteria for accreditation of a body for monitoring codes of conduct and of a certification body.
- Conduct the accreditation of a body for monitoring codes of conduct and of a certification body.
- Authorize contractual clauses and provisions referred to in Article 46(3).
- Approve binding corporate rules.
- Contribute to the activities of the European Data Protection Board (EDPB).
- Keep internal records of infringements of the GDPR and of measures taken in accordance with Article 58(2).

- Fulfill any other tasks related to the protection of personal data.*

Each data protection supervisory authority must facilitate the submission of complaints referred to in Point (f) by measures such as a complaint submission form that can also be completed electronically, without excluding other means of communication.†

The performance of the tasks of each data protection supervisory authority must be free of charge for the individual data subject and, where applicable, for the data protection officer.‡

Investigative Powers

Pursuant to the new GDPR, each data protection supervisory authority has the following investigative powers

- To order the controller and the processor and, where applicable, the controller's or the processor's representative to provide any information it requires for the performance of its tasks.
- To carry out investigations in the form of data protection audits.
- To carry out a review on certifications issued pursuant to Article 42(7).
- To notify the controller or the processor of an alleged infringement of the GDPR.
- To obtain, from the controller and the processor, access to all personal data and to all information necessary for the performance of its tasks.

---

* GDPR Article 57(1).

† GDPR Article 57(2).

‡ GDPR Article 57(3). Where requests are manifestly unfounded or excessive, in particular because of their repetitive character, the data protection supervisory authority may charge a reasonable fee based on administrative costs, or refuse to act on the request. The data protection supervisory authority must bear the burden of demonstrating the manifestly unfounded or excessive character of the request. GDPR Article 57(4).

- To obtain access to any premises of the controller and the processor, including to any data processing equipment and means, in accordance with EU or member state procedural law.*

Corrective Powers

Each data protection supervisory authority has the following corrective powers

- To issue warnings to a controller or a processor that intended processing operations are likely to infringe provisions of the GDPR.
- To issue reprimands to a controller or a processor where processing operations have infringed provisions of the GDPR.
- To order the controller or the processor to comply with the individual data subject's requests to exercise their rights pursuant to the GDPR.
- To order the controller or the processor to bring processing operations into compliance with the provisions of the GDPR, where appropriate, in a specified manner and within a specified period.
- To order the controller to communicate a personal data breach to the individual data subject.
- To impose a temporary or definitive limitation, including a ban on processing.
- To order the rectification or erasure of personal data or restriction of processing pursuant to Articles 16 through 18 and the notification of such actions to recipients to whom the personal data have been disclosed pursuant to Article 17(2) and Article 19.
- To withdraw a certification or to order the certification body to withdraw a certification issued pursuant to Articles 42 and 43 or to order the certification body not to issue certification if the requirements for the certification are not or are no longer met.
- To impose an administrative fine pursuant to Article 83 in addition to, or instead of, the measures referred to in this

* GDPR Article 58(1).

paragraph, depending on the circumstances of each individual case.
- To order the suspension of data flows to a recipient in a third country or to an international organization.*

Authorization and Advisory Powers

Each data protection supervisory authority has the following authorization and advisory powers

- To advise the controller in accordance with the prior consultation procedure referred to in Article 36.
- To issue, on its own initiative or on request, opinions to the national parliament, to the member state government, or, in accordance with member state law, to other institutions and bodies as well as to the public on any issue related to the protection of personal data.
- To authorize the processing referred to in Article 36(5) if the law of the member state requires such prior authorization.
- To issue an opinion and approve draft codes of conduct pursuant to Article 40(5).
- To accredit certification bodies pursuant to Article 43.
- To issue certifications and approve criteria of certification in accordance with Article 42(5).
- To adopt the standard data protection clauses referred to in Article 28(8) and in Article 46(2)(d).
- To authorize the contractual clauses referred to in Article 46(3)(a).
- To authorize the administrative arrangements referred to in Article 46(3)(b).
- To approve binding corporate rules pursuant to Article 47.†

The exercise of the powers conferred on the data protection supervisory authority pursuant to this Article must be subject to appropriate

---

* GDPR Article 58(2).
† GDPR Article 58(3).

safeguards, including effective judicial remedy and due process, set out in EU and member state law in accordance with the EU Charter.*

Each member state must provide by law that its data protection supervisory authority must have the power to bring infringements of the GDPR to the attention of the judicial authorities and where appropriate, to commence or engage otherwise in legal proceedings to enforce the provisions of the GDPR.†

Each member state may provide by law that its data protection supervisory authority must have additional powers to those referred to in this section. The exercise of those powers must not impair the effective operation of Chapter VII of the GDPR.‡

Independence

Chapter VI of the GDPR refers to the independent data protection supervisory authorities. The reference to and emphasis on their independent status are noteworthy. The independence of data protection supervisory authorities (from political interference or influence) has been questioned in a number of instances. The GDPR assists in emphasizing the need for independence.

Data protection supervisory authorities§ and the complete independence of data protection supervisory authorities are referred to in Recitals 121 and 153 and Articles 4, 51, and 52. Chapter VI, Section 1 of the GDPR refers to their "independent status." Each member state must provide for one or more independent public authorities to be responsible for monitoring the application of the GDPR so as to protect the fundamental rights of natural persons in relation to processing and to facilitate the free flow of personal data within the EU (data protection "supervisory authority").¶ Each data protection supervisory authority must contribute to the consistent application of the GDPR throughout the EU. For that purpose, the data protection supervisory

---

* Charter of Fundamental Rights of the European Union.
† GDPPR Article 58(5).
‡ GDPR Article 58(6).
§ Such as the Data Protection Commissioner (DPC) in Ireland and the Information Commissioner's Office (ICO) in the UK. The data protection supervisory authorities were previously called *data protection authorities* (DPAs).
¶ GDPR Article 51(1).

authorities must cooperate with each other and the EU Commission in accordance with Chapter VII.*

Where more than one data protection supervisory authority is established in a member state, that member state must designate the data protection supervisory authority that is to represent those authorities in the EDPB and must set out the mechanism to ensure compliance by the other authorities with the rules relating to the consistency mechanism referred to in Article 63.†

Each data protection supervisory authority must act with complete independence in performing its tasks and exercising its powers in accordance with the GDPR.‡ The member or members of each data protection supervisory authority must, in the performance of their tasks and exercise of their powers in accordance with the GDPR, remain free from external influence, whether direct or indirect, and must neither seek nor take instructions from anybody.§ Member or members of each data protection supervisory authority must refrain from any action incompatible with their duties and must not, during their term of office, engage in any incompatible occupation, whether gainful or not.¶

Each member state must ensure that each data protection supervisory authority is provided with the human, technical, and financial resources, premises, and infrastructure necessary for the effective performance of its tasks and the exercise of its powers, including those to be carried out in the context of mutual assistance, cooperation, and participation in the EDPB.** Each member state must ensure that each data protection supervisory authority chooses and has its own staff, which must be subject to the exclusive direction of the member or members of the data protection supervisory authority concerned.†† Each member state must ensure that each data protection supervisory

---

* GDPR Article 51(2).
† GDPR Article 51(3). Each member state must notify to the EU Commission the provisions of its law that it adopts by May 25, 2018 and, without delay, any subsequent amendment affecting them. GDPR Article 51(4).
‡ GDPR Article 52(1).
§ GDPR Article 52(2).
¶ GDPR Article 52(3).
**GDPR Article 52(4).
††GDPR Article 52(5).

authority is subject to financial control that does not affect its independence and that it has separate, public annual budgets, which may be part of the overall state or national budget.*

There have been a number of cases taken in relation to ensuring that data protection supervisory authorities are sufficiently independent in their roles as required under EU law.†

Cooperation with National Data Protection Supervisory Authorities

Article 31 of the GDPR makes provision in relation to cooperation with the data protection supervisory authority. It provides that the controller and the processor and, where applicable, their representatives must cooperate, on request, with the data protection supervisory authority in the performance of its tasks.

Enforcement Powers of Data Protection Supervisory Authority

The data protection supervisory authorities have a number of powers of enforcement available to them. These include the following.

Investigations by National Data Protection Supervisory Authorities

National data protection supervisory authorities will investigate any complaints the data protection supervisory authority receives from individuals who feel that personal information about them is not being treated in accordance with the law, unless the data protection supervisory authority is of the opinion that such complaints are "frivolous or vexatious." The data protection supervisory authority notifies

---

* GDPR Article 52(6).
† For example, *Commission v Germany*, Case C-518/07 (March 9, 2010); *Commission v Austria*, Case C-614/10 (October 16, 2012). There is also a recent case filed in Ireland by Digital Rights Ireland. Note, for example, Schütz, "Comparing Formal Independence of Data Protection Authorities in Selected EU Member States," Fourth Biennial ECPR Standing Group for Regulatory Governance Conference (2012); Balthasar, "'Complete Independence' of National Data Protection Supervisory Authorities—Second Try: Comments on the Judgement of the CJEU of 16 October 2012, Case C-614/10 (*European Commission v Austria*), with Due Regard to its Previous Judgement of 9 March 2010, C-518/07 (*European Commission v Germany*)," *Utrecht Law Review* (2013) (9:3) 26.

the complainant in writing of their decision regarding the complaint. The data protection supervisory authority's decision can be appealed to court.

The data protection supervisory authority may also launch investigations on its own initiative where the data protection supervisory authority is of the opinion that there might be a breach of the data protection rules, or it considers it appropriate to ensure compliance with the data protection laws.

Power to Obtain Information

The data protection supervisory authority may require any person to provide it with whatever information the data protection supervisory authority needs to carry out its functions, such as to pursue an investigation. The data protection supervisory authority exercises this power by providing a written notice, called an *information notice*, to the person.

Power to Enforce Compliance with the Data Protection Laws

The data protection supervisory authority may require a controller or processor to take whatever steps the data protection supervisory authority considers appropriate to comply with the terms of the data protection laws. Such steps could include correcting the data, blocking the data from use for certain purposes, supplementing the data with a statement that the data protection supervisory authority approves, or erasing the data altogether. The data protection supervisory authority exercises this power by providing a written notice, called an *enforcement notice*, to the controller or processor. A person who receives an enforcement notice has the right to appeal it to court. It is an offense to fail or refuse to comply with an enforcement notice without reasonable excuse.

Power to Prohibit Overseas Transfer of Personal Data

The data protection supervisory authority may prohibit the transfer of personal data from a member state to a place outside the member state. The data protection supervisory authority exercises this power by providing a written notice, called a *prohibition notice*, to the controller or processor. In considering whether to exercise this power, the data protection supervisory authority must have regard to the need to facilitate international transfers of information.

A prohibition notice may be absolute or may prohibit the transfer of personal data until the person concerned takes certain steps to protect the interests of the individuals affected. A person who receives an enforcement notice has the right to appeal it to the court. It is an offense to fail or refuse to comply with a prohibition specified in a prohibition notice without reasonable excuse.

Powers of Authorized Officers to Enter and Examine

The data protection supervisory authority may appoint an authorized officer to enter and examine the premises of a controller or processor to enable the data protection supervisory authority to carry out its functions, such as to pursue an investigation. The authorized officer, on production of written authorization from the data protection supervisory authority, has the power to

- Enter the premises and inspect any data equipment there.
- Require the controller, processor, or staff to assist in obtaining access to data and to provide any related information.
- Inspect and copy any information.
- Require the controller, processor, or staff to provide information about procedures on complying with the law, sources of data, purposes for which personal data are kept, persons to whom data are disclosed, and data equipment on the premises.

It is an offense to obstruct or impede an authorized officer; to fail to comply with any of the requirements set out in the preceding list; or knowingly to give false or misleading information to an authorized officer.

Prosecution of Offenses

The data protection supervisory authority may bring summary proceedings for an offense under the data protection rules. The data protection supervisory authority also has the power to prosecute offenses in relation to unsolicited marketing.

Formal undertaking agreements can also arise, whereby the organization agrees to do or not do certain things. The US Federal Trade Commission has also issued many consent agreements in relation to breach issues.

Notifying Data Breach to Data Protection Supervisory Authority

As soon as the controller becomes aware that a personal data breach has occurred, the controller should notify the personal data breach to the data protection supervisory authority without undue delay and, where feasible, not later than 72 hours after having become aware of it, unless the controller is able to demonstrate, in accordance with the accountability principle, that the personal data breach is unlikely to result in a risk to the rights of natural persons. Where such notification cannot be achieved within 72 hours, the reasons for the delay should accompany the notification, and information may be provided in phases without undue further delay.* Also see Chapter 29 on data breach issues.

European Data Protection Board

The new EDPB has been established. This effectively replaces the Article 29 Data Protection Working Party (WP29). References to the previous WP29 must be construed as references to the EDPB established by the GDPR.

Background Guidance

To promote the consistent application of the GDPR, the EDPB should be set up as an independent body of the EU. To fulfill its objectives, the EDPB should have legal personality. The EDPB should be represented by its chair. It should replace the Working Party on the Protection of Individuals with Regard to the Processing of Personal Data established by 1995 data protection directive (DPD95). It should

---

* GDPR Recital 85.

consist of the head of a data protection supervisory authority of each member state and the European Data Protection Supervisor (which deals mostly with issues regarding the EU official bodies) or their respective representatives. The EU Commission should participate in the EDPB's activities without voting rights, and the European Data Protection Supervisor should have specific voting rights. The EDPB should contribute to the consistent application of the GDPR throughout the EU, including by advising the EU Commission, in particular on the level of protection in third countries or international organizations, and promoting cooperation of the data protection supervisory authorities throughout the EU. The EDPB should act independently when performing its tasks.*

Legal Rule

Article 68(1) provides that the EDPB is established as a body of the EU and must have legal personality. The EDPB must be composed of the head of one data protection supervisory authority of each member state and of the European Data Protection Supervisor (which deals with EU bodies) or their respective representatives.† Article 69 refers to the independence of EDPB. Article 70 refers to the EDPB tasks.

Chapter VII, Section 3 of the GDPR provides for the EDPB. The EDPB is established as a body of the EU and must have legal personality.‡ The EDPB must be composed of the head of one data protection supervisory authority of each member state and of the European Data Protection Supervisor (dealing with issues regarding the EU bodies) or their respective representatives.§ The EDPB must act independently when performing its tasks or exercising its powers.¶

Conclusion

The role, activities, and powers of the data protection supervisory authorities will be critical to how data protection operates in practice.

---

* GDPR Recital 139.
† GDPR Article 68(3).
‡ GDPR Article 68(1).
§ GDPR Article 68(3).
¶ GDPR Article 69(1).

Organizations will inevitably interact with the data protection supervisory authorities on a regular basis in terms of queries, advice, and notifications regarding the data protection officer, but also in terms of problem issues that might arise, such as data breaches and complaints.

KEY CONCEPTS

The data protection supervisory authorities are central to the operation of the data protection rules. The data protection supervisory authorities are important for organizations to deal with not only in terms of normal processes but also in cases of problem issues or even contentious matters. The guidance that data protection supervisory authorities issue will be of assistance to organizations. Similarly, the guidance from the EDPB will also assist organizations.

KEY WORDS

- Data protection supervisory authorities in EU member states.
- Govern, regulate, and enforce data protection regime in member states.
- Investigations.
- Enforcement and fines.
- Promote data protection and rights awareness.
- Promote compliance.
- Audit compliance.
- Investigate breach and data loss incidents.
- Tasks.
- Investigative powers.
- Corrective powers.
- Authorization and advisory powers.
- Independence.

FURTHER READING

- Balthasar, "'Complete Independence' of National Data Protection Supervisory Authorities—Second Try: Comments on the Judgement of the CJEU of 16 October 2012, Case C-614/10 (*European Commission v Austria*), with due Regard to its Previous Judgement of 9 March 2010, C-518/07 (*European Commission v Germany*)," *Utrecht Law Review* (2013) (9:3) 26.
- Greenleaf, "Independence of Data Privacy Authorities (Part 1): International Standards," *Computer Law & Security Review* (2012) (28) 3.

41

THE DATA PROTECTION OFFICER

Introduction

Now, organizations need to have a designated data protection officer to deal with the data protection compliance obligations, handling individual data subject access requests, and so on. This can be in addition to the privacy officer, whom many organizations may have already appointed. That is not to say that the responsibility of the board of the organization for data protection compliance is in any way lessened. Organizations are now required to have a data protection officer. In addition, the role and task requirements are now more explicit. The data protection officer must also have an appropriate independence in their activities and cannot be compromised or dictated to in a manner that undermines their role and duties in relation to personal data. It is now clear that the profession of the independent and expert data protection officer has arrived.

New Data Protection Officers

The General Data Protection Regulation (GDPR) refers to the new requirement for data protection officers in organizations. Chapter IV, Section 4 of the new GDPR refers to the new role and requirement of data protection officers and the obligation for organizations to appoint data protection officers. Article 37 is headed "Designation of the Data Protection Officer." Article 37(1) states that the controller and the processor must designate a data protection officer in any case where

- The processing is carried out by a public authority or body, except for courts acting in their judicial capacity.
- The core activities of the controller or the processor consist of processing operations that, by virtue of their nature, their

scope, and/or their purposes, require regular and systematic monitoring of individual data subjects on a large scale.
- The core activities of the controller or the processor consist of processing on a large scale of special categories of data* and personal data relating to criminal convictions and offenses.†

The data protection officer must in the performance of their tasks have due regard to the risk associated with processing operations, taking into account the nature, scope, context, and purposes of processing.‡

Where the controller or the processor is a public authority or body, a single data protection officer may be designated for several such authorities or bodies, taking account of their organizational structure and size.§

The controller or processor or associations and other bodies representing categories of controllers or processors may or, where required by EU or member state law must designate a data protection officer. The data protection officer may act for such associations and other bodies representing controllers or processors.¶

The data protection officer must be designated on the basis of professional qualities and, in particular, expert knowledge of data protection law and practices and the ability to fulfill the tasks referred to in Article 39.**

The data protection officer may be a staff member of the controller or processor or fulfill the tasks on the basis of a service contract.††

The controller or the processor must publish the contact details of the data protection officer and communicate them to the data protection supervisory authority.‡‡

---

* Pursuant to GDPR Article 9.
† Referred to in GDPR Article 10.
‡ GDPR Article 39(2).
§ GDPR Article 37(3).
¶ GDPR Article 37(4).
**GDPR Article 37(5).
††GDPR Article 37(6).
‡‡GDPR Article 37(7).

Position

The controller and the processor must ensure that the data protection officer is involved, properly and in a timely manner, in all issues that relate to the protection of personal data.*

The controller and processor must fully support the data protection officer in performing the tasks referred to in Article 39 by providing the resources necessary to carry out those tasks and access to personal data and processing operations, and to maintain their expert knowledge.†

The controller and processor must ensure that the data protection officer does not receive any instructions regarding the exercise of those tasks. They must not be dismissed or penalized by the controller or the processor for performing their tasks. The data protection officer must directly report to the highest management level of the controller or the processor.‡

Data subjects may contact the data protection officer with regard to all issues related to processing of their personal data and to the exercise of their rights under the GDPR.§

The data protection officer must be bound by secrecy or confidentiality concerning the performance of their tasks, in accordance with EU or member state law.¶

The data protection officer may fulfill other tasks and duties. The controller or processor must ensure that any such tasks and duties do not result in a conflict of interests.**

Article 39 Tasks

The data protection officer must have at least the following tasks

- To inform and advise the controller or the processor and the employees who carry out processing of their obligations pursuant to the GDPR and to other EU or member state data protection provisions.

---

* GDPR Article 38(1).
† GDPR Article 38(2).
‡ GDPR Article 38(3).
§ GDPR Article 38(4).
¶ GDPR Article 38(5).
**GDPR Article 38(6).

- To monitor compliance with the GDPR, with other EU or member state data protection provisions, and with the policies of the controller or processor in relation to the protection of personal data, including the assignment of responsibilities, awareness-raising and training of staff involved in processing operations, and the related audits.
- To provide advice where requested as regards the data protection impact assessment and monitor its performance pursuant to Article 35.
- To cooperate with the data protection supervisory authority.
- To act as the contact point for the data protection supervisory authority on issues relating to processing, including the prior consultation referred to in Article 36, and to consult, where appropriate, with regard to any other matter.*

The data protection officer must in the performance of their tasks have due regard to the risk associated with processing operations, taking into account the nature, scope, context, and purposes of processing.†

The data protection officer may fulfill other tasks and duties. The controller or processor must ensure that any such other tasks and duties do not result in a conflict of interests.‡

The data protection officer will also supervise, advise, and/or assist in relation to data protection impact assessments, monitor performance, and make recommendations. They will also monitor and deal with any requests from the data protection supervisory authority and will also be the designated contact for the data protection supervisory authority.

It is important that the data protection officer has regard to the risks that may arise specific to the organization in relation to personal data and processing issues (including security issues). Depending on the sector, there may also be code of conduct and or certification issues for the data protection officer to be concerned with. Data protection seals and certification are meant to help organizations demonstrate compliance.

---

* GDPR Article 39(1).
† GDPR Article 39(2).
‡ GDPR Article 38(6).

Group Data Protection Officer

A group of undertakings may appoint a single data protection officer provided that a data protection officer is easily accessible from each establishment.*

Where the controller or the processor is a public authority or body, a single data protection officer may be designated for several such authorities or bodies, taking account of their organizational structure and size.†

The controller or processor or associations and other bodies representing categories of controllers or processors may or, where required by EU or member state law must designate a data protection officer. The data protection officer may act for such associations and other bodies representing controllers or processors.‡

Qualifications and Expertise

The data protection officer must be designated on the basis of professional qualities and, in particular, expert knowledge of data protection law and practices and the ability to fulfill the tasks referred to in Article 39.§

The data protection officer may be a staff member of the controller or processor or fulfill the tasks on the basis of a service contract.¶

Contact Details

The controller or the processor must publish the contact details of the data protection officer and communicate them to the data protection supervisory authority.**

Individual data subjects may contact the data protection officer with regard to all issues related to the processing of their personal data and to the exercise of their rights under the GDPR.††

---

* GDPR Article 37(2).
† GDPR Article 37(3).
‡ GDPR Article 37(4).
§ GDPR Article 37(5).
¶ GDPR Article 37(6).
** GDPR Article 37(7).
†† GDPR Article 38(4).

Duty of Confidentiality

The data protection officer is bound by secrecy or confidentiality concerning the performance of their tasks, in accordance with EU or member state law.*

Reporting

The data protection officer must directly report to the highest management level of the controller or the processor.†

Independent in Role and Tasks

The controller and processor must ensure that the data protection officer does not receive any instructions regarding the exercise of those tasks. They must not be dismissed or penalized by the controller or the processor for performing their tasks.‡ There should be no conflict. There should also be no directing or dictating orders to the data protection officer, whether from middle managers or senior managers who may prefer a particular commercial decision less favorable to or ignoring data protection considerations.

Resources

The controller and processor must support and assist the data protection officer in performing the tasks referred to in Article 39 by providing the resources necessary to carry out those tasks and access to personal data and processing operations, and to maintain their expert knowledge.§ The work of the data protection officer must not be compromised or restricted indirectly by withholding resources (which would include staffing) from the data protection officer.

---

* GDPR Article 38(5).
† GDPR Article 38(3).
‡ GDPR Article 38(3).
§ GDPR Article 38(2).

Data Protection by Design and Data Protection by Default

Article 25 of the GDPR refers to data protection by design. It also refers to data protection by default. These are increasingly important requirements in data protection. The data protection officer will promote education and adherence in relation to both of these new concepts within the organization.

Article 25(1) introduces this topic by saying that taking into account the state of the art, the cost of implementation, and the nature, scope, context, and purposes of processing as well as the risks of varying likelihood and severity for rights of natural persons posed by the processing, the controller must, both at the time of the determination of the means for processing and at the time of the processing itself, implement appropriate technical and organizational measures, such as pseudonymization, which are designed to implement data protection principles, such as data minimization, in an effective manner and to integrate the necessary safeguards into the processing to meet the requirements of the GDPR and protect the rights of individual data subjects.

The controller must implement appropriate technical and organizational measures for ensuring that, by default, only personal data that are necessary for each specific purpose of the processing are processed. That obligation applies to the amount of personal data collected, the extent of their processing, the period of their storage, and their accessibility. In particular, such measures must ensure that by default, personal data are not made accessible without the individual's intervention to an indefinite number of natural persons.[*]

An approved certification mechanism pursuant to Article 42 may be used as an element to demonstrate compliance with the requirements set out in paragraphs 1 and 2 of this Article.[†] The data protection officer will be active in monitoring the existence of appropriate codes within the industry sector appropriate to the organization. This will apply similarly to any other developments in relation to standards for data protection and data protection awareness in respective industries.

---

[*] GDPR Article 25(2).
[†] GDPR Article 25(3).

Conclusion

So, organizations must designate a data protection officer, including to

- Monitor internal compliance with the GDPR regime and
  rules
  - Where the processing is undertaken in the public sector;
    or
  - Where the processing requires regular and systematic
    monitoring of individual data subjects on a large scale; or
  - Where the processing is on a large scale of special cat-
    egories of data pursuant to Article 9 and data relating to
    criminal convictions and offenses
- Ensure the governance of the organization's data management.
- Draft and update compliant data protection policies.
- Implement systems, changes, and functions in terms of being
  compliant.

The data protection officer should be qualified and have particular
expertise in data protection law and practice. They need to be able to
fulfill their tasks in compliance and conformity with the GDPR. It
appears that they may be either an employee or a contractor.

The data protection officer's details must be made available publicly, and the data protection supervisory authority should be notified.

The organization must involve the data protection officer in a timely
manner in relation to all issues relating to the protection of personal
data and individual data subject issues. Proper and adequate resources
must be supplied to the data protection officer by the organization so
that they can undertake their tasks. There is an obligation that the
data protection officer has independence in their role and functions,
and that they cannot be controlled, micromanaged, or instructed in
relation to their tasks.

The data protection officer will report to the board of the organization or highest management level as appropriate. This also emphasizes
the increasing importance attached to data protection understanding
and compliance.

The data protection officer advises the organization and employees
in relation to their data protection obligations under national law and

the GDPR. They will also monitor compliance with the data protection legal regime as well as internal policies. They will also be involved in assigning responsibilities, raising awareness, and staff education and training.

Data protection officers should be involved in highlighting ongoing changes and the new GDPR to the organization. Key issues need to be identified to appropriate management. New and ongoing change and compliance issues need appropriate resourcing. The data protection officer should assess what personal data the organization collects and processes, for what purpose, and where they are located and secured. Particular attention is needed with outsourcing issues and contracts with processors. Contracts, including service-level agreements in relation to information technology (IT) systems, the cloud, and so on may be assessed. The various IT hardware, software, and systems that employees use need to be considered.

The structure of the organization or groups needs to be considered as well as jurisdiction and location issues. The life cycle, storage, and disposal of personal data are also an important consideration for the new data protection officer.

The processes, policies, and documentation must be maintained by the organization, which places particular obligations on the data protection officer to consider the different documentation sets.

Further details and commentary on data protection officers can be found in the book *The Data Protection Officer: Profession, Rules and Role*.* Undoubtedly, the role and importance of the data protection officer will continue to grow, as will the tasks and activities of the data protection officer.

KEY CONCEPTS

To assist in data protection compliance, assist regulators, and assist individual data subjects, it is increasingly necessary for organizations to appoint data protection officers. The GDPR enhances this obligation.

---

* Lambert, *The Data Protection Officer: Profession, Rules and Role* (Routledge, Taylor & Francis, 2017).

KEY WORDS

- Data protection officer.
- Independence is key.
- Appropriate and necessary resources are key.
- Regulating compliance of data protection within organizations.
- Risk.
- Assessments.
- Advising and reporting to organization board level.
- *The Data Protection Officer: Profession, Rules and Role*.

FURTHER READING

- Edwards and Waelde (eds), *Law and the Internet* (Hart, 2009) 539.
- Gough, ed., *Data Protection for Financial Firms: A Practical Guide to Managing Privacy and Information Risk* (Risk Books, 2009).
- Kuner, *European Data Protection Law: Corporate Compliance and Regulation* (Oxford University Press, 2007).
- Matthews, *Data Protection Toolkit* (2014).
- Morgan and Boardman, *Data Protection Strategy, Implementing Data Protection Compliance* (Sweet & Maxwell, 2012).
- Room, *Data Protection and Compliance in Context* (British Computer Society, 2007).

Appendix I: The Sources of Data Protection Law

What are the various sources of data protection law? Organizations, data protection officers, and individuals need to consider a number of sources of the law, policy, and practice underpinning the data protection regime. In addition, there is a growing number of sources of interpretation and understanding of data protection law. Reliance on the data protection rules alone can, therefore, be insufficient. Data protection is, therefore, arguably quite different from many other areas of legal practice. In order to fully understand the data protection regime, one has to look beyond the text, or first principles, of the data protection rules and GDPR. What are the sources of data protection law and policy? Some of these are referred to below.

National Data Protection Laws/Acts

Primarily, the data protection regime is governed by the data protection rules and new GDPR. In addition, it is also necessary to have regard to a number of other sources of law, policy, and the interpretation of the data protection regime. It is also necessary to look out for any amendments to these.

National Secondary Legislation

In addition to the data protection rules, the legal statutory instruments need to be considered.

EU Data Protection Law

The main sources of EU data protection laws include

- GDPR.
- DPD95.
- ePrivacy Directive* and proposed replacement entitled *Proposal for a Regulation on Privacy and Electronic Communications* (2017).
- Regulation re processing of personal data by the EU institutions and bodies.†

It is also necessary to look out for any amendments to these.

The new GDPR is the most important development in EU data protection since 1995. There are significant implications for organizations and data protection practice.

Data Protection Convention

The Council of Europe Data Protection Convention in relation to data protection is also important

- Convention for the Protection of Individuals with Regard to Automatic Processing of Personal Data at Strasbourg on 28 January 1981.

---

* As amended by Directives 2006/24/EC and 2009/136/EC. Directive 2002/58/EC of the European Parliament and of the Council of 12 July 2002 concerning the processing of personal data and the protection of privacy in the electronic communications sector (Directive on privacy and electronic communications)(as amended by Directives 2006/24/EC and 2009/136/EC).

† Regulation (EC) No 45/2001 of the European Parliament and of the Council of 18 December 2000 on the protection of individuals with regard to the processing of personal data by the Community institutions and bodies and on the free movement of such data, Regulation (EC) No 45/2001, OJ L 8, 12.1.2001, at http://eur-lex.europa.eu/LexUriServ/LexUriServ.do?uri=OJ:L:2001:008:0001:0022:en:PDF.

Caselaw

Increasingly, data protection cases (and cases that involve direct or indirect reference to personal data and information impacting the data protection regime) are coming to be litigated and determined before the courts.

One of the reasons is that individuals are increasingly aware of and concerned about their rights under the data protection regime. A further reason is that technological developments have enhanced the potential abuse of personal data, from non-transparent collections of personal data, spam, unsolicited direct marketing, hacking, data loss, phishing, email and Internet scams, online abuse, offline abuse, data transfers, access to personal data, and so on, as well as litigation related access to personal data, and so on. Personal data access requests are permissible, even in the case of ongoing litigation.

The caselaw that can be relevant to applying and interpreting the data protection regime include

- Cases in EU countries.
- Documentation from the data protection supervisory authorities.
- Case complaints adjudicated by the data protection supervisory authorities.
- Cases in England and Wales and Scotland.
- EU Court of Justice (ECJ/CJEU*) cases.
- EU Court of Human Rights (ECHR) cases.
- Relevant cases in other EU member states.
- Relevant cases in other common law jurisdictions.

Investigations

Investigations by the data protection supervisory authority can occur as a result of complaints or via proactive data protection supervisory authority investigations. The data protection supervisory authority is

---

* Note: The ECJ is now known as the Court of Justice of the European Union (CJEU).

also able to carry out investigation of their own volition without having to wait on the receipt of a complaint.*

National Data Protection Supervisory Authority Guides

The EU national data protection supervisory authorities provide many guides and interpretations in relation to specific data protection issues and industry sectors.† Some examples include

General Issues

- Getting organized for data protection.
- Key definitions.
- Website privacy statements.
- Personal data.
- Parental guide to Internet security—from the Office of Internet Security (OIS).
- Manual data and relevant filing system.
- Age of consent.
- Back-up systems.
- Data security.
- Data protection and CCTV.
- Data protection and the use of body worn cameras.
- Data protection and drones.
- Data protection and cloud.
- Guidance note for controllers on purpose limitation and retention.
- Guidance note for controllers on the release of personal data to public representatives.
- Guidance note for controllers on purpose limitation and retention in relation to credit/debit/charge card transactions.
- Guidance note on data protection in the electronic communications sector.
- Data sharing in the public sector.

---

* Increasingly investigations by the EU data protection supervisory authorities can have potentially worldwide significance.

† See Irish data protection supervisory authority (DPC), at http://dataprotection.ie/ ViewDoc.asp?fn=%2Fdocuments%2Fguidance%2Fdefault%2Ehtm&CatID=6&m=m.

- Guidance note on canvassing, data protection, and electronic marketing.

Marketing

- Direct marketing: A general guide.
- Guidance note on data protection in the electronic communications sector.
- Restrictions on the use of publicly available data for marketing purposes.
- Data protection in the telecommunications sector.
- Guide to the use of the National Directory Database for direct marketers.
- Guidance note for electronic communications service providers on direct marketing telephone calls to their subscribers and former subscribers.
- Guidance note for entities considering the use of Bluetooth technology for direct marketing purposes.
- A consumer guide to dealing with unsolicited direct marketing.
- Subscriber FAQs on the National Directory Database.

Employment Related

- Access requests and personnel.
- Staff monitoring.
- Considerations when vetting prospective employees.
- Biometrics in the workplace.
- Whistleblower.
- Transfer of ownership of a business.

Medical Related

- The medical and health sector.
- Access to medical records on a change of medical practitioner.
- Referral of medical consultant's clinical notes for review without their or the patients' consent.
- Guidance note on research in the health sector.

Education

- Biometrics in schools, colleges, and other educational institutions.

Organizations should consult the data protection supervisory authority websites for guidance on specific issues.

Data Protection Supervisory Authority Determinations

In addition, there is a body of decided decisions in relation to complaints filed by individuals with the national data protection supervisory authorities on various issues. These can assist in considering identical and similar situations regarding issues of data protection compliance.* Many organizations have altered various data protection related practices pursuant to the data protection supervisory authority audits, with certain issues ongoing.

Legal Textbooks and Further Reading

There is an increasing number of data protection legal textbooks and guides. There are also relevant learned journals and articles published in relation to data protection compliance and developing data protection issues.

European Data Protection Board

In terms of the interpretation and understanding of the data protection regime, the EDPB† is also required to be consulted. This is an influential body in relation to addressing and interpreting the data protection regime, as well as problem areas in data protection practice. It is also influential as it is comprised of members from the respective data protection authorities in the European Union.

The previous WP29 issued working papers, opinions, and related documentation, available at: http://ec.europa.eu/justice/data-protection/article-29/documentation/opinion-recommendation/index_en.htm.

---

* In relation to the national data protection supervisory authorities generally regarding data protection not DPD95; and also Greenleaf, "Independence of Data Privacy Authorities (Part 1): International Standards," *Computer Law & Security Review* (2012)(28) 3.
† Previously the EU Article 29 Working Party (WP29), established under Article 29 of the DPD95.

European Data Protection Supervisor

The European Data Protection Supervisor, which deals in the main with data protection issues regarding the EU official bodies (and therefore not commercial organizations directly), is also worth consulting and is arguably increasing in prominence and importance. Details are available at: https://secure.edps.europa.eu/EDPSWEB/edps/EDPS/cache/offonce?lang=en.

Council of Europe

There are various important reference materials in relation to data protection and privacy emanating from the Council of Europe, such as

- Council of Europe Convention on data protection, No. 108 of 1981 (Data Protection Convention).
- Amendments to Convention.*
- Recommendation CM/Rec (2016)1 of the Committee of Ministers to member states on protecting and promoting the right to freedom of expression and the right to private life with regard to network neutrality.
- Recommendation CM/Rec (2015)5 of the Committee of Ministers to member states on the processing of personal data in the context of employment.
- Recommendation CM/Rec (2012)4 of the Committee of Ministers to member states on the protection of human rights with regard to social networking services.
- Recommendation CM/Rec (2012)3 of the Committee of Ministers to member states on the protection of human rights with regard to search engines.
- Recommendation CM/Rec (2010)13 of the Committee of Ministers to member states on the protection of individuals

---

* Amendments approved by the Committee of Ministers, in Strasbourg, on 15 June 1999, see https://rm.coe.int/CoERMPublicCommonSearchServices/DisplayDC TMContent?documentId=090000168008c2b8; Amendment to Convention ETS No 108 allowing the European Communities to accede; Additional Protocol to Convention ETS No 108 on data protection supervisory authorities and trans-border data flows.

with regard to automatic processing of personal data in the context of profiling.

- Recommendation No R(2002) 9 on the protection of personal data collected and processed for insurance purposes.
- Recommendation No R(99) 5 for the protection of privacy on the Internet.
- Recommendation No R(97) 18 on the protection of personal data collected and processed for statistical purposes.
- Recommendation No R(97) 5 on the protection of medical data.
- Recommendation No R(95) 4 on the protection of personal data in the area of telecommunication services, with particular reference to telephone services.
- Recommendation No R(91) 10 on the communication to third parties of personal data held by public bodies.
- Recommendation No R(90) 19 on the protection of personal data used for payment and other operations.
- Recommendation CM/Rec (2015)5 (replacing Recommendation No R(89) 2 on the protection of personal data used for employment purposes).
- Recommendation No R(87) 15 regulating the use of personal data in the police sector.
- Recommendation No R(86) 1 on the protection of personal data for social security purposes.
- Recommendation No R(85) 20 on the protection of personal data used for the purposes of direct marketing.
- Recommendation No R (97) 5 (replacing Recommendation No R(81) 1 on regulations for automated medical data banks).
- Resolution (74) 29 on the protection of individuals vis-à-vis electronic data banks in the public sector.
- Resolution (73) 22 on the protection of privacy of individuals vis-à-vis electronic data banks in the private sector.
- Declaration of the Committee of Minister on risks to fundamental rights stemming from digital tracking and other surveillance technologies.*

---

* These and other documents are available at: http://www.coe.int/t/dghl/standardsetting/dataprotection/Default_en.asp.

The Data Protection Convention* of 1981 pre-dates the DPD95 and the new GDPR and is incorporated into the national law of many EU and other states—even prior to the DPD95. The Council of Europe is reviewing and updating the Data Protection Convention.[†]

Other Data Protection Supervisory Authorities

Issues that may not yet be decided or formally reported on can sometimes have been considered elsewhere. It can, therefore, be useful to consider the decisions and logic behind decisions, reports, and opinions of the

- Data protection supervisory authorities of other EU member states.
- Data protection supervisory authorities of EU member states.
- Data protection supervisory authorities of other states (for example, Canada).

Sometimes non-EU states will follow or are influenced by the EU data protection regime[‡]

---

* Data Protection Convention, at http://www.coe.int/t/dghl/standardsetting/data-protection/Default_en.asp. Draft convention for the protection of individuals with regard to automatic processing of personal data, *International Legal Materials* (1980) (19) 284.

† See Kierkegaard et al., "30 Years On: The Review of the Council of Europe Data Protection Convention 108," *Computer Law & Security Review* (2011)(27) 223. Greenleaf, "Modernising Data Protection Convention 108: A Safe Basis for Global Privacy Treaty," *Computer Law & Security Review* (2013)(29) 430; de Hert and Papakonstantinou, "The Council of Europe Data Protection Convention Reform: Analysis of the New Text and Critical Comment on Its Global Ambition," *Computer Law & Security Review* (2014)(30:6) 633. de Terwangne, "The Work of Revision of the Council of Europe Convention 108 for the Protection of Individuals as Regards the Automatic Processing of Personal Data," *International Review of Law, Computers & Technology* (2014)(28:2) 118.

‡ This includes the DPD95 and, potentially in time, the GDPR. The complaints and issues raised in *EU Article 29 Working Party on Data Protection and Data Protection Authorities/Google*, Privacy Policy Change [2012] were endorsed by the Asia Pacific Privacy Authorities. So, the new GDPR and new EDPB may have wider significance and influence.

The European Data Protection Supervisor (which deals with issues regarding the official EU bodies) provides links to the data protection authorities in the EU at

- http://ec.europa.eu/justice/policies/privacy/nationalcomm/ index_en.htm.

Other Official Sources

Government or official reports can be beneficial and applicable on certain data protection topics. Industry codes that may be agreed with the data protection supervisory authority can also be relevant to those industries, for example, the industry sector codes of practice in relation to data protection.

Related issues can sometimes arise under freedom of information legislation.

Industry bodies also publish recommendations and information regarding aspects of data protection.

Tribunals can also be relevant, including the Leveson Inquiry in terms of protection for personal data, security, deliberate breaches, hacking, and so on, and the data protection supervisory authority investigation (Operation Motorman).

Data Protection Websites and Blogs

There are many privacy and data protection websites and blogs, such as Datonomy (http://www.datonomy.eu/); Irish Internet Association (www.iia.ie); Data Protection Forum; Society of Computers and Law (www.scl.org); Association of Data Protection Officers; and International Association of Privacy Professionals.

Other Laws

Other laws can also be relevant in considering personal data and privacy.* Examples include

---

* See review of particular laws in Delfino, European Union Legislation and Actions, *European Review of Contract Law* (2011)(7) 547, which includes reference to data protection law.

- IT law.
- Contract law.
- Consumer law.
- eCommerce law.
- Distance selling law.
- Financial services law.
- Gaming law (gambling).
- Computer game law.
- Health and medical law and obligations.
- Child law.
- Criminal law.
- Succession law.
- Drones, drone licensing, and drone registration.

This is by no means a complete list.

Conferences

There are a variety of conferences, annual events, and training organizations related to data protection. Some are organized by professional conference firms, while others are non-profit technology, legal, or related organizations. Various commercial organizations arrange training, audits, testing, and conferences.

Reference Websites

Useful reference material is available as set out below:

The EU Commission is at

http://ec.europa.eu/justice/data-protection/index_en.htm

The WP29 is at

http://ec.europa.eu/justice/data-protection/article-29/
index_en.htm
http://ec.europa.eu/justice/policies/privacy/workinggroup/
index_en.htm

This is being replaced by the EDPB.

The EU Court of Justice website is at

http://europa.eu/about-eu/institutions-bodies/court-justice/
index_en.htm

EU Court of Justice cases* are at

http://curia.europa.eu/jcms/jcms/j_6/
The ECHR website is at
http://www.echr.coe.int/Pages/home.aspx?p=home
Society of Computers and Law:
www.scl.org

Legislation

Data Protection Directive 1995:

http://eur-lex.europa.eu/LexUriServ/LexUriServ.do?uri=CEL
EX:31995L0046:en:HTML

Proposed Data Protection Regulation:

http://ec.europa.eu/justice/data-protection/document/
review2012/com_2012_11_en.pdf

Proposed Data Protection Directive:

http://ec.europa.eu/home-affairs/doc_centre/police/docs/
com_2012_10_en.pdf

Final version Data Protection Regulation (Regulation (EU) 2016/679):

http://ec.europa.eu/justice/data-protection/reform/files/
regulation_oj_en.pdf

Proposed Data Protection Network and Information Security Directive:

http://ec.europa.eu/dgs/home-affairs/what-is-new/news/
news/2013/docs/1_directive_20130207_en.pdf

---

* Tzanou, Balancing Fundamental Rights, United in Diversity? Some Reflections on the Recent Case Law of the European Court of Justice on Data Protection, *CYELP* (2010)(6) 53.

European/International Legislation

- Aarhus Convention on Access to Information, Public Participation in Decision making and Access to Justice in Environmental Matters 1998.
- Charter of Fundamental Rights of the European Union.
- CIS Convention on the Use of Information technology for Customs Purposes 1995.
- Commission Decision 2004/91 of December 7, 2004 amending Decision 2001/497 as Regards the Introduction of an Alternative Set of Standard Clauses for Transfer of Personal Data to Third Counties.
- Commission decision 2004/535 on the Adequate Protection of Personal Data Contained in Passenger Name Record of Air Passengers Transferred to the United States Bureau of Customs and Border Protection.
- Convention for the Processing of Individuals with Regard to the Automatic Processing of Personal Data 1981.
- Convention on Mutual Assistance Between Customs Administrations 1967.
- Convention on Mutual Assistance in Criminal Matters 2000.
- Council of Europe Convention 1981.
- Council Decision 2004/496 on the Agreement Between the European Community and the United States of America on the Processing and Transfer of PNR Data by Air carriers to the United States of America on the Transfer and processing of PNR data by Carriers to the United States Department of Homeland Security, Bureau of Customs and Border Protection.
- Council Directive 73/148 (Council Directive 73/148/EEC of 21 May 1973 on the abolition of restrictions on movement and residence within the Community for nationals of member states with regard to establishment and the provision of services).
- Council Directive 89/552 (Council Directive 89/552/EEC of 3 October 1989 on the coordination of certain provisions laid down by Law, Regulation or Administrative Action in member states concerning the pursuit of television broadcasting activities).

- Council Directive 95/46 (Directive 95/46/EC of the European Parliament and of the Council of 24 October 1995 on the protection of individuals with regard to the processing of personal data and on the free movement of such data)(DPD95).
- Council Directive 1997/7/EC (Directive 97/7/EC of the European Parliament and of the Council of 20 May 1997 on the protection of consumers in respect of distance contracts—Statement by the Council and the Parliament re Article 6(1)—Statement by the Commission re Article 3 (1), first indent)(Distance Selling Directive).
- Council Directive 97/66 (Directive 97/66/EC of the European Parliament and of the Council of 15 December 1997 concerning the processing of personal data and the protection of privacy in the telecommunications sector)(Telecoms Data Protection Directive).
- Council Directive 98/34 (Directive 98/34/EC of the European Parliament and of the Council of 22 June 1998 laying down a procedure for the provision of information in the field of technical standards and regulations and of rules on Information Society services).
- Council Directive 98/48 (Directive 98/48/EC of the European Parliament and of the Council of 20 July 1998 amending Directive 98/34/EC laying down a procedure for the provision of information in the field of technical standards and regulations).
- Council Directive 99/5 (Directive 1999/5/EC of the European Parliament and of the Council of 9 March 1999 on radio equipment and telecommunications terminal equipment and the mutual recognition of their conformity).
- Council Directive 2000/31 (Directive 2000/31/EC of the European Parliament and of the Council of 8 June 2000 on certain legal aspects of information society services, in particular electronic commerce, in the Internal Market) ("Directive on electronic commerce") (eCommerce Directive).
- Council Directive 2002/21 Directive 2002/21/EC of the European Parliament and of the Council of 7 March 2002 on a common regulatory framework for electronic communications networks and services (Framework Directive).

- Council Directive 2002/22 (Directive 2002/22/EC of the European Parliament and of the Council of 7 March 2002 on universal service and users' rights relating to electronic communications networks and services) (Universal Service Directive).
- Council Directive 2002/58 (Directive 2002/58/EC of the European Parliament and of the Council of 12 July 2002 concerning the processing of personal data and the protection of privacy in the electronic communications sector [Directive on privacy and electronic communications])(ePrivacy Directive).
- Council Directive 2003/98 (Directive 2003/98/EC of the European Parliament and of the Council of 17 November 2003 on the re-use of public sector information).
- Council Directive 2009/136/EC (Directive 2009/136/EC of the European Parliament and of the Council of 25 November 2009 amending Directive 2002/22/EC on universal service and users' rights relating to electronic communications networks and services, Directive 2002/58/EC concerning the processing of personal data and the protection of privacy in the electronic communications sector and Regulation (EC) No 2006/2004 on cooperation between national authorities responsible for the enforcement of consumer protection laws).
- Council Regulation (EC) 2299/89 (Council Regulation (EEC) No 2299/89 of 24 July 1989 on a code of conduct for computerised reservation systems).
- Council Regulation 1035/97 (Council Regulation (EC) No 1035/97 of 2 June 1997 establishing a European Monitoring Centre on Racism and Xenophobia).
- Council Regulation 2725/2000 (Council Regulation (EC) No 2725/2000 of 11 December 2000 concerning the establishment of "Eurodac" for the comparison of fingerprints for the effective application of the Dublin Convention).
- Council Regulation 2424/2001 (Council Regulation (EC) No 2424/2001 of 6 December 2001 on the development of the second generation Schengen Information System (SIS II).
- Council Regulation 2580/2001 (Council Regulation (EC) No 2580/2001 of 27 December 2001 on specific restrictive

measures directed against certain persons and entities with a view to combating terrorism).

- Council Regulation 45/2001 (Regulation (EC) 45/2001 of the European Parliament and of the Council of 18 December 2000 on the Protection of Individuals with Regard to the processing of personal data by the Community Institutions and Bodies and on the Free Movement of Such Data).
- Council Regulation 2252/2004 (Council Regulation (EC) No 2252/2004 of 13 December 2004 on standards for security features and biometrics in passports and travel documents issued by member states).
- Council Regulation 871/2004 (Council Regulation (EC) No 871/2004 of 29 April 2004 concerning the introduction of some new functions for the Schengen Information System, including in the fight against terrorism).
- Cybercrime Convention.
- Decision 2001/497 of 15 June 2001 on Standard Contractual Clauses for the Transfer of Personal Data to Third Countries under Directive 95/46.
- Directive 95/46 on the Protection of Individuals with Regard to the Processing of Personal Data and on the Free Movement of the Data.
- Directive 97/7 on the Protection of Consumers in Respect of Distance Contracts.
- Directive 97/66 Concerning the Processing of Personal Data and the Protection of privacy in the Telecommunications Sector (Telecommunications Directive).
- Directive 98/48 amending Directive 98/34 (Directive 98/48/EC of the European Parliament and of the Council of 20 July 1998 amending Directive 98/34/EC laying down a procedure for the provision of information in the field of technical standards and regulations).
- Directive 99/67 amending Directive 93/49 (Commission Directive 1999/67/EC of 28 June 1999 amending Directive 93/49/EEC setting out the schedule indicating the conditions to be met by ornamental plant propagating material and ornamental plants pursuant to Council Directive 91/682/EEC).

- Directive 2002/19 on Access to and Interconnection of Electronic Communications Networks and Associated Facilities.
- Directive 2002/21 on a Common Regulatory Framework for Electronic Communications Networks and Services.
- Directive 2002/22 on Universal Service and Users' Rights Relating to Electronic Communications Networks and Services.
- Directive 2002/58 Concerning the Processing of Personal Data and the protection of Privacy in the Electronic Communications Sector Privacy and Electronic Communications Directive.
- Directive 2002/96 on Waste Electrical and Electronic Equipment (WEEE).
- Directive 2003/4 Public Access to Environmental Information
- Directive 2005/18 on the Retention of Data Generated or processing in Connection with the Provision or Publicly Available Electronic Communications Services or of Public Communications Networks.
- Directive 2006/24 on the Retention of Data Generated or Processed in Connection with the Provision of Publicly Available Electronic Communications Services or of Public Communications Networks and Amended Directive 2002/58.
- Dublin Convention 1990 (Convention determining the State responsible for examining applications for asylum lodged in one of the member states of the European Communities—Dublin Convention).
- EEA Agreement.
- EC Treaty.
- EU Charter of Fundamental Rights.
- Eurodac Convention 1996.
- Europol Convention on the Establishment of a European Police Force.
- European Convention for the Protection of Human Rights and Fundamental Freedoms 1950.
- Europol Convention.
- Lisbon Treaty.

- Mutual Assistance Convention.
- Nice Charter of Fundamental Rights 2000.
- Regulation 515/97 on Mutual Assistance Between Administrative Authorities of the Member States.
- Regulation 45/2001 on the Protection of Individuals with Regard to the Processing of Personal Data by the Community Institutions and Bodies and on the Free Movement of Such Data.
- Regulation 343/2003 (Dublin II Regulation).
- Regulation 1987/2006 (Schengen II/SIS II).
- Rome EC Treaty 1957.
- Single European Act 1987.
- Strasbourg Convention.
- Treaty 108 of the Council of Europe Convention for the Protection of Individuals with Regard to Automatic Processing of Personal Data 1981.
- Treaty of Amsterdam.
- Treaty on European Union.
- Treaty on European Union consolidated.
- UNCITRAL Model Law on Electronic Commerce.

Data Retention

The EU Court of Justice also pronounced on the often contentious area of official data retention. This is the obligation placed by countries on Internet service providers (ISPs) to retain certain customer data in relation to telephone calls, Internet searches, and so on, so that (certain) official agencies can ask to access or obtain copies of such data in future. Debate frequently surrounds whether this should be permitted at all, and if so, when and under what circumstances, how long ISPs must store such data, and so on. The strongest argument for an official data retention regime may relate to the prevention or investigation of terrorism. Serious crime might come next. There are certainly legitimate concerns that the privacy and data protection costs are such that official data retention, if permitted, should not extend to "common decent crime." On one end of the spectrum is the EU Court of Justice decision in *Digital Rights Ireland* striking down the EU Data Retention Directive as invalid.* By implication this also undermines many national data retention measures.† It remains to be seen how challenges to new data retention legislation may transpire, and how courts and policymakers will react. This remains, if anything, a contentious issue. The various Snowden revelations and their ripple effects lean against the data retention regime, or at least an overly broad and overreaching one. In addition to debate in relation to legitimate data retention, there is a separate but related debate (especially in the United States and the United Kingdom) in relation to encryption, encryption by default, encryption by service providers, personal encryption, and encryption back doors for law enforcement authorities.‡ However, every time there is a terror related event, and at the time of writing we are in the aftermath of attacks, calls and arguments for data retention/extended data retention are at their

---

* Judgment in Joined Cases C-293/12 and C-594/12, *Digital Rights Ireland* and *Seitlinger and Others*, Court of Justice, 8 April 2014. Directive 2006/24/EC of the European Parliament and of the Council of 15 March 2006 on the retention of data generated or processed in connection with the provision of publicly available electronic communications services or of public communications networks and amending Directive 2002/58/EC (OJ 2006 L105, p 54). Rauhofer and Mac Sithigh, "The Data Retention Directive Never Existed," *SCRIPTed* (2014)(11:1) 118.

† Such as the Regulation of Investigatory Powers Act 2000 (RIPA) in the UK. The UK government proposed a new amending regulation entitled the Data Retention and Investigatory Powers Act 2014 (DRIPA). However, two MPs (David Davis and Tom Watson), successfully challenged DRIPA in the High Court. The court held that sections 1 and 2 of DRIPA breached rights to respect for private life and communications and to the protection of personal data under Articles 7 and 8 of the EU Charter of Fundamental Rights. The decision gave the (UK) government until March 2016 to rectify the DRIPA problems. The Queen's speech has also promised a "snooper's charter" which would replace DRIPA. See Whitehead, "Google and Whatsapp Will be Forced to Hand Messages to MI5," *Telegraph*, 27 May 2015. Since then a draft of the Communications Data Bill has issued. No doubt argument, debate and research will ensue. In relation to "Data Protection as a Fundamental Right," see, for example Rodata, Data protection as a fundamental right, in Gutwirth, Poullet, de Hert, de Terwangne and Nouwt, *Reinventing Data Protection?* (Springer, 2009) 77.

‡ A Harvard study suggests, *inter alia*, that an encryption back door would in any event be ineffective. See Schneier, Siedel and Vijayakumar, *A Worldwide Survey of Encryption Products*, (Harvard, 11 February 2016). Also Barrett, "Bill Aims to Stop State Level Encryption Before It Starts," *Wired*, 10 February 2016. Also note Grauer, "The Government Wants to Listen in on Your Smartphone," *Wired*, 14 February 2016, referring to connected Internet of things (IOT) devices in the home.

strongest.* While the issues of *official data retention* are important, it is a separate subject to *data protection*. This book focuses on data protection alone.

---

* Prime Minister Cameron (as he then was) made statements to advance data retention proposals, in particular the Communications Data Bill, labelled by some as a "snooper's charter." Critics also increasingly suggest that research is indicating that data retention does not demonstrate that data retention works. However, official sources in various jurisdictions refer to terror attacks being prevented and that retained data is invaluable. The link or proof of positive effect is not necessarily specified. This debate also crosses over with issues of unauthorized access or tapping by official agencies of technology companies and their customers' data, and public and industry arguments that official access must be regulated, transparent, and proportional.

Appendix II: How to Comply with the Data Protection Regime

How does an organization comply with the data protection regime? What are the different components of compliance? The tables below set out assistance how to comply with the data protection regime.

COMPLYING WITH DATA PROTECTION

All organizations collect and process at least some personal data as defined under the Data Protection Acts and the data protection regime. Therefore, an organization must ensure it only collects and processes personal data if complying with

- The obligation to only collect and process personal data if in compliance with the data protection laws.
- The principles, also known as the "data quality principles."
- The legitimate processing conditions.
- The requirement that processing of personal data be "legitimate" under at least one of the legitimate processing conditions.

- The transparency and prior information requirement obligations.
- Recognizing the two categories of personal data covered by the data protection regime, namely, sensitive personal data and non-sensitive general personal data.
- In the case of sensitive personal data, complying with the additional sensitive personal data legitimate processing conditions.
- Ensuring the fair obtaining of all personal data collected and processed.
- The security conditions.
- The notification and registration conditions (as applicable).
- The data breach notification conditions.
- The personal data outsourcing and processor conditions.
- Implementing formal legal contracts when engaging or dealing with third-party processors (e.g., outsourcing data processing tasks or activities).
- Complying with the separate criteria in relation to automated decision-making processes or automated decisions.
- The personal data transfer ban or trans-border data flow restrictions. The transfers of personal data outside of EU is strictly controlled. Personal data may not be transferred outside of the EU unless specifically permitted under the data protection regime.
- Complying with the legal criteria for direct marketing.
- The individual data subject rights, including access, deletion, and so on.
- Access requests, or requests by individuals for copies of their personal data held by the organization, must be complied with (unless excepted).
- A duty of care exists in relation to the individual data subjects whose personal data the organization is collecting and processing.
- Queries, audits, and investigation orders from the data protection supervisory authority.
- The time limits for undertaking various tasks and obligations.

- Implementing internal privacy policies and terms.
- Implementing outward-facing privacy policies for customers, and so on.
- Implementing outward-facing website privacy statements (generally a data protection policy covers organization-wide activities, whereas a website privacy statement governs only the online collection and processing of personal data).
- Implementing device, mobile, computer, and Internet usage policies.
- Implementing data loss, data breach, incident handling and incident reporting policies, and associated reaction plans.
- Data incidents, losses, and breaches need to be reported to the data protection supervisory authority (unless exempted).
- Keeping abreast of the increasing trend toward sector/issue specific rules, for example spam; direct marketing.
- Industry codes of conduct in relation to personal data.
- Children and personal data issues.
- Data protection impact assessments and privacy consultations.
- Data protection by design and by default.
- Complying with new legal developments.

DATA PROTECTION PRINCIPLES

The new GDPR sets out the data protection principles as follows, namely that personal data must be

- Processed lawfully, fairly, and in a transparent manner in relation to the Individual data subject ("lawfulness, fairness, and transparency").
- Collected for specified, explicit, and legitimate purposes and not further processed in a way incompatible with those purposes; further processing of personal data for archiving purposes in the public interest, scientific and historical research purposes, or statistical purposes must, in accordance with Article 83(1), not be considered incompatible with the initial purposes ("purpose limitation").

- Adequate, relevant, and limited to what is necessary in relation to the purposes for which they are processed ("data minimisation").
- Accurate and, where necessary, kept up to date; every reasonable step must be taken to ensure that personal data that are inaccurate, having regard to the purposes for which they are processed, are erased or rectified without delay ("accuracy").
- Kept in a form that permits identification of Individual data subjects for no longer than is necessary for the purposes for which the personal data are processed; personal data may be stored for longer periods insofar as the data will be processed solely for archiving purposes in the public interest, scientific and historical research purposes, or statistical purposes in accordance with Article 83(1) subject to implementation of the appropriate technical and organizational measures required by the Regulation in order to safeguard the rights and freedoms of the Individual data subject ("storage limitation").
- Processed in a way that ensures appropriate security of the personal data, including protection against unauthorized or unlawful processing and against accidental loss, destruction, or damage, using appropriate technical or organizational measures ("integrity and confidentiality").

The controller must be responsible for and be able to *demonstrate* compliance with the above ("accountability").

In summary, personal data must be

- Lawful, fair, and transparent.
- For a specified, explicit, and legitimate purpose (and not further processed).
- Adequate, relevant, limited (necessary) to the purpose.
- Accurate, kept up to date with inaccurate data erased or rectified.
- Kept no longer than necessary.
- Protected by appropriate security.
- And must demonstrate compliance with above.
- Controllers must also give a copy of personal data to any individual, on request (i.e., a data access request).

Appendix III: General Data Protection Regulation Sections

Chapters

There are 11 chapters to the General Data Protection Regulation. These chapters and their subject matter are:

Chapter I: General provisions
Chapter II: Principles
Chapter III: Rights of the data subject
Chapter IV: Controller and processor
Chapter V: Transfer of personal data to third countries or international organisations
Chapter VI: Independent supervisory authorities
Chapter VII: Co-operation and consistency
Chapter VIII: Remedies, liability, and penalties
Chapter IX: Provisions relating to specific data processing situations
Chapter X: Delegated acts and implementing acts
Chapter XI: Final provisions

GDPR Provisions

General Provisions

The Chapter I general provisions refer to:

Article 1: Subject matter and objectives
Article 2: Material scope
Article 3: Territorial scope
Article 4: Definitions

Principles

The Chapter II principles refer to:

Article 5: Principles relating to processing of personal data
Article 6: Lawfulness of processing
Article 7: Conditions for consent
Article 8: Conditions applicable to child's consent in relation to information society services
Article 9: Processing of special categories of personal data
Article 10: Processing of personal data relating to criminal convictions and offences
Article 11: Processing which does not require identification

Rights of the Data Subject

Chapter III, referring to the rights of data subjects, contains five sections, as follows:

Section 1: Transparency and modalities
Section 2: Information and access to data
Section 3: Rectification and erasure
Section 4: Right to object and automated individual decision making
Section 5: Restrictions

Section 1, referring to transparency and modalities, contains the following:

Article 12: Transparent information, communication, and modalities for the exercise of the rights of the data subject.

Section 2, referring to information and access to personal data, contains the following:

Article 13: Information to be provided where personal data are collected from the data subject.
Article 14: Information to be provided where personal data have not been obtained from the data subject.
Article 15: Right of access by the data subject.

Section 3, referring to rectification and erasure, contains the following:

Article 16: Right to rectification
Article 17: Right to erasure (right to be forgotten)
Article 18: Right to restriction of processing
Article 19: Notification obligation regarding rectification or erasure of personal data or restriction of processing
Article 20: Right to data portability.

Section 4, referring to right to object and automated individual decision making, contains the following:

Article 21: Right to object
Article 22: Automated individual decision making, including profiling

Section 5, referring to restrictions, contains:

Article 23: Restrictions

Controller and Processor

Chapter IV, referring to controllers and processors contains five sections, as follows:

Section 1: General obligations
Section 2: Security of personal data
Section 3: Data protection impact assessment and prior authorisation
Section 4: Data Protection Officer
Section 5: Codes of conduct and certification

Section 1, referring to general obligations, contains the following:

Article 24: Responsibility of the controller
Article 25: Data protection by design and by default
Article 26: Joint controllers
Article 27: Representatives of controllers or processors not established in the Union
Article 28: Processor
Article 29: Processing under the authority of the controller and processor
Article 30: Records of processing activities
Article 31: Co-operation with the supervisory authority

Section 2, referring to security of personal data, contains the following:

Article 32: Security of processing
Article 33: Notification of a personal data breach to the supervisory authority
Article 34: Communication of a personal data breach to the data subject

Section 3, referring to data protection impact assessment and prior consultation, contains the following:

Article 35: Data protection impact assessment
Article 36: Prior consultation

Section 4, referring to Data Protection Officers, contains the following:

Article 37: Designation of the Data Protection Officer
Article 38: Position of the Data Protection Officer
Article 39: Tasks of the Data Protection Officer

Section 5, referring to codes and certification, contains the following:

Article 40: Codes of conduct
Article 41: Monitoring of approved codes of conduct
Article 42: Certification
Article 43: Certification bodies

Transfer to Third Countries or International Organisations

Chapter V, referring to transfer of personal data to third countries or international organisations, contains the following:

Article 44: General principle for transfers
Article 45: Transfers on the basis of an adequacy decision
Article 46: Transfers subject to appropriate safeguards
Article 47: Binding corporate rules
Article 48: Transfers or disclosures not authorized by Union law
Article 49: Derogations for specific situations
Article 50: International co-operation for the protection of personal data

Independent Supervisory Authorities

Chapter VI, referring to independent supervisory authorities, contains the following sections:

Section 1: Independent status
Section 2: Competence, tasks and powers

Section 1, referring to independent status, contains the following:

Article 51: Supervisory authority
Article 52: Independence
Article 53: General conditions for the members of the supervisory authority
Article 54: Rules on the establishment of the supervisory authority

Section 2, referring to competence, tasks, and powers, contains the following:

Article 55: Competence
Article 56: Competence of the lead supervisory authority
Article 57: Tasks
Article 58: Powers
Article 59: Activity reports

Cooperation and Consistency

Chapter VII, referring to cooperation and consistency, contains the following sections:

Section 1: Co-operation
Section 2: Consistency
Section 3: European Data Protection Board

Cooperation

Section 1, referring to cooperation, contains the following:

Article 60: Cooperation between the lead supervisory authority and the other supervisory authority
Article 61: Mutual assistance
Article 62: Joint operations of supervisory authority

Consistency

Section 2, referring to consistency, contains the following:

Article 63: Consistency mechanism
Article 64: Opinion of the Board
Article 65: Dispute resolution by the Board
Article 66: Urgency procedure
Article 67: Exchange of information

European Data Protection Board

Section 3, referring to the European Data Protection Board, contains the following:

Article 68: European Data Protection Board
Article 69: Independence
Article 70: Tasks of the Board
Article 71: Reports
Article 72: Procedure

Article 73: Chair
Article 74: Tasks of the chair
Article 75: Secretariat
Article 76: Confidentiality

Remedies, Liability and Sanctions

Chapter VIII, referring to remedies, liability, and sanctions, contains the following:

Article 77: Right to lodge a complaint with a supervisory authority
Article 78: Right to an effective judicial remedy against a supervisory authority
Article 79: Right to an effective judicial remedy against a controller or processor
Article 80: Representation of data subjects
Article 81: Suspension of proceedings
Article 82: Right to compensation and liability
Article 83: General conditions for imposing administrative fines
Article 84: Penalties

Provisions for Specific Data Processing Situations

Chapter IX, referring to provisions relating to specific processing situations, contains the following:

Article 85: Processing and freedom of expression
Article 86: Processing and public access to official documents
Article 87: Processing of the national identification number
Article 88: Processing in the context of employment
Article 89: Safeguards and derogations relating to processing for archiving purposes in the public interest, scientific or historical research purposes or statistical purposes
Article 90: Obligations of secrecy
Article 91: Existing data protection rules of churches and religious associations

Delegated Acts and Implementing Acts

Chapter X, referring to delegated acts and implementing acts, contains the following:

Article 92: Exercise of the delegation
Article 93: Committee procedure

Final Provisions

Chapter XI, referring to final provisions, contains the following:

Article 94: Repeal of Directive 95/46/EC
Article 95: Relationship to Directive 2002/58/EC
Article 96: Relationship with previously concluded Agreements
Article 97: Commission reports
Article 98: Review of other Union legal acts on data protection
Article 99: Entry into force and application

Index

Automated decision-making and
  profiling
  background guidance, 222
  legal rule, 222–223
  overview, 221

Background Recital 13, 375
Biometric data, 386
Biometric personal data, 116–117
Bring your own device (BYOD), 299
BYOD. *see* Bring your own device
  (BYOD)

Call line identification (Article 8),
  399
Cavoukian, Ann, 329
CERTs. *see* Computer emergency
  response teams (CERTs)
Children, and data protection
  codes of conduct and
    certification, 248
  legal rules
    age, 245–247
    consent and conditions for,
      247–248

legitimate interest processing
  of, 247
merit specific protection, 244–245
overview, 243–244
supervisory authority, 249
transparency and, 245, 248
Codes of conduct
  certification seals and marks, 268
  children, and data protection, 248
  description, 263–265
  details of, 266–268
  legal rule, 268–269
  monitoring of approved, 265–266
  overview, 263
Computer emergency response
  teams (CERTs), 134
Computer hardware, disposal of, 302
Computer security incident response
  teams (CSIRTs), 134
Confidentiality (Article 5), 398
Council of Data Protection
  Convention, 344
Courts
  background guidance, 416–419
  civil sanctions, 414–416

data subjects representation,
423–424
GDPR remedies/legal rules/
damage/compensation,
419–420
jurisdiction issues, 425–428
controller/processor in
EU, 425
controller/processor not in EU,
425–426
investigation and evidence, 428
main establishment, 426–428
monitoring, 426
organizational privacy groups,
424–425
overview, 413–414
right to compensation and
liability, 420–422
right to effective judicial remedy
against controller or
processor, 420
against data protection
supervisory authority,
422–423
right to lodge complaint, 422
Cross-border data transfers
adequate protection exception,
352–353
assessing ban, 363–365
creating adequacy, 354–355
cross-border flows, 342–343
exceptions, 361–362
issues, 362–363
legal rule, 349
not authorized by EU law, 359
overview, 341–342
and Privacy Shield, 365–368
and Safe Harbor arrangement,
365–368
and Schrems, 365–368
transfer agreements and
mechanisms, 343–349
via adequacy decision, 350–352

via appropriate safeguards,
353–354
via Binding Corporate Rules
(BCRs), 355–358
via derogations for specific
situations, 359–361
Cross-border processing, of personal
data, 119
CSIRTs. *see* Computer security
incident response teams
(CSIRTs)

Data breaches, 28–29
communication to data
subject, 309
description, 306
employee, 310
incidents
in context, 305–306
response, 312
notifications
to data protection supervisory
authority, 307–308
to individual data subjects,
306–307
and measures, 307
processes, 310
timelines, 310
overview, 305
requirements to report, 29–30
security standards, 310–311
Data concerning health, 117,
385–386
Data portability
background guidance on
automated processing and,
229–230
legal rule, 230–231
overview, 229
Data protection. *see also* Personal
data
breach and loss, 28–29
concepts, 76–78

criteria for data processing, 78
by default, 463
  assessments, 337–338
  certification, 339
  legal rule, 337
  overview, 337
definitions, 79
description, 64–66
by design, 463
  background, 329–330
  legal rule, 331–333
  overview, 329
  principles of, 330–331
and fines, 28
impact assessment, 284–286
  characteristics, 323–325
  consultation and risk, 326–327
  description, 316–318
  high risks, 315
  legal rule, 318–321
  overview, 315
  reasons for, 321–323
  reports, 323
  steps and methodologies, 325–326
importance of, 1–6
  benefits, 26–27
  digitization, 25
  fundamental right, 24–25
  online abuse, 25–26
  overview, 23–24
inward-facing, 69–73
issues, 74–76
legal instruments of
  background recitals, 89–94
  and consent, 94–96
  and DPD95, 84–85
  and GDPR, 85–86
  lawfulness of processing, 88–89
  laws of, 83
  principles, 86–87
legitimate processing, 79

national data protection
  supervisory authorities, 74
new processing rules of
  context of GDPR, 100
  controllers and processors, 104
  exemptions, 106–108
  formal nature of regulations and directives, 101
  fundamental legal right, 101
  issues for organizations, 102–103
  joint controllers, 105–106
  overview, 99–100
  processing not allowing identification, 106
  processing not requiring identification, 104
  processing of criminal convictions and offenses data, 104
  processing under authority of controller and processor, 106
  repeal of DPD95, 100
  responsibility of controller, 105
and organizations, 27
outward-facing, 67–69
parties, 62–63
principles
  background guidance, 132–136
  data collection, 140
  description, 136–139
  overview, 131–132
  processor, 140
proactive official audits, 31
profiling, 116
and prosecutions, 31
purpose of updating
  EU Commission, 37–42
  new and enhanced provisions, 42–57
  overview, 35–36

regime, 66–67
restriction of processing, 115
rights-based, 73
US–EU similarities
  description, 13–15
  history of, 9–12
  similarity bridges, 15–20
Data protection directive 1995
    (DPD95), 57, 393
  and ePD, 396
Data Protection Directive of
    1997, 394
Data protection officer
  Article 39 tasks, 459–460
  contact details, 461
  data protection
    by default, 463
    by design, 463
  description, 457–458
  group, 461
  independent in role and
    tasks, 462
  overview, 457
  position, 459
  qualifications and expertise, 461
  reporting, 462
  resources, 462
  secrecy/confidentiality, 462
Data protection supervisory
    authorities
  authorization and advisory
    powers, 446–447
  corrective powers, 445–446
  enforcement powers of, 449
  European Data Protection Board
    (EDPB), 452–453
  independence, 447–449
  investigative powers, 444–445
  national, 74
  national data protection
    supervisory authorities
    cooperation with, 449
    investigations by, 449–450

notifying data breach to, 452
  overview, 441–442
  and personal data, 118
  powers of authorized officers to
    enter and examine, 451
  power to enforce compliance, 450
  power to obtain information, 450
  power to prohibit overseas
    transfer of personal data,
    450–451
  prosecution of offenses, 451–452
  tasks, 442–444
Data subject, 124–125
Data transparency
  background guidance, 375–380
  legal rule, 380–383
  overview, 375
Deceptive emails, 405
Default, data protection by, 463
  assessments, 337–338
  certification, 339
  legal rule, 337
  overview, 337
Design, data protection by, 463
  background, 329–330
  legal rule, 331–333
  overview, 329
  principles of, 330–331
Digitization, and data
    protection, 25
Direct marketing
  and ePD, 400–401
    and existing customers'
      email, 404–405
    limited, 404
  right to prevent
    background guidance,
      225–226
    legal rule, 226
    overview, 225
Directories (Article 12), ePD, 400
DPD95. *see* Data protection
    directive 1995 (DPD95)

ECommerce Directive, 437

EDPB. *see* European Data Protection Board (EDPB)

EEA. *see* European Economic Area (EEA)

Effective compensation, 421

Email
  and organizational security awareness, 297

Employees
  data breaches, 310
  and organizational security awareness, 296–297
  and personal data security, 288–289

Employment data, 430

Enforcement notice, 450

Enterprise, and personal data, 117

EPD. *see* EPrivacy Directive (ePD)

EPrivacy Directive (ePD)
  background, 394–395
  call line identification (Article 8), 399
  confidentiality (Article 5), 398
  deceptive emails, 405
  direct marketing, 400–401
    and existing customers' email, 404–405
    limited, 404
  directories (Article 12), 400
  and DPD95, 396
  and ePrivacy Regulation, 406–407
  international spam, 402
  location data, 400
  marketing emails, 405–406
  marketing protection for organizations, 406
  national marketing opt-out registers, 405
  non-itemized billing, 399
  overview, 393–394
  security (Article 4), 397–398

spam problem, 402
traffic data, 399
unsolicited communications, 402–403
EPrivacy Regulation, 406–407

EU Commission, 37–42

European Data Protection Board (EDPB), 263, 345

European Economic Area (EEA), 363

Federal Trade Commission (FTC), 367

Filing system, personal data, 125

Fines and penalties
  background guidance, 251–252
  enforcement, 260
  general conditions for imposing administrative, 257–259
  impact, 256
  for non-compliance with data protection supervisory authority order, 254–256
  overview, 251
  of ten million, 253
  of twenty million, 254

FTC. *see* Federal Trade Commission (FTC)

General Data Protection Regulation (GDPR)
  churches and religious associations, 437
  eCommerce Directive, 437
  employment data, 430
  freedom of expression and information, 431–432
  general registration/notification requirement removed, 437–438
  Obligations of Secrecy, 436–437
  processing national identification numbers, 431

processing of personal data,
431–432
public authorities, 431
safeguards and derogations,
432–436
specific data processing
situations, 429–430
Genetic data, 386
Genetic personal data, 116
Group of undertakings, 117

Health data
biometric data, 386
data concerning health, 385–386
genetic data, 386
health research, 388–389
overview, 385
profiling, 387
pseudonymization, 386–387
right to erasure, 389
special data, 387–388
Health research, 388–389

Impact assessment, data protection
characteristics, 323–325
consultation and risk, 326–327
description, 316–318
high risks, 315
legal rule, 318–321
overview, 315
reasons for, 321–323
reports, 323
steps and methodologies, 325–326
Information notice, 450
Information society service, 119
International organization, 119
International spam, 402
Internet access, and organizational
security awareness, 297
Internet service provider (ISP), 415
Internet social media, 298
Inward-facing data protection, 69–73
ISP. *see* Internet service provider (ISP)

Legal instruments of data protection
background recitals, 89–94
consent
conditions, 94–96
freely given, 94–95
withdrawing, 96
general provisions
in DPD95, 84–85
in GDPR, 85–86
lawfulness of processing, 88–89
laws of, 83
principles, 86–87
Legislative data protection
reviews, 291
Legitimate processing conditions
lawfulness of
general conditions, 152–154
personal data conditions,
154–156
overview, 151
Location data privacy, 400

Main establishment, 117
Marketing emails privacy, 405–406
Marketing protection, for
organizations, 406

National data protection supervisory
authorities, 74
National marketing opt-out
registers, 405
New processing rules, of data
protection
context of GDPR, 100
controllers and processors, 104
exemptions, 106–108
formal nature of regulations and
directives, 101
fundamental legal right, 101
issues for organizations,
102–103
joint controllers, 105–106
overview, 99–100

processing not allowing identification, 106
processing not requiring identification, 104
processing of criminal convictions and offenses data, 104
processing under authority of controller and processor, 106
repeal of DPD95, 100
responsibility of controller, 105
Non-itemized billing privacy, 399
Notifications, data breaches
  to data protection supervisory authority, 307–308
  to individual data subjects, 306–307
  and measures, 307
  processes, 310
  timelines, 310

Online abuse, 25–26
Organizational security awareness
  appraising employees, 296–297
  bring your own device (BYOD), 299
  connecting hardware, 298
  email, 297
  general policy, 297
  identifying and controlling, 295–296
  internet access, 297
  internet social media, 298
  mobile telephones and devices, 297
  password security, 298
  remote access, 298
  software installation and management, 298
  vehicles, 297
Outsourcing to third-party data processors
  background guidance, 234–236
  controller records, 239

legal rule, 236–237
overview, 233–234
processing under authority, 237–238
processor records, 240–241
requirements, 238–239
and security, 238
Outward-facing data protection, 67–69

Password security, 298
PbD. *see* Privacy by Design (PbD) approach
Personal data, 61–62. *see also* Data protection
  background guidance, 121–122
    breaches, 274–275
    high risks, 275
    risk and damage, 272–274, 276–277
    risk evaluation, 275
  binding corporate rules, 118
  biometric, 116–117
  breach laws to consider, 300–301
  breach of, 116
  categories of, 111–112
  and child, 120
  communication of personal data breach to data subject, 283–284
  and controller, 125
  cross-border processing of, 119
  data concerning health, 117
  data protection impact assessment, 284–286
  and data protection supervisory authority, 118
  data subject, 124–125
    consent of, 126–127
  definition of, 120
  disposal of computer hardware, 302
  employees and, 288–289

and enterprise, 117
filing system, 125
    relevant, 127
general, 112
genetic, 116
group of undertakings, 117
information society service, 119
international organization, 119
legal rule, 122–124, 277–287
legislative data protection
        reviews, 291
main establishment, 117
notification of data breach to
        data protection supervisory
        authority, 282–283
organizational security awareness
    appraising employees,
        296–297
    bring your own device
        (BYOD), 299
    connecting hardware, 298
    email, 297
    general policy, 297
    identifying and controlling,
        295–296
    internet access, 297
    internet social media, 298
    mobile telephones and
        devices, 297
    password security, 298
    remote access, 298
    software installation and
        management, 298
    vehicles, 297
overview, 271–272
prior consultation, 286–287
processing, 125
and processor, 126
processors and security issues,
        289–291
pseudonymization, 116
and recipient, 126

relevant and reasoned
        objection, 119
representative, 127
security awareness, 292
Security Directive, 291
security measures, 287–288
    organizational, 299–300
sensitive, 112–115, 120–121
specific public interest prior
        consultations, 291
supervisory authorities guides,
        292–294
supervisory authority concerned,
        118
and third party, 126
third-party security providers,
        301–302
use and compliance, 63–64
Working Party (WP29)/EDPB,
        294–295
Principles, data protection
    background guidance, 132–136
    data collection, 140
    description, 136–139
    overview, 131–132
    processor, 140
Prior information conditions
    and GDPR, 143–144
    indirectly obtained data, 146–148
    overview, 143
    requirements, 145–146
    timing of information, 148–149
Privacy by Design (PbD) approach,
        330
Privacy Impact Assessment Code of
        Practice, 333
Privacy Shield, 365–368
Proactive official audits, 31
Processors and security issues,
        289–291
Profiling, 387
    data protection, 116

Prohibition notice, 451
Prosecutions, and data
        protection, 31
Pseudonymization, 116, 386–387

Record keeping
    maintaining, 159–161
    overview, 159
    principles requirement, 162–163
    requirement, 161–162
    responsibility and liability, 159
Relevant and reasoned objection,
        119
Remote access, and organizational
        security awareness, 298
Representatives/non-EU
        controllers
    article requirement, 166–167
    background guidance, 165–166
Restriction of processing, 115
Right of access
    background guidance, 183–184
    dealing with requests, 186–187
    exceptions and issues, 188–189
    legal rule, 184
    making request for, 185–186
    overview, 182–183
    response to requests, 187–188
    time limits for, 185
Rights of confirmation
    background guidance, 180–181
    description, 179
    legal rule, 181–182
    overview, 179
Rights of individual data subjects
    background guidance, 172–173
    issues, 170–172
    legal rules and rights, 173–174
    overview, 169
    recipients of, 170
Right to erasure, 219, 389
    background guidance, 197–200

legal rule, 200–204
overview, 197
Right to object to processing
    background guidance,
        213–215
    legal rule, 215–216
    overview, 213
Right to prevent direct marketing
    background guidance, 225–226
    legal rule, 226
    overview, 225
Right to rectification
    background guidance, 191–193
    legal rule, 193
    overview, 191
Right to restriction of processing
    background guidance, 209–210
    on methods to restrict
        processing, 210
    legal rule, 211
    overview, 209

Safe Harbor arrangement,
        365–368
Schrems, Max, 365–368
Schrems v Commissioner, 365
Security awareness, 292
Security Directive, 291
Security measures, personal data,
        287–288
    organizational, 299–300
Security standards, 310–311
Software installation and
        management, 298
Spam problem, 402
Special health data, 387–388
Supervisory authorities guides
    personal data security, 292–294

TEFU. *see* Treaty on the
        Functioning of the
        European Union (TFEU)

Third-country safeguards
    Background Recital 39, 371–373
    legal rule, 373–374
    overview, 371
Third party, and personal data, 126
Traffic data privacy, 399
Treaty on the Functioning of
        the European Union
        (TFEU), 252

Unsolicited communications,
    402–403

Vehicles, and personal data
    security, 297
VTech, 415
Working Party (WP29)/EDPB,
    294–295